£24·50

Law, Resistance, and the State

Gerald Strauss

Law, Resistance, and the State

The Opposition to Roman Law
in Reformation Germany

PRINCETON UNIVERSITY PRESS — PRINCETON, NEW JERSEY

Published by Princeton University Press, 41 William Street, Princeton, New Jersey
08540
In the United Kingdom: Princeton University Press, Guildford, Surrey

Library of Congress Cataloging in Publication Data will be found on the last
printed page of this book

ISBN 0-691-05469-X

This book has been composed in Linotron Sabon

Printed in the United States of America by Princeton University Press,
Princeton, New Jersey

for Daphne

CONTENTS

PREFACE

RESISTANCE to Roman law occurred nearly everywhere in early modern Europe, and many scholars have touched on it, most often in passing. My own interest in the subject goes back a good many years to the time when I began to see that, in early modern Germany at least, the conflict over Roman law brought deep-seated social antagonisms to the surface. The focus on "written" law and "learned" lawyers, I suspected, was largely symbolic in function. To explain why this was so, it has seemed best to me to proceed in this book from the particular to the general, from the words of scorn, derision, and detestation lavished upon the legal profession to the constitutional and religious setting that gives these outbursts weight and meaning. My aim has been to let the story unfold gradually until the whole of the context lies exposed. This has meant a move also from the simple to the complex, which is why the last two chapters, on the Reformation and on estate assemblies, are the longest. My chief object has been to give as full and circumstantial an accounting of opposition to Roman law in early modern Germany as I could. Of course there is a point of view as well. Whether I have seen things correctly or not is for my readers to judge.

It could be said that my book is a long commentary on a text taken from a recent article by the distinguished legal historian Helmut Coing:

> Because ideas always exert their influence through human beings, it is important to remind ourselves that, from the late middle ages in Europe, public affairs such as administration and politics have been for the most part in the hands of jurists, and that since antiquity law has always been regarded as the decisive means of giving direction to state and society.[1]

The accession of jurists to this controlling position in the management of people and affairs pitted innovators against traditionalists in a struggle for supremacy and survival in which the nature of law itself was the great matter at issue. In so innately conservative a society as sixteenth-

[1] "Das Recht als Element der europäischen Kultur," *HZ* 238:1 (1984), 13. Coing attaches a *limitatio*. It is no special advantage to European culture that law has played such a prominent part in it. "No one," he says, "knows better than the jurist the weaknesses of a social system in which law is prevalent. No one knows better that law can function only when it is framed by moral and religious obligations" (*ibid.*, 15).

century Germany, with the Lutheran Reformation to heighten the public sense of crisis, the conflict over new ideas (as they were taken to be), and over lawyers as their agents, was bound to be sharp and divisive. Each side in this encounter had its unworldly ideal: the legal intellectual's *communitas perfecta* created and upheld by the supremely rational Roman law versus the populist's projection of a "natural" community based on time-tested customs. Each side cherished its distorted image of the other: the common caricature of lawyers wedded to their adversary model of human relations and indifferent to all questions of right and wrong versus the jurist's contempt for folkish obscurantism and ignorance. As always, the conflict turned as much on perceptions as on the objectively real. Its denouement, of course, is well known. To us, looking back, this outcome seems to have been a foregone conclusion. To contemporaries, however, it was anything but that: hence the resistance.[2]

It is a pleasure to be able to record here my gratitude for the generous financial assistance I received in the various stages of my work on this book. A fellowship from the National Endowment for the Humanities enabled me to begin archival research in 1979-1980, and grants from the American Philosophical Society and the American Council of Learned Societies let me continue it during the summer of 1981. In the fall term of 1983 I was a member of the Institute for Advanced Study in Princeton, where the first half of the book was written in the perfectly congenial and supportive conditions created by that splendid institution. A stipend from the American Bar Foundation gave me time to complete the manuscript during the spring and summer of 1984. Finally, a grant-in-aid from the Office of Research and Graduate Development of my university covered the cost of preparing the typescript. I am deeply grateful for all this help. Assistance of another, no less essential, kind was given me by a host of archivists and librarians in East and West Germany, Austria, and the United States. They must remain anonymous here, but their support of my work is evident in the notes, where a scholar's real debts are acknowledged.

[2] Some of the themes with which this book is concerned are touched on by Bruce Lenman and Geoffrey Parker, "The State, the Community and the Criminal Law in Early Modern Europe" in V.A.C. Gatrell, Bruce Lenman, and Geoffrey Parker, eds., *Crime and the Law. The Social History of Crime in Western Europe Since 1500* (London, 1980), Chapter One. The chronological and geographical range of this article is so large, however, that the image it presents of the interaction of law and society remains unfocused.

LIST OF ABBREVIATIONS

BHStA Mu	Bayerisches Hauptstaatsarchiv München
HStA St	Hauptstaatsarchiv Stuttgart
HZ	*Historische Zeitschrift*
LA Tir	Landesarchiv Tirol, Innsbruck
Sehling	Emil Sehling, ed., *Die evangelischen Kirchenordnungen des 16. Jahrhunderts*, vols. 1-5 (Leipzig, 1902-13); vols. 6ff continued by the Institut für evangelisches Kirchenrecht der evangelischen Kirche in Deutschland zu Göttingen (Tübingen, 1955-).
StA Bamb	Staatsarchiv Bamberg
StA Dr	Staatsarchiv Dresden
StA Nbg	Staatsarchiv Nürnberg
StA Wei	Staatsarchiv Weimar
WA	*D.Martin Luthers Werke. Kritische Gesamtausgabe* (Weimar, 1883ff; reprint 1964-68).
WA Br	*D.Martin Luthers Werke. Briefwechsel* (Weimar, 1930ff).
WA DB	*D.Martin Luthers Werke. Deutsche Bibel* (Weimar, 1906ff).
WA TR	*D.Martin Luthers Werke. Tischreden* (Weimar, 1912ff).
ZRG	*Zeitschrift für Rechtsgeschichte*
	Germ.Abt. *Germanistische Abteilung*
	Kan.Abt. *Kanonistische Abteilung*
	Rom.Abt. *Romanistische Abteilung*

Law, Resistance, and the State

CHAPTER ONE

Lawyers: A Profession under Indictment

POWER and position invite hostility. The ill will displayed toward a particular group or profession is often an index of that body's perceived place in society. In the abundant literature of antipathy aimed since ancient times at professional men and their vocations, lawyers and the law must be the leading recipients of ridicule, abuse, rage, and scorn, and in the sixteenth century the perplexed resentment with which their careers and activities were viewed by a large segment of the public reached a high point. What was said about them reflects the social and political power to which lawyers had risen; implicitly it also reveals the authority and prestige conferred by this power, the arrogance they exhibited toward their fellow men, and the flimsiness and artificiality of the legal edifice itself and of the operations that kept it standing.[1] Jests and anecdotes convey the prevailing attitude. An angry prince warns his court jurist: "I'll be an ungracious lord to you!" "Then I shall be an ungracious doctor of laws to *you*," answers the lawyer, and the prince gives in.[2] In another story a jurist demands of his sovereign that a mountain be moved because it blocks his view of the sunrise from his study window.[3] A peasant woman sees young scholars issuing from a lecture hall. Who are they? Law students, she is told, who in time will be doctors of law, advocates, procurators, and notaries. "Pity us poor folk," she wails. "In my village we have only one advocate, the sexton, and he has confused us all and made a muddle of things. Once this horde of young men has been let loose, poor people like us will never have peace again."[4] If God were in litigation against Satan, goes the question in a contemporary joke, who would win? Answer: the devil, for he has all the lawyers on his side.[5] A page in an emblem book shows

[1] See Stith Thompson, *Motif-Index of Folk Literature* (*Indiana University Studies* XXII [1935]), X 311-18.

[2] Quoted in Roderich Stintzing, *Geschichte der deutschen Rechtswissenschaft* (Munich and Leipzig, 1880-1910) I, 61.

[3] Quoted in Werner Vogel, *Franz Hotman und die Privatrechtswissenschaft seiner Zeit* (Freiburg im Breisgau, 1960), 94.

[4] From the 1545 edition of Johann Pauli, *Schimpf und Ernst* (first published Strasbourg, 1522) II, No. 787. Cf. Stith Thompson, *Motif-Index* X 311.

[5] Quoted in Adolf Weissler, *Geschichte der Rechtswissenschaft* (Leipzig, 1905; reprint Frankfurt am Main, 1967), 246.

a peasant entering a lawyer's office bearing gifts: a rabbit, sausages, eggs. The lawyer is bent over a table, eating ravenously from delicacies served by a young woman, while behind him an apothecary inserts a huge clyster into his bottom. "What are you doing?" asks the peasant. "What I always do," replies the lawyer, "taking from both sides at once."[6] "The more rigid the law, the greater the injustice," it was commonly said;[7] on the other hand, "there is no law without a hole in it for him who can find it."[8] "I appeal," cries the expiring lawyer on his death bed, or, in another version of this story, applies for a delay, confident that it will be granted.[9]

The serious substance of these taunts suggests something of the misgivings stirred up in society by the phenomenon of proliferating legal experts and their growing prominence in public and private life. This book concerns itself with Germany—that is to say, the German-speaking regions of the Holy Roman Empire—but the problem, as it was understood at the time, touched all Europe in the early modern period, and most notably in the sixteenth century, the century of state building and dramatic realignments in the association of state and church. During this time, it has been observed, "lawyers became the technicians of politics and administration,"[10] increasing greatly in number and consolidating their corporate organization as a profession and their position as a class. A large army of experts with legal training was active in society, among whom holders of law doctorates from major European universities formed the proud elite. Earning a good income and gaining high honors in state, church, and municipal office, they developed a sense of themselves as indispensable to the functioning of a modern government.[11] Even without holding a degree, a man who had heard law lectures was respectfully referred to as "learned." If he held a doctorate he became "most learned" as well as "noble," addressed as "*Edel und hochgelert Herr* so-and-so, *der Rechten Doctor*,"[12] a title

---

[6] Arthur Henkel and Albrecht Schöne eds., *Emblemata. Handbuch zur Sinnbildkunst des 16. und 17. Jahrhunderts* (Stuttgart, 1967), 1,050.

[7] Günter Grundmann et al., *Rechtssprichwörter* (Leipzig, 1980), 18.

[8] *Ibid.*, 19.

[9] Stith Thompson, *Motif-Index* X 315. See also the massive repertoire of common sayings in Karl Friedrich Wander, *Deutsches Sprichwörter-Lexikon* (Leipzig, 1867-1880) under *Advocaten, Gerechtigkeit, Gesetz, Jurist, Procurator, Recht*. The overwhelming number of them are unfavorable.

[10] Carlo M. Cipolla, "The Professions: The Long View," *The Journal of European Economic History* 2 (1973), 49.

[11] Karl Heinz Burmeister, *Das Studium der Rechte im Zeitalter des Humanismus im deutschen Rechtsbereich* (Wiesbaden, 1974), 294.

[12] This title is given with many others in a two-volume manuscript *Tyttelbuch* in Stadtarchiv Augsburg, *Nachlässe*.

proclaiming his profession's ascent to the ranks of the aristocracy.[13] It was a good time for ambitious young men to choose the bar as a career. Martin Luther (though he himself had renounced it and elsewhere said some very nasty things about lawyers) made this argument a prominent part of the plea for academic schooling he issued in 1530. There has never been a better moment than this to let your sons study law, he exhorted parents. "Those who are students today will soon be in great demand. Two princes and three cities will compete for every one with a degree. Look around you," he went on, "countless positions are waiting to be filled by the learned" for whom good pay is in store

> and much dignity in addition to honest rewards. For chancellors, secretaries, and jurists sit at the top, advising, counselling, ruling. . . . In truth, they are lords on earth, though neither by birth nor by estate were they made for such rank.[14]

No wonder there was swift and lasting response. Throughout the fifteen hundreds, enrollment in law schools swelled, with the greatest increase coming in the last third of the century.[15] The adage *Dat Justinianus honores* seemed to be borne out by experience, and many young men gambled on the prospect, exchanging years of tedium sitting over Justinian's *Institutes* and *Digest* for the promise of an exciting and lucrative career in the halls of power.

The German side of this story of a profession's climb to eminence accompanied by mounting resentment and distrust is of special interest. State building proceeded swiftly in Germany as political and ecclesiastical authority was concentrated as a result of the religious split in both Protestant and Catholic sections of the empire. Bureaucracies and bureaucratic procedures were rapidly advanced by this development. The deliberate effort on the part of church and state agents during the Reformation to reorient the thinking and alter the behavior of ordinary men and women brought the high issues of politics and doctrine down to the ward and village, where they aroused controversy and often heated passions. Lawyers—jurists, legal practitioners, functionaries with some legal training—played a leading role in these events, which is why their place and, more important, the principles governing their

---

[13] In the records of the Bavarian estates, for example, doctors of law are always listed among the nobles in rosters of committee members.

[14] Luther, *Eine Predigt, dass man Kinder zur Schule halten solle* (1530), WA 30^{II}, 566.

[15] Ferdinand Elsener, *Die Schweizer Rechtsschulen vom 16. bis zum 19. Jahrhundert* (Zurich, 1975), 110. The same phenomenon has been noted in Spain by Richard L. Kagan, "Lawyers and Litigation in Castile 1500-1750" in Wilfred Prest ed., *Lawyers in Early Modern Europe and America* (London, 1981), Chapter 9, especially chart on page 188.

actions in courts, councils, and consistories, fell under so much questioning and met with such intense opposition. A full explanation of this resistance to law—specifically Roman law—and its agents will be unfolded in the course of the following chapters. The present one will illustrate the phenomenon itself.

"THE word of God shall be preached faithfully and truthfully in the land, and all sophistry and lawyering [*Juristerey*] shall be rooted out and all their books burned."[16] Article Seven of Michael Gaismair's draft constitution of 1526 for the County of Tyrol, part utopia, part reform plan, written in the immediate aftermath of the great German peasant war, points to the ultimate source of distaste among laymen for professional law and jurisprudence. Truth and law—man-made law, that is—were opposites; faith and the legal mind stood as adversaries. So sweeping a rejection was, of course, not an inevitable or a universal lay reaction to the practice of law. In normal times law was accepted, utilized, even welcomed. But at moments of crisis, in adversity, a deepseated, if latent, inclination to legal nihilism rose to the surface, not often declared with Gaismair's ruthlessness, but profoundly felt, and giving powerful expression to basic anarchic tendencies in society. To quote another instance, more obscure but no less evocative than Gaismair's, of the common disposition to see truth and law as antitheses: "We would dearly love to live by God's Word. . . . But jurists and advocates are against it, for their law contradicts the Lord's command to 'do unto others as you would have them do unto you.' "[17] Thus Argula von Grumbach, a Bavarian noblewoman, in a pamphlet describing the many burdens "with which Christ's people are being oppressed." Counterposing the enactments of men to divine commandments was a commonplace of preachers and theologians. Catholic and Protestant churchgoers were familiar with the accusation that jurists "stick to their texts" while ignoring "the principles and reasons of what is right and what is wrong."[18] This explains the frequent citation of the ancient proverb *summum ius, summa iniuria*, regarded as a platitude as long ago as Cicero, but useful to sixteenth-century theologians and lay people as an argument for the superiority of equity over positive law.[19]

[16] Michael Gaismair, *Landesordnung 1526*, Article 7 in Günther Franz ed., *Quellen zur Geschichte des Bauernkrieges* (Munich, 1963), No. 92, p. 286.

[17] Argula von Grumbach, *Ein christenliche schrifft einer erbarn frawen vom Adel . . .* (n.p., 1523), bᵛ-cʳ. The short pamphlet is dedicated to Duke Wilhelm IV of Bavaria.

[18] Burmeister, *Studium der Rechte*, 24, quoting the Tübingen theologian Konrad Summenhardt.

[19] *De officiis* 1.10.33. On the problem of law versus equity, see the fine discussion by

Trust and fidelity cannot flourish in the presence of human law; conversely, where faith and loyalty abound, no laws are needed. The equation epitomizes the moral gulf between the present time and better ages in the past. "Old chronicles," writes Johann Eberlin in *A Lamentable Complaint Addressed to the Christian Roman Emperor* of 1521, tell us how healthy our nation used to be. Now, however, we are beset by

> false and bad faith, from which there is no escape because it is upheld by Roman law and church legislation so that no one can now be certain of his case owing to the loopholes that can always be found in it, through which common people are chased from pillar to post. Jurists and advocates go to school to learn such tricks, and they make good money from it. This is why our ancestors had little law, though they had much faith, which they kept well.[20]

When commands of piety need to be circumvented for the sake of profit, the jurist's learning can show the way. Thomas Murner, the indefatigable Catholic publicist and pamphleteer, a doctor of laws himself but one who catered in most of his writings to common prejudices, made this one of his charges against the profession:

> And if a thing that God abhors
> You wish to gain and hold by force,
> Depend upon the jurist's books.

Law books, Jewish intrigues, and women's wiles, he says, quoting an old proverb, are the three destroyers that keep cities and countries divided against themselves.[21]

> And even if the text is sound
> A crooked gloss is quickly found,[22]

an allusion to the familiar complaint that judicial interpretation serves mainly to twist and subvert the law. "Let us therefore take our direction more from ancient customs than from the written laws," wrote Duke Georg of Saxony in an instruction to the justices of his appellate court in 1532, "seeing that these laws, needing interpretation, have come

---

the sixteenth-century jurist Johann Oldendorp in his *de iure et aequitate* of 1541: Hans-Helmut Dietze, *Johann Oldendorp als Rechtsphilosoph und Protestant* (Königsberg, 1933), 77-78.

[20] Johann Eberlin von Günzburg, *Ein klägliche klag an den christlichen Römischen kayser . . . (Der erst bundtsgenoss)* 1521 in *Neudrucke deutscher Litteraturwerke des 16. und 17. Jahrhunderts* No. 139 (Halle, 1896), 10.

[21] Thomas Murner, *Narrenbeschwörung* (first published Strasbourg, 1512): "*Fuss halten*" in *Neudrucke deutscher Litteraturwerke* Nos. 119-124, pp. 98-99.

[22] *Ibid.*, 100.

down to us as fabricated opinions [*gemachte opinion*]."[23] For this reason, both poets and jurists are banished from the perfected societies masquerading as dream visions that were so popular as a sounding board for reform ideas at the time: both are purveyors of fiction.[24] In one of the most far-reaching of these scenarios to appear in Germany on the eve of the Reformation, a long narrative poem called *Welsch Gattung*, first printed in Strasbourg in 1513, law, particularly Roman law, is portrayed as one of the chief promoters of misfortune and wickedness in the land. It crushes right and suppresses truth by enabling lawyers to turn bad into good and good into bad. "Poor old Justice" is shown as a forlorn exile, cast out of a world that has been taught to prosper without her:

> They say I'll not be missed among
> The great and eminent who throng
> High councils, learned men of fame
> Who put plain honesty to shame.
> In jurisprudence they are schooled,
> Experts in how the world is ruled.
> Against my judgment, straight and true,
> They send forth an appeal or two
> And win it in another court:
> I'm no match for this wily sort.
> For councils also I'm unfit,
> Where none but "Highly Learned" sit
> With stacks of books and a degree
> From Padua in Italy.
> They call me simple, less than bright,
> Unfit to say what's fair and right, . . .[25]

because guile and cunning are the only qualities now in demand.

Said to have turned against the ideals of truth and justice, jurisprudence was held in deep suspicion by social reformers striving to improve men and women by raising the conditions of their lives. As a human artifact, law could be no better than men themselves. Legal codes and their interpreters cannot therefore contribute to the betterment of humankind. True justice needs no stated rules and no explanations,

---

[23] Printed in Woldemar Goerlitz, *Staat und Stände unter den Herzögen Albrecht und Georg 1485-1539 (Sächsische Landtagsakten* I, Leipzig and Berlin, 1928), 190-92.

[24] E.g., *Die Welsch Gattung*, ed. Friedrich Waga (*Germanistische Abhandlungen* Heft 34 (Breslau, 1910), lines 655-56 (p. 188): "*Hie bleibt auch niendert kain Jurist, / Es hat auch kain Poet hie statt, / Hie leidt man auch kain advocat.*"

[25] *Ibid.*, lines 2326-2346 (pp. 232-33), somewhat compressed in my translation.

while written law inevitably creates occasions for deceit. "Hence the proverb *inventa lege, mox fraus inventa est*," wrote Justin Gobler in 1550, in the preface, addressed to the emperor Charles V, to his *Mirror of Laws*, "which means that as soon as law and justice are brought into being, Dame Duplicity joins the company."[26] As a jurist in high position in the city of Frankfurt, Gobler believed that adequate internal safeguards were available to protect the law from human self-serving. But laymen often thought otherwise, seeing the written law as both a product of, and an incentive to, nefarious manipulation.

These suspicions were formidably reinforced by the rhetoric of the religious reformers, especially by Martin Luther himself, who—as will be shown in detail in a later chapter—although remaining ambivalent on the social function of law and lawyers, frequently allowed his instinctive distaste for the profession to darken his references to them.[27] Luther was emphatic on the intimate links that wedded law to power. "Whoever holds the law in his hands has power," he said, "and only God knows whether such power is right." He added: "Law rests on the fist. Turn the word *ius* inside out, and it spells *vis*, might."[28] Lacking inherent moral force, the law can offer no instruction to wielders of power. "This is why I have no laws to suggest to a ruler. I wish only to inform his heart"[29]—an organ open to the preacher but inaccessible to legal counsel. It was Luther's theological starting point that laws were the consequence of mankind's fallen condition and cannot therefore contribute to its improvement. "Politics and law," he preached, "don't follow from grace; they are the products of wrath."[30] In his preface to the Old Testament of 1523 he declared that "God gave the imperial laws [that is to say Roman, or "common," law] for the sake of the wicked. . . . They are laws to defend ourselves with, not laws that can teach us anything."[31] Like the code laid down by God through Moses, the laws of civil society serve to ensure "that man learns through the law how false and evil is his heart, how far he is still from God."[32] Lu-

---

[26] Justin Gobler, *Der Rechten Spiegel . . .* (Frankfurt am Main, 1550), ii^r.

[27] For a brief survey of Luther's expressed views on law and lawyers, see Gerald Strauss, "Luther as Barabbas" in Peter N. Brooks ed., *Seven-Headed Luther* (Oxford, 1983), 166-75.

[28] WA TR 6, No. 7016; 3, No. 3793.

[29] Luther, *Von weltlicher Oberkeit, wie weit man ihr Gehorsam schuldig sei* (1523), WA 11, 273.

[30] Sermon of 13 January 1544, WA 49, 316.

[31] WA DB 8, 16-17 ("*nur Wehrgesetz, mehr denn Leregesetz*").

[32] Sermon on Galatians 3:23-29 (*Kirchenpostille* [1522]), quoted in F. Edward Cranz, *An Essay on the Development of Luther's Thought on Justice, Law, and Society* (Harvard Theological Studies XIX. Cambridge, 1959), 99.

ther sometimes spoke admiringly of cultures that managed to live without written codes, informed solely by their spiritual resources,[33] and he
held right reason to be a standard much superior to positive law. But
where, he asked, would we today find lawgivers capable of rational legislation? In the absence of reason, we must resort to written laws for
the *pöbel*, the common crowd.[34] Melanchthon (who was later to develop a much more subtle view) advanced the same argument in his *loci
communes* of 1521. "Laws and courts are necessary in order to coerce
evil men," he wrote.[35] Coercion aiming at control, then, not enlight-
enment leading to amelioration, is the object of legislation: a starkly
negative view of the place of law in human affairs. This constricted
sense accounts for Luther's and other reformers' frequently expressed
disdain for civil lawyers, "whose office it is . . . to teach and judge nothing but mortal, fleeting, wretched, worldly things such as lending at interest, especially where the text offers them opportunities for quibbling
and hair splitting."[36] So dismal a view so often and so forcefully expressed did much to sharpen older suspicions and prejudices in the
community.

Cued and seconded by the theologians, lay critics accused the law of
favoring the dishonest and courting the rich. People were warned
against going to court even in the best of causes, because—so it was
suggested—justice can always be outwitted, ensnared in technicalities,
deceived by cunning, and confused by lies.[37] Speaking truth in a righteous cause does not help. "Don't you see how craftily and slily your
opponents can convert a bad case into a winning argument? You are
much too simple to argue with advocates and learned judges. . . . Better
abandon your claim to justice. Patch up your quarrel with the other
party. Even if you lose in the bargain you'll be better off than if you
were trapped in litigation."[38] Jurists disputed the accuracy of this description, but it was offered as sage advice throughout the century.

[33] E.g., his allusion to the Turks in *An den christlichen Adel deutscher Nation* (1520),
WA 6, 459. At other times, however, Luther expressed admiration for the Roman empire
as a well-ordered state.

[34] WA TR 6, No. 6955.

[35] Melanchthon, *Loci communes theologici* (1521) translated by L. J. Satre in Wilhelm
Pauck, ed., *Melanchthon and Bucer* (*Library of Christian Classics* XIX. London, 1969),
128.

[36] Luther, *An die Pfarrherrn, wider den Wucher zu predigen* (1540) WA 51, 343.

[37] Hans Sachs, *Ein gesprech, die verblendet Gerechtigkeyt vor dem gericht betreffend*
(1539) in Adelbert von Keller, ed., *Hans Sachs 7* (*Bibliothek des litterarischen Vereins
Stuttgart*, 1873 [reprint Hildesheim, 1964]), p. 250, ll. 33-6. Warnings for Christians
against going to law extend back to the New Testament. E.g., I Cor. 6:7 and Mat. 5:40.

[38] *Hans Sachs 7*, 250, ll. 11-21; p. 251, ll. 1-3.

More easily substantiated were complaints about exorbitant costs and the claim that litigation was effectively unavailable to the poor, impoverished the middle sort, and benefited only the rich. People of wealth could hire an advocate, apply to a law faculty for an expert opinion, defray the cost of transferring records from one court to another.[39] Those at the bottom of society had neither the means nor the connections to avail themselves of this kind of help. If you want to go to court, warned the north-German attorney Bartholomäus Sastrow in his autobiography, written at the end of the sixteenth century,

> you must bring with you three sacks, one filled with money, the other to hold documents, and the third containing patience. And the longer your case takes, the lighter will be the money bag, the heavier the stack of papers, and the shorter your patience.[40]

Horror stories of ten- or twenty-year-long suits may have been cautionary tales trading on exaggeration.[41] But too many voices in the literature of secular reform speak of the unconscionable delays achieved by resourceful lawyers, and of the financial ruination to which this established practice reduced clients, for the charge to be an entire fiction.[42] Governments sometimes gave their subjects due notice of the hazards awaiting them upon entering litigation. The town of Schlaggenwald in Bohemia, for example, warned burghers in the columns of its civil code that "anyone considering legal action is reminded that cases at law are apt to be long drawn out, costly, and uncertain in their outcome."[43] Decades of complaints at all levels and in all forums of the community underpin the cogency of this advice. In 1514, the estates of Württemberg, meeting in diet in the city of Tübingen, pressed their duke to

[39] Heinrich Mitteis, *Deutsche Rechtsgeschichte* (11th ed. by Heinz Lieberich, Munich, 1969), 201.

[40] [Bartholomäus Sastrow], *Bartolomäi Sastrowen Herkomen, Geburt und Lauff seines gantzen Lebens . . .* ed. Gottlob Friedrich Mohnike (Greifswald, 1823-1824) I, 258.

[41] E.g., the cartoon of a peasant about to visit his lawyer in Hans Fehr, *Kunst und Recht* I: *Das Recht im Bilde* (Erlenbach-Zurich, 1923), Plate 216 and pp. 165-66; Ulrich von Hutten, *Praedones* in *Auserlesene Werke*, ed. and tr. Ernst Münch, III (Leipzig, 1823), 408.

[42] E.g., Johann Eberlin von Günzburg, *Der erst bundtsgenoss* (1521) (*Neudrucke deutscher Litteraturwerke* 139), 13. Eberlin urged Charles V "*das man kain recht handel, auch am wältlichen rechten, uber ein jar umb ziehe dem armen man zu verderbnis.*"

[43] *Rechtsbuch der kayserlichen freien Bergstadt Schlackenwald* Titulus VIII, paragraph 2. Manuscript copy in Germanisches Nationalmuseum Nuremberg, Hs. 17.471, fol.7^r.

attend to our grievances concerning the learned jurists whose presence on the courts of our entire land grows daily more harmful, to wit, that a man obliged to go to court can now expect to pay fees of ten gulden or more where only twelve years ago it cost him less than ten shillings. This brings great hardships to the ordinary man and creates an unprecedented situation in the land.[44]

Several measures were taken to reduce the expense of legal action in Württemberg.[45] But the complaints continued there and elsewhere of "excessive court costs, *per diem* expenses, notary's and scrivener's charges, sealing fees, and other payments imposed in violation of ancient customs and usages."[46] Those with money to spend could speed procedures by greasing appropriate palms; but the poor suffered delays. As the proverb said: "Much money, a short time. Little money, a long time."[47] "A poor man gets no justice," protested the peasant deputies of Salzburg in 1525; "without money you are given neither help nor redress."[48] Those who tried anyway often found themselves ruined. Advice books on the problems of daily life therefore urged people strongly to refrain from involving themselves with the law. Among the "Nine Vices That Make a Poor Man of You," going to law is number five, according to Hans Sachs, the Nuremberg versifier and moralist.[49] And of "The Three Golden Teachings of Chilon the Sage," the third— following "Know Thyself" and "Keep Measure in All Things"—is "Don't Start a Law Suit."[50] "It is better to suffer a small injustice than to go to court," the proverb said,[51] because

> Whether you're plaintiff or defending
> There's no end to your money spending,

[44] *Württembergische Landtagsakten* 1. Reihe (ed. Wilhelm Ohr and Erich Kober, Stuttgart, 1913) I, 174.

[45] In 1583, after many years of strenuous protests, steps were taken to shorten and streamline legal procedures. See HstA St A34 Bü 18ᵈ (with unnumbered leaves).

[46] LA Tir, *Tiroler Landtagsakten*, Fasz. 9, no pagination, relating to the year 1577. Identical complaints about "*übermessige Gerichts Cossten*" occur throughout the 1570s and in later decades. In 1646, the Tyrolean estates' *gravamina* objected to "*viele unnotwendige assessorn und beystaender*" whose presence on the courts drive up the cost of trials. *Landtagsakten* Cod. 2929 (no pagination).

[47] Quoted in Winfried Trusen, *Anfänge des gelehrten Rechts in Deutschland . . .* (Wiesbaden, 1962), 181.

[48] *24 Artikel gemeiner Landschaft Salzburg* (May-June, 1525) in Günther Franz, *Quellen* No. 94, p. 307.

[49] Hans Sachs, *Neun Stück bringen in Armut* in Keller and Goetze eds., *Hans Sachs* 20, 501-02.

[50] Hans Sachs, *Die drey gülden leer Chilonis des philosophi* in *ibid.*, 5, 344.

[51] Quoted in Hans Fehr, *Die Dichtung im Recht* (Bern, 1936), 177.

Not counting worry, fear, and doubt;
And this goes on year in, year out,
While jurists, lawyers, clerks purloin
Your treasure down to your last coin.[52]

The dishonesty and greed of lawyers were proverbial, always attributed at base to their alleged indifference to moral questions, a lack of concern for the truth deliberately nurtured, it was suggested, by their legal training. In Jost Amman's well-known depiction of the world's *Estates*, published in 1568, the "Procurator" is alone among the book's more than one hundred trades and social conditions in possessing corrupt qualities. Only the "Jew" is presented as equally disagreeable. "I'm a procurator," the lawyer says in Hans Sachs's verses that provide the captions for Amman's woodcuts, "and it's my job in court to speak for bad causes. Sophistical logic, deceit, trickery, and intrigue help me draw a case out indefinitely, and even if I'm unsuccessful in the end, and my client loses, it doesn't hurt me because I have had plenty of time to fill my pockets with his money."[53] In the same vein, Holbein's designs for the *Dance of Death* show death surprising a judge and an advocate in the act of accepting bribes for their professional favors.[54] Given a chance for a few final words, a jurist pictured in another *Dance of Death* comes to the last-minute realization—in the nick of time for contrition—that "Justice is a gift of God, and no jurist should try to twist it; he should instead hate lies and love truth."[55] The strong feelings against lawyers that rise so often to the surface in sixteenth-century reform writings are motivated in large part by the conviction that they are insensitive to questions of right and wrong. "If they favor someone, they find justice on his side," charged Johann Hergot, author of a deeply pious proposal for a truly Christian society, drafted in anger and frustration a year or two after the defeat of the great peasant revolution:

Right or wrong [he continues] it makes no difference to them because their written codes tell them how to win in all circumstances. The Holy Spirit does not teach this. He teaches only truth and justice. This is why he is an enemy of all learning, while the learned them-

[52] Hans Sachs, *Neun Stück bringen in Armut* (as note 49), 502, ll. 2-9.
[53] Jost Amman, *Eygentliche Beschreibung Aller Stände auff Erden . . .* (Frankfurt am Main, 1568), Nos. 14 (*Procurator*) and 30 (*Der Jud*). Hans Sachs's verse is in Keller, ed., *Hans Sachs* 23, 277.
[54] Holbein, *Dance of Death* (first published Lyons, 1538), Nos. 18 and 19.
[55] Quoted in Franz Heinemann, *Der Richter und die Rechtspflege in der deutschen Vergangenheit* (Jena, 1924), 82.

selves take for fools those of us who wish to decide matters by the light of the Spirit and judge by the truth.

"I believe that God gives more wisdom to an unlettered old man than he grants to a learned young doctor,"[56] Hergot added, expressing his general disenchantment with book knowledge, a disappointment widespread at the time and clearly one of the sources of the public aversion to law and legal thinking. But intellectuals, too, and especially theologians, tended to see law and conscience as opposites. Luther was insistent on drawing this contrast. "I write for the sake of conscience, not law," he declared, discussing a point in the law of marriage,[57] and, again: "Law should serve conscience, and not the reverse. Conscience does not serve the law. If both cannot be served, your duty is with conscience."[58] Elsewhere he let it be known that "Truth and Law are always enemies to each other":[59]

> Show me the jurist [he said] who studies to find the true cause of things so that he might discover the truth and learn from it what is right and what is not right, and how to honor God and serve his fellow men. No, they study law only for the profit it brings them, namely high honors and great riches![60]

More specific accusations were voiced in statements of grievance issued by territorial parliaments (these are discussed at length in Chapter Eight) and in governmental legislation trying to meet these complaints. Rulers regularly issued mandates attempting to control the activities of legal practitioners. These edicts, and the protests to which they respond, reveal both the intensity and the ubiquity of public feelings against lawyers. Lawyers were called quarrelsome ("abusive language," "*ad hominem* insults"), given to feints and tricks ("dangerous stratagems"), garrulous ("tongue-flapping rabulists"), long-winded ("bombastic circumlocutions"), impudent ("lacking in proper respect"), and immoral ("knowingly defending a bad cause").[61] A Court

[56] Johann Hergot, *Von der newen Wandlung eynes christlichen Lebens* (Leipzig, 1526 or 1527) in Adolf Laube *et al.*, eds., *Flugschriften der Bauernkriegszeit* (Berlin [East]), 1975), 553. On Hergot and his plan, see also Chapter Four, below. On the question of authorship, see note 130 to that chapter.
[57] Luther, *Von Ehesachen* (1530), WA 30[III], 245.
[58] *Ibid.*, 246.
[59] WA TR 3, No. 3,793 (1538).
[60] WA TR 1, No. 349 (1532).
[61] All these from *Canzley Acta. Die Advocaten-Ordnung* issued by Saxony in 1598. StA Dr, Loc. 30501. The same complaints were made throughout the second half of the sixteenth century, as recorded in the Saxon estates documents in Dresden. For a similar list, see StA Dr, Loc. 9362: "Erledigung der Gravaminam . . . 1609," 40r-41r.

and Chancellery Ordinance published in Marburg in 1563 cautioned
advocates and procurators on pain of disbarment to "show the court a
decent respect, avoid offensive gestures and insulting behavior, refrain
from using abusive, derisive, or provocative language, and abstain
from long addresses which serve only to prolong the trial, waste time,
and delay the proceedings."[62] The city of Regensburg swore procurators to the avoidance of "deception, fraud, falsehood, and dishonesty"
and the performance of their duties without regard to profit and favors.[63] In Switzerland they were instructed to refrain from "unnecessary and useless palavering, needling, mocking, and taunting."[64] In
Saxony,

> the city of Dresden reports [in 1601] that a plague of peace-hating,
> quarrelsome advocates has descended on the town, who . . . can be
> seen every day milling about the town hall, and when they see two
> parties leaving court, they attach themselves to the one showing signs
> of dissatisfaction with our verdict and incite him to appeal against
> it. . . .

The Dresden city fathers' complaint about this practice concluded with
the common charge that "all this they do to make money from it."[65]
But clearly the resentment lay much deeper. It was the very idea of an
appointed advocate and court officer encouraging subjects to proceed
against their legitimate overlords that dismayed the authorities. Late in
the sixteenth century, this was still a novel and disturbing phenomenon
on the European political scene. The gravamen of the case against lawyers, therefore, was not so much the charge that they made a practice
of "goading parties to move against each other, thereby plunging both
sides into great and unnecessary costs,"[66] as the accusation that "they
stir people up and traduce them."[67] "They have their henchmen,"

[62] *Marburgische Hofgerichts- und Kanzleiordnung* 1563 in Franz Gundlach, *Die hessischen Zentralbehörden von 1247 bis 1604* (*Veröffentlichungen der historischen Kommission für Hessen und Waldeck* XVI, Marburg, 1930-1932) II, 122-23: "Von Procu-
ratoren."

[63] Quoted in Herrmann Knapp, *Alt-Regensburgs Gerichtsverfassung, Strafverfahren
und Strafrecht bis zur Carolina* (Berlin, 1914), 69.

[64] Quoted in Ferdinand Elsener, *Die Schweizer Rechtsschulen*, 249. The date was
1544.

[65] From *Landtags Sachen oder Verzeichnis aller Gravamina* submitted to the government of Saxony in 1601. StA Dr, Loc. 9359, 26ʳ and ᵛ.

[66] From *Hofratsordnung* 1590 of Duke Wilhelm V of Bavaria, quoted in Manfred
Mayer, *Quellen zur Behörden-Geschichte Bayerns* I: *Geschichte der Neuorganisationen
Albrechts V* (Bamberg, 1890), 175-76. This is repeated verbatim in Duke Maximilian's
Hofratsordnung of 1604: *ibid.*, 215.

[67] Grievances of knights and cities in Saxony, 1582: StA Dr, Loc. 9350, No. 10, 24ᵛ.

wrote the Saxon jurist and court official Melchior von Osse, speaking of advocates in a scathing review of the Saxon judicial system, "who go about the wine and beer shops and prod people into grumbling and fretting against their hereditary lords and other superiors."[68] To the extent that this charge was true, the professional lawyer represented a potentially alarming intrusion into the bilateral relationship between governors and the governed. He was under suspicion of having brought divisive and adversary habits into a traditionally harmonious association, and this—though it does not survive historical examination—was a serious indictment.

Most such suspicions and accusations relate not so much to lawyers in general, as to advocates and "procurators" in particular. This is because their place in the legal community, while no longer new and unfamiliar, had as late as the sixteenth century by no means won general acceptance. Advocates had been active in German civil law procedure since the late twelve hundreds. Parties were entitled, were in fact encouraged, to be represented by counsel, called *Vorsprecher, prolocutor*, or *procurator*, who spoke for litigating individuals and offered advice on all legal matters, especially with respect to the drawing up of documents and the conduct of trials.[69] Formally assigned to a client by the court before which he was entitled to practice, the *Vorsprecher*— also called *Redner* or, in an attempt to bestow classical dignity, *orator*—was theoretically enjoined from taking a case he could not support in good conscience; this rule, however, was soon—perhaps had always been—regarded as a pious fiction, and the counsel's chief and defining responsibility was taken to be the promotion of his client's interests: in other words, helping him win his case. The ambivalence implicit in this double role—responsibility to court and loyalty to client— was the source of all accusations of hypocrisy, double-dealing, and moral obtuseness made by critics and reformers to whom the ethical issue was both paramount and pure.

By the sixteenth century, in response to the growth of legal activity, the office of counsel had become a bit more stratified. *Vorsprecher* (or *Fürsprech, Vorreder*) pleaded on behalf of parties having legal business in the inferior courts of towns, regional administrative districts (*Äm-*

---

[68] Melchior von Osse, *Welchergestalt ein cristliche obrikait . . . ein gotselige, weisliche, vornunftige und rechtsmessige justicien erhalten kan . . .* (1556) in Oswald Artur Hecker ed., *Schriften Dr. Melchiors von Osse* (Leipzig and Berlin, 1922), 442. Osse includes in his survey all the charges and criticisms made by laymen against lawyers: *ibid.*, 441-44.

[69] On the role of the *Vorsprecher* in medieval German law, mainly according to the *Sachsenspiegel*, see J. W. Planck, *Das deutsche Gerichtsverfahren im Mittelalter* (Braunschweig, 1879; reprint Hildesheim, 1973), 194-217.

ter), and private seigneurial jurisdictions. These were nearly always laymen whose chief qualification for their job was the practical experience they had gained while attending legal and administrative trials. At the higher judicial levels of the princely appellate courts (*Hofgerichte*), advocates assisted parties with their briefs and all other aspects of trial preparation, while "procurators" or *Redner* argued the client's case before judge and jury.[70] These distinctions tended, however, to be blurred in practice. In many regions no differentiation was made between solicitors and barristers.[71] Most advocates and procurators had formal legal training; some were notaries or scriveners. Advocates, especially, tended to be licentiates at least. But to the holders of doctorates of one (civil) or both (civil and canon) laws, they were all dilettantes. Academic jurists like Melchior von Osse were scornful of "failed artisans too lazy to do honest work, sextons and other riffraff run away from their jobs, who make themselves out to be procurators, many of them incapable even of reading a law book."[72] This would appear to be an exaggeration. On the other hand, the many vernacular "Law Mirrors," "Trial Books," "Institutes," "formularies," and summaries, the publication of which in the sixteenth century tells us so much about the preoccupation in European society with legal matters,[73] were written for just such a public.[74] Justin Gobler hoped that his *Gerichtlicher Process*, published in 1578 to explain procedure, would be useful to procurators, "especially those who have not studied law in their days but wish to learn their craft from easily accessible

[70] The sixteenth-century legal writer Kilian König gives the following definition: "Der wirdet im Rechten ein Procurator oder Vorsprecher genant, der frembde hendel aus befelh der Herrn gutwilliglich [i.e., voluntarily] zu handeln auf sich nimmt. . . . Un als dann ist einer ein Anwald oder Procurator, wenn er den befelh oder Mandat von dem, welches sachen er faren sol vor gericht, mündlich oder durch briefe willig empfangen und angenomen hat. Dann niemandts mag wider seinen willen zu Anwalden gesatzt . . . werden." *Practica und Prozess* . . . (Bautzen, 1555), Chapter 10 (no pagination).

[71] The pattern presented in the above sketch prevailed in Albertine Saxony in the early sixteenth century. See Woldemar Goerlitz, *Staat und Stände*, 177. With minor regional variations, the pattern holds for most other German territories. See Adolf Weissler, *Geschichte der Rechtsanwaltschaft*, 110-339, who emphasizes regional variations. For more on advocates and procurators, see Chapter Six below.

[72] Melchior von Osse, *Welchergestalt ein . . . obrikait . . .* (as in note 68), 442.

[73] E.g., Justin Gobler, *Der Rechten Spiegel* (Frankfurt am Main, 1550) and *Gerichtliche Process* (Frankfurt am Main, 1578), Andreas Perneder, *Gerichtlicher Process* (Ingolstadt, 1573, preface dated 1544) and *Institutiones* (Ingolstadt, 1573; Perneder's writings were first published posthumously by Wolfgang Hunger in 1544). On popular legal writings of this kind, see Chapter Three, below.

[74] Hans Rudolf Hagemann, "Rechtswissenschaft und Basler Buchdruck an der Wende von Mittelalter zur Neuzeit," *ZRG* 77 (1960), *Germ.Abt.*, 251-55.

books."[75] As a jurist, Gobler seems genuinely to have been upset at what he called the "excessive use of trickery, fraud, insinuation, sycophancy, and calumny by both advocates and procurators"[76] in the courts of his day, and his book was meant to improve this situation. A similar volume of popular legal instruction, the *Gerichtlicher Process*, by the Bavarian councillor and civil servant Andreas Perneder, was praised because its author had omitted from his text all "cavils, cautels, or other such fraudulent and deceptive tricks" and, instead, "shows [his readers] only the open, honest, honorable path to right justice."[77] Basic to this attempt to make the practice of law conform to higher standards was the formal requirement that no attorney take a case he could not represent with a clear conscience.[78] In Saxony, for example, the statutes governing practice before the duchy's superior courts gave the following oath formula to be pronounced by all advocates:

> I swear that I will advise, assist, and represent before this court only parties whose matters are, by my understanding and faith, right, just, and truly founded. I also swear that I will demand, accept, or receive no money or gifts from any party other than that allowed me by the presiding judge or his assessors.[79]

Most court constitutions in Germany enjoined lawyers to give such guarantees. But the oath seems to have remained a perfunctory gesture. It does not appear that it, any more than the improving books of Perneder and others, made the hoped-for impact on legal practice. The unending flood of complaints and protests from the later years of the sixteenth century suggests that the use of "cavils, cautels, and other fraudulent tricks" by advocates continued unabated. "Advocate, Badvocate" expressed the general sentiment,[80] and, in a clever play on Matthew 22:14, it was said that *multi enim sunt advocati, pauci vero electi, scilicet, ad vitam aeternam.*[81]

---

[75] Justin Gobler, *Gerichtliche Process, auss geschriebenen Rechten, und nach gemeinen, im Heiligen Reich Teutscher Nation gebrauch und übung* (Frankfurt am Main, 1578), unnumbered leaf before A[r].

[76] Justin Gobler, *Spiegel der Rechten* (Frankfurt am Main, 1573), 23[v].

[77] Wolfgang Hunger in his dedication to Wilhelm IV of Bavaria, dated 1544, of Andreas Perneder's *Gerichtlicher Process . . .* (Ingolstadt, 1573), leaf ./. iii[v].

[78] *Ibid.*, CLXXV[v].

[79] Quoted in Christian Gottfried Kretschmann, *Geschichte des churfürstlich-Sächsischen Oberhofgerichts zu Leipzig* (Leipzig, 1804), 80-81.

[80] The German is *Advocat, Schadvocat.*

[81] "For many are called, but few are chosen." "For there are many advocates, but few are chosen, i.e., to eternal life." Quoted in Georg Philipp Harsdörffer, *Ars apophthegmatica . . .* (Nuremberg, 1655), No. 1153.

Nor did the profession's detractors make careful discrimination between amateur practitioners and learned jurists with a lofty view of their calling. Critics argued as vehemently for the removal of "doctors" as they clamored for the control of procurators. "Doctors are no servants of justice. They are paid hirelings interested only in their own profit. . . , [and] they shall not sit on any court or give a verdict," proposed the so-called Heilbronn program, a draft proposal to guide the deliberations of a peasant assembly in 1525.[82] According to the proverb *nemo jurista nisi Bartolista*, all jurists were held to be quibblers, hairsplitters, and obscurantists, traits associated in lay opinion with the fourteenth-century Italian Bartolus, a founding father of legal science.[83] Their involuted Latinate speech and Roman tags were a common source of humor in shrove-tide plays, where a court scene featuring a peasant or merchant taking absurd German meanings from misunderstood fragments of fake Latin was always good for a laugh. It was money, however, that seems to have been at the root of the resentment. "An advocate and a wagon wheel want to be greased" was an often-quoted saying,[84] and the legal profession's reputed susceptibility to corruption is epitomized by a medal showing, on one side, an open hand full of coins, surmounted by the legend "If you come to me with these," and, on the obverse, the robed figure of a judge looking through his wide-spread five fingers and saying "I'll do this."[85] The emblem for an honest judge was a man without hands.[86] In sixteenth-century popular comedy, the *Redner* or *procurator* who, for a price, could be hired to do or say anything was a favorite figure.[87] Johann Pauli, the compiler of a best-selling anthology of tales and anecdotes, *Schimpf und Ernst*, first published in 1522, points the moral of one such story as follows:

A scale has two trays, one on each side, and up above a tongue, and the tongue always points toward the heavier of the two trays. In the same way, the lawyer has two hollow hands, and these he holds in front of him, and his tongue is up high in his mouth. And the tongue

[82] Printed in Adolf Laube *et al.*, *Flugschriften*, 74.

[83] Quoted, for example, in Jürgen Bücking, *Kultur und Gesellschaft in Tirol um 1600* . . . (Lübeck and Hamburg, 1968), 72.

[84] Günter Grundmann *et al.*, *Rechtssprichwörter* (Leipzig, 1980), 13.

[85] Illustrated in Guido Kisch, *Recht und Gerechtigkeit in der Medaillenkunst* (*Abhandlungen der Heidelberger Akademie der Wissenschaften, philosophisch-historische Klasse, Jahrgang 1955-1956*), Plate VIII.

[86] Shown in Henkel and Schöne eds., *Emblemata*, 1039.

[87] An example: "Consistori Rumpoldi" (c. 1510) in *Fünfzehn Fastnachts-Spiele aus den Jahren 1510 und 1511* ed. Olswald Zingerle (Vienna, 1886). For jokes on this theme see G. P. Harsdörffer, *Ars apophthegmatica* (1655), Nos. 1584-1585.

goes toward the hand which receives the most money, you can depend on it.[88]

Lawyers, wrote Duke Maximilian of Bavaria, cautioning his son and successor against corrupt advocates, "grow fat on slow-moving court proceedings as a physician gets rich on a lingering disease."[89] The analogy would have seemed aptly chosen to the duke's contemporaries, some of whom were, as we shall see, ready to perform radical surgery.

READERS of the moralistic literature of the later middle ages will recognize the venal judge, the legal brain for hire, the advocate without a conscience as familiar *topoi*.[90] But more than literary conventions were at work in their depiction. Elmar Mittler concludes from his survey of medieval sources that

> a considerable number of medieval works concern themselves intensively with law and the person of the law expert. In part these works paint a dark picture in which judges are portrayed as unjust and rapacious. Others, on the other hand, give a more differentiated impression of how things were, and most of these were written by authors who themselves had more or less intimate knowledge of legal procedure and for this reason concentrated their criticism on particular problems and endeavored to find solutions to them. More and more it is the use of written codes, especially of the Roman law, that was seen as the solution. Law books are therefore recommended, the unschooled amateur juror being held unqualified to give a judgment based on the facts. . . . With this attitude, a development is under way that was to lead gradually to the reception of Roman law in Germany.[91]

But the professionalization of law so described (and to be dealt with in Chapter Three) generated more difficulties than it could handle. Above all, it accelerated the rampant legalism of the late medieval and

---

[88] Johannes Pauli, *Schimpf und Ernst*, No. 128 (I, 87).

[89] Christian von Aretin ed., *Maximilian I. . . . Anleitung zur Regierungskunst* (Bamberg, 1822), 65.

[90] The image of the lawyer in late medieval literature is surveyed by Erich Genzmer, "Hugo von Trimberg und die Juristen" in *L'Europa e il diritto Romano. Studi in memoria di Paolo Koschaker* I (Milan, 1954), 289-336; id., "Kleriker als Berufsjuristen im späten Mittelalter" in *Études d'histoire du droit canonique dédiées à Gabriel LeBras* 2 (Paris, 1965), 1207-1236; Elmar Mittler, *Das Recht in Heinrich Wittenwilers "Ring"* (Freiburg i.B., 1967), 164-79; Arpad Stephan Andreànsky, "Wittenwilers 'Ring' als Quelle der mittelalterlichen Sozialgeschichte," *Archiv für Kulturgeschichte* 60:1 (1978), 94-98; 119-20.

[91] Elmar Mittler, *op. cit.*, 174.

early modern periods—itself one of the reasons for long-standing anti-judicial attitudes among the laity. This excessive—as it was thought to be—recourse to legal mechanisms was not, in fact, the fault of jurists and lawyers, who were themselves its products. Commercial capitalism was responsible, as was, above all, and with massive effect, the early modern state with its spreading bureaucracy and its dependence on administrative enactments and legal constraints.[92] Law-dominated government and frequent, often bitter, contentions among competing and conflicting jurisdictions encouraged the proliferation of legal experts, who, in time, came to penetrate society from the high benches and privy councils of ruling princes and state churches down to the private seigneurial courts and village tribunals. This is how it happened that, by the early sixteenth century, it could be said—as the Württemberg estates complained at their diet in 1514—that "if an end is not made of this [development], every village will in time have to have one or two doctors to advise people on the law and their rights."[93]

The other consequence of professionalization was the conversion of the legal adviser—at that time still called *Rechtsetzer* or *Rechtsprecher* (one who ascertains or determines and provides information about the law)—into a judicial technician whose habits of mind and social orientation differed fundamentally from those who took his counsel. Of all the specialist's qualities, it was his moral neutrality or—as it was more often interpreted—his indifference that was most upsetting to the laity: hence the attempts, just mentioned, on the part of state governments to set standards of conscientious behavior for counsellors. But these endeavors were largely unavailing, as we have seen, and a society still disquieted by the idea that advisers and helpers should accept fees in exchange for their service[94] grew increasingly alarmed at the sight of law and justice slipping from people's hands into the grasp of legal experts of dubious character and suspect loyalties.

In Utopia there were no lawyers. Nothing illustrates better the common misgivings about the shift from amateur to specialist's law than the emphatic exclusion of the legal profession from all plans for an imaginary or hoped-for society. Thomas More's ban of lawyers (he

[92] Cf. the remarks on the spread of lawyers through English society by E. W. Ives, "The Common Lawyers in Pre-Reformation England," *Transactions of the Royal Historical Society* Fifth Series 18 (1968), 154-55.

[93] *Landtag* in Tübingen, 1514 in *Württembergische Landtagsakten* 1. Reihe I (Stuttgart, 1913), 174.

[94] This point is made for the twelfth and thirteenth centuries by Erich Genzmer, "Hugo von Trimberg" (as in note 90), 229. It seems to me that it is valid for the sixteenth century as well.

was, of course, one himself) from Utopia, the good place that was, as yet, no place, is well known. But the arguments he presented for it in 1516 deserve to be quoted here for their appositeness to the present discussion. The Utopians, More writes,

> have very few laws because very few are needed for persons so educated. The chief fault they find with other peoples is that almost innumerable books of laws and commentaries are not sufficient. They themselves think it most unfair that any group of men should be bound by laws which are either too numerous to be read through or too obscure to be understood by anyone. Moreover they absolutely banish from their country all lawyers, who cleverly manipulate cases and cunningly argue legal points. They consider it a good thing that every man should plead his own cause and say the same to the judge as he would tell his counsel. Thus there is less ambiguity and the truth is more easily elicited when a man, uncoached in deception by a lawyer, conducts his own case, and the judge skillfully weighs each statement and helps untutored minds to defeat the false accusations of the crafty. To secure these advantages in other countries is difficult, owing to the immense mass of extremely complicated laws. But with the Utopians each man is expert in law. First they have, as I said, very few laws and, secondly, they regard the most obvious interpretation of the law as the most fair interpretation.[95]

Utopia has no lawyers because they are not needed and because, if present, they would destroy what has been achieved. Rules governing public conduct and relationships are few and simple, and everyone learns them; lawyers would only confound this "natural" state of affairs by indoctrinating citizens in adversary habits. Utopia was therefore a tempting paradigm for all who were perplexed by the age's growing social disarray. One such observer was Johann Eberlin. An intensely serious, reform-minded Franciscan preacher and early adherent of the Lutheran movement, Eberlin wrote his indignation and his hopes into "A New Order of Worldly Society Brought by Psitacus from the State of Wolfaria." Wolfaria—Welfare-land—is another imaginary but—Eberlin thought in 1521—by no means unattainable society where everyone fares well, owing in large part to the absence of legal machinations, the freedom from which was guaranteed to the Wolfarians. In Wolfaria a citizen's rights and duties are established by public discussion and assent. "No one can be a householding burgher until he

[95] Thomas More, *Utopia*, ed. Edward Surtz, S.J. and J. H. Hexter, *The Complete Works of St. Thomas More* 4 (New Haven, 1965), 195.

has made himself familiar with the common customs and rights." All "imperial" (i.e., Roman) and church laws—alien, imposed laws, that is—have been abolished, the old law books and codes destroyed. "Every individual is obligated to know what is fair and what is unfair." No jurist or advocate disturbs the social peace. "If a man cannot speak for himself, let him take along his neighbor." Penal statutes agree with the law of Moses, "for man shall not punish more severely than God."[96]

The exclusion of lawyers from Utopia[97] was intended to remove two current evils, both deeply upsetting to proponents of social and moral regeneration. Jurist's law, arbitrary and depending on compulsion, upheld the coercive order so repellent to evangelical reformers. Secondly, lawyers' stratagems perpetrated the manipulations and official meddling that tended to alienate the ordinary person from his own society. Their banishment was therefore thought to be a realistic move toward a society grounded in the principles of voluntarism, association, non-interference, and freedom from constraint. Wherever a better world was contemplated, lawyers were kept at arm's length.[98] The Reformation, especially, raised concrete hopes of such a new world abuilding, and many Protestant reformers, Luther leading them, were distinctly unfriendly to law and lawyers. In the best of all possible worlds, no lawyer's shadow ever darkened Saint Peter's door. The satirist Sebastian Brant—another jurist who shared some of the age's jaundiced views of his own profession—tells a story about St. Yves, patron saint of lawyers and an honest man who, in life, had helped the poor and counselled the unfortunate, waiting year after year for a lawyer to arrive at the door to heaven; none, however, appears.[99]

---

[96] Johann Eberlin von Günzburg, *Ein newe ordnung weltlich standts das Psitacus anzeigt hat in Wolfaria beschriben. Der XI. bundtsgenoss* (*Neudrucke deutscher Litteraturwerke* No. 141), 122, 127-28, 130.

[97] The phenomenon is a general one not limited to the two by More and Eberlin discussed here. See, for example, Anton Francesco Doni, *The New World* (1553) as discussed in Paul F. Grendler, *Critics of the Italian World 1530-1560* (Madison, 1969), 174.

[98] Two contrasting examples: (1) Leipzig, 1525: a rebellion in the city led by Michael Rumpfer demanded, among other changes, that all jurists should be removed from government service. Cited in R. W. Scribner, "The Reformation as a Social Movement" in *Stadtbürgertum und Adel in der Reformation* ed. Wolfgang J. Mommsen (Stuttgart, 1979), 73; (2) In 1529, the Spanish crown banned all lawyers from the new colony of Peru. See Richard L. Kagan, *Lawsuits and Litigants in Castile 1500-1700* (Chapel Hill, 1981), 19.

[99] Quoted by Karl Heinz Burmeister, "Der hl. Ivo und seine Verehrung an den deutschen Rechtsfakultäten," *ZRG* 92 (1975), *Germ.Abt.*, 62. On St. Yves as a cultic figure—significant in people's attitudes toward law and litigation—see Hans Christoph

"Leave our towns and villages to their ancient courts, meetings, and customs," the estates of Württemberg begged their duke at the time of the rebellion called "Armer Konrad" in 1514, "as these have been passed down to us from the days of our forefathers, despite the efforts of the doctors."[100] Lawyers were seen as foes of the traditional order, eager destroyers of familiar routines, "modernizers" undermining a culture deeply attached to accustomed ways. Lawyers were outsiders to the social body, unsympathetic to its often irrational folkways, ignorant and contemptuous of its workings. Their technical know-how and command of law idiom gave them a powerful instrument for innovation. Lay judges and jurors had to be reminded "to stick to the old customs and pay no heed to the doctors."[101] Their cliquishness mocked their claim to impartiality. "One moment they act as advocates," the estates of Bamberg complained to their lord-bishop, "the next we see them sitting with the judges, offering them help and advice. It's easy to imagine," they add, "what the common man thinks of such practices."[102]

The weightiest of the reproaches against them, however, was the widely held suspicion that they acted as the advance guard of the forces of political and ecclesiastical centralization. Their codes, their rigid formalism, and their levelling procedures were seen as a juggernaut poised to crush diversity and flexibility in society so that the way might be made smooth for the uniform rules of the authoritarian state. Jurists— and in the sixteenth century this designation carried automatic association with the Roman law—were believed (not in every instance fairly, as we shall see) to be the chief promoters of autocracy.[103] They were also the most visible agents of ruling princes and governing magistrates in the struggle to broaden and increase sovereign jurisdictions over lesser authorities. The documents in which the incidents of this struggle are recorded are full of complaints about courts by-passed, judgments disallowed, venues changed, briefs transferred, jurisdictions removed; of protests against arrogant officials guilty of summary actions against long-standing rights, abrogation of established guarantees, unjustified

Heinerth, *Die Heiligen und das Recht* (Freiburg i.B., 1939), 13-19; on St. Yves as patron saint of lawyers, *ibid.*, 76-96.

[100] Grievances of Württemberg *Landschaft* 1514 in Günther Franz, *Quellen* No. 8, p. 50.

[101] Counsellors of the city of Nuremberg to the city's *Schöffen*, 1505, quoted in Hermann Knapp, "Das alte Nürnberger Kriminalverfahren bis zur Einführung der Karolina," *Zeitschrift für die gesamte Staatswissenschaft* XII (1892), 258.

[102] From grievances presented by estates of Bishopric of Bamberg, 1521, StA Bamb B28, No. 13, 4ᵛ.

[103] A good example of this belief in practice is given by Quentin Skinner, *The Foundations of Modern Political Thought* (Cambridge, 1978) II, 132-33.

imposition of fees and taxes, of petitions for relief from arbitrary regulations, unprecedented fees, and inquisitorial investigations—all ending in the refrain "which goes against the old traditions, freedoms, and customs guaranteed to us since ancient times," and always lamenting the loss of time and the heavy out-of-pocket expenses borne by those on the receiving side of *neuerung und ännderung*.[104] Jurists and lawyers were instigators as well as executors of these "innovations and alterations." This, in any case, was what was believed: they were at once the ideologues proposing the restructuring of society in the direction of autocracy and the technocrats who oversaw the enactment of this scheme.[105]

The loudest and most sustained response to this threat came from the group that stood to lose most from the disappearance of traditional rights: the aristocracy, whose survival as a class depended critically on the repulsion or deflection of every such "innovation and alteration." Anxiety was gravest in the lower ranks of the nobility, and it was there that resistance to the alarming drift was most vociferous. In every region and territory, representatives of the imperial knights led the opposition to the new law and its agents. Especially galling was the elevation of jurists to comparable social rank. Since the middle of the fourteenth century, doctors of law were counted as members of the lower nobility: *milites legalis militiae*. Seeing these newcomers replace them in the service of their states—in the political fabric of which petty nobles were increasingly anachronistic figures at the very time when *Fürstendienst*, state service, gained greater favor as a career choice[106]— knights excoriated lawyers in tones in turn plaintive and outraged.

Protesting against the presence of "so many of the learned" on their

[104] The quotations in this summary are from protest by spokesmen for the *Gerichte* (i.e., districts) in Tyrol against violations of old traditions by agents of the Habsburg *Regierung*, 1547: LA Tir, *Tiroler Landtagsakten* Fasz. 375 (no foliation).

[105] In the often-quoted first note to his *The Old Regime and the Revolution*, Alexis de Tocqueville argues vehemently that "the singular availability of the Roman law—which was a slave law—for the purposes of monarchs, who were just then establishing their absolute power upon the ruins of the old liberties of Europe, was the true cause" of the triumph of the foreign over the domestic law. He continues: "Kings naturally embraced it with enthusiasm, and established it wherever they could throughout Europe; its interpreters became their ministers or their chief agents. Lawyers furnished them at need with legal warrant for violating the law. They have often done so since. Monarchs who have trampled the laws have almost always found a lawyer ready to prove the lawfulness of their acts—to establish learnedly that violence was just, and that the oppressed were in the wrong." Translation by John Bonner (New York, 1856), 272-73. On this question generally see Erwin Riezler, *Die Abneigung gegen die Juristen* (*Münchener Juristische Vorträge* Heft 2, Munich, 1925), 7-8, 15-16.

[106] Hans Hattenhauer, *Geschichte des Beamtentums* (*Handbuch des öffentlichen Dienstes* I, Cologne, 1980), 72.

duchy's high court (*Hofgericht*) around 1500, the Bavarian *Ritterschaft* denounced the

> great oppression of our common rights . . . inflicted on us. The benches of the high courts are no longer occupied as they used to be in the old days, but have now come into the hands of the learned. And hardly a locally born man [*landmann*] is found on the court who knows where the book is kept by which judgment should be given, which the foreigners [*auslender*] know nothing about and hold in contempt; and out of this contempt new laws are made, unheard of in the days of our forefathers and mortal to our common rights and customs.[107]

The duke's reply to this complaint shows how far the change in the empire's legal order had penetrated into its territories.

> A great number of doctors sit on our high courts [wrote the duke] because they have superior knowledge of the law. And because their legal understanding is greater than that of laymen, their judgments are more correct and in better agreement with the law. Thus our people are not harmed by faulty verdicts which, when appealed to the Imperial Chamber Court, would be rejected there.[108]

It was a good argument. "As long as the successive stages of appeal went from the territorial high court to the Imperial Chamber Court, whose bench was occupied by doctors of law," comments the historian of the Bavarian administrative system, "it was only sensible to fear that verdicts prepared without the help of jurists and without due attention to the foreign law, would always be overruled at the highest instance."[109] But the nobles' protest was not merely directed against a few "doctors" sitting on appellate courts. It attacked the whole scheme of political reorganization of which jurists were the strategists. A huge distance separated the nobility's idea of "ancient rights" from the

---

[107] The Bavarian *Ritterschaft* to the government, 1497, printed in Franz von Krenner ed., *Baierische Landtags-Handlungen in den Jahren 1429 bis 1513* (Munich, 1803-1805), XIII, 8-9. In Bavaria, the *Hofgericht*, or Duke's aulic court, sat in the chief cities of the subdivisions of the duchy. It was presided over by the duke himself, or by his deputy, the marshal or the major domo. The presiding officer's *Beisitzer*, assessors, consisted of nobles, an occasional burgher, and—increasingly in the later fifteenth century—ducal councillors, a growing number of whom were jurists. See Eduard Rosenthal, *Geschichte des Gerichtswesens und der Verwaltungsorganisation Baierns* (Würzburg, 1889-1906; reprint Aalen, 1968) I, 134-48.

[108] Reply drafted by Bavarian councillors to a repetition of the above complaint, 1501. Printed in Krenner, *Landtags-Handlungen* XIII, 191.

[109] Eduard Rosenthal, *op. cit.*, I, 144.

state's plans for a well-ordered polity. In 1534 the associated knights in the Bishopric of Bamberg defended as "a right guaranteed by ancient tradition" their practice of despoiling the churches in their lands. It may be old custom (*alt herkomen*), said the bishop in response to their defense of this right, but now it goes against the spirit and violates the letter of common and imperial laws.[110] Nothing in the new law recognized the legal solipsism claimed by the Bamberg knights. No lawyer whose understanding of politics derived from Justinian's code could evince much sympathy for the kind of free-wheeling particularism in which the nobility's privileges were rooted. All estates were conscious of the enormous gulf between these two positions—this is what made resistance to law and lawyers a general, rather than a class- or place-specific phenomenon. Thus the cities of Württemberg argued at their caucus for the *Landtag* of Tübingen in 1514 that "doctors" should be excluded from their prince's council whenever the matter under discussion touched the duchy's common concerns.[111] The larger issue motivating this and similar protests—resistance to the invasive force of the new state—will be discussed in later chapters. The point here is the singling out of "doctors," and of their less learned colleagues, as the villains in the piece.

The most intemperate outburst against them came from one who considered himself the leading spokesman for his class, Ulrich von Hutten, whose dialogue *Praedones*—"Robbers"—written in 1521, brought together nearly all accusations aimed at lawyers in his time. Of the four degrees of "robbers" pilloried in this tract, only priests are worse—so Hutten contends—and thicker on the ground. "Legal experts [*iureconsulti*] are the soul of all that goes on in the world now . . . ; no state can be governed without them. They build up governments and then tear them down again, just as they please." Good princes are corrupted by them: it was by his lawyers that Charles V allowed himself to be convinced that an edict should be issued against Martin Luther. Their only aim is to enrich themselves. Although stupid, they have duped ordinary people into respecting them as learned men. But their so-called art is nothing but idle chatter, and their intelligence serves only to quibble, cheat, and mislead. We allow them to turn our heads with a string of citations from thick tomes, but in our hearts we know that it is all a bag of tricks. Conscience means nothing to them; they care only for words. Mere words decide whether a man is to go free or will be ruined. Their books allow them to prove anything they

---

[110] StA Bamb, B28, No. 2, 95ʳ.
[111] *Württembergische Landtagsakten* 1. Reihe, ed. Ohr and Kober, I, 139.

wish to prove; they bend the law to their designs as a goldsmith shapes a lump of wax. The most successful of them are those who can turn the worst case into the greatest victory. Harmony among men is loathsome to them; they therefore incite people to endless litigation. No fairness, no equity exist for these men, who should be expelled from all the courts and chancelleries that they now infest, and their books burned. But our rulers have too little courage to send them packing. Princes should look in their hearts for justice; instead they rely on the texts of their jurists who, having usurped the nobility's place at the side of princes, govern unimpeded, growing richer by the year and plundering everything in sight. No conquering tyrant could rule Germany more despotically than these villainous manipulators of justice who now oppress the land. They are, indeed, "Germany's misfortune." It is high time, says Hutten, that we followed the example of our ancestors, who, when they wanted to rid themselves of this pest, cut out their tongues and sewed up their lips.[112]

Hutten's invective could scarcely be escalated in its ferocity. From his lines speaks the anger of his class as well as the rage of the national patriot. That many jurists in high administrative and judicial positions were foreigners did not enhance their image. To be sure, "foreign" (*fremd, auslendig*) was a generously construed designation in sixteenth-century usage. Not many of the doctors came from abroad, though the Habsburgs brought Spaniards into their Austrian and Tyrolean domains, a practice that provoked vigorous protest from their estates. "For many years now the government has been in the hands of foreigners ignorant of the German nation and the German tongue, and ill informed on matters touching Germany and the empire."[113] The answer to this complaint was that appointment to state offices was the prince's prerogative,[114] and rulers regularly made use of this right to attract "foreign learned and able people"[115] to their governments. Many of these "foreigners" were, however, Germans with degrees from Italian or French universities, a condition that made them strangers in the eyes of the territory's estates, to whom only an indigenous person with

[112] Ulrich von Hutten, *Praedones* in Eduard Böcking, ed., *Ulrichi Hutteni . . . opera* 4 (Leipzig, 1860), 378-86. In German translation: *Die Räuber* in Ernst Münch, ed. and tr., *Ulrich von Hutten. Auserlesene Werke* III (Leipzig, 1823), 394-410.

[113] From Grievances of the Protestant estates at Passau, 1552, quoted in Eduard Rosenthal, "Die Behördenorganisation Kaiser Ferdinands I. Das Vorbild der Verwaltungsorganisation in den deutschen Territorien," *Archiv für österreichische Geschichte* 69 (1887), 76.

[114] *Id., Geschichte des Gerichtswesens . . . Baierns*, 552.

[115] *Id.*, "Behördenorganisation," 171-72.

property on the soil, and not very much travel abroad, was a *landkind*, a native son. "Cities and lands are never so ruined as when foreigners are taken into the government" was a favorite adage, and "the native-born must always be preferred to any others."[116] But "foreign" and "other" referred more often to Germans from a different region in the empire, or even to a local man with foreign ties, than to a genuine import like Doctor Salamanca, the Spanish finance minister of Ferdinand I who aroused great indignation in Tyrol.[117] Thus the frequent complaints about "foreign" provenance and an "alien" cast of mind must be understood in the context of the age's tenacious localism, by whose wisdom a person from a neighboring territory or city—especially one of the imperial cities—was an outsider. It was a man's roots in a place that made him a native. The study and practice of law, inevitably linked in the sixteenth century to its Italian origins and international ties, tended—at least at moments of stress—to stamp a person as a "foreigner," revoke his native status, and generally place him under suspicion.

DEEPER currents therefore swelled the flood of complaints, protests, and denunciations. Feeding the ill will and driving the attacks on the legal profession was a growing public sense of alienation from the drift of political life. A profoundly traditional society reacted in this way to an intruding ideology whose promoters were perceived as agents of change. As such they appeared to pose a threat to the stability, some thought the survival, of familiar social patterns. In the sixteenth century these fears crested. The transmutation of jurists into powerfully placed bureaucrats, and the evident linkage between bureaucracy and the would-be autocratic state (which, from the 1540s or so, included the church, and not only in Protestant countries), heightened suspicions and stiffened resistance. Forceful and pervasive as it was, this opposition is somewhat blurred, and the evidence for it clouded, by the usefulness of the new law to all sides in the struggle.[118] To the resisters no less than to the aggressors, law was at times an indispensable tool and the learned counsel an invaluable ally. Their utility, however, scarcely neutralized the threat they seemed to pose. To their contemporaries,

---

[116] Both proverbs quoted in Eduard Graf and Mathias Dietherr, *Deutsche Rechts-sprichwörter* (Nördlingen, 1864), 517-18.

[117] Article 46 of the 1525 Meran Articles demanded Dr. Salamanca's expulsion from Tyrol. Cf. Günther Franz, *Quellen*, 283.

[118] For a survey of positive attitudes toward Roman law among estates and municipalities, see Georg von Below, *Die Ursachen der Reception des römischen Rechts* (Munich and Berlin, 1905), 67-101. More on this in Chapter Eight, below.

they stood for a transformation coming to pass in their time, the symptoms and portents of which aroused deep distress. For reasons still to be examined, law and lawyers therefore became a symbol for much that appeared worrisome, distasteful, or upsetting in society, a kind of objective correlative to vaguely defined, but keenly felt, dissatisfactions. A universal phenomenon not unfamiliar to students of other periods and countries,[119] the movement of opposition to law reached special intensity in the German-speaking regions of the Holy Roman Empire around the time of the Protestant Reformation. The following chapters will attempt to explain why this was so.

[119] For example: E. Meynal, "Remarques sur la réaction populaire contre l'invasion du droit romain au France aux XIIe et XIIIe siècles," *Romanische Forschungen* XXIII (1907), 557-84; Richard L. Kagan, "Lawyers and Litigation in Castile" (as in note 15), 195-96; Peter Burke, *Popular Culture in Early Modern Europe* (New York, 1978), 183; Christopher Hill, *The World Turned Upside Down: Radical Ideas During the English Revolution* (London, 1972), 82-83, 92, 107-08, 259, 308, 332; E. J. Hobsbawm, *Primitive Rebels* (New York, 1965 [first published 1959]), 22; Eugen Weber, *Peasants into Frenchmen. The Modernization of Rural France 1870-1914* (Stanford, 1976), 50-51.

CHAPTER TWO

Law: Views and Disputes

THERE is a folktale, at home in many cultures, of a king who watches in disguise as a child improvises a game recreating the crux of a difficult legal case, and playfully solves it.[1] The story touches the nerve of the controversy over law in the sixteenth century as seen by the weak and the obscure. In this perspective, all the conundrums of legal science are the inventions of cunning and ambitious men. Their effect—indeed, their purpose—is to cloud evident truth and open the obvious to doubt. Left to themselves, issues are simple and clear: matters of right and wrong. Plain folk could solve them by trusting their instincts and obeying their common sense. Read in this context, the story, in which the king comes to recognize the superior virtue of artlessness and innocence in the solution of conflicts, is an emblem of the cultural distance separating professional from lay approaches to the "speaking of law."

Popular ideas about law must be inferred. But from the pens of the educated came explanations in large number of the nature of law and its function in a world perfectly governed by God but very imperfectly lived in by his creatures. It is interesting to see how pointedly such expositions of judicial principles raise the same ethical questions that were asked outside the circle of law experts, only to side-step their implications by incorporating them in declarations legitimizing the established order. The preface to Ulrich Tengler's *Layman's Mirror* of 1510, for example, begins with natural rights, ends with the "two swords," and bridges the distance between these two poles by a tidy sequence of arguments. As he created Adam and Eve, Tengler begins, God poured natural rights (*natürlich recht*) into the very spirit of life (*geist des lebens*) so that, had mankind remained in its original condition, the knowledge of these rights "would have been sufficient for peaceful association, and all things would have been held in common among men." But with the fall came "unbridled greed . . . , wrangling and bickering every day, discord against peace," and in these new circumstances "the faded natural law [*das verblichen natürlich gesatz*] was no longer enough." The inner spring of lawful conduct having run dry, an

[1] Stith Thompson, *Motif-Index of Folk Literature* (revised edition, Bloomington, Ind., 1955-1958) J 123.

external force had to be applied. "In his divine solicitude, God therefore resolved to teach and subdue [*underweisen und bezwingen*] men by means of commandments of law, [instructing them] how they should live honestly, do injury to no one, and give to each person his due." Roman and imperial laws (*die gemeinen recht*) were promulgated to support these commandments, the spiritual and worldly swords appointed to uphold them, and "new statutes and edicts issued whenever the situation created an honest need for them." All this, Tengler assures his readers, has been explained at length, "in hard-to-understand Latin," by "learned men who are wise in matters of law."[2]

It is true, as Tengler says, that these philosophical subjects received ample discussion in the academic tongue. From the beginning of professional jurisprudence, legal writers had discoursed, usually in explanation of the opening titles of Justinian's *Institutes* (1.1-2), on the origins, purpose, scope, and formal arrangement of law. What is remarkable is that so many authors should have thought these matters worth imparting to a wider circle of lay readers, in the common tongue. Their effort was no doubt impelled by the urgent need to justify the existing legal system—and the political order underlying it—in the face of expressed and anticipated objections to it on historical as well as on moral and religious grounds. The Christian tradition made such justification both necessary and easy, and most authors offered it in similar terms, dressing it in images and phrases familiar for centuries as the conservative rationale for aggressive law-making and law-enforcing.

On the one hand, so runs this argument, we have an inborn sense of right and wrong, which is the active part of that divine gift of natural rights on which all our entitlements are based. "Natural right is what all creatures possess by nature. . . . From this right come freedom and the common ownership of all things." (The words are the Saxon jurist Melchior Kling's, in the preface to his edition of the territorial law of Saxony.)[3] Because man has been created in God's image, these rights can never entirely vanish from a world governed by Providence. For this reason "statutes cannot invalidate natural rights"[4] and "a law does not stand if it prohibits or fails to acknowledge the true nature of things and actions."[5] When violence is done to natural rights, we are promptly

---

[2] Ulrich Tengler, *Layenspiegel. Von rechtmässigen ordnungen in Burgerlichen und peinlichen regimenten* . . . (Strasbourg, 1510), unnumbered leaves following Aiiii.

[3] Melchior Kling, *Das gantze Sechssisch Landrecht . . . in eine richtige ordnung gebracht* . . . (Leipzig, 1571), iv^v-v^r.

[4] Günter Grundmann *et al.*, *Rechtssprichwörter* (Leipzig, 1980), 27.

[5] From Justin Gobler's translation of Constantine Harmenopoulos, *Handbuch und Auszug kayserlicher und Bürgerlicher Rechten* . . . (Frankfurt am Main, 1564), viii^r.

and spontaneously made aware of the injury. How is it, asks Justin Gobler, a prolific legal writer and prominent jurist in mid-sixteenth century, that we can tell with such certainty right from wrong, fair from unfair? "We know it [he replies] by the light and natural understanding implanted and infused in man from the beginning. Owing to this light, if a thing goes against the law of nature, it cannot long endure in the laws of men."[6]

Here Gobler's argument makes an easy transition from natural rights to positive laws. The same natural understanding that sounds an instinctive warning when something is wrong also impels us to accept the need for positive laws. Gobler continues:

> As all sensible people can count and reckon, and know that two are more than one and four are more than two, so it is natural, that is to say innate to our nature, to acknowledge laws. In other words, it is a function of our nature to recognize that there must be [objective] law and that there must be order. And from this inborn knowledge, natural perception, and sound reason come all the excellent codes, regulations, and constitutions discovered and set down by experienced, wise, learned men in the service of our governments.

Codifying the true nature and relations of things into laws is an act as natural as the love parents express for their children. When such "natural, inborn inclination and love" is "put in writing, set in good arrangements, and displayed in formal patterns," Gobler says, we call the result *ius positivum*,[7] which is "a body of law enacted by governments and magistrates and intended by them as an addition and able assistant [*zusatz und Gehülff*] to the natural law," "an aid and comfort"—in the words of another jurist—"to the law of nature and to good customs."[8] Gobler gives the punishment for theft as an example of how this "addition and assistance" works in practice:

> Natural right sets it down as a general proposition that theft must be punished. Governments and magistrates extend this principle by determining how punishment shall take place, and what the penalty shall be, namely, that a thief shall be brought before the court, tried, and hanged.

---

[6] Justin Gobler, *Spiegel der Rechten* (Frankfurt am Main, 1573), 17ͬ.

[7] "*Ius positivum*" is actually a misnomer, dating back to about the twelfth century, for *ius positum*, "posited"—i.e., "set down" or "laid down" law, from *legem ponere*.

[8] ". . . *dem natürlichen rechten und der guten gewonheit zu hülff*." From the glosses by Christoph Zobell to the *Sechssisch Weychbild und Lehnrecht* . . . (Leipzig, 1537), Aiiiͮ.

It does not matter that the positive law varies from country to country. "The important thing is that it must never go against natural right."[9]

The implicit circularity in Gobler's exposition (and in that of all other legists who wrote on the subject) arises from a second assumption, one that effectively undercuts the implications of his initial postulate concerning natural rights. The post-lapsarian corruption of all human beings necessitates a social order ready to inhibit and restrain them. This conclusion, which seems to have been more firmly accepted the higher one rose in society, was the ground on which all political edifices stood. Men being wicked, they need a firm hand to hold them back. God provides for these constraints. Having made his world, he does not walk away from his creation, says Gobler; instead he "preserves and governs the human race day by day." *Oberkeyt und regenten*, and the laws and institutions made by them, are God's tools for sustaining this ceaseless governance. Christoph Zobell, a Saxon jurist, explains how this mission is carried out:

> Listen now to how the laws we call "written" have come about. In the far distant past, some people followed the natural laws while others did not. This division resulted in two kinds of customs, one honest and praiseworthy—and this was the way of the good people, rooted in nature—the other the way of the wicked, going against nature. . . . Because of the conflict between these two kinds of customs, the need arose for written laws to be set over them, and this was the work of noble emperors who, coming to the aid of the good and their worthy customs, . . . made a code, which we call "the written law," and which began when the emperor chose from between the two kinds of custom the most honest and best and made a code of law to support it.[10]

Rulers know "what God demands of them and what their office is," namely, the protection of the pious and the punishment of the wicked.

And in order that they may proceed in this task without losing their way [writes Gobler], not straying too far either to the left or to the right, but walking straight in the middle path, they have, from the

---

[9] Justin Gobler, *Spiegel der Rechten*, 17v. On the appropriate punishment of thieves there existed a controversy among jurists. The question was whether Exodus 22:1-4 or the provisions of Roman law should apply. The former listed a number of varieties of theft but said nothing about the death penalty for any of them. Melanchthon touches on this issue in his 1528 *Unterricht der Visitatoren an die Pfarrherrn im Kurfürstentum zu Sachsen* (in Robert Stupperich ed., *Melanchthons Werke in Auswahl* I (Gütersloh, 1951), 233-34.

[10] Christoph Zobell in *Sechssisch Weychbild* Aiiiv.

very beginning of human association and common life, made laws, ordinances, and statutes, by the enforcement of which as a divine and necessary instrument rulers and governments fulfill their office.[11]

Gobler dismisses the claim that positive laws are products of human cunning, serving mainly to oppress the poor and exploit the weak:

> No . . . , God has ordained and established [written laws] as a precious instrument for the preservation of government, community, and neighborly association so that tranquility and peace may reign among men under the watchful eyes of emperor, kings, princes, and lords, whose high task it is to keep and champion the laws, for which office we must regard them as God's loving gift to mankind, and by no means dishonor them or bring them into contempt.[12]

Without the strong bonds of the written law, and the authority of the lawgiver to back it, the wickedness of men would run free. General injunctions—to live honestly, to hurt no one, to give every man his due—could not by themselves "curb men's evil will" and crush the "wrangling, trouble making, fighting, and mutual hatred" resulting from it (this was said by Kilian König, in the preface to a treatise on procedure). Only the *ius positivum* stands between civilized society and chaos.[13] Good government is the suppression of uncontrolled human drives by "using the will of the written law to overcome human self-seeking."[14]

Tengler's, Gobler's, König's, Zobell's, and their colleagues' explanations of the legal order never descended from the heights of these sweeping terms. Their emphasis on the normative laws *ought* to be in harmony with natural rights; rulers *should* perform their duties mindful of their role as servants of God gave their works an air of philosophical detachment. But clearly these men were, and considered themselves to be, spokesmen for established authorities in German cities and principalities, and they chose their arguments and cases in point to make the established order appear rational, godly, and inevitable. As in Gobler's example of the proper fit between positive and natural law, in which the hanging of a thief stands as the correct enactment of an unalterable natural principle, their explanations sought to forestall any possible misunderstanding of social arrangements as being either cir-

---

[11] Justin Gobler, *Der Rechten Spiegel* (Frankfurt am Main, 1550), a^r-aii^r.

[12] *Ibid.*

[13] Kilian König, *Practica und Prozess* (Bautzen, 1555) preface (n.p.).

[14] ". . . *dass man durch des gesetzten rechts willen, menschliche dürstigkeit bezwung . . .*": Christoph Zobell in a gloss on *Sechssisch Weychbild*, Aii^v.

cumstantial or contingent. In their depiction of it, the established order is not only ordained and, for this reason alone, unshakable; it is, as well, the result of rational processes at work in nature. Things are what they are by God's inscrutable design, but also by right reason, which is a universal faculty shared by us all. Newly redacted collections of law usually opened with statements of definition (often taken from classical jurisprudence) in which legislation is linked to such lofty legitimizing principles. The "Patrimonial Court Constitution for Saxony," for example, began with the declaration (paraphrased from opening passages in Justinian's *Institutes* and *Digest*) that "*Justicia*, called *Gerechtigkeit* in German, is a constant, unassailable, perpetual will apportioning to each what is his or what has been given to him by God and by right."[15] The implied suggestion here is that the ensuing statutes must be taken as embodying the noble principle announced in the preamble. Whenever possible, jurists demonstrated that their draft laws, verdicts, or advisory opinions were grounded in a harmonious concordance of divine revelation, the rules of reason, written law, and the demands of equity (*Billigkeit*). Arguments were deployed to prove this point, showing, for instance, that a local statute should be upheld "because it is in agreement with reason and fairness, and is not directly contradicted by the common [*gemeine*, i.e., Roman] law."[16] To find against it would impair the concordance of laws and rights that was, according to the jurists, the key to responsible legislation. This principle could be stated positively—"the law of nature commands us to live honestly, to do injury to no one, and to give everyone his right and due"[17]—or negatively, as when the Bavarian state councillor Octavianus Schrenck, introducing Andreas Perneder's *New Criminal Code*, contended that a country's laws must do more than merely ensure "that everyone is safe in the possession of what is rightfully his." They must also, he wrote, warrant "that both in respect of his property and in respect of his body and life, no man is aggrieved contrary to fairness, to the divine law, or to the workings of nature, which will not permit a creature made in the image of the Almighty to be in any way injured or distressed."[18]

Two agencies were required to guarantee compliance with this prescription: legitimate authority and skilled jurists. Rulers, for their part,

---

[15] From an *Ehegerichtsordnung* (*Ehe* = *Hege-gericht*; see Chapter Eight, below) for Amt Stollberg, Saxony, 1556. StA Dr, Loc. 8832, "Amt Stolbergks Acta," 19r.

[16] StA Dr, Loc. 9665: "Leipziger Schöffensprüche und andere Rechtsgutachten," 18v.

[17] Melchior Kling, preface to *Sechssisch Landrecht*, vr. See also Ulrich Tengler, *Layenspiegel*, Jr.

[18] Octavius Schrenck, preface to *Ain newe Halsgerichtsordnung* . . . (Ingolstadt, 1573), Ddd iir.

relished their position as supreme heads of the legal edifice in their realms; they routinely affirmed their love of justice "to which before our Lord God we are duty-bound as well as personally inclined."[19] As for jurists, they made much of their acknowledged indispensability to the judicial and administrative process. Law being "a general commandment or decree, the counsel of wise men, . . . a divine creation,"[20] it was the "counsel of wise men" that made the difference between good and bad law in a given state. Ulpian's praise of his vocation, included in the *Digest* (1.1.1; 10) was often quoted: "*Ius* is the art of what is good and fair. Of this art we may deservedly be called the priests." There is no doubt that the sixteenth-century jurist's pride of place, and his ambition to rise beyond it, rested on this exalted view of his calling. At a time when jurists and theologians were vigorously, sometimes bitterly, competing to be heard on the great questions affecting human life and destiny, this claim to a priestly office in secular affairs was not frivolously made, nor was it passively received.

As EXERCISES in legitimation, statements like Gobler's and Tengler's must have carried a certain reassurance in the ears of established authorities. At the other end of the political spectrum, however, their authority was severely diminished by their failure to confront the most crucial of social questions, the interconnections between law and power. That law *was* power is ancient wisdom, to which Luther and other religious reformers gave new currency, as we have seen. But the proposition that legal norms always mirror existing power structures was scarcely ever articulated by writers with official connections, although some radical notions about this were beginning to surface during the turbulent years of the Reformation.

A lively interest in equity sometimes led a writer to the obvious conclusion that "right" was whatever the laws said. In the old days, according to Johann Oldendorp, a jurist from the north of Germany and a legal educator long active in the government of Hessen, people always equated "fair" and "good." They never asked "What is fair and *right?*" but strove instead to do "What is fair and *good.*" This natural way of pursuing justice came to an end when positive laws were introduced, and with them the substitution of "legal" for "just." Now, Oldendorp says, most people imagine that "fair" has no other meaning than "ac-

---

[19] From instructions of Landgrave Wilhelm to the jurist Jacob Lersner upon his appointment to the Marburg *Hofgericht* in 1552, quoted in Franz Gundlach, *Die hessischen Zentralbehörden von 1247 bis 1604* (*Veröffentlichungen der historischen Kommission für Hessen und Waldeck* XVI, Marburg, 1930-1932), II, 15.

[20] From Justin Gobler's translation of Hermenopoulos's *Handbuch und Auszug*, viii^r.

cording to law." In fact, the two are far apart. Ask "What is right?" and you will be told what is prescribed by the letter of the written law. But this is very different from "what is fair," which is a judgment flowing from "a decision made by natural reason" drawn from the principle of the Golden Rule. Oldendorp makes a point of denying that such judgments can be taken from law books. "It's a trial," he wrote, "taking place in your heart or conscience," in which you take all appropriate circumstances into consideration.[21] But while he is emphatic on the superiority of equity over written codes—equity is, he says, "the best part of law"—Oldendorp never alludes to the connections between law making and access to political power.

To critics less prominently placed than Oldendorp, however, these links were self-evident. If law is the imposition of order on collective life, a society's legal system will always favor those in a position to impose. The normative maxims sanctioned by official legal philosophy— whether drawn from natural law ("law must accord with fairness") or quoting the Roman code ("justice is a constant, unfailing disposition to give everyone his legal due")[22]—therefore offered no guarantee of fair dealing in a society fragmented by the clash of concrete and vital interests.[23]

In official circles, the starting point for considering problems of legitimacy was always the question "What does the law say?" But those who lacked position and power, or who saw themselves as their victims, began with a much more basic question. They asked "What is just?" Legal experts were of little help in addressing this fundamental concern in other than platitudinous terms, though they were not reluctant to be heard on the subject. Their answers, as we have seen, were set in patterns that affirmed the existing order of things. Before this or-

[21] Johann Oldendorp, *Wat byllick und recht ys, eyne korte erklaring, allen stenden denstlick* (Rostock, 1529), 11-15. See the discussion of Oldendorp's scholarly writings on equity by Hans-Helmut Dietze, *Johann Oldendorp als Rechtsphilosoph und Protestant* (Königsberg, 1933), 78-90.

[22] Ulpian in *Digest* 1.1.10. Charles Henry Monro, tr., *The Digest of Justinian* (Cambridge, 1904-09).

[23] Modern definitions are apt to beg the question, too. E.g., Helmut Coing, *Epochen der Rechtsgeschichte in Deutschland* (Munich, 1967), 2: "The point of justice [*Recht*] is to find for a given community an arrangement of laws that guarantees peace and security, and establishes according to the principles of justice the relations among citizens themselves as well as between them and their political organization." But who defines "the principles of justice" and determines when the legal arrangement meets their demands? For an interesting and useful survey of modern German definitions of law and justice (*Recht*), see Gerhard Köbler, *Das Recht im frühen Mittelalter* . . . (Cologne and Vienna, 1971), 5-11.

der could be attacked, therefore, the jurists' defense of it had first to be broken, and this could be done only by shifting the ground of the discussion. This move was initiated most often by the charge, implicit in the story opening the present chapter, that positive, objective, manmade laws, far from being—as the jurists claimed—a just "extension" or commensurate "addition" and "support" of ineluctable natural rights, were in fact counterfeit alterations of benign pristine conditions. The natural human state is, so it is contended, to be peaceful, helpful, and trusting. In their natural setting people know and do what is right. The ideal situation is one without laws of any kind. Laws always falsify the artless essence of things. By introducing definitions and establishing rules, they turn what is naturally just and fair into a contrived set of arbitrary standards. Imagine a situation, says Hans Sachs in one of his cautionary rhymes, in which brothers confide in each other, neighbors live in friendship and mutual support, and husbands and wives exchange love, fidelity, and comfort. What could a code of civil and criminal law contribute to such an idyll?[24] It would only destroy it by substituting ingenuity for innocence, artifice for spontaneity, interference and manipulation for sound human impulses.

In contrast to the opinion of the experts, popular notions about the origin of human laws did not lay such heavy emphasis on the corruption of mankind's inborn goodness. Our native sense of what is right, and our capacity for recognizing it in real-life situations, remain essentially unimpaired. Folk wisdom insisted on this, and many appeals were made to the good sense of ordinary people, whose innate aptitude for telling right from wrong seemed a better guarantee of social equity than the codes of learned academics. The idea of a "law inscribed in the hearts of men," a favorite of spiritualist theologians,[25] was a fundamental truth for populist critics of learned jurisprudence. Their position was that people—ordinary people—have a native capacity for "finding" what is right. As the just order of things is given, established for all time, and the moral realm has objective reality in God's universe, it must be possible to "find," understand, and act upon its precepts. Jurists and politicians, while not accused of denying this simple truth, were suspected of distorting it by embedding it in pro- and prescriptive rules. For the community, the effect of this perversion has been lamentable. The remedy, critics thought, was to bring fresh and innocent

[24] Hans Sachs, *Drey Stück, so Gott und den menschen gefallen* in Adelbert von Keller, ed., *Hans Sachs* IV, 295-96.

[25] See on this Ulrich Bubenheimer, *Consonantia Theologiae et Iurisprudentiae. Andreas Bodenstein von Karlstadt als Theologe und Jurist zwischen Scholastik und Reformation* (Tübingen, 1977), 266-80.

minds to bear on the resulting human and social problems. The application of artless, direct habits of thought and of plain speech gave promise of a liberating approach.

In the vision offered by this program, justice among men would replicate the divine world order. The subjective rights of men do not differ from the laws established by God as part of his plan of creation. Infringements of these rights are violations of God's law. Long ago, in the distant historical past, this was not only recognized but also accepted and observed. For this reason, old laws are usually good laws. Innovations are nearly always for the worse. "The idea of the 'good old law,' " comments Otto Brunner, "is the most vigorous expression of a form of legal thought in which right and justice are the same as right and law, and in which all 'law,' all enactment, ordinance, and commands are held to be valid only within the concept of 'right,' that is, within the conviction held at the grass roots of society that ideal law and positive law cannot and must not be separated."[26] To be sound, positive law must be both "old" and "good"—Fritz Kern's characterization of medieval concepts of law[27] is even more apposite to the spirit of sixteenth-century protests against "official" law making and "learned" jurisprudence. "Old" meant having ancient origins, conforming to pre-existing standards of legitimacy. "Good" signified close approximation to norms of morality and fairness rooted in the conscience. Together, "old" and "good" assured stability. "Old" and "good" laws had stood the test of time; for this reason they were held to be permanently true, not subject to change or distorting interpretation. Honest people had lived by these laws in the past, not because they had been chained to them by "written" codes backed by force, but because they had accepted them in their hearts. They honored God as their only true law giver; beside him they revered only a handful of wise and upright kings and statesmen who had drawn a few uncomplicated precepts from the divine law as secular equivalents of the Decalogue. The state did not then disturb the trusting relations between people and law. Nor was it necessary to acquire "learning" in order to know the law and advise on its use. People had not been reduced to the lamentable position of the

[26] Otto Brunner, *Land und Herrschaft. Grundfragen der territorialen Verfassungsgeschichte Österreichs im Mittelalter* (5th ed. Vienna, 1965),155-65.

[27] Fritz Kern, "Recht und Verfassung im Mittelalter," *HZ* 120 (1919), 1-79. Kern's interpretation aroused considerable controversy and has been refuted as far as the early middle ages are concerned by Gerhard Köbler, *Das Recht im frühen Mittelalter* (Cologne and Vienna, 1971) *passim*, esp. 1-2, 222-26. On this controversy, see the review of Köbler's book by Gerhard Dilcher in *ZRG* 90 (1973) *Germ.Abt.*, 267-73. Dilcher agrees with Köbler that the Kern thesis must be modified.

modern lay person, who was "encumbered and bewildered by a profusion of words."[28] Conscience alone informed the good men who, in days of yore, acted as *Rechtsprecher*, "law speakers," resolvers of doubts, and arbitrators of conflicts in the community.

The radical primitivism of this scenario has been rightly pilloried when it surfaced again in the nineteenth century as an idealization of a mythical peasant folk.[29] But it would be foolish to underestimate the ideological force which, in the sixteenth century, made it the engine of a widespread protest against the age's dominant juristic culture. At a time when, in the perception of ordinary people,

> Our ancient law has gone to rot,
> The poor get nothing, the rich a lot[30]

primitivism—the determined, sometimes ruthless, redirection of values to an imagined uncorrupted past—held out the promise of a complete turnabout. Powerfully fuelled by the early, popular phase of the Lutheran Reformation, this promise was not an empty one, and the response to it a far from unrealistic gesture.

Legal primitivism was of a piece with the religious and moral reorientations attempted, many of them successfully in some respects, in the age of Reformation. Law was the reigning paradigm for conceptualizing social organization and moral relations. So deeply had legal ideas penetrated Christian thought in the course of the middle ages[31] that speculations on the problems of human society tended to take the form of reflections on legal obligations. This was true of the political and moral science of the period,[32] of theology,[33] and, no less, of the unpretentious, often tangled, romantic conjectures of popular critics and prophets. The quest of these would-be reformers was for a way of turn-

---

[28] From a gloss by Christoph Zobell, *Sechssisch Weychbild*, Aii[r].

[29] See Peter Burke, *Popular Culture in Early Modern Europe* (New York, 1978), 21-22. The most important and influential formulation of the view in the nineteenth century is found in Jacob Grimm, "Von der Poesie im Recht" in *Kleinere Schriften* 6 (Berlin, 1882), 152-91.

[30] *Das edle Recht ist worden krank / Dem Armen kurz, dem Reichen lang.* Quoted in H. Hantsch, *Der deutsche Bauernkrieg* (Würzburg, 1925), 52.

[31] For an extended development of this argument, see Walter Ullmann, *Law and Politics in the Middle Ages. An Introduction to the Sources of Medieval Political Ideas* (Ithaca, N.Y., 1975), Chapter 1: Introduction.

[32] On this point see the works of Donald R. Kelley, especially "Vera Philosphia: The Philosophical Significance of Renaissance Jurisprudence," *Journal of the History of Philosophy* XIV:3 (1976), 267-69.

[33] See Brian Tierney, *Religion, Law, and the Growth of Constitutional Thought 1150-1650* (Cambridge, 1982).

ing universal moral norms into practical precepts for a working Christian community. That the end of this search would see the abandonment of present attachments and the readoption of older, more authentic loyalties was a foregone conclusion. Their "primitivism" thus expressed itself as a pledge to return to what they held to be the elementary Christian principles of trust, innocence, and good faith, supported by a conviction that a viable social order could be built on these. The "godly law" of the New Testament and the "good old laws" of their forefathers were to be the chief constituent elements of this new order.

In the year 1517 the distinguished French scholar-jurist Guillaume Budé gave reasoned and dignified exposition to these notions, thereby revealing them to be in their own time a far weightier proposition than the mere folk atavism suggested by the above synopsis. Writing to Thomas Lupset, in a letter that found its way into the prefatory matter for the second edition of Thomas More's *Utopia*, published in Paris that same year, Budé touched the very themes that were agitating common people around that time. Even the humanist's calm voice cannot obscure the evangelical radicalism of his analysis—an iconoclastic position on which Budé was by no means prepared to act, but whose ideological appeal might well, if given broader dissemination, induce action in others. Budé's letter is interesting also as evidence of the extent to which values were shared among divergent social groups, and of the ability of the Christian social ethic to cross class and occupational lines. In the fervently honest response they made to some very basic questions, Budé's elegant Latin sentences are a fair representation of ideas widely held in his time.

What if we were to judge our laws by the standard of truth and by the command of the gospel to be simple, Budé asks. "Anyone with a spark of intelligence and sense would admit, if pressed, that there is a vast difference between true equity and law . . . as expressed in civil statutes and royal decrees." You would find that true justice is "nowhere in evidence" or, at best, is "treated . . . like a scullery maid." Rulers and governments like to claim that their laws are expertly drawn from "that real and world-old justice which is called the natural law." In truth, however, they are of a very different kind, an order "according [to which] the stronger a man is the more he should possess, and the more he does possess the more eminent among his fellow citizens he ought to be." How can this be called "natural" or "godly"?

Christ seems to me to have abolished, among his own at least, the whole arrangement set up by the civil and canonical law of fairly recent date in contentious volumes. This law we see today holding the highest position in jurisprudence and controlling our destinies.

The country of Utopia, Budé continues, coming to the occasion of his present reflections, has found a way to liberate itself from this stranglehold by adopting "the customs and the true wisdom of Christianity for public and private life" and by having kept this wisdom uncorrupted.

> It has done so by holding in close combat (as they say) to three divine principles: (1) the equality of all things, good and bad, among fellow citizens . . . ; (2) the resolute and tenacious love of peace and quiet; and (3) the contempt of gold and silver. These are the three overthrowers, I may say, of all frauds, impostures, swindles, rogueries, and wicked deceptions.

If these three divine principles were adopted wherever men call themselves Christians, "the golden age of Saturn would return." But this cannot be done as long as we are under our present governance, in which it is assumed that "each person's case usually is right insofar as it satisfies the demands of the law or insofar as it is supported by the law."[34] Laws always reproduce a given society's power relations. "The demands of the law" can never be just to those who do not happen to be strong. "What the laws say" and "what is just" are very different matters.

Thus Budé, most eloquently. But few among the powerless in society needed a humanist to deliver this lesson to them. They were beginning on their own to see more and more clearly that laws and social conventions favored the rich and the strong. For the *arme mann*—the humble commoner—hope rested not in the magistrate's statutes but in the law of God.

ASKED to name the varieties of law in use in their time, jurists—following the lead of the *Institutes*—usually gave three: the law of nations (*ius gentium*), the civil law (*ius civile*), and the law of nature (*ius naturale*).[35] Laymen also named three, but differently: the godly law, the natural law, and the written law.[36] The last of these referred to the written, by

---

[34] Guillaume Budé to Thomas Lupset, 1517, in *The Complete Works of St. Thomas More* IV: "Utopia," ed. Edward Surtz, S.J. and J. H. Hexter (New Haven, 1965), 6-11.

[35] E.g., Johann Oldendorp, *Lexicon iuris* (Lyons, 1549), 189-93; also the glosses by Christoph Zobell on *Sechssisch Weychbild*, Aii^r - Aiii^r; also the jurist Konrad Peutinger in a memo written for the Augsburg City Council, 1534. Stadtarchiv Augsburg Literalien 1534, Nachtrag I, No. 15, 16^r.

[36] *"Göttliche, natürliche und geschriebene Recht." Rechtbuch der kayserlichen freien*

now mostly printed, law books to which judges and jurors turned for reference, and upon which academic lawyers exercised their jurisprudence: municipal codes, criminal codes like the *Halsgerichtsordnung* of Bamberg, and, of course, the body of Roman law and legal opinion known as the *corpus iuris Justiniani*, parts of which had been in print since 1468. "Written law" and "natural law" had always been treated as separate, though interdependent, entities. Differentiating the "godly law" from the law of nature, on the other hand, was a recent practice gaining currency in the aftermath of evangelical preaching, with its elevation of the gospel to the position of sole and exclusive norm.

In the early sixteenth century, legal theoreticians responded to this redoubled interest in Scripture as law by exploring the relations between decalogue, gospel, and natural rights.[37] For laymen, to the contrary, the concern was entirely practical. God's law and the law of nature established moral norms. Both were characterized by constancy. The positive laws of each individual state, on the other hand, "are subject to frequent change, either by the tacit consent of the people or by the subsequent enactments of another statute" (*Institutes* 1.2.11). In other, less formal, words, "a written law stands only as long as another law does not come along to cancel it."[38] This mutability made "written laws" inherently vulnerable to degradation. As for the natural law, although it contained the essential prescriptions of basic human rights, it was weakened in its applicability by a certain inherent vagueness. The New Testament, however, was explicit and concrete as a statement of God's intentions for humankind. Theologians differed sharply on the propriety of using the gospel as a guide to the everyday business of a Christian's secular life; and after the events of 1525 many preachers who had before that year exhorted their audiences to act in the name of the gospel changed their minds.[39] But no attentive listener to the sermons of the early Reformation, no careful reader of Matthew, Acts, and Paul, could doubt that *göttliche Gerechtigkeit, iustitia dei*, the godly justice of which the gospel was the message, closely matched his own intuitive sense of what is, or should be, fair and right in the world.

Bergstadt Schlackenwald, manuscript copy in Germanisches Nationalmuseum Nürnberg Hs. 17.471, 32ᵛ.

[37] See especially the works of the north German jurist and educator Johann Oldendorp, active at the court of Philip of Hesse from 1543 to his death in 1567: *Isagoge iuris naturalis, gentium et civilis* (1539); *De iure et aequitate* (1541); *Lexicon iuris* (1549), 189-90; and the popular work *Wat byllick und recht ys* (Rostock, 1529). On Oldendorp see Hans-Helmut Dietze, *op. cit.*, who offers analyses of the works mentioned.

[38] *Sechssisch Weychbild*, Ggiiiiᵛ.

[39] The best study of this turnabout is Justus Maurer, *Prediger im Bauernkrieg* (Stuttgart, 1979).

"The origin of the idea of a 'godly law,' " comments Winfried Becker, "is found in the realm of intentions, emotions, and intuitions, and in people's spontaneous desire to help bring about a renewal."[40] This was the inner source of its ideological power. "Godly law" became symbol and slogan of a great transformation, an effort at renewal proceeding from a testing of all existing rules for their agreement with the gospel.

In the revolution of 1525 the idea of the godly law operated as the chief legitimizing principle of rebelling peasants.[41] Their manifestos indicate how this law was intended to be used and what the alternative society built on its provisions would be like. Equal treatment of all before the law was the major rectification to be achieved by the turn to the divine law as a single legal canon. The brotherhood of men was its absolute essence.[42] "It would be well," wrote Friedrich Weygandt in his proposal for an equitable imperial constitution, "if all secular laws used in the empire were to be abolished, and the godly and natural law . . . put in its place. If this were done, the poor would have as much justice as the powerful and the rich. . . ."[43] Existing, man-made law was the chief obstacle to the adoption of God's law; lawyers and other "learned" men—theologians especially—were its most determined foes. Weygandt therefore reduced their competences severely. "Doctors, whether of the spiritual or of the secular kind, shall not sit in any prince's council or court of laws, neither to advocate, nor to advise or officiate. They must be altogether removed from such employment so that a change may be made from man-made laws to divine Scripture." Weygandt was prepared to tolerate jurists on the faculties of a few universities, "where princes or other courts may obtain advice." But from judging and arbitration they were to be excluded, "because jurists do not serve the cause of justice, but are hirelings who pursue their own interest." Deep misgivings about university-trained intellectuals under-

---

[40] Winfried Becker, " 'Göttliches Wort,' 'Göttliches Recht,' 'Göttliche Gerechtigkeit.' Die Politisierung theologischer Begriffe?" in Peter Blickle, ed., "Revolte und Revolten in Europa." HZ Beiheft 4 (N.F., 1975), 232-63. The quotation is on p. 253.

[41] For an excellent discussion of the "godly law" in relation to traditional concepts of natural law, see Peter Bierbrauer, "Das göttliche Recht und die naturrechtliche Tradition" in Peter Blickle ed., Bauer, Reich und Reformation. Festschrift für Günther Franz (Stuttgart, 1982), 210-34.

[42] Winfried Becker in loc. cit., 256, comments: "The only kind of injustice known to the 'godly law' is man's refusal to recognize another as his brother. Such refusal is interpreted as a denial of the evangelical command of brotherly love which makes everything free, common, and peaceful."

[43] Friedrich Weygandt's Reichsreformentwurf of May 1525 is printed in Günther Franz, ed., Quellen zur Geschichte des Bauernkrieges (Munich, 1963), No. 124. Quotations from 376-77.

lie this exclusionary impetus. It was an old populist suspicion, gaining momentum in the sixteenth century. "The door to justice is shut to doctors; not one of them knows where to find the key to it. . . . But the layman has the key in his pocket, and in good time he will unlock the door and bring out the law."[44] The promise of this liberation of law from its academic prison offered the best hope for a fair society.

An interesting exchange on the two opposing systems of law took place during negotiations by the leader of a peasant group in Upper Swabia, Ulrich Schmid, with emissaries of the Swabian League, which was preparing to subdue the rebellion. It is a revealing moment because it shows us just how tangible a moral code the law of God was believed to be. When Schmid inquired as to the law by which the league proposed to judge the merits of the peasants' complaints, the league's spokesman answered "the Chamber Court," meaning the "imperial" or common, i.e., Roman, law to which the Imperial Chamber Court was bound. When the officials then put to Schmid the same question, namely, "what law he desired,"

> Ulrich answered "the godly law, which instructs every estate in what it should do and what it should not do." In response to this, the lords said, mockingly: "My good man, you are asking for God's law. Tell us, who will interpret this law for us? We doubt that God will soon come down from heaven to hold a judgment day." To this Ulrich made answer: "My dear sirs, it is hard for me in my simplicity here and now to come up with the names of judges or pronouncers of the law. But in about three weeks I will give them to you, and in the meantime I call upon our parish priests to offer heartfelt prayer to God, trusting that he will point out and apportion to us some wise, pious men able to judge and to decide these matters according to the meaning of divine Scripture."[45]

The list of "judges" eventually submitted by the peasants was headed by Martin Luther and included such prominent Reformation figures as Zwingli, Osiander, Jacob Strauss, Johann Brenz, and Matthäus Zell. Only Philip Melanchthon, whose name is coupled with that of Luther on the list, could have been regarded as a partisan of "imperial" law, but the rebel leaders may not have known this. What they looked for in

[44] From an anonymous reform pamphlet attributed to the emperor Frederick III. On the disputed authorship of this work, see Otto Schiff, "Die unechte Reformation Kaiser Friedrichs III. Forschungen zur Vorgeschichte des Bauernkrieges," *Historische Vierteljahrschrift* 19 (1919), 189-219.

[45] From the narrative of events given by Johann Kessler in his *Sabbata*. Excerpt printed in Günther Franz, *Quellen*, No. 31. Quotations from pp. 146-47.

their "law speakers" was a general acknowledgment of the Bible as an exclusive touchstone for judging a right or an obligation. What was found fair and just by this standard they were prepared to accept as their bounden duty. On this point no distinction separated Lutherans from Catholics. A group of Bavarian peasants wrote to their duke in 1525 that "it is our unanimous will and opinion that we will obey our ecclesiastical and worldly superiors in all that we are obliged to give and do, as judged by the godly laws."[46] And this, in turn, echoes the more famous undertaking given in the Twelve Articles that "if any one or more of these articles is not in agreement with God's word (which we doubt) . . . we will abandon it when this is proved by the Bible."[47] The drafters of these articles, and their followers, accepted the full implications of this promise.

No Catholic or Protestant could, of course, allow himself to deny the normative sway of the divine law in Christian life. But norms are tied to actions by complex linkages, and these, for the realist, severely restrict the golden rule's utility. In the practical view—the view above all of lawyer bureaucrats, whose training and experience had taught them not only the inadequacy of men, but also the infinite complexity of things—the expectations placed upon God's law so far exceeded human possibilities that its dictates could only be treated as counsels of perfection. Its decrees might govern a better life in the future; the present one, however, demanded less generous, more watchful, tougher controls. Against this guarded and suspicious disposition—the mind-set of governing elites everywhere at the time—it was difficult to maintain that people were ready to accept God's will and take it as the measure of their lives.

How was the divine law to be dispensed? Some urged that godly principles should be allowed to work themselves out without human interference. Justice has an objective existence. It only needs to be "found," and simple people know where to look for it. Legal parables made this point:

> Two peasants quarrelled before court over an ox, each claiming to be its owner. The honorable jurors found that the ox should be taken to the communal fountain to drink, there blindfolded and, after

[46] In *ibid.*, No. 60, p. 210.

[47] "Conclusion" from "The Just and Fundamental Articles of All the Peasantry." Translation by Thomas A. Brady, Jr. and H. C. Erik Midelfort, in Peter Blickle, *The Revolution of 1525. The German Peasants' War from a New Perspective* (Baltimore, 1981), 200-01. For the latest scholarship on the Twelve Articles, see Peter Blickle, "Nochmals zur Entstehung der zwölf Artikel im Bauernkrieg" in *id.*, ed., *Bauer, Reich und Reformation*, 286-308.

drinking and his eyes uncovered again, allowed to wander off on his own. And he to whose house he returned should be known as his owner. And so the ox went home to his rightful owner.[48]

Nature and instinct are the best guides. Leave things alone and they will right themselves. "Let the law go its own way," says a peasant to a judge in a shrovetide play, pleading for justice.[49] The phrase encapsulates the minimalist position on the judicial process.

But this was too homely a remedy for a society a long way from the imagined simplicity of the tribal village. The more reasonable alternative was to conform to the spirit of natural justice by adhering as closely as possible to "old," "traditional" (*hergebrachte*) customs by which people had conducted themselves from immemorial times. "Custom," it was said, "is always the best interpreter of laws and rights."[50] With a deeply held conviction, most people seem to have believed in a past in which nature was less infected by private and public vices. The ways of the forefathers, therefore, must be better ways. In the form of old charters, time-honored conventions, these ancient arrangements were still in use, though in recent times they had been coming under attack from proponents of the newer, "written" and "learned" law. It was this seasoned and venerable "right" that the jurors in the story about the disputed ox had "found." Most people in towns and countryside thought of justice in this way.

But in the early sixteenth century, this "finding" mode,[51] with its lay jurors and its informal, open procedures, was being supplanted by an altogether different legal ethos, one based on formulating, defining, and "setting" (*setzen*) the law into binding codes to be administered by experts. When the jurisconsults of the city of Nuremberg spoke of themselves as "doctors and finders of the laws," they were guilty of what, to laymen, was a contradiction in terms.[52] Doctors could make or "compose" the law, but "finding" was a job for amateurs. This change from "finding" law—i.e., a pre-existing law not created by judges—to "making" law—where those who brought it into being ob-

---

[48] Johann Pauli, *Schimpf und Ernst* (1522) ed. Johannes Bolte (Berlin, 1924), No. 121.

[49] From *Vaschang* (c. 1511), an Austrian carnival play, in *Fünfzehn Fastnachts-Spiele aus den Jahren 1510 und 1511*, ed. Oswald Zingerle (Vienna, 1886), 235.

[50] This is an often-cited principle. See, for example, Georg von Rotschitz, *Tractatus von der Mitgift . . .* (Leipzig, 1598), B^r.

[51] On "finding" law see Gustav Klemens Schmelzeisen, "Rechtsfindung im Mittelalter?" *ZRG* 91 (1974), *Germ.Abt.*, 73-89 and Götz Landwehr, " 'Urteilfragen' und 'Urteilfinden' nach spätmittelalterlichen Rechtsquellen," *ibid.*, 96 (1979), 1-37.

[52] " . . . *doctorn und erfindern der recht.*" Legal opinion by Dr. Peter Dotzler (1521), StA Nbg, *Ratschlagbücher* No. 3, 20^r.

viously acted on behalf of the dominant forces in society—had far-reaching consequences.[53] Not that it was always forced upon unwilling subjects. "Written law" often began when groups of anxious peasants or town dwellers called upon their superiors to "set down" long-observed but hitherto unconfirmed and unwritten customs. In due course, however, the initiative shifted, as governments undertook the collection of rights for the purpose of framing them in a comprehensive code drawn up by jurists, sanctioned by ruler or magistrate, and published as an act of state. The enlargement of regalian prerogatives was a salient motive of all early modern governments in first participating in this process, then taking it over. With its official seals, the new code had the force of law backed by whatever power a particular government could muster to ward off challenges to its authority. Facing so well entrenched an opponent, aggrieved groups looked to natural and divine law in an effort to challenge and, where possible, halt this—to them—disastrous shift in the location and exercise of power. A modern student of this phenomenon, Karl-Heinz Burmeister, comments:

> The call for natural law is a necessary consequence of the transition from custom to codified law. . . . When the former was dominant, a demand for natural law would have made no sense, for rights and justice were always present, needing neither to be created nor to be justified. It is the *making* of law that creates a legal dynamic: newly made law, being a *new* law, needs to be justified. Before it is accepted as binding, it must be tested by the criterion of eternal legal principles, which is to say, by the natural law.[54]

This double call for a setting down of rights, combined with an appeal to divine and natural justice as a universal touchstone, became the characteristic expression of movements of protest and resistance in the sixteenth century. Their circumstances will be considered in later chapters where, it is hoped, the texture of political life in sixteenth-century German territories and towns will be revealed. Here it is important to emphasize the tense ambivalence characterizing the legal situation in the empire. The most widely quoted of the many legal proverbs of the time, "He never does wrong who insists on his right," was cited with equal conviction by all sides in the period's constitutional and jurisdictional contentions. Insisting on one's rights was a passion as much as a strategy. Rights defined a person's social being. The defense of them

[53] I follow Karl Heinz Burmeister, "Genossenschaftliche Rechtsfindung und herrschaftliche Rechtssetzung. Auf dem Weg zum Territorialstaat" in *HZ* Beiheft 4 (N.F.), 171-85.
[54] *Ibid.*, 183-84.

was basic self-protection, carried on at all levels of personal and collective life and with characteristic unwillingness to allow distinctions between important and trivial (as they would seem to us) causes.

The richly detailed literature of grievance produced in huge bulk throughout the century (it will be discussed in Chapter Eight) gives us our best clues to what the struggle over law and freedom was really about: down-to-earth utilitarian matters, for the most part. Everyone had rights at stake, and at many points of contact among individuals and groups they were in conflict. Everyone, it seems, was fighting over something. At one time or another, nearly everyone was in litigation. If there was a philosophical position on this—mostly verbal—rivalry, it was contained in the often-heard advice to keep measure and moderation in pressing one's case. Sebastian Brant, who—it will be remembered—was a jurist by trade but is best known as a satirical moralist, took this position in 1510 in his rhymed preface to Ulrich Tengler's *Layman's Mirror*:

> There is a limit, measure, pace
> To guide your steps in every case;
> He who does more than these permit
> Helps justice not, but hinders it.
> A written law prescribed of old
> You must forever keep and hold
> Unless new circumstances give
> You grounds for change, and only if
> Good equity and fairness guide
> Your ingenuity and pride,
> And if your action, suit, or cause
> Does not impugn our common laws.[55]

But this was weak counsel, for most debates turned precisely on the question of how "circumstances" (*Umbstend*) affected the law or right at issue, one side arguing that it was clear and capable of direct application, the other citing conditions requiring careful qualification. *Die Umbstend* always made the difference:

> What, who, where, when, and lastly why:
> That's where the grounds of judgments lie.[56]

---

[55] Ulrich Tengler, *Layenspiegel*, Aiii[r].

[56] Hans Sachs, *Das weyse Urteyl künig Salomonis* in Adelbert von Keller ed., *Hans Sachs* 1, 245. For a professional jurist's discussion of the role of circumstances in equity, see Johann Oldendorp, *De iure et aequitate*, discussed in Hans-Helmut Dietze, *op. cit.*, 78-88.

In fact, no claim was beyond challenge on principle, and few actions passed without such challenges being made and vigorously pursued through courts and chancelleries. This is why drafters of opinions, judgments, arguments, promulgations, edicts, and constitutions tended to cite as many as possible of the available sources of authority: ". . . stated in the written law and affirmed as well in nature . . .";[57] ". . . according to the common laws, the opinions of most of the jurists, the statutes and the written laws of our ancestors, and the immemorial customs observed in our land . . .";[58] ". . . by the pure divine word of Christ, the teachings of the prophets and apostles, also by the Constitutions of the Christian emperors and common imperial laws, which are in accord with the word of God and not contrary to it, and in addition by the praiseworthy ancient customs of our principality and lands."[59] A ruling so amply based and massively supported was difficult to challenge and dangerous to oppose.

THE broad outlines sketched in the present chapter yield a confusing picture. Shifts in power relations brought on sharp antagonisms and increasingly hostile confrontations among social and political groups. Disputes over law were at the heart of these struggles. The right to make law, interpret it, and administrate it was the universal bone of contention. But law was also the symbol for the conflict as a whole. Like its agent, the lawyer, who personified much of what was feared and resented, law was the emblem representing the whole of society in the complexity of its inner stresses, and in its problematic relationship with its rulers and its God. Opposition to an existing social, political, or religious authority inevitably meant turning against the laws that upheld and shielded it. Concepts of law differed widely among the contesting camps, and little consensus existed on how the basic but vaguely understood premises concerning justice should be cast into legal precepts capable of giving structure and cohesion, as well as desirable direction, to society. The evangelical rhetoric of Reformation preachers added passion to the arguments and exacerbated the mood of urgency that had been gathering in Germany since the late fifteenth century. A sense of doom merged with anticipations of reform: here, too, law

[57] From a *Ratschlag* (legal advice) prepared by Konrad Peutinger for the city of Memmingen. Stadtarchiv Augsburg, *Peutinger 1523-1569*, 211ʳ.

[58] From a *Schöffenspruch* issued by the Leipzig *Schöffen*. StA Dr, Loc. 9665 "Leipziger Schöffensprüche," 35ʳ.

[59] From *Ordnung und reformation ecclesiastici consistorii zu Jena . . . Anno 1569* printed in Emil Sehling ed., *Die evangelischen Kirchenordnungen des XVI. Jahrhunderts* I (Leipzig, 1902), 236.

functioned as a token for the whole, for in contemporary usage *Reformation* was the technical term for revisions made in a legal code or a set of ordinances. At the same time, the word served as the most general name for the hoped-for renewal of everything from local customs to the whole complexion of public and private life.

All talk about "reform" and "reformation" therefore carried associations of law and jurisdiction and, inevitably, of the many controversies raging round these. But the battle lines were not clearly drawn. None of the ideas or notions mentioned in this chapter was adopted exclusively or consistently. Principles were embraced, discarded, espoused, combined, and amalgamated by participants whenever strategy demanded or opportunity suggested. Peasants and knights pleaded from briefs prepared by learned counsel according to the rules of formal procedure. Dukes and emperors appealed to the divine law and argued for the validity of ancient usages. Ideological purity was prized neither in justifying the struggle for social justice, nor in the tactics adopted for waging or resisting it in a particular instance.

All this makes for a blurred picture. But it is one with a rich texture, the "feel" of which is, it seems to me, our best clue to a sympathetic understanding of what was going on in the Holy Roman Empire at the time of the Reformation. Legal proverbs, a favored device for disseminating ideas about law, reflect the prevailing state of uncertainty. Most of them were coined and launched by law teachers and practicing jurists in order to put legal principles into memorable forms as "sentences" or "topics" with which to argue or conclude a disputed point.[60] When translated into vernacular aphorisms, they served to make legal propositions appear like perennial truths. An apposite adage or precept was always at hand to advance or gainsay a controversial contention. To show that law is an inseparable part of divine righteousness: "God himself is just, therefore he loves justice"; "He who loves God loves

---

[60] Scholarship on legal proverbs is torn between accepting them as spontaneous creations of anonymous folk wisdom, or as the deliberate coinage of jurists and other legal professionals eager to spread legal principles among the people. The trend of interpretation is in the direction of the latter view. See especially Ferdinand Elsener, " 'Keine Regel ohne Ausnahme.' Gedanken zur Geschichte der deutschen Rechtssprichwörter," *Festschrift für den 45. deutschen Juristentag* (Karlsruhe, 1964), 23-40; Albrecht Foth, "Gelehrtes römisch-kanonisches Recht in deutschen Rechtssprichwörtern" in *id., Juristische Studien* (Tübingen, 1971). For the older view: Hans Fehr, *Die Dichtung im Recht* (Bern, 1936), esp. 163-80; Eberhard von Künssberg, *Rechtliche Volkskunde* (Halle, 1936); Eugen Wohlhaupter, *Die Rechtsfibel* (Bamberg, 1956). The best collection of legal proverbs is by Eduard Graf and Mathias Dietherr, *Deutsche Rechtssprichwörter* (Nördlingen, 1864). An older collection is Johann Friedrich Eisenhart, *Deutsches Recht in Sprichwörtern* (Helmstädt, 1759), new edition by Dr. Waldmann (Berlin, 1935).

justice"; "Justice is truth, truth is justice"; "Where the powerful reign, justice is silent"; "All power is unjust"; "Law helps those who cannot help themselves."[61] To claim instead that law expresses the will of worldly rulers: "Justice is the king's law"; "The emperor's will is law"; "Justice is what the king says"; "New king, new laws"; "Might makes right"; "A new statute cancels an old law."[62] It could be shown that custom rules: "Where there is custom there is justice"; "An old custom is stronger than a sealed decree"; "Law is old and has been many years coming down to us"; "As it has come to us, so we must pass it on"; "This is how we found it, this is how it must remain."[63] Or it could be argued that justice demands the displacement of custom: "Where the law is honest, custom gives way"; "Custom makes way for law"; "Other times, other customs"; "New times demand new customs"; "A bad custom does not make a thing good"; "Law conquers custom."[64] To demonstrate the superiority of ancient law: "First in time, first in law"; "First to arrive at the mill, first to grind his corn"; "A year and a day will last forever."[65] Or to break the rule of antiquity: "A hundred years of wrong do not equal a single hour of right"; "What is wrong today will not be right tomorrow."[66] To urge that the law be relaxed: "Necessity knows no law." Or to justify severity to the letter: "The law is the law."[67] To offer hope: "He who has justice on his side will win in the end."[68] Or to play the legal realist: "Petty thieves are hanged, big thieves go free."[69]

Two basic positions, however, can be detected among these disparate notions about law, justice, judicial process, jurisprudence, and their function in the world. One of these placed confidence in positive law as by far the best guarantor of peace and order. Its text was a passage in the introduction to Justinian's *Digest*: ". . . there is in all things nothing found so worthy of respect as the authority of enacted law, which disposes well things both divine and human, and expels all iniquity. . . ."[70] This lapidary statement was elaborated into paeans to the certainty and constancy of objective law:

[61] These and many similar ones in Graf and Dietherr, 1-6.
[62] *Ibid.*, 17-21.
[63] *Ibid.*, 10-14; Eisenhart, 13-14.
[64] Graf and Dietherr, 10-14.
[65] *Ibid.*, 25, 94.
[66] *Ibid.*, 94.
[67] Eisenhart, 177.
[68] Graf and Dietherr, 418.
[69] Eisenhart, 180.
[70] *The Digest of Justinian*, tr. Charles Henry Monro, xiii.

. . . for law is not a thing that is changeable or subject to human opinion or fantasy. On the contrary, it has been set, instituted, and defined into incontrovertible words and formalities which, following consideration of all possible circumstances, establish common principles for all to obey and observe. This is what the imperial [Roman] law is and does, as long as it is approached in a learned and fair-minded spirit and not interpreted ignorantly or maliciously.[71]

This was the view from the palace and the high court bench. Observed from a lesser eminence, the statutes of enacted law often seemed more like marks of deeply rooted injustice and oppression in society. Partisans of this outlook denounced the law for its lack of compassion and its indifference to wrong-doing in the world. They saw the "learned" law's briefs, summonses, rulings, decisions, and mandates, and the formal methods of its procedures, as a smoke screen to hide the profound inequity at work. Quoting from the Sermon on the Mount, they admonished the lawyers to "Let your speech be 'yes, yes; no, no.' What is more than this is of evil."[72] This disposed of the whole lore of jurisprudence: a clean sweep that could be justified only by affirming "that we owe greater obedience to God than to men."[73] In submission to this higher duty, "let judges be ordered to give their judgments and verdicts by the Bible and the holy word of God, so that the poor will fare just as well as the rich."[74] To accomplish this feat, "let all [worldly] laws conform to the will of God."[75]

So radical an alternative, and so broad a challenge, would scarcely have won so much support at an earlier moment in European history. The wave of opposition to "enacted" law in the early decades of the sixteenth century must be explained in part by the agitation leading up to the Lutheran and Zwinglian reformations and by the enormous public excitement accompanying their initial phase as an evangelical movement. But there was another, deeper, cause of the polarization in legal thinking described in this chapter. Established law was a formidable presence at the opening of the sixteenth century. Endowed with a powerful intellectual structure by the legal science of Rome and Italy, embraced by the leaders of state and church as the organizing principle of

---

[71] Justin Gobler, *Spiegel der Rechten* (Frankfurt am Main, 1573), 22ʳ.

[72] Matt. 5:37.

[73] *46 Artickel, so die gemeyn einem ersamen rath der . . . stadt Franckenfurt . . . fürgehalten* (1525) in Adolf Laube et al., eds., *Flugschriften der Bauernkriegszeit* (Berlin [East], 1975), 59.

[74] From the Eleven Articles of Mühlhausen (1524) in *ibid.*, 80.

[75] No. 39 of Huldreich Zwingli's *67 Conclusiones* (1523) in *Zwingli Hauptschriften* 4, ed. Oskar Frei (Zurich, 1952), 112.

their realms, and extolled by men of letters as a supreme achievement of the human spirit, it loomed on the European scene as an immense and well-nigh irresistible force for social change. Only a shift in the basic concepts of law could hope to cut down this colossus. Only a stubborn clinging to tradition offered protection from it. As we shall see, these were the means chosen to resist the political consequences in Germany of the process known as the "Reception of Roman Law."

CHAPTER THREE

Reception: The New Law in Germany

IN THE course of the fourteenth and fifteenth centuries, the legal and judicial structure of the Holy Roman Empire underwent a major transformation. Known as the "Reception of Roman Law," this sweeping change altered permanently the ways in which Germans thought about law, litigated, judged, and governed. Given the permeation of society by legal attitudes, this change affected, in one way or another, most areas of public and private life. It created new conditions in which the claims of politics became paramount: in this sense it is part of the history of the modern state. It directly affected the Lutheran Reformation, which, as it established itself from the 1530s onward, and as the Catholic Church had done centuries earlier, discovered in Roman law a useful store of principles, arguments, and techniques for governing. Questions of jurisdiction and obedience, super- and sub-ordination, civic obligations and personal rights, were rethought and reformulated. Tentative at its beginning, the process of romanization in Germany became irresistible by the end of the fifteenth century, and the first half of the sixteenth saw it take its place as the dominant legal culture wherever there was a center of authority and power.

All debates and controversies reviewed in the preceding chapters were aspects of the national response to the Roman law's rise to dominance. Scholars of the phenomenon—and the reception has had an immense historiography[1]—have always agreed on its intrinsic significance

[1] The historiography of the reception of Roman law in Germany is enormous in volume. The following titles are intended only to introduce the subject: Helmut Coing, *Römisches Recht in Deutschland* (*Ius Romanum medii aevi* Pars V, 6, Milan, 1964); *id., Die Rezeption des römischen Rechts in Frankfurt am Main* (Frankfurt am Main, 1939); Winfried Trusen, *Anfänge des gelehrten Rechts in Deutschland. Ein Beitrag zur Geschichte der Frührezeption* (Wiesbaden, 1962); Paul Koschaker, *Europa und das römische Recht* (Munich and Berlin, 1947); Hermann Krause, *Kaiserrecht und Rezeption* (*Abhandlungen der Heidelberger Akademie der Wissenschaften, philos.-hist. Klasse*, Jahrgang 1952, Heidelberg, 1952). For the older literature, see Georg von Below, *Die Ursachen der Rezeption des römischen Rechts in Deutschland* (Munich and Berlin, 1905). For brief but suggestive surveys in English, see Wolfgang Kunkel, "The Reception of Roman Law in Germany. An Interpretation" and Georg Dahm, "On the Reception of Roman and Italian Law in Germany," both in Gerald Strauss, ed., *Pre-Reformation Germany* (London, 1972), 263-81; 282-315. The most exhaustive treatment of the whole subject of law in

and its far-reaching impact on German political and cultural life. But opinions have differed on whether the effects should be judged good or bad. It used to be argued that the absorption of Roman law had been injurious to the social health of the German people. Taking their cue from sixteenth-century opposition to romanization, later critics have accused jurists, and those who employed them during the time of reception, of having undermined the robust, native, folk- and soil-based, history-tested customary law by first infiltrating, and then imposing, an alien code uncongenial to the German character and experience, and fatally destructive of the essential organic union between a people's character and the law by which it lives. An attack in these terms was first launched in the early nineteenth century by the historical school of jurisprudence led by the legal scholar Friedrich Karl von Savigny, who contrasted a vigorous national system of justice, spontaneously generated and continuously creative ("originating in common morality and belief . . . , made by inner, anonymously active forces"), to synthetic products of politically motivated "academic jurisprudence [at the service of] the arbitrary power of a lawgiver."[2] Liberal-national and Romantic-folkish ideas later in the nineteenth century fleshed out this sketch of a critique of the alien import. Their language bristled with allegations of "perversion of justice," "suppression of freedom,"[3] subjugation by a "hard-hearted" culture whose law was "as different from the German as fire is from water,"[4] "contempt for the national law," submission to "slavish doctrines," and an "ill-fated deformation of the German idea of justice."[5] These and similar charges are laid out at

late medieval and early modern Europe is to be found in a collaborative scholarly enterprise of which Helmut Coing is the general editor: *Handbuch der Quellen und Literatur der neueren Europäischen Privatrechtsgeschichte*, vol. I: *1100-1500* (Munich, 1973), vol. II: *1500-1800* (Munich, 1976-1977).

[2] Friedrich Karl von Savigny, *Vom Beruf unsrer Zeit für Gesetzgebung und Rechtswissenschaft* (Heidelberg, 1814), 14. Savigny, however, explicitly disavowed the notion that Roman law had spoiled or driven out German law. He admired the law of the Romans because—unlike the Napoleonic Code—it "sich fast ganz von innen heraus, als Gewohnheitsrecht gebildet hat" (p. 20). On German law as spontaneous creation, see also Otto von Gierke, who described the law-creative process thus: "Es strömte aus seiner Seele wie Volksgesang." Quoted by Gerhard Köbler, *Das Recht im frühen Mittelalter* . . . (Cologne, 1971), 13. See also Gierke's *Der Humor im deutschen Recht* (Berlin, 1871), 18, 60. A good brief recent survey of the Savigny school in its European legal and historical context is Donald R. Kelley, *Historians and the Law in Post-Revolutionary France* (Princeton, 1984), Chapter 6.

[3] Wilhelm Zimmermann, *Geschichte des grossen Bauernkrieges* (first published 1856; I use Naunhof and Leipzig, 1939), 94-95.

[4] Karl Lamprecht, *Deutsche Geschichte* V (2nd ed. Berlin, 1896), 102.

[5] Johannes Janssen, *Geschichte des deutschen Volkes seit dem Ausgang des Mittelal-*

length and with much passion in Johannes Janssen's *History of the German People at the Close of the Middle Ages*,[6] the most extravagant of the nineteenth-century "Germanist" treatments of this and related matters. They have often been voiced since then by historians[7] and legal scholars[8] to whom the sixteenth-century battle between two opposed types of justice and law was anything but a dead issue.[9] It is interesting to reflect that analogous controversies in the early modern history of other nations—the argument over the "Norman Yoke" in England, the "Anti-Tribonianism" in France during the period of religious wars[10]— did not provoke anything like this sustained historiographical debate.[11] Although most recent German scholarship on the reception has deliberately avoided the emotionalism and touches of xenophobia once aroused by the subject, the discussion is still, to those who participate in it, of much more than antiquarian interest. It is no longer a story told in metaphors of ruthless conquest and violated or duped victim. But even in the most rigorously scholarly accounts of the reception the sense of drama is not lacking, and few historians offer their explanations of the Roman law's rapid advance without asking what was being

ters (13th ed. Freiburg im Breisgau, 1887) I, 484, 488, 504. Adolf Stölzel calls the Roman law an "antinationale fremde Recht." *Die Entwicklung der gelehrten Rechtssprechung* (Berlin, 1901-1910) II, 812.

[6] English translation by M. A. Mitchell and A. M. Christie (2nd ed. London, 1908) II, 137-88; German edition (as in note 5) I, 459-513.

[7] E.g., Hans Spangenberg, *Vom Lehnstaat zum Ständestaat* (Munich, 1912; reprint Aalen, 1964), 118-19.

[8] Otto Stobbe, *Geschichte der deutschen Rechtsquellen* (Leipzig, Braunschweig, 1860-1864; reprint Aalen, 1965) II, 37-39; 115-17; 123; Adolf Stölzel, *Die Entwicklung des gelehrten Richtertums in den deutschen Territorien* (Stuttgart, 1872; reprint Aalen, 1964) I, 142; Rudolph Sohm, *Das Recht der Eheschliessung* ... (Weimar, 1875), 250; Hans Liermann, "Nürnberg als Mittelpunkt deutschen Rechtslebens," *Jahrbuch für fränkische Landesforschung* 2 (1936), 5; Georg Dahm, "Zur Rezeption des Römisch-italienischen Rechts," *HZ* 167 (1943), 229-58 (English translation as in note 1, especially p. 314); Adalbert Erler, *Thomas Murner als Jurist* (Frankfurt am Main, 1956), 97-98.

[9] A strong revival of the "Germanist" position occurred in Germany in the 1930s when National Socialist propaganda made much of the reputed incompatibility between native and foreign culture, including law. See, for example, the comments by Dr. Waldmann (no first name given) in his edition of Johann Friedrich Eisenhart's *Grundsätze der deutschen Rechte in Sprichwörtern* (Berlin, 1935), *passim*.

[10] On the "Norman Yoke" see Christopher Hill, *Puritanism and Revolution* (New York, 1964 [originally published 1958]), 50-122. On Anti-Tribonianism in France, see Julian H. Franklin, *Jean Bodin and the Sixteenth-Century Revolution in the Methodology of Law and History* (New York, 1963) and Quentin Skinner, *The Foundations of Modern Political Thought* (Cambridge, 1978) II, 269-75.

[11] See, for example, the attack on the Savigny position by Rudolf von Ihering, *Der Kampf ums Recht* (Vienna, 1872; I use Darmstadt, 1963), 11-12. The most sweeping rejection of the Germanist position is offered by Georg von Below, *Die Ursachen*, 67-101.

lost. Explicitly or by implication, the question of what happened, and why, and with what results, links the modern scholar with the sixteenth-century participant.

Nothing about the reception would make sense if one did not begin with an appreciation of the inherent qualities of the system of law and jurisprudence that made its apparently irresistible way across the German (as well as most of the continental European) legal scene near the end of the middle ages.[12] The virtues of Roman law have been often told. Here they must be conveyed in terms that were meaningful to those who came to value them over the shortcomings—as they thought them to be—of their own legal institutions.

Its astonishing originality is the first of its merits: no other ancient peoples developed their laws into a comparable system of jurisprudence. Romans knew this, and their emulators in later centuries knew it as well; in any case, from the fifteenth century onward, the disposition created by the Renaissance respect for things Roman built admiration into the pursuit of every aspect of Latin civilization, including law. More impressive even than its sheer inventiveness is the cumulative nature of Roman legal thought (and a society as conservative as that of the Holy Roman Empire is bound to have responded positively to this appeal). Built up over time in the form of opinions, interpretations, commentaries on old and new laws stretching from the Twelve Tables through republic and principate to the early and late empire, Roman legal science developed into a remarkable instrument for practicing the *ars boni et aequi*, the art of determining what is just and fair, in concrete everyday situations, keeping pace with vast changes in every aspect of national life while holding on to what was considered the essential strength of the old law's origins in the *mores maiorum*, the ways of venerable ancestors. For reasons peculiar to Roman society,[13] this legal craft dealt in the main with civil, rather than criminal, law (the latter being left to the authority of administrative officials), and it was into the civil law practice of succeeding societies that Roman ideas and Roman procedures made their way in the early phases of the reception. Their impact on public law and administration came later.

---

[12] The best general survey in English of the history of Roman law in antiquity is Wolfgang Kunkel, *An Introduction to Roman Legal and Constitutional History*, tr. J. M. Kelly (2nd ed. Oxford, 1972). An excellent brief sketch of the character of Roman law is J.A.C. Thomas, *Text Book of Roman Law* (Amsterdam and New York, 1976), Chapter 1: "The Claims of Roman Law." For a succinct appreciation of the intellectual and cultural value of Roman law see Woldemar Engelmann, *Die Wiedergeburt der Rechtskultur in Italien durch die wissenschaftliche Lehre* (Leipzig, 1939), 28-41.

[13] J.A.C. Thomas, *op. cit.*, 4.

As the product of a highly developed and sophisticated urban society, Roman law was well suited to adoption by a late medieval European city culture near the take-off point. That is to say, it embodied legal ideas about property useful to an emerging commercial and manufacturing elite;[14] at the same time its uniform methods for the protection and management of possessions appealed to a growing corps of technicians engaged in these tasks. As we shall see, lawyers, notaries, scriveners, and other such functionaries played an important role in the spread of Roman law from the fourteenth century on. The Roman insistence on putting everything in writing engaged the enthusiasm of municipal secretaries, councillors, and urban solicitors. In due course, these men became the leading promoters of city and territorial "reformations," which were revisions of older law codes with more or less massive infusions of Roman elements in both substance and procedure. All these groups and individuals responded to the Roman law's unique combination of three elements: tradition, the continuing vitality of this tradition as a result of interpretation, and a resolute pragmatism in the rendering of opinions. These characteristics not only made the Roman law an effective practical instrument; they recommended it to intellectuals as an exciting and rewarding occupation. It also created for many of these men a place in the political thick of things—and this happened at a crucial time of state building and church reformation in the Holy Roman Empire.

To the intellectual, the Roman law's greatest attraction lay in the clarity and force of its conceptualizations. This, in turn, lent it the character of a timeless doctrine, a perennially valid formulation of the *fundamenta iuris*, the mere citation of which clinched an argument. Unhistorical as this use of Roman law was, jurists habitually resorted to it. "The *fundamenta iuris* need little defense, especially when they are laid before a learned judge," declared the Nuremberg jurist Dr. Christoph Scheurl. "Nor do they admit contradiction. Let the opposing party dispute and make what arguments it will, the judge has the text before his eyes and rests his verdict on it."[15] Such homage tended to raise the law to the plane of objective truth. The Roman law, wrote a German translator of Justinian's *Institutes*, contains "what the most excellent and experienced jurists have unanimously agreed, reasoned, and pro-

---

[14] The (commonly accepted) argument for this point is most aggressively made by Perry Anderson, *Lineages of the Absolutist State* (London, 1974), 22-29, especially 26-27. For an older voice with this point of view, see Karl Lamprecht, *Deutsche Geschichte* V (2nd ed. Berlin, 1896), 100-04.

[15] From a *Ratschlag* given in 1527 relating to a dispute between Nuremberg and Bamberg. StA Nbg, *Ratschlagbücher* No. 5, 296ʳ.

nounced to be good and just,"[16] and most serious students did indeed conclude that the Roman law embodied permanently valid norms of individual conduct and social organization.

Two circumstances in its long history account for this ineradicable—until modern times—tendency to think of Roman law in terms of absolutes. One is its development as an intellectual discipline; the other has to do with its having become known to Europeans almost exclusively through the so-called *corpus iuris Justiniani*, the codification of Roman law carried out under the aegis of the emperor Justinian in the early sixth century A.D. As to the former, it is generally acknowledged that the Roman law's best claim to universal validity (a claim first advanced in the politically charged scholarly milieu of thirteenth- and fourteenth-century Italian commentators) is the large body of interpretations written over the centuries, especially during its "classic" period in the first and second centuries A.D., by legal experts who were private citizens with a serious and informed interest in public affairs, and who had the vision to extend the law's substance to meet changing circumstances while preserving its traditional forms. The writings of these men, though always produced in the context of practical litigation rather than academic analysis, gave Roman legal thought its intellectual bent. The most distinguished of their opinions and commentaries were later gathered into the fifty books of Justinian's *Digest*, published in 533 (called *Pandecta* in Greek, from "to take in everything"). This collection was the "jurist's law" that so impressed sixteenth-century lawyers. "The great strength of the Roman mind," comments the legal historian Wolfgang Kunkel, "lay not in theoretical construction but in the technically accurate mastering of actual individual cases. . . . With sublime sureness of touch [Roman jurisconsults] deployed the methods of logical reasoning, the techniques of procedural formulas,[17] and the complicated rules and conventions growing out of the existence side by side of legal institutions old and new, civil and magistral, casual and strictly formalistic."[18] In their own time, these authors exerted influence by virtue of their social position near the center of power in Roman life. They were, as J.A.C. Thomas has noted, "men whose opinions and rulings would be accepted by their fellow citizens because they were who they were."[19] In later centuries, their authority as expoun-

---

[16] Ortholph Fuchsberger, *Justinianischer Instituten warhaffte Dolmetschung* (Augsburg, 1536), Aii^v. Fuchsberger's translation was first published in Augsburg in 1535.

[17] A *formula* was a written synopsis of claims and counter-claims made by litigants, addressed to a judge and drafted with the advice of jurists.

[18] Wolfgang Kunkel, *op. cit.*, 111.

[19] J.A.C. Thomas, *op. cit.*, 5. For the historical circumstances under which Roman ju-

ders, systematizers, and justifiers of law came to depend entirely on the intrinsic merits, real or supposed, of their work (always remembering the enhancing effect given to any and all products of classical antiquity by the Renaissance predisposition to look to ancient Rome as a universal paradigm). "Rational," "objective," "orderly," "logical," "prudent," and "philosophic"—these qualities came automatically to be associated with Roman legal science, and this science in turn formed the conceptual frame within which the promoters of the reception argued in favor of "the rule of law" as opposed to the shifty and capricious rule of men.

The second circumstance conditioning European attitudes to Roman law was its assimilation during the middle ages in the form of the *corpus iuris civilis*. Virtually all we now know about the legal thought of ancient Rome is based upon this collection, produced, on the order of Justinian, by a commission whose chairman was Tribonian. In less than a decade this team compiled, in addition to the *Digest*, a textbook for law students—the *Institutes*—and the twelve books of the *Codex*, which contain the emperors' edicts and decisions.[20] The imperial connection is important in appreciating the appeal of Roman law to medieval German monarchs, who treasured their identification with ancient predecessors (as they took them to be). Much more significant, however, in its rise to a dominant position over European law was its reintroduction in the eleventh century as a closed body of thought conveying a strong impression of system and integration. Among its admirers in the sixteenth century, the methodical orderliness of the ancient law won special praise. Native law making was exasperatingly untidy by contrast. As the Saxon jurist Melchior Kling wrote to his duke,

> The confusion and disorder in our Saxon territorial law must be well known to Your Electoral Grace. Oftentimes a single article will contain a variety of unrelated matters, such as criminal and civil, per-

rists—and some jurists more than others—acquired the authority to interpret the law, see Alan Watson, *Sources of Law, Legal Change, and Ambiguity* (Philadelphia, 1984), 1-11.

[20] In the course of the middle ages, this mass of material was enlarged by the addition of supplementary imperial laws, the *Novellae*, as well as a body of feudal laws of the twelfth and thirteenth centuries, the *Libri feudorum*. All these materials formed the *corpus iuris civilis* taught at medieval universities. See Ernst Levy, "Vulgarization of Roman Law in the Early Middle Ages," *Medievalia et Humanistica* Fasc. I (1943), 14-40. An excellent general survey of the circumstances under which codification took place is Franz Wieacker, "Allgemeine Zustände und Rechtszustände gegen Ende des weströmischen Reichs," *Ius Romanum medii aevi* Pars I, 2, a (Milan, 1963).

taining to persons or to things, etc., so that a man can never find quickly what he wants, no matter how good his memory.[21]

To an academic lawyer like Kling (he had degrees in civil and canon law from Wittenberg and was one of the most outspoken of Lutheran admirers of the Roman law), the *corpus iuris* was the model and the incentive for all attempts to standardize and rationalize the indigenous law of his territory. Uniformity of legal principles and procedures became a desideratum in all centers of government, and the *corpus* was the means of accomplishing it. The "New Territorial Code of the Principality of Württemberg" of 1555 draws a vivid picture of conditions clamoring for such standardizing:

> Whereas we have now established equal and uniform measures and weights . . . in our territory, therewith putting an end to the old inequality and dissimilarity of things, and whereas we see from day to day even greater ill effects arising from contradictory and unfair statutes, customs, and traditions in the towns and villages of our duchy, leading to constant unrest, bickering, and lawlessness in our courts, to confusion, bewilderment, and perversion of judges' verdicts, and thus to the prevention of equal law and justice for all, we have therefore considered how, with the help of the Almighty, we might establish a common, honorable, fair, and uniform law for all subjects and residents of our duchy, for the purpose of improving, if not wholly abolishing and preventing, the above-mentioned abuses, disputes, and disruptions.[22]

This was in the middle of the sixteenth century. In the early days of the reception, the need for uniformity in national, regional, and urban law was not so clearly acknowledged. Nevertheless, the initial perception of the *corpus* as an exemplar of successful coordination contributed greatly to its paradigmatic force and remained one of its strongest sources of appeal to jurists and statesmen alike.

Closely related to this view was the understanding of the *corpus iuris Justiniani* as imperial law, and therefore as a promoter of authority, not to say authoritarianism. This, again, was in good part a misreading of the sources. While the *Codex* presupposes the emperor as possessor of law-making and law-administrating power and the text here and there

[21] Dedication in *Sechsisch Landrecht mit Text und Gloss, in eine richtige Ordnung gebracht durch Doctor Melchior Klingen* (Leipzig, 1571), ii[r].

[22] *Neu Landrecht des Fürstentumbs Württemberg . . .* (1555) in Franz Beyerle, Wolfgang Kunkel, Hans Thieme, eds., *Quellen zur neueren Privatrechtsgeschichte Deutschlands* I, 2 (Weimar, 1938), 81-82.

offers an extravagant affirmation of his position as *dominus mundi* (e.g., *Digest* 14.2.9), the opinions gathered in the *Digest* were in fact carefully balanced on the question of the ruler's power. They award no license to would-be absolutists. Nonetheless, the *corpus* did furnish a number of passages that offered legal sanction to supreme power and justified a ruler's exercise of it. J. W. Allen's comment is pertinent here. "Two conceptions were found in the *corpus iuris*," he writes,

> the conception of a sovereign law-making *princeps* and the conception of the princeps as delegate of a sovereign people. The stress might be laid on one or the other, or even alternately on both. The study of the *Corpus iuris* did not necessarily turn men into royal absolutists.[23]

Yet often just this happened, and it is a fact that whenever the need was felt for order and discipline in life and the drift of public policy was for submission to such a regime, the Roman law was acclaimed as the most reliable guarantor of social peace.

Philip Melanchthon offered such an appraisal in his revision of Johann Carion's *Chronicle from the Beginning of the World*, a popular history first published in Wittenberg in 1532, and many times thereafter, in both German and Latin. "There is no doubt," Melanchthon writes, "that rulers are obliged to provide their peoples with a definitive, formal, written system of justice [*ius recte scriptum et certum*] so as to hold people in constraint and discipline [*Zwang und Zucht*] and to enable courts to arrive at uniform and unanimous verdicts." For these reasons God himself made the gift of a "written law" to the state of the Hebrews (*politia Israel; Jüdische Polizey*). Among the Romans, written law, and the wise and sober men who interpreted it, were held in highest esteem, as jurists to this day are distinguished by special honors, and the greatest of their law books, the *Digest (Auszug der Rechten)*, is "filled with high wisdom and art."

> It often happens, however, that some hotheads make a big noise, not only against the law, but against all worldly authority. They say they want the community of goods, and demand that no one should have anything to call his own. . . . They reject all government, law, courts of justice, due punishments, claiming that these are nothing more than sinful acts.

[23] J. W. Allen, *A History of Political Thought in the Sixteenth Century* (London, 1928), 281.

Such people, says Melanchthon, pretend that the Decalogue is the only law by which Christians should judge. They abolish the *bürgerliche Recht*, the civil law, wherever they are in a position to do so. But what ignorance this is, what folly, and what confusion! The righteousness taught by the gospel has nothing to do with the rules of authority laid down for civic life. All this, Melanchthon adds, is necessary for him to explain in the context of his outline of the history of the late Roman Empire, "for it is useful at times to look back and discover how the majesty of worldly government, and even the law itself, have everywhere been under attack by hordes of rebels."[24] Among the secular means at hand to combat such madness—a danger to which all governments were alert in the sixteenth century—the written law was by far the most reliable weapon.

THE first important stage in the Roman law's march to victory in Germany was the constitution of the Imperial Chamber Court in 1495. By the provisions of this document, judges and assessors on the empire's highest appellate bench were to "make and explain their decisions in accordance with the common laws of the empire,"[25] that is to say, by the Roman law. Put more precisely, the Roman law was to function from then on as a subsidiary law for all superior secular courts. When older, local statutes were silent, or unclear, or in contradiction, Roman law was to apply as a *ius commune*. This rule would have been meaningless without a cadre of trained lawyers to put it into effect, and, indeed, by the end of the fifteenth century the legal profession was firmly in place in Germany. Four hundred years earlier, Roman law had been virtually unknown in Teutonic lands, and jurists non-existent. The process of gradual adoption and adaptation leading to 1495 is what constitutes the "reception."[26] The events of these centuries have been

[24] I cite according to *Chronicon Carionis* edited and enlarged by Philip Melanchthon in *Philippi Melanthonis opera . . .* , ed. G. Bretschneider (*Corpus Reformatorum*) XII (Halle, 1844), 1050-1052, and Johann Carion [Philip Melanchthon, further expanded by Caspar Peucer], *Chronica . . . von Anfang der Welt bis auf Keiser Carolum den Fünfften* (Wittenberg, 1573), 357-58. On Melanchthon's and Peucer's roles in the publication of Carion's chronicle see Gerald Strauss, "The Course of German History: The Lutheran Interpretation" in Anthtony Molho and John A. Tedeschi, eds., *Renaissance Studies in Honor of Hans Baron* (Florence, 1971), 678-80, with bibliography. Peucer's third and fourth parts of the Carion-Melanchthon chronicle were first published in 1562 and 1565.
[25] Karl Zeumer, *Quellensammlung zur Geschichte der deutschen Reichsverfassung in Mittelalter und Neuzeit* (Tübingen, 1913), No. 174.
[26] On the ambiguities of the term "reception," see Erich Genzmer's general introduction to *Ius Romanum medii aevi* Pars I, l, d (Milan, 1961), 138.

most carefully examined by legal historians,[27] and, although nothing one could call a consensus exists concerning the relative weight to be given to the different factors in the course of the reception, the story's main outline is not open to dispute.

Systematic study of Roman law was revived at the University of Bologna shortly after a complete manuscript of the *Digest* had been discovered at the end of the eleventh century. The name of Irnerius is commonly associated with this first period of intense occupation with the *Digest*. He was a teacher of liberal arts at Bologna who, with his pupils, developed techniques that were to govern the study of law texts for centuries: writing notes, called glosses, to solve problems posed by the text. For reasons remaining somewhat mysterious to us, but probably having to do with the growing admiration in Europe for all things Roman, the "glossators'" program of study attracted followers from many countries, including Germany. Thus was initiated a vogue for legal scholarship in much of Europe, and a convergence of enthusiasts on Italy took place. This development reached major proportions when the glossators were succeeded by a new school, the so-called commentators or conciliators, who specialized in restoring to the Roman law its original practical orientation by utilizing it in their "commentaries"— i.e., interpretations—and advice (*consilia*) on current legal problems, especially the relationship of the *ius scriptum*, the formal Roman law, to the informally gathered statutes of Italian city-states. In the process, the commentators elaborated a new theory. They argued that in view of the multifarious variety of local and regional European laws the Roman law (along with the Church's canon law) must be taken as a common system of justice for all countries formerly part of the Roman empire. When local statutes gave no basis for judgment, this law was to be called on as subsidiary or underlying.[28] The *mos italicus*, as this "Italian" way of understanding and using the Roman law came to be called, and its leading proponents, Bartolus and Baldus, two fourteenth-century academic jurists, were later disavowed by practitioners of a rival discipline, the so-called French manner, or *mos gallicus*, who investigated the law of the Romans as a historical phenomenon and who brought to this activity a primarily scholarly interest in the culture of antiquity. But it was Bologna that restored legal studies to the rank of

[27] Above all, now, by Helmut Coing, *Römisches Recht in Deutschland* in *Ius Romanum medii aevi* Pars V, 6 (Milan, 1964). See also Friedrich Merzbacher, "Römisches Recht und Romanistik im Mittelalter. Zum gegenwärtigen Stand der Forschung," *Historisches Jahrbuch* 89:1 (1969), 1-32.

[28] On Roman and canon law as a European *ius commune* see Helmut Coing, "Das Recht als Element der europäischen Kultur," *HZ* 238:1 (1984), 1-15.

honorable occupations not unlike the status they had enjoyed in antiquity, and it was in Italy that the most significant recovery of Roman law in European history occurred.[29]

German law students began crossing the Alps in the thirteenth century, and from then on, and into the early modern period, the practically oriented *mos italicus* dominated German jurisprudence.[30] Civil law in the Italian manner was taught from 1388 in Cologne, and at other German universities—Erfurt, Rostock, Greifswald, Leipzig, Heidelberg—from the early fifteenth century.[31] (Italy, France, and Spain had had law faculties since the 1200s.) Their course of study completed, graduates found employment in city governments and the chancelleries of territorial rulers, and the reception was advanced substantially by the experience and outlook these men brought to their tasks.[32] Until the fifteenth century, most of them were clerics, moved to the study of Roman law by their familiarity with the law of the Church, the basic text of which was a Bologna product as well, the twelfth-century *Decretum Gratiani*, which, as supplemented by later papal decretals, came to constitute a body of ecclesiastical laws subsequently referred to as the *corpus iuris canonici*.[33] From its beginnings, the canon law contained large amounts of Roman material, the Christian Roman emperors having legislated for Church and clergy according to Ulpian's

[29] See the positive interpretation of the *mos italicus* given by Donald R. Kelley, "Civil Science in the Renaissance: Jurisprudence Italian Style," *The Historical Journal* 22:4 (1979), 777-94. See also the recent account of the beginnings of legal scholarship in Italy by Ferdinand Elsener, *Die Schweizer Rechtsschulen vom 16. bis zum 19. Jahrhundert* (Zurich, 1975), 3-19, with excellent bibliography. The best treatment of the revival of Roman law in Italy is to be found in Woldemar Engelmann, *Die Wiedergeburt der Rechtskultur in Italien* . . . (Leipzig, 1939). The most recent treatment is by Helmut Coing *et al.* in *Handbuch der Quellen und Literatur der neueren Europäischen Privatrechtsgeschichte* I (Munich, 1973), 129-313. There is an informative description of the method followed by post-glossators in Wolfgang Kunkel, "Das römische Recht am Vorabend der Rezeption" in *L'Europa e il diritto romano. Studi in memoria di Paolo Koschaker* I (Milan, 1954), 1-20. On this topic see also Walter Ullmann, *Law and Politics in the Middle Ages. An Introduction to the Sources of Medieval Political Ideas* (Ithaca, 1975), Chapter 3. Georg Dahm's article cited in note 1 above is very good on the circumstances under which Roman law was first received in Italy. See especially pp. 296-302.

[30] Wolfgang Kunkel, "Das römische Recht am Vorabend der Rezeption" in *loc. cit.*, 18-20. Georg Dahm in *loc. cit.*, argues that German and Italian law converged upon each other in the period before 1495.

[31] Helmut Coing, *Römisches Recht in Deutschland*, 70.

[32] See the notes on this by Friedrich Merzbacher, "Römisches Recht und Romantik im Mittelalter" in *loc. cit.*, 27.

[33] For an introduction to the history of canon law, see Walter Ullmann, *Law and Politics in the Middle Ages*, Chapters 4-5.

dictum that "Public law relates to sacred rites, ministers of religion, and public officials" (*Digest* 1.1.1). Experts in ecclesiastical law (called "canonists," whereas specialists in the Roman civil law were "legists" or "civilians") worked for bishops, monasteries, or cathedral chapters as notaries, clerks, judges, and legal officers. In view of the overlapping of ecclesiastical and worldly jurisdictions in medieval life, competence in secular law became essential for these functionaries, just as a knowledge of canon law proved indispensable for lay jurists holding office in civic or regional governments. The two bodies of law thus influenced each other substantially.[34] By custom, each was subsidiary to the other: a lacuna or obscurity in one law was repaired by referring to the other. A fully trained jurist was expected to have degrees in both kinds of law (in the sixteenth century a legal scholar who knew only one law was sometimes called *monoculus*—one-eyed). The "man learned in both laws"—*iuris utriusque doctor*, or *J.U.D.*—was at the top of his profession.

This interpenetration of Roman and canon law endured even into the Protestant Reformation. It was a thorn in Luther's flesh that evangelical jurists (for instance the aforementioned Melchior Kling) refused to join him in denying authority to the law of the Church. But to the trained lawyer, the two codes had too common a history, and reinforced each other at too many points, to be arbitrarily pried apart.[35] Thus Roman civil law and the Church's canon law together came to make up what, from the fourteenth century, was taken by all jurists to

[34] Erich Genzmer, "Kleriker als Berufsjuristen im späten Mittelalter," *Études d'histoire du droit canonique dédiées à Gabriel LeBras* 2 (Paris, 1965), 1207-36. For the best recent discussion of the role of ecclesiastical law in promoting Romanization, see Wilfried Trusen, *Anfänge des gelehrten Rechts in Deutschland*, 14-68, and Ferdinand Elsener, "Die Einflüsse des römischen und kanonischen Rechts in der Schweiz," *Historisches Jahrbuch* 76 (1957), 133-47, esp. 136-40. Hans Hattenhauer, *Geschichte des Beamtentums* (*Handbuch des öffentlichen Dienstes* I, Cologne, 1980), 11-19 gives a succinct but helpful account. The most up-to-date discussion of the activity of canon lawyers and the interpenetration of canon and civil law is Brian Tierney, *Religion, Law, and the Growth of Constitutional Thought, 1150-1650* (Cambridge, 1984).

[35] Harold J. Berman makes the point that all "the great national revolutions of the past—the Russian Revolution of 1917, the French and American Revolutions of 1789 and 1776, the English Revolution of 1640, the German Reformation of 1517—eventually made peace with the legal tradition that they or some of their leaders had set out to destroy." *Law and Revolution. The Formation of the Western Legal Tradition* (Cambridge, Mass., 1983), 5, 10. See, however, 29-30, where it becomes clear that Berman's understanding of the German Reformation's effect on law and politics rests on an appreciation of the reformers' intentions, rather than an analysis of institutions and how they operated. For some highly suggestive remarks on the subtle, and not unambiguous, relationship of canon law and Roman law, see *ibid.*, 204-05.

be the West's *ius commune,* the common body of legislative rules and legal opinions defining and interpreting private and public relations. Of this common law, the essential part for the secular lawyer was the law of the Romans, based almost entirely on Justinian's *corpus,* the complete text of which was put into print by the Nuremberg publishing house of Koberger in the years 1482-1504.[36] This law was the *ius scriptum,* the written, now printed, formally organized, disposed, thought-through, and integrated—and for these reasons stable—body of laws and judicial opinion. As a law of general application it tended to eclipse less formal and much less systematized customs and statutes of merely local application and of unstable authority owing to the absence of legal scholarship brought to bear on them. It was the source and origin of all subsequent codes. "All written laws come from Roman law," asserted a German jurist,[37] and this was believed by most of its admirers. In the courts of the fifteenth century, this written, common law took on the additional designation of "imperial" law (*kaiserliches Recht*) as jurists separated this label from medieval German codes to which it had originally referred[38] and attached it instead to the codified law of the Caesars and Augusti whose successors the German monarchs, as Roman kings and Holy Roman emperors, claimed to be. Ultimately, these "common," "written," and "imperial" laws gained the distinction of being known, simply, as *die Rechte,* "the laws."[39]

The imperial connection is one of the chief reasons for the influence gained by Roman law over the conduct of justice and public administration in German lands. Emperors had promoted the revival of the an-

[36] Copies of the complete text became available in the fourteenth century. The *Institutes* were first printed in Mainz in 1468, with fifty-four editions to follow in the remainder of the fifteenth century, twelve of them in Germany. Koberger published the *Digest* in 1482, the *Institutes* in 1486, and the *Codex* in 1488. See Ralf Michael Thilo, "Drucke des Corpus Iuris Civilis im deutschen Sprachraum," *Gutenberg Jahrbuch* 59 (1985), 52-66.

[37] Christoph Zobell in his glosses on *Sechssisch Weychbild und Lehnrecht* (Leipzig, 1537), Ggiii^v.

[38] As territorial codes, such as the *Sachsenspiegel* and *Schwabenspiegel,* were usually ascribed to particular rulers such as Charlemagne and Barbarossa, they too had been known as *Kaiserrecht.* This is how it happened that in the reform literature of the fifteenth century, "*Kaiserrecht*" had two contradictory meanings: it referred to Roman law as well as to an anti-Roman, older, indigenous "emperors' law." On all aspects of Kaiserrecht, see Hermann Krause, *Kaiserrecht und Rezeption* (*Abhandlungen der Heidelberger Akademie der Wissenschaften, phil.-hist. Klasse,* 1952), 15-125.

[39] E.g., in the work of the Frankfurt jurist Johann Fichard. Quoted in Otto Stobbe, *Geschichte der deutschen Rechtsquellen* II (Braunschweig, 1864; reprint Aalen, 1965), 324.

cient law from its very beginnings in Italy. "Imperial politicians," comments Helmut Coing,

> discovered in the legists' teachings a concept of law capable not only of legitimizing their claims [for empire and against the Church] but of being employed in addition as the instrument of a new power politics. Two historical forces were thus brought into contact: the science of Roman law and the ambitions of the Hohenstaufen dynasty. They seemed destined to work together.[40]

The idea of an uninterrupted Roman imperium carried forward by German emperors was a precondition of the peculiar nature of the German reception. Where the empire persisted, the imperial law would also reign. *Kaiserrecht*—imperial law—was the "Trojan horse" (in the words of an unsympathetic critic) of the German reception.[41] From the emperors' point of view, and in the opinion of all those who proposed using the Roman code aggressively, there was nothing foreign about imperial law: "Germany is the Roman empire, and Justinian reigned here, too, in former times."[42] Included in lists of "German" lawgivers were "King Constantine and the noble Emperor Justinian and the worthy Emperor Charles and his son Louis and the latter's son, the noble Lothair." The rules and statutes of "written law" had been proclaimed by these and later emperors, "and for this reason they are good and enduring above all regional laws, for the Roman King is lord and sovereign of all Christians."[43] It was another Lothair, the Saxon emperor Lothair II, who was credited with having revived legal studies in Italy:

> After the Goths, Lombards, and Franks had brought the ancient laws of their forefathers to Italy, . . . the Emperor Lothair the Saxon was persuaded by a distinguished jurist, Irnerius, who had studied for many years in Constantinople and heard the lectures of famous jurists there, to have a search made for the digest or collection of all the jurists' books, called *Pandects*, and to order public lectures given on this book in Bologna, and to have all matters under dispute settled by reference to it. This is how it happened that the teachings of the ancient jurists were brought from Constantinople to Italy.[44]

[40] Helmut Coing, *Römisches Recht in Deutschland*, 30.

[41] Hermann Krause, *op. cit.*, 13.

[42] This was said by Johann Stephan Pütter, *Litteratur des Teutschen Staatsrechts* I (Göttingen, 1776), 88.

[43] Quoted in Hermann Krause, *op. cit.*, 90-91.

[44] Johann Carion and Philip Melanchthon, *Chronica* (Wittenberg, 1573), 357.

Roman law and medieval empire thus lived in intimate association from the beginnings of the former's revival to the early modern period.[45] In the fifteenth century, this symbiosis began to establish itself also in territorial principalities and urban magistracies. It is not difficult to see how this came about. As Helmut Coing explains, legists provided sovereigns with

> an ideological basis for their ambitions. . . . The body of law the jurists had made the subject of their scholarly research reflected the legal system of an absolute, though not arbitrary, monarchy, which was also autonomous, not to say dominating, vis-à-vis the Church. Moreover, it contained the principles of a tightly centralized bureaucratic state with the help of which one could make an effective stand against the dangers inherent in the feudal system.[46]

These features were no less relevant to the policies of dukes and electors than they had been to the aims of emperors. For this reason, the "imperial" law became a trusted weapon in the struggle of territorial princes against secular and ecclesiastical opponents of regional centralization. Coing offers the following summary of the Roman law's ideological utility to a ruler, or to a magistrate, engaged in this fight: The *imperium* comes directly from God; it requires no mediation through the *sacerdotium*. Its possessor, the emperor, is *dominus mundi*, inspired by God. Moreover, as Roman *princeps* he has received his power as well from the people, via the *lex regia*. As personified law—*lex animata*—the emperor determines what is right and legitimate. Finally, he is inviolable in his own person.[47] One needs only to state these points to make a case for the extraordinary usefulness to ambitious and embattled sovereigns of a legal system offering ancient and honorable sanction for each of these claims.

This "ideological opulence" (as Walter Ullmann has called it)[48] made the Roman law "an indispensable instrument of government" with which to strengthen the hands of rulers struggling to assert themselves against rival claimants, especially against those who maintained the su-

[45] Percy Ernst Schramm stresses the significance of the idea of "revival" or "renewal" for an understanding of this close association of empire and law: *Kaiser, Rom und Renovatio* . . . (Leipzig and Berlin, 1929), 275-89.

[46] Helmut Coing, *Römisches Recht in Deutschland*, 31-32.

[47] *Ibid.*, 32-33, with references to the *corpus iuris civilis*. Walter Ullmann stresses the absolutist tendencies of the Justinian law in *Law and Politics in the Middle Ages*, Chapter 3: "The law that was primarily studied [at Bologna] (and this applies with equal force to canon law) exhibited an unadulterated monarchic system of government the hallmark of which was the descending-theocratic theme in relation to the creation of law."

[48] *Id., Medieval Foundations of Renaissance Humanism* (London, 1977), 37.

periority of ecclesiastical rule. This is why the Roman law's period of greatest influence upon public affairs coincided with the approach and establishment of the Reformation in Germany, a time when princes and magistrates seized all available means of securing public acceptance of both the primacy and of the sanctity of secular authority. Of this primacy, the *Code* supplied the enactments by which it had been established in the days of the Christian Roman emperors, and the *Digest* furnished an ample body of supporting opinions. Winfried Trusen has shown how German princes made use of these enabling arguments as early as the fourteenth century, notably in an effort—successful in most instances—to enlarge their personal jurisdiction as "highest judge," which was one of the functions of the *Landesfürst*.[49] Tentatively, and never without arousing strong vocal and, sometimes, physical resistance (as will be shown in the following chapters), the Roman law's—later celebrated—authoritarian precepts were employed to augment the prerogatives of princes and lesser rulers. While the claim that *rex est imperator in regno suo* was not explicitly advanced in these expansions, this is, in fact, the political principle underlying the usurpation by all regional rulers of non-traditional rights and powers.[50] *Quod principi placuit, legis habet vigorem* (*Digest* 1.4.1; *Institutes* 1.2.6) and *Princeps legibus solutus est* (*Digest* 1.3.31) were—always out of context, but, given the enormous respect accorded to ancient pronouncements, no less persuasive for that—quoted to support large and small pretensions to new or greater prerogatives tending toward centralization of power.[51] The fact that a living emperor stood above the *Landesfürst* in the empire's political hierarchy had little restraining effect on the elaboration of these claims.

One must not, however, exaggerate the impact of such Roman power boosts on German states. No systematic theory of monarchism was ever worked out, or even imagined. Utilizing Roman law to enhance authority was a matter of selecting quotations to serve *ad hoc* objectives. Allusions to *merum imperium, summa potestas,* and *lex*

[49] Winfried Trusen, *Anfänge des gelehrten Rechts*, 209-20.

[50] *Ibid.*, 210. "Ein jeder Herr ist Kaiser in seinem Land" existed as a legal proverb as early as the thirteenth century. See Johann Friedrich Eisenhart, *Deutsches Recht in Sprichwörtern*, 202.

[51] But this rarely happened without calling out contrary arguments taken from the same *corpus*. E.g., *Codex* 1.14.4: "It is an acknowledgment worthy of the emperor to admit that he is bound by the laws, for our authority is derived from the authority of law. And an emperor who submits himself to the law is thereby more respected than by his power." Myron P. Gilmore emphasizes the unhistorical, anachronistic use made of the *corpus iuris* in his *Arguments from Roman Law in Political Thought 1200-1600* (Cambridge, Mass, 1941), 37.

animata presupposed no commitment to a considered doctrine of political absolutism. Most jurists in fact rejected such a posture in favor of a traditional constitutional role for their prince or magistrate. To the bold assertion "A prince . . . is not subject to the laws; that is to say, if he transgresses, he is not punished," Justin Gobler added the gloss (from *Institutes* 2.17.8): "But he submits himself willingly to the laws."[52] In Augsburg, a municipal counsellor gave the same caution to a city father who was weighing a reversal of a previously announced decision: "Even an emperor," he advised in his memorandum on the matter, "though he is above the law, is obliged to keep his contracts and agreements."[53] Still, even the denials of authoritarian rule tended in the sixteenth century to be supported with arguments from *Digest* and *Institutes*. No other secular source had equal weight. Wherever significant political power was gathered, Roman law and lawyers sat beside those who wielded it. The alliance of these two forces—the institutional and the intellectual—had become indispensable and was to prove indissoluble.

VITAL though its promotion by centralizing, aggrandizing rulers was for the spread of Roman law, the reception should not be presented as a unilateral imposition from above. It has often been portrayed in this way.[54] But the true story is much more complex and much more interesting, as research in legal history has been demonstrating for the past forty years.[55] "Reception" proceeded by a push from below as well as by the will of authorities in positions to command. Scarcely a segment of German society failed to be drawn, at one time or another, to the utility of the Roman law. A brief survey of these non-governmental sources of support will reveal the reception's broad base in fifteenth- and sixteenth-century Germany. It should also indicate something of the tensions inevitably created in the body social by so fundamental a structural change in legal and political relations.

Before we continue, a reminder is in order of a cultural factor affect-

[52] Justin Gobler, *Handbuch und Auszug kayserlicher und Bürgerlicher Rechten* (Frankfurt am Main, 1564), ix^v.

[53] Hieronymus Rott to Augsburg Council, 1530. Stadtarchiv Augsburg *Literalien* 1534, Nachtrag I, No. 20, 17^r.

[54] For example by Tullius von Sartori-Montecroce, *Über die Reception der fremden Rechte in Tirol . . . (Beiträge zur österreichischen Reichs- und Rechtsgeschichte* I, Innsbruck, 1895), and, recently, by Perry Anderson, *Lineages of the Absolutist State* (1974), 22-29.

[55] See the titles cited in note 1, above, and especially the works of Helmut Coing. A catalogue of older views of the causes of the reception is offered by Georg von Below, *Die Ursachen*, 1-30. Below's own view is stated on pp. 106-64.

ing in the most elemental way all thoughts about past, present, and future in early modern society. This is the all-embracing concept of "reform." Since at least the late fifteenth century, this paradigm idea had shaped public opinion in Germany. In varying ways—that is to say, with different points of reference and emphasis—it swayed all classes and groups of people in their understanding of events and their reading of the signs. Law had been tied to the idea of renewal from the very beginning of its post-classical history. To Carolingian and Saxon emperors it was a vital aspect of the restoration of the ancient empire, the universality and permanence of which were fittingly represented by a timeless code of law taken as *ratio scripta*, as recorded reason.[56] In the world-wide monarchy of the Habsburg emperor Charles V, the theme of renewal was less fresh, but no less forcefully advanced.[57] Several generations of humanists going back to Lorenzo Valla and Jacob Wimpheling had, by then, placed their philological, historical, and textual studies at the service of a reconstruction of antiquity, a revival they saw as the most solid foundation on which to build a reformed society. Given its anti-Bartolist (i.e., opposed to the *mos italicus*) prejudices, this humanist scholarship made little impact on the course and nature of the German reception.[58] On the other hand, humanist propaganda for a general rejuvenation of culture contributed greatly to the intellectual atmosphere in which the classical law (as it was taken to be) was restored.[59] As pointed out on an earlier page, "law" and "reformation" had, by the late fifteenth century, become closely linked. *Reformatio* was renewal, including renewal of law. Whatever had become *de*formed in the course of time was in need of *re*formation, and this could never be innovation—departure in new directions—but must be restoration, going back to something true and permanent, firmly located in the past.

Roman law provides a case in point of how such a restoration re-

[56] Percy Ernst Schramm, *Kaiser, Rom und Renovatio*, 275-89.

[57] Peter Rassow, *Die Kaiser-Idee Karls V dargestellt an der Politik der Jahre 1528-1540* (Berlin, 1932; reprint Vaduz, 1965), vii-viii.

[58] Franz Wieacker, "Einflüsse des Humanismus auf die Rezeption. Eine Studie zu Johannes Apels Dialogus," *Zeitschrift für die gesamte Staatswissenschaft* 100 (1939), 423-56, especially 454-56.

[59] On humanism and reception, see Franz Beyerle, "Rezeption, Rezeptionsreife und Überwindung [1942]," *ZRG* 95 (1978), *Germ.Abt.*, 115-20 and, more generally, Donald R. Kelley, "The Rise of Legal History in the Renaissance," *History and Theory* 9 (1970), 174-94, especially 176-82. A useful survey is Quentin Skinner, *The Foundations of Modern Political Thought* I, 105-06; 201-08, based chiefly on Donald R. Kelley, *Foundations of Modern Historical Scholarship: Language, Law and History in the French Renaissance* (New York, 1970).

sponded to a consensus existing among contemporaries. This consensus, Wolfgang Leiser has pointed out,

> was an essential factor in creating the psychological precondition of a reform of law based on the *corpus iuris civilis*. . . . Whenever a change or improvement was made in a law during these years, the label *Reformatio* was attached to it. Beginning with the early fifteenth century, one finds innumerable large and small law codes either entitled *Reformation* or given this designation in the preamble or text. Examples can be named from Bavaria to Hamburg, among them imperial laws, urban and territorial laws, domainial constitutions, secular and ecclesiastical codes. In the end, *Reformatio* is simply a synonym for "law."[60]

Leiser's last sentence may convey the wrong impression. "Reformation" suggested much more than "law." The many associations ringing in this powerfully charged word could not have gone unheeded in so crisis-ridden a time as the early sixteenth century. Everyone was waiting for a *reformatio*, though grounds for longing for it varied. To many of those sharing this expectant mood, the best procedure they could imagine for accomplishing the reform was an alteration of the laws.[61] "*Verenderung der gesetz*" were announced in almost every prognostication issued for these troubled years, and the mass market cultivated by astrologers and almanac makers for their predictions must have reacted with sympathetic anticipation. This, in turn, created an accommodating ambience for legal change in the land, even at the grass roots.

This cultural atmosphere provided a welcoming setting for the reception. The much more aggressive role of instigator was played by professional men who took to the study of law as the best preparation for careers in state and church. Clerics preceded their lay colleagues on this path. In the thirteenth century, German ecclesiastics were found at Italian, and later at French, universities, making themselves experts in canon and civil law, then taking up positions as judicial officers for bishops and cathedral chapters. Some rose high in the church; others functioned as canons and priors. It was not long before secular governments availed themselves of their services—the city of Nuremberg employed a qualified jurist as *Stadtschreiber* in the 1370s. Soon the law

---

[60] Wolfgang Leiser, " 'Kein Doctor soll ohn ein solch Libell sein.' 500 Jahre Nürnberger Rechtsreformation," *Mitteilungen des Vereins für Geschichte der Stadt Nürnberg* 67 (1980), 1-16.

[61] "Was in disem 1562 Jar von den himmlischen Einflüssen in gemein bedeutt werde" in a manuscript *prognosticatio* in Germanisches Nationalmuseum Nuremberg Hs. 16.573, 3ᵛ.

faculties of Italian and French universities enrolled large contingents of lay students from Germany.[62] From the early fifteenth century on it was possible to study law also in a number of German universities, as we have seen, but Italy remained the preferred training ground for ambitious professionals. Almost every name with a reputation among sixteenth-century German jurists had been matriculated at Bologna, Padua, Perugia, Bourges, Toulouse, or Orléans, and many had degrees from these schools.[63] More than ten years of study beyond the M.A. were required for the doctorate in law; a jurist was likely to be in his early thirties before he was fully qualified.[64] For obvious reasons, only a minority of entering law students made it to the doctorate; but even those who did not finish found opportunities in church and state administrations, where their mastery of law nomenclature and their legalistic mind-set made them suitable for employment in the proliferating echelons of the state and judicial bureaucracy.

These men introduced Roman methods into German law. In a process known in German scholarship as *Verwissenschaftlichung*, they succeeded over the course of a century or so in transforming native law and legal procedure by making it learned, scholarly, professional, "scientific," enriching it with these qualities in keeping with their academic preferences. Procedural law especially was changed in their handling of court business: it became more formal and rigid, but also more expeditious and predictable. Everything was put in writing. Institutions like guardianship, adoption, inheritance, custody, property, the laws of proof, evidence, and witnesses—to name a few—were enhanced with Roman material.[65] Important terms were latinized: complaint became *actio*; reply, *receptio*; property, *possessio*; and so on. From the *iuris*

[62] Winfried Trusen, *Anfänge des gelehrten Rechts*, 102-24; Ferdinand Elsener, "Die Einflüsse des römischen . . . Rechts in der Schweiz" in *loc. cit.*, 136-40; Ulrich Bubenheimer, *Consonantia Theologiae et Jurisprudentiae*, 40-48; Otto Stobbe, *Geschichte der deutschen Rechtsquellen* II, 11-16; René David (tr. and ed. Günther Grasmann), *Einführung in die grossen Rechtssysteme der Gegenwart. Rechtsvergleichung* (Munich and Berlin, 1966), 39-55.

[63] On the names and numbers of Germans studying in Italy and France, and later in Germany, see Adolf Stölzel, *Die Entwicklung des gelehrten Richtertums in den deutschen Territorien* (Stuttgart, 1872; reprint Aalen, 1964) I, 45-111. Stölzel's list covers the fourteenth through seventeenth centuries, and the universities of Bologna, Padua, Pavia, Perugia, Siena; Bourges, Toulouse, Strasbourg, Orléans; Heidelberg, Cologne, Erfurt, Leipzig, Rostock, Freiburg, Greifswald, Basel, Ingolstadt, Mainz, and Wittenberg. Perugia alone (*ibid.*, Appendix 2) had 225 Germans enrolled in the sixteenth and seventeenth centuries, most of them law students.

[64] Karl Heinz Burmeister, *Das Studium der Rechte im Zeitalter des Humanismus im deutschen Rechtsbereich* (Wiesbaden, 1974), 200-04.

[65] Ferdinand Elsener, *Die Schweizer Rechtsschulen*, 26-27.

utriusque doctor saturated with the dignity of Roman jurisprudence down to the self-trained village notary copying phrases from his *summa artis notariae*, "learned" and "semi-learned" legal practitioners transformed old processes in both substance and practice by introducing their acquired *modus operandi*.[66] Adolf Stölzel has reconstructed in great detail the circumstances that eventually brought the majority of judgeships in German territories into the hands of "learned" law graduates or near-graduates. Rulers and nobles with jurisdictional rights over court appointments named judges and jurors to benches formerly filled by election. "Thus 'freely chosen' judges turned into 'freely chosen and appointed,' ultimately simply into 'appointed' judges."[67] This transition suited rulers in many ways, although their immediate objective was the promotion of skill in the administration of courts.

Such developments tended to reinforce each other. The introduction of written procedures, for example, made trials an ordeal for illiterate jurors, leaving them ill able to resist competition from the learned who, in the end, replaced them. Requirements for properly executed documents created a need for notaries, a flourishing profession from the fifteenth century onward, licensed by a grant of official authority and closely tied in their business to the Roman procedural system. Imposition of a regular sequence of instances for appeals weakened local courts still functioning under amateurs by frustrating them with frequent reversals of judgments at a higher level. Even in municipal territories, the trial functions of country judges were usurped by city courts. The city of Zwickau, in Saxony, for example, transferred rural cases to the municipal bench, where Roman law was in use, because the councillors suspected native Saxon law of being too lenient.[68] In this fashion, the impression gradually spread that justice was in better hands when practiced by the learned. Many legal historians have emphasized the poor performance of amateur-run courts in the age of the reception.

[66] On the role of "semi-learned" paralegal personnel in carrying out the German reception, see especially Roderich Stintzing, *Geschichte der populären Literatur des römisch-kanonischen Rechts in Deutschland am Ende des 15. und im Anfang des 16. Jahrhunderts* (Leipzig, 1867), *passim*, especially xix–xxiii. On the role of the notary in particular, see Franz Beyerle, "Rezeption, Rezeptionsreife und Überwindung," *ZRG* 95 (1978) *Germ.Abt.*, 116. For an interesting account of the reception in twelfth-century France in similar terms, see Jan Rogoziński, *Power, Caste, and Law. Social Conflict in Fourteenth-Century Montpellier* (Cambridge, Mass., 1982), 107-13 and Appendix II.

[67] Adolf Stölzel, *Die Entwicklung des gelehrten Richtertums* I, 138.

[68] The evidence for this practice is contained in the record book of Zwickau's appointed judicial officer, the *Schultheiss*, over countryside courts. See Susan Karant-Nunn's forthcoming book, *Zwickau in the Age of the Reformation*.

Jurors were often named for no more than one court session at a time, and this limited their practical experience when experience was all they had to draw on in doing their jobs.[69] They also suffered from a serious lack of common rules for conducting hearings and trials. Such conditions have been seen as a major cause of the shift of loyalty to the learned, written law. Confusion spread in the lower courts. "Every petty point of law was referred to a higher bench; superior courts, for their part, handed down decisions without giving reasons, speaking like oracles, *ex cathedra*, while at about the same time the jurists routinely provided *rationes decidendi* for all their judgments."[70] Thus the notion gained ground among affected parties that indigenous law was *ius incertum*, resting on subjective impressions, in contrast to Roman law, which, as *ius certum*, was brought into action whenever particular laws were in a state of conflict.[71] As the vogue for the new law gained strength, this recourse was more frequently taken, especially by the well to do, who were most often in litigation and who had most at stake in pursuing it successfully. Already an object of reverence as the "law of emperors," the merits of which were generally acknowledged, if not clearly understood,[72] Roman law became increasingly the law of choice.

But what was welcomed as a businesslike method for succeeding in court was often discovered—especially when decisions went against one—to be an unfamiliar, if not actually hostile, system of adjudication. In many small and large ways, the reception drastically altered German law both in substance and in procedure, and this change was not—or, at any rate, seemed in the end not to be—in the interest of those who were most in need of protection.

We can observe this tension in Saxony, where the old territorial code, the *Sachsenspiegel*, had long performed as a subsidiary body of law to settle inadequacies and contradictions among local laws.[73] By the opening of the sixteenth century, however, this indigenous law had received some rather rough handling by learned interpreters and commentators. In 1518 the estates complained of "new articles" in the code which, they said, "go against the common custom, also they are ob-

---

[69] Friedrich Wilhelm Unger, *Geschichte der deutschen Landstände* (Hannover, 1844), 212.

[70] Franz Beyerle, "Rezeption, Rezeptionsreife . . ." in *loc. cit.*, 118. The strongest case for chaotic conditions in German law is made by Georg Dahm, "On the Reception of Roman and Italian Law" (for reference see note 1), *passim*, especially 293.

[71] Otto Stobbe, *Geschichte der deutschen Rechtsquellen* I, 651.

[72] *Ibid.*, 640.

[73] *Ibid.* II, 4-6.

scure and ambiguous." They asked for explanations.[74] The request was repeated in every subsequent diet:

> The said *Sachsenspiegel* contains a number of articles that go against our common custom and usage and are in part obscure and ambiguous, that is to say, subject to different and contradictory interpretations. . . . For the sake of our common land and people [we ask] that the *Sachsenspiegel* be corrected and explained in its erroneous and obscure articles, as well as generally improved.[75]

"Dark and obscure" passages confused local courts, whose improperly rendered verdicts were then nullified at the elector's superior bench. "The Saxon law that is used in [the duchy's *Hofgericht*, or high appellate court] needs explanation on many points, and we beg Your Electoral Grace to have it examined and explained by men experienced and knowledgeable in the law; also, the Latin words contained therein should be put into easy-to-understand German. For it happens very often, owing to the ignorance and lack of understanding now so widespread, that the jurors' bench [*Schöffen*] in Leipzig and the Electoral High Court [*Hofgericht*] arrive at differing and even contradictory judgments in many cases."[76]

Ungleichheit der urteil—conflicting judicial opinions based on divergent principles—were the chief concern of the authors of such complaints.[77] They resulted from the practice of appealing almost every decision of local and patrimonial tribunals to a higher court in hopes of obtaining satisfaction. Even petty *Bauernsachen*—peasant trivia— were moved to superior benches. Rapacious lawyers were said to hang on every courtroom to goad litigants into making appeals.[78] Lack of certainty by lay jurors on what the laws meant, and on how the laws related to each other, was chiefly responsible. All this resulted in a "great burdening of people's consciences, leading to disobedience toward their lords and unfriendly strife among neighbors," as the knights of Meissen and Thuringia complained at their diet in Jena, in 1518,

[74] From meetings of estates at Jena, 1518 in C.A.H. Burckhardt ed., *Ernestinische Landtagsakten* I: *Die Landtage von 1487-1532* (*Thüringische Geschichtsquellen* N.F. 5, Jena, 1902), No. 238.

[75] StA Wei Reg Q No. 17, 134ᵛ-135ʳ.

[76] Grievance addressed to Elector August by association of knights, joined by cities, meeting in Leipzig in 1554. StA Dr, Loc. 9356: "Beratschlagung der Landgebrechen . . . ," 17ᵛ-18ʳ.

[77] For a clear impression of this, see the summary of estate deliberations in Saxony from 1495 to 1588: "Summarischer Extract aller Handlungen . . ." in StA Dr, Loc. 9349, No. 7, 156ᵛ, 164ᵛ, 167ʳ, 191ᵛ, etc.

[78] Complaint of Saxon *Ritterschaft* 1602, StA Dr, Loc. 9359 *passim* in entire volume.

asking for a "new ordinance."[79] In many cases the judgments ultimately handed down by higher courts were harmful to local interests. New trial procedures were also objected to, especially innovations regarding evidence and proof. "Put an end to excessive *interrogatoria* in examining witnesses."[80] None of this means, however, that traditional legal ways disappeared in Saxony and elsewhere. Even while judicial process underwent steady "modernization" and "rationalization," customs continued to dominate the way people actually lived—a fact acknowledged with some distaste by Dr. Melchior Kling in his attempt to make Saxon territorial law conform "to a right order."[81] The complaints and protests we have been examining in these pages had their origin in just this friction between the two kinds of law in use. It was not that the learned law was automatically rejected or resisted. On the contrary, as we have seen, there was much about it that gained it a loyal following. But tension was inevitable in this intricate process of social adjustment, and at many points of contact the familiar law, to which people were accustomed, was in conflict with the jurisprudence taught at the university and practiced at the high courts.

As the Saxon example shows, this conflict occurred most conspicuously in the rivalry between local and superior benches, and between lay judges and learned jurists attached to university faculties and sitting on the elector's appeals courts. Two developments brought contentions to a head in the sixteenth century. One was the gradual replacement of the old and originally lay *Oberhof* by a newer *Hofgericht* or aulic court. This was another long step toward the professionalization of justice, as appeals and referrals were redirected from benches with traditional authority in the older law (*Oberhöfe* existed in Leipzig, Magdeburg, Lübeck, Freiburg in the Breisgau, and Frankfurt am Main, cities whose law codes enjoyed wide recognition among the lay courts in surrounding regions) to the superior courts of territorial states where "learned" justice reigned. The second development was the habit—vigorously promoted by governmental directives—of applying to distinguished academic lawyers for opinions, or even for verdicts, on difficult points of law. Otto Stobbe has traced this gradual, but one-directional, transition in a number of German territories. Everywhere he found a weakening of traditional laymen's tribunals in favor of professionally

---

[79] StA Wei Reg Q, No. 17, 122ᵛ-124ʳ.

[80] StA Dr, Loc. 9349, No. 7, 203ʳ. The complaint relates to the spread of inquisitorial proceedings.

[81] Melchior Kling, *Das gantz Sechssisch Landrecht . . .* (Leipzig, 1571), iiᵛ-iiiʳ.

staffed courts.[82] The same process is described by Adolf Stölzel as it was at work in the Electorate of Brandenburg, where the early years of the sixteenth century saw the elector's learned councillors replace *Schöffen* as "instructors"—*Rechtsbelehrer*—of lower courts in points of law. To meet the competition, lay jurors had to become "learned" themselves. By the time of the Reformation, all had received some legal training; by the beginning of the next century, the entire Brandenburg *Schöffen* bench had become professionally "juristic," as had the more famous *Schöffen* tribunal in the city of Magdeburg.[83]

The already noted inadequacy of amateur *Schöffen* (lay jurors, always men of high local standing chosen by local authorities to the honorary office of court assessor)[84] in the face of their increasingly complex legal responsibilities[85] was only one factor in this debilitation. Another was the insistence of territorial princes on keeping legal business within their own states. Referrals to trans-territorial *Oberhöfe* were interdicted and the sequence of instances rerouted to state superior courts as the benches of final appeal.[86] *Hofgerichte* occupied by academically qualified jurists appeared in all German territories in the last decades of the fifteenth and the early years of the sixteenth centuries.[87] Saxony had one such court in Leipzig and another in Wittenberg. One third of the judges serving on these benches were *doctores*. Later in the sixteenth

[82] Otto Stobbe, *Geschichte der deutschen Rechtsquellen* I, 64-109. See Stobbe's second volume for special consideration of how the process worked itself out in the territory of Hessen. A good description of how a *Schöffengericht*—in this case the court in Frankfurt am Main—operated is found in Alfons Vogt, "Die Anfänge des Inquisitionsprozesses in Frankfurt am Main," ZRG 69 (1951), Germ.Abt., 267-77. Helmut Coing, *Die Rezeption des römischen Rechts in Frankfurt am Main* shows in detail how *Schöffen* were replaced by professional judges in that city.

[83] Adolf Stölzel, *Die Entwicklung der gelehrten Rechtssprechung* I, 186-87, 191, 279 81, 293.

[84] For a discussion of the history of *Schöffen* (scabini, échevins) in Europe, particularly Germany, see John P. Dawson, *A History of Lay Judges* (Cambridge, Mass., 1960), 94-115. Dawson's pages on Germany are based almost entirely on Adolf Stölzel, *Die Entwicklung des gelehrten Richtertums*. See also Otto Stobbe, *Geschichte der deutschen Rechtsquellen* I, 274-443.

[85] A good illustration of the unwillingness of local courts to judge matters for themselves by the middle of the sixteenth century is offered in a detailed study of a single village court over time: Hans Tütken, *Geschichte des Dorfes und Patrimonialgerichtes Geismar bis zur Gerichtsauflösung im Jahre 1839* (*Studien zur Geschichte der Stadt Göttingen* 7, 1967), especially 252.

[86] Jürgen Weitzel, *Der Kampf um die Appellation ans Reichskammergericht* (Cologne and Vienna, 1976) shows in detail how territorial and urban rulers attempted to inhibit appeals to the Imperial Chamber Court.

[87] For the fifteenth-century beginnings of this process, see Winfried Trusen, *Anfänge des gelehrten Rechts in Deutschland*, 213-21.

century, a "faction of doctors" (*Doktorenpartei*) at the elector's court tried to purge all non-learned members of the old *Schöffen* bench in Leipzig.[88] In Mecklenburg, the *Reformation* of 1558 turned the duke's *Hofgericht* into a professional judicial body; at about the same time litigating parties were encouraged to submit their cases to arbitration by learned councillors who, of course, used Roman law in their decisions.[89] On the Palatinate's court in Heidelberg, five of eleven members were jurists.[90] In Bavaria, the question of "doctors" on the duchy's high courts led to bitter altercations between duke and estates, as will be shown in another chapter. Half of Württemberg's superior court judges were "learned in the law." Of the thirty-eight assessors sitting on the high court of Hessen in Marburg during the first two decades of the sixteenth century, twelve were doctors, one a magister, and another a licentiate.[91] The courts of Oldenburg became professional in the late 1520s; by 1573 this process was complete.[92] In the Archbishopric of Mainz, five of the *Hofgericht*'s ten assessors were "learned"; the others, who were nobles, took their duties so lightly that the jurists usually met without them. In the seventeenth century the "noble bench" vanished altogether.[93]

With few exceptions, this was the pattern of developments in all the empire's territories.[94] Roman law and its practitioners served rulers well in accomplishing this transition to a professionally qualified and politically integrated system of justice. Jurists supported these moves because they made for efficiency and economy. Melchior von Osse, an important judicial figure in Saxony, argued vigorously that litigants,

[88] Hermann Theodor Schletter, *Die Constitutionen Kurfürst Augusts von Sachsen vom Jahre 1572* (Leipzig, 1857), 36-37. The "party" was unsuccessful at the time, and in 1574 all the academic lawyers were removed from the Leipzig *Schöppenstuhl*.

[89] Hermann Krause, *Die geschichtliche Entwicklung des Schiedsgerichtswesens in Deutschland* (Berlin, 1930), 47.

[90] The situation in the Palatinate has recently been investigated by Herbert Helbig, "Fürsten und Landstände im Westen des Reiches im Übergang vom Mittelalter zur Neuzeit" in Heinz Rausch ed., *Die geschichtlichen Grundlagen der modernen Volksvertretung* II: *Reichsstände und Landstände* (Darmstadt, 1974), 167-69. On the role of the university of Heidelberg, and the Palatinate government's eagerness to have its law faculty play this role, see Gerhard Ritter, *Die Heidelberger Universität* I (1936), 439ff.

[91] Karl E. Demandt, *Der Personenstaat der Landgrafschaft Hessen im Mittelalter. Ein Staatshandbuch Hessens vom Ende des 12. bis zum Anfang des 16. Jahrhunderts* (Marburg, 1981), *passim*.

[92] Werner Hülle, *Geschichte des höchsten Landesgerichts von Oldenburg* (Göttingen, 1974), 11-25.

[93] Hans Goldschmidt, *Zentralbehörden und Beamtentum im Kurfürstentum Mainz vom 16. bis zum 18. Jahrhundert* (Berlin and Leipzig, 1980), 156.

[94] Otto Stobbe, *op. cit.*, 91-101.

and especially the poorer sort, would be much better off if the procedure in use at Saxon superior courts were also adopted at all other courts—district, urban, ecclesiastical, and patrimonial—with no exceptions allowed.[95] From the middle of the fifteenth century on it also became customary to refer troublesome matters to distinguished legists and university law faculties for authoritative (though not necessarily binding) opinions.[96] This practice received an enormous boost from the publication of the imperial criminal code, the *Carolina* (so named after Charles V, who issued it in 1532), whose concluding article obliged lay judges who were "not learned, experienced, or practiced in our imperial laws . . . to seek counsel" in criminal matters "at the nearest university, city, or other source of legal knowledge."[97] The mid- and late-sixteenth century was the time of greatest demand for this consulting jurisprudence, the writing of *consilia*, opinions, and judgments for the use of courts and litigating parties.[98] University statutes accorded to law professors—called *iurisconsulti* for this side of their activity—the *ius respondendi*, the right to render this professional service.[99] Most German territories followed the example of the *Carolina* in encourag-

---

[95] Melchior von Osse, *An Hertzog Augustum . . . Ein unterthäniges Bedencken . . . welchergestalt ein . . . obrigkeit . . . ein . . . rechtmessige Justicien erhalten kan* (1555) in *Schriften Dr. Melchiors von Osse*, ed. Oswald Artur Hecker (Leipzig and Berlin, 1922), 455-56.

[96] E.g., in the judicial constitution for Lower Bavaria issued in 1520, which permitted litigating parties to obtain *Ratschläge* "von bewärten doctoren oder andern Schriften, darin die Recht angezeigt werden, den Richtern zu einer Unterricht, damit sie desto gewisser und rechtmässiger Urteil schöpfen und Recht sprechen mögen." Quoted in Eduard Rosenthal, *Geschichte des Gerichtswesens und der Verwaltungsorganisation Baierns* (Würzburg, 1889-1909) I, 74.

[97] *Die peinliche Gerichtsordnung Kaiser Karls V von 1532 (Carolina)*, ed. Gustav Radbruch (Munich, 1975), article 219. On the ambiguous role of the *Carolina*, and its predecessor and source, the so-called *Bambergensis*, in the standardization of criminal law in the empire, see Hellmuth von Weber, "Die peinliche Halsgerichtsordnung Kaiser Karls V," *ZRG* 77 (1960) *Germ.Abt.*, 292-99.

[98] For an excellent bibliography of collections of such *consilia*, see Helmut Coing, ed., *Handbuch der Quellen und Literatur der neueren Europäischen Privatrechtsgeschichte* II (1976-1977), part 2, 1,362-92. A highly interesting collection of *Rechtsgutachten*, mostly from the seventeenth century, and of inordinate length, is in StA Dr, Loc. 9665.

[99] Alois Schikora, *Die Spruchpraxis der Juristenfakultät zu Helmstedt* (Göttingen, 1973), 86. See *ibid.* 11-22 for a general picture, with good bibliography, of the *Spruchtätigkeit*, the rendering of legal opinions by the law faculties of German universities. See also Gerhard Pötzold, *Die Marburger Juristenfakultät als Spruchkollegium* (Marburg, 1966); Norbert Hasselwander, *Aus der Gutachter- und Urteilstätigkeit der alten Mainzer Juristenfakultät* (Wiesbaden, 1956); Helmut Wolff, *Geschichte der Ingolstädter Juristenfakultät 1472-1625* (Berlin, 1973); Karl Konrad Finke, *Die Tübinger Juristenfakultät 1477-1534* (Tübingen, 1972).

ing such consulting, for example the state of Braunschweig, whose prince declared in 1548 that

> Our councillors are authorized, if requested to do so by the parties or for any other necessary reasons, to send trial records to a distinguished university in order to be instructed in the law in the respective case, and to do so in our name and in our matter, but always at the parties' own expense and costs.[100]

In principle, lower courts could disregard judicial "instruction," but in fact this rarely happened, as studies of particular courts, for example in Württemberg, have shown.[101] In complicated cases, local jurors limited themselves to investigating the facts, then simply sent the documents to a law faculty for judgment.[102] A similar trend had been under way for some time in the operation of arbitration courts—long influenced by Roman and Italian practices—where the lay *Schiedsrichter* retired in favor of the learned *arbiter* or *compromissarius* whose opinions in disputed matters carried much more weight.[103] Such developments were found to distance the prevailing legal culture even further from its amateur base. "Law finding" was becoming a matter for the expert, while—as Georg Dahm has noted—"the court itself turned into a forum for announcing the decision, a mouth piece for legal scholars and other professional jurists."[104] Although this happened most often in criminal justice, the entire legal system was affected. Even in civil matters, litigants who could afford to do so applied to a law professor for expert counsel on their case. Cowed by the weight of such expertise, jurors usually found in accordance with the learned opinion.[105]

Thus the endeavor of imperial and regional legislators earlier in the century to rationalize legal institutions in Germany had borne fruit. The Imperial Chamber Court of 1495[106] and the appellate benches

---

[100] From a *Kanzleiordnung* of 1548 quoted in Alois Schikora, *op. cit.*, 83.

[101] F. Graner, "Zur Geschichte der Kriminalrechtspflege in Württemberg," *Württembergische Vierteljahrshefte für Landesgeschichte* 37 (1931), 49-52.

[102] This is shown by Hans Tütken, *op. cit.*, 252.

[103] Hermann Krause, *Die geschichtliche Entwicklung des Schiedsgerichtswesens in Deutschland* (Berlin, 1930).

[104] Georg Dahm in *loc. cit.*, 288.

[105] Otto Stobbe, *op. cit.*, 82. Woldemar Goerlitz, *Staat und Stände unter den Herzögen Albrecht und Georg 1485-1539* (*Sächsische Landtagsakten* I, Leipzig, 1928), 176-77, shows how widespread the practice of consulting university jurists was among the rural administrators and urban judges of Albertine Saxony.

[106] On the Imperial Chamber Court see Rudolf Smend, *Das Reichskammergericht* I: *Geschichte und Verfassung* (Weimar, 1911; Jürgen Weitzel, *Der Kampf um die Appellation ans Reichkammergericht.* On the roots of the court as constituted in 1495 see Otto

which, in rapid succession and in response to the demands of this body,[107] appeared in the territories, had, through their use of Roman law and academic jurisprudence, changed the country's entire legal culture. The "reformed" codes issued throughout the sixteenth century by states and cities in the empire brought this long process of reception, adaptation, and transformation to its apogee.

IF ONE is to believe their preambles, municipal and territorial "reformations" were undertaken in Germany for one overriding reason: to end the uncertainty affecting all areas of law by replacing the old rules with a single code combining the virtues of clarity and uniformity. Men are fickle, so asserts the preface to the *Reformation* of the city of Worms published in 1498; human society is unstable. Customs are easily forgotten, and reason pulls us in different directions. This being so, the principles of law and order, if they are to endure, must be given definite form, which can be done only "with the counsel and help of men learned in the law."[108] Constantly repeated, this explanation became the conventional rationale for legal centralization. God himself, notes Ortholph Fuchsberger in his translation of the *Institutes*, laid down the law to Adam and Eve, but, alas, they did not keep it. Moses, Draco, Solon, Mercury, Romulus had the same experience. "Each thought he had given his people a good law but found that they did not want to live by it, bending it instead to suit their whims and fancies."[109] A fixed, authoritative written text of an internally consistent law—a *ius certum*—is the only safeguard against such human mutability. In the past, the fatal tendency of men to unsteadiness produced a chaos of singular rules and customs. So many diverse, overlapping, redundant, and contradictory usages exist in the land, it was stated in the Brandenburg *Reformation* of 1527, that "it is impossible now to give good judgments. Thus the multifarious practices of each and every particular place . . . have deprived many people of their due justice."[110] Remedies for this defect must be most carefully prepared and expertly carried out.

---

von Franklin, *Das Reichshofgericht im Mittelalter* (Weimar 1867-69; reprint Hildesheim, 1967).

[107] For the formative role played by the appeals procedure in sixteenth-century German law, see Adolf Stölzel, *Die Entwicklung der gelehrten Rechtssprechung* II, 72-170.

[108] Franz Beyerle *et al.*, *Quellen zur neueren Privatrechtsgeschichte Deutschlands* I,1,97. Almost literally repeated in Ulrich Zasius's code for Freiburg, 1520: *ibid.* I,1,243.

[109] Ortholph Fuchsberger in the postscript to his German translation of the *Institutes: Justinianischer Instituten warhaffte Dolmetschung* (Augsburg, 1536), Ziv[r].

[110] Beyerle *et al.*, eds., *Quellen* I,2 (1938), 71.

The reformation of Württemberg law in the 1550s shows how this was ordinarily done. "A common, honorable, fair, and equitable law for all subjects and residents of our principality" is what the *Neu landrecht* of 1555 was intended to provide.[111] To this end its framers, who included the Tübingen professor Johann Sichard, a jurist well-known in Germany,[112] collected and sifted thousands of local statutes and customs with a view to discovering common denominators. This was not an action imposed willynilly on an uncooperative country. In 1552 the Württemberg estates, meeting in diet, had voted to have this collection made, agreeing to let a commission of experts, appointed by Duke Christoph, conduct a close examination of what was found. They were driven to this decision, the estates explained, by "many and sundry troublesome dissimilarities, . . . and, in addition, lengthy and circumstantial procedures whenever a thing is taken to court, also great costs and useless efforts."[113]

What was brought together by the compilers makes a fat tome as the territory's *Codex consuetudinum*.[114] Looking through this "great heap" (*grosse hauffen*), the estates' deputies, who had their own legal advisers helping them in negotiating with the duke,[115] found the duchy's laws "wholly dissimilar and, in addition, mutually contradictory and, in sum, for the most part in conflict with the common written law and also with equity." The cure, they suggested to the duke, was to issue instructions

> that first and foremost (and without regard to what laws or customs this or that town or village has practiced heretofore) a common, uniform and well-founded [*begrundten*] law should be made, modeled on the common written laws and on human equity, by which all actions and cases are to be argued, counselled, and settled, and to be brought from point to point into good sequence and order.[116]

The need for a revision of procedural law was even more urgent. What was desired was "a summary and efficient mode of conducting trials, . . . so that the disorder and harmful confusion we have been suffering in our courts may be abolished and prevented, and no man be denied

---

[111] *Neu Landrecht des Fürstenthumbs Würtemberg* . . . (1555) in *ibid.* I,2,81.

[112] *Ibid.* I,1 (1936), xxii.

[113] HstA St *Tomi actorum provincialium Wirtembergicorum* 2a, 89ᵛ-90ʳ.

[114] In the Württembergische Landesbibliothek Stuttgart.

[115] They were D. Caspar Beer as *Rat und Redner* and Melchior Kurrer as *Schreiber*. HStA St *Tomi actorum* 2a, 317ʳ and ᵛ.

[116] *Ibid.*, 123ᵛ-124ʳ.

equal, expeditious, convenient, and auspicious access to the law."[117] In a familiar refrain to close their petition, the estates "plead submissively and earnestly to be left safe in possession of their honorable customs and ancient traditions, which are indispensable to them in preserving their native manner [*Landsart*] and livelihood."[118] But this request fell on deaf ears. The "fair, uniform law, statutes, and ordinance [*Ordnung*] conceived and assembled by several of our appointed learned councillors and the law faculty in Tübingen"[119]—the code delivered by the jurists to Duke Christoph in 1554 and published a year later—was one of the most ruthlessly romanizing codes of the early modern period. Scholars have found only traces of old Württemberg customs in the *New Territorial Law* which, wherever possible, pointed judges to the text of the *corpus* and the provisions of the imperial law.[120]

The results of "reformations" varied from place to place.[121] The Württemberg model was followed in the Palatinate, Baden, the small County of Solms, and the cities of Frankfurt and Nuremberg.[122] Saxony took a somewhat different direction. In 1565 the estates complained there, too, of diverse and conflicting verdicts. They suggested that a board composed of jurists and nobles be empowered to "restore things to right order and certainty."[123] But the elector, August I, instead ordered the combined law faculties of the universities of Leipzig and Wittenberg to undertake the task of sifting and revising. The result of their labors was the so-called *Constitution*, published in 1572 and sent to all courts in the land. Less romanizing than the Württemberg code, the new Saxon code left intact all indigenous territorial laws that had been found to agree with each other. Only where these proved inadequate did the framers resort to the imperial law.[124] The territorial law of Solms, on the other hand—the work of Johann Fichard, the renowned jurist of Frankfurt am Main—was a thoroughgoing romanizing product. Its preamble, dated 1571 under the names and seals of the Counts of Solms, makes a succinct argument for this move:

[117] *Ibid.*, 125ʳ.

[118] *Ibid.*, 130ʳ.

[119] Franz Beyerle *et al., Quellen* 1, 2, 82.

[120] *Ibid.* I,1, xxvi; Otto Stobbe, *Geschichte der deutschen Rechtsquellen* II, 384-89.

[121] For an excellent bibliography of sources and scholarly literature on law codification in the empire and its territories and cities, see Helmut Coing *et al., Handbuch der Quellen und Literatur* II, part 2, 310-21 (for the empire), 357-70 (Saxony), 377-84 (Hessen), 392-96 (Palatinate), 401-06 (Württemberg), 406-13 (Bavaria), 425-28 (Tyrol).

[122] Franz Beyerle *et al., Quellen* I,1, xxvi.

[123] *Ibid.* I,1, 257.

[124] Hermann Theodor Schletter, *Die Constitutionen Kurfürst Augusts von Sachsen*, especially 196-222 and Conclusions: 342-43.

Although the common, old, written, imperial statutes and laws have been established and accepted everywhere in the Holy Roman Empire for its subjects and residents to observe as a definitive and uniform law . . . , we have found that this same imperial law, being somewhat verbose, is incomprehensible to the common man so that the latter has adhered to the common unwritten customs of this land which, in the course of time, have crept into the country (as also into the domains of other princes). These customs, although not in all their points at variance with law and equity (for which reason it is difficult to detach the common man from them) are nevertheless in most respects false, inconsistent, open to doubt and argument, and self-contradictory, thus causing many troublesome mistakes and confusions to occur in courts, in verdicts, and in diverging interpretations, resulting in not insignificant disadvantages to all our subjects.

The solution was "to reduce the above-mentioned uncertain and disputable customs to a state of certainty, so that henceforth our subjects may live by uniform laws and, through these, in greater unity."[125] The resulting code included a provision for handling future actions not covered by the reformed law: "Let all such actions be decided and judged not by the above-mentioned, old, and now abolished usages or customs, but by the common, written, imperial law."[126]

In Frankfurt am Main, the city for which we have Helmut Coing's pioneering analysis of the historical transition from one law to another,[127] Roman elements coming in by way of canon law had been modifying the highly developed, if only minimally formalized, native law since about 1490, leading to the general adoption of written procedures, at least in the more important cases. Local law held its place where it could be definitively established. But in cases of uncertainty—and the jurists' judgment on this point was not without prejudice—the *gemeine Recht* became the law of preference.[128] This shift happened gradually, by a kind of fusion of the two bodies of law (Coing calls it a *Verschmelzungsvorgang*),[129] much encouraged when the Imperial Chamber Court met in the city for a few years after 1495, and culminating in the first Frankfurt reformation of 1509, the work of Adam Schönwetter, a jurist with close personal links to the city's patriciate.

[125] Franz Beyerle *et al., Quellen* I,2,175.
[126] *Ibid.,* 176; Otto Stobbe, *op. cit.* II, 379-84.
[127] Helmut Coing, *Die Rezeption des römischen Rechts in Frankfurt am Main.*
[128] For examples of this, see *ibid.,* 121, 142, 144-45 and *passim.*
[129] *Ibid.,* 147.

Sixty years later, Johann Fichard found this revision "very confused, obscure in many places, and faulty,"[130] and persuaded the City Council to call a commission for working out a fresh revision. Completed in 1578, *The City of Frankfurt's New Reformation* was the most comprehensive of all German municipal codes. It was, needless to say, thoroughly Roman, correcting the chief faults found in the earlier revision, namely that "many customs and practices [in it] do not conform to the common laws" and that "these customs and practices are nowhere precisely described and therefore impossible to demonstrate, except by citing general usage."[131] In all cases of doubt, reference was from now on to be made to the written (imperial) law.[132]

Like the Württemberg code of 1555, the romanized law of Frankfurt became a model for revisions in other places. Everywhere laws were being brought up to date. The city of Nuremberg, whose reformation of 1479 was the first municipal code to be printed in Germany (in 1484) revised and republished its law code in 1522 and again in 1564.[133] Even villages often received their new *Dorfgerichtsbuch* from the hands of whoever enjoyed the right of jurisdiction over their courts, "so that peace and concord, uniformity and justice may be furthered and upheld among my subjects."[134] In all such codifications the Roman law was the predominating presence. At its lowest level of authority, it was subsidiary to all other statutes. Thus the "Saxon Judicial Constitution" for the Appellate court in Wittenberg declared that "Saxon laws, insofar as they do not stand against God's Word and have not been abolished by the Christian Church, shall be observed. But in cases where the Saxon law does not ordain or decree anything, let the common written law be used."[135] This was the usual formula,[136] which had been given as early as 1495, in the Constitution establishing the Imperial Chamber Court. In the County of Tyrol, one of the last territories to adopt the rule of subsidiariness in principle,[137] it was prescribed as late as 1619:

[130] Otto Stobbe, *op. cit.* II, 318.

[131] Franz Beyerle *et al.*, *op. cit.* I,1, 223.

[132] Otto Stobbe, *op. cit.* II, 324-26.

[133] *Ibid.* II, 297-306, and Wolfgang Leiser, " 'Kein Doctor soll ohn ein solch Libell sein.' . . ." in *loc. cit.*, 1-16.

[134] From *Dorfgerichtsbuch, darinnen die Ordnung, wie es im Dorf Pomersfelden, dem Edlen und ehrnvesten Christoph Truchsessen daselbsten zustending, gehalten und gehandelt werden solle . . .* (1565), ms. in Germanisches Nationalmuseum Nuremberg Hs. 4576, 1ʳ.

[135] Otto Stobbe, *op. cit.* II, 125.

[136] Other examples: *ibid.* II, 126-33.

[137] Tullius von Sartori-Montecroce, *Über die Reception der fremden Rechte in Tirol*

> Whenever the territorial ordinances and particular statutes are silent, let recourse be had to the *ius commune*, especially when the old customs stray from fairness and reasonableness. This practice is the usual one now in all well-founded governments and polities.[138]

Such provisions gave Roman law a power base from which to lengthen its reach. The extension came swiftly and with finality as Roman law gained a position of near-absolute preeminence in a significant number of codes: Württemberg, as we have seen, Wolfenbüttel (1559), where the superior court "is to conduct itself not by Saxon, but instead by the common written imperial laws,"[139] Trier, where in 1537 the Lord-Archbishop issued a new *Gerichtsordnung* without having consulted his estates and imposed heavy fines on all who ventured to adhere to their *alte Landrechte und Gewohnheiten*,[140] and several others.[141] In time, even the rule of subsidiariness was turned against the indigenous law as the latter was interpreted more and more strictly (on the principle *statuta stricte sunt interpretanda*), while "common law" provisions were given the widest possible latitude.[142] Sharing in the glory and the rewards of the new law's eminence were its learned interpreters, who were being made indispensable by the controlling position that Roman law had come to occupy in central and local courts. Their lack of sympathy for the older indigenous law—in large part owing to their ignorance of its texts and usages (as has often been pointed out)[143]—sealed its slippage into subordinate place. Given the intimate ties between law and every other aspect of early modern society, the transition from the "old" to the "new" law altered substantially the quality of life for many, who found that a move they once had favored for reasons of utility or convenience had, in fact, transformed some essential elements of their social existence.

There was no longer any question as to which law was uppermost. "When we say 'law,' without adding any other word, we always mean the common, written, imperial law," explained Justin Gobler in the

---

und die Tiroler Landes-Ordnungen (*Beiträge zur österreichischen Reichs- und Rechtsgeschichte* I, Innsbruck, 1895), 76.

[138] LA Tir, *Tiroler Landtagsakten* Cod. 2902, 96.

[139] Otto Stobbe, *op. cit.* II, 126.

[140] Herbert Helbig, "Fürsten und Landstände im Westen des Reiches . . ." in *loc. cit.*, 166-67.

[141] For these, see Otto Stobbe, *op. cit.* II, 130-33.

[142] Heinrich Mitteis, *Deutsche Rechtsgeschichte* (11th ed. by Heinz Lieberich, Munich, 1969), 201.

[143] Woldemar Engelmann, *Die Wiedergeburt der Rechtskultur*, 8-14.

Book of Statutes he edited in 1553.[144] Echoed by his colleagues in the mid-sixteenth-century juristic establishment—standing higher now than ever before in honors, rewards, and appointed tasks—Gobler exulted in the universality of this law. "There is not an item or particle in the whole of secular and civic life," he declared, "on which the Roman and imperial laws do not lay down honest, good, and helpful teachings and instruction."[145] So all-encompassing a reach could be justified only by the law's innate nobility. "Roman imperial common laws rest on the true ground of the highest and fairest equity," insisted Andreas Perneder, adding the assurance that "we could not wish for a more even-handed and praiseworthy law."[146] Without it, wrote Ortolph Fuchsberger,

> no one would be able to distinguish what is his own from what belongs to another, or protect his patrimony and his children's rightful inheritance. All fairness and decency would vanish from human affairs, and we would be returned to that original wild and brutish existence in which solitary men and women fed in the woods on acorns and the stronger freely forced his will upon the weaker.[147]

To Ulrich Zasius, the law was *sanctissima*[148] and the care of it, to Melanchthon, a "holy office (*sanctum officium*)."[149] The Saxon jurist Melchior von Osse described it as a special grace of God, and the best means "of keeping the dispositions of rulers and judges on the right path":

> When you reflect on the utility of these God-given well-ordered, written laws and statutes, you will find them to be one of the greatest blessings and most precious gifts granted to us in this life. For these excellent statutes and laws were made long ago by wise and experienced men following the most careful reflection and deliberation. These men sought no one's favor and intended no one's harm. Their minds were free from distortion by disorderly passions or inclinations. For in those days men gave no thought to a particular person's

[144] Justin Gobler, *Statutenbuch, Gesatz, Ordnungen und Gebräuch Keyserlicher, allgemeyner, und etlicher besonderer Landt und Stett Rechten* (Frankfurt am Main, 1572), Aii.

[145] Justin Gobler, *Spiegel der Rechten* (Frankfurt am Main, 1573), 22.

[146] Andreas Perneder, *Institutiones. Auszug und Anzeigung etlicher geschriebenen kayserlichen und des heiligen Reichs Rechte* (Ingolstadt, 1573), χiii.

[147] Ortolph Fuchsberger, *Justinianischer Instituten . . . Dolmetschung*, Aii.

[148] Cited in Adalbert Erler, *Thomas Murner als Jurist* (Frankfurt am Main, 1956), 96.

[149] Melanchthon in the peroration of his *oratio de legibus*, 1525. Printed in Guido Kisch, *Melanchthons Rechts- und Soziallehre* (Berlin, 1967), 208.

advantage or injury. They aimed only at what contributes to the common good.[150]

The case for the Roman law's objective rationality could scarcely be made more strongly. To hold this law unswervingly to the tracks laid down by the venerable *corpus* was the principal mission of the fraternity of jurists. Osse presses a vigorous argument against any move by laymen to mitigate (*mildern*) "the discipline of written laws and statutes by means of ideas of equity [*billikeit*] carried in everyone's head." Such meddling, he writes, adulterates "the severity of the laws" (*Schärfe der recht*) with "ideas of fairness and equity as understood by the laity" (*mit der billikeit und equitet leiisch verstandes*). If this were done, interpreting the law would become a matter of bending (*bigen*) it to suit each partisan opinion, "and the pursuit of justice would be invaded by all those desires, inclinations, and passions with which nature has encumbered human understanding." To be sure, "rational law" has its source "in the true fountain and spring of natural equity." But

> no single individual has an understanding so pure and excellent that his reason should be preferred to written laws and statutes that have been made, following objective [*unparteisch*] consideration, by the harmonious agreement of many wise and prudent men.

"One must never, therefore, deviate from expressly mandated common laws merely for the sake of fairness and equity," asserts Osse, and "a written law, no matter how severe and hard it may seem to be, shall always be preferred to considerations of fairness not explicitly stated in the laws." Easily swayed and misled, blinded by "disorderly inclinations," men cannot trust their instincts. What seems fair to one or to a few may in truth be "in the highest degree unfair and wrongful, and for this reason, an individual's human understanding must always be subordinated to the stated order of law flowing from humanity's common wisdom."[151]

Joining most members of the governing class in a deep suspicion of what was assumed to be human nature, and placing, like all his fellow intellectuals, his trust in written documents and ancient texts, Melchior von Osse made a forceful argument for governance by formal law. After a century and a half of "reception" in Germany, his plea was no longer a mere exhortation. By the 1550s it had become agreed doctrine

---

[150] Melchior von Osse, *An Hertzog Augustum . . . Ein unterthäniges Bedencken* (1555) in *Schriften*, 280.

[151] *Ibid.*, 286-88. Osse adds, however, that in the presence of two conflicting written codes, the judge is to prefer the one that seems fairer and milder (*ibid.*, 288).

resting on established political and legal institutions and on the participation in these of a strategically placed professional elite. Osse heaps
scorn upon critics who carped at relinquishing the administration of
justice to a corps of experts. "A devilish opinion," he calls their protest,
and "a pestilence by which clever, experienced, worldly-wise men have
always been plagued, in the old days, today, and at all times." The de-
lusion that anyone can know what is right and wrong has been responsible for destroying many a well-ordered realm through the tyranny of
rulers as well as the rebelliousness of their peoples. History is full of
"gruesome examples" of this, writes Johann Oldendorp. "You can always tell a fool: he is one who trusts his own counsel."[152] Osse is more
vehement: "This is the very poison against which Almighty God has
given us the medicine of definitive, reasonable laws transmitted by
knowing and wise men whose nature his divine omnipotence strengthens and maintains at all times." It is from these laws that we draw our
ideas of what is right, fair, and equitable. Once "the *ius arbitrarium* has
invaded a land," Osse continues, referring to a situation in which everyone governs according to his own will and "disorderly inclinations,"
"you will have as many kinds of justice as there are heads in the government."[153] Only a fixed body of law kept uncorrupted by a dedicated
cadre of learned jurists can prevent this descent into lawlessness and
chaos.

This was the view from the top of the political edifice. At ground
level, Osse's case must have seemed a good deal less compelling. "Humanity's common wisdom," "notions of fairness and equity," "severity
of the laws" were slogans that rang with very different associations
when heard at a distance from council chambers, superior courts, and
university. Neither the logic nor the eloquence of Osse's argument silenced his critics, as we shall see. To the end of the century, jurists felt
embattled in their guardianship of the sacred law. Dr. Jacob Lersner's
*Reply . . . to the Question: Is it Better to judge and govern by definite,
certain, written, proven, and accustomed Laws, Ordinances, and
Usages, or by one's own Reason, Sense, Wit, Discretion, Sense of Fairness, and Conscience*, which had been first published in 1542, was reprinted late in the sixteenth century, giving the jurist's response to the
persistent populist notion "that written laws and legal experts are not
needed."[154] He has heard this said, Lersner notes, sadly, by many peo-

---

[152] Johann Oldendorp, *Von ratslagende . . .* (Rostock, 1530), 3-4.

[153] Melchior von Osse, *op. cit.* in *loc. cit.*, 288-89.

[154] *Antwort . . . auf die Frage, ob es besser sei, nach gewissen beschriebenen und sonst
bewährten bräuchlichen Rechten, Gesetzen, Ordnungen und Gewohnheiten, oder nach*

ple, even at court and in the university. Expressing genuine concern, he seeks to refute these "misonomists or haters of written laws"[155] and, in general, allay public anxiety about the great legal transformation that had taken place.

Like Gobler and Osse, Lersner rests his case on the inherent fair-mindedness he claims for the written law. When the Roman decemvirs were given the task of framing a code of laws for their people, he explains, they went to Greece to obtain it "in order to prevent by this move all mistrust of their motives and so that no Roman might suspect his laws of favoring or disfavoring anyone, out of preference or hatred, prejudice or envy." In Rome even the emperors placed themselves under the law "so as to avoid the suspicion that written laws profit law makers and deprive and oppress their subjects." Rome's extraordinary success as a state is directly due to these excellent laws. How could the Romans have lived and acted so honestly without instruction and discipline? And whence could they have taken this instruction and discipline but from their constant laws? All that is good and fair in subsequent legislation has been drawn from these "constant" laws, and this proves, says Lersner, "that no government or administration can be upheld without certain, written laws and firmly declared legal principles." He insists that these are neither harsh nor oppressive. Far from it.

> They are excellent, honest, fair, reasonable, natural, feasible, necessary, and useful laws. They agree with every country's special nature and with the circumstances of every age. And they are made not to serve anyone's selfish gain but to seek the common good of territories and cities and the welfare, improvement, peace, and unity of their peoples.

It is not true, Lersner assures his readers, that jurists wish to suppress or inhibit popular customs and rights, "an intention wrongly attributed to them nowadays." There may be dishonest, intolerant jurists in the land, he admits. But to destroy the entire law because of a few such men is as foolish as it would be to reject the Bible for a bad preacher. Indeed, most jurists are "excellent and true men, like Papinian." Their help is indispensable if the written laws are to accomplish their noble purpose. For this reason

> I declare and affirm that it is best to govern and judge by written and in other ways certain, honest, reasonable, fair, and proven laws and

---

eigener Vernunft, Sinn, Witz, Gutdünken und selbst gefassten Billigkeit und eigenem Gewissen zu urteilen, zu regieren . . . (Augsburg, 1542), Aiiʳ.

[155] *Ibid.*, Eiiᵛ.

statutes found and framed [*erfunden und auffbracht*] by pious, honorable, fair-minded, objective, learned, and experienced men and lawgivers with their implanted sense of fairness, reason, understanding, decency, and conscience.[156]

But even in the face of rhetoric as ardent as Lersner's, the suspicions and accusations against which he tilted persisted. To see why this was so, and to catch the contrasting resonances of an enduring passionate argument, we must descend from the heights of theoreticians and power wielders to the dispersed locations of political activity in the German landscape. From this lower vantage point we shall gain a very different perspective on the reception and on the problems it had created for society in the empire.

[156] *Ibid.*, Bii^r-Eii^v.

CHAPTER FOUR

Custom, Privilege, Freedom: The Conservative Society

IF CONCENTRATION was the strategy at the summits of political power, the rule at ground level was dispersion. Diversity still defined the reality of legal life after a century or more of reception in the Holy Roman Empire. To men and women whose existence was circumscribed by locality and a short life span, the loss of even a single accustomed usage was cause for alarm. But those who stood above the motley scene judged its obstinate particularism to be untidy, muddled, and obscure. No one could be expected to know, let alone understand and accept, the limitless variety of customs in the land. Melchior Kling rigorously excluded them from the large tome he edited of *The Whole of the Saxon Territorial Law . . . Put into Right Order* of 1571. "Many people have told me that I ought to include customary rights in my book," he wrote in his dedication to Elector August. "But this I cannot do. In every town they have special statutes, and in the countryside particular practices, no two of which are alike, and with which I am unfamiliar." His collection, he said, is confined to the *Sachsenrecht*, the common law of the Saxons. As to the *consuetudines speciales*, the customs of each particular place and group, "no educated man can know what these are."[1]

In his barely concealed contempt for the conventions of ordinary life, Kling spoke for his peers. Men such as he were unimpressed by the claim of antiquity made for almost every usage. "Whatever serves the interest of someone is called 'an ancient custom' and insisted upon with fierce determination."[2] Most such "customs," they believed, would not stand the test of historical scrutiny. As often as not they drew a respectable cloak over private greed in its plunder of *gemeiner nutz*, the general welfare—a slippery term in the sixteenth century, often appropri-

---

[1] Melchior Kling, *Das gantze Sechssisch Landrecht . . . in eine richtige ordnung gebracht . . .* (Leipzig, 1571), ii^v-iii^r.

[2] Reply by councillors speaking for Ferdinand II of Tyrol to complaints by Tyrolean estates in 1573 concerning transfers of cases from local courts. LA Tir *Tiroler Landtagsakten* Codex 45, 323^r and ^{v}.

ated by governments to discredit a particular privilege.[3] Whatever rulers and magistrates might have meant by "the common welfare," they were agreed that its objectives were best served by uniform laws and tight administrative controls. Where these prevailed, "common welfare" was objectively indistinguishable from *Landeshoheit*—territorial sovereignty embodied in a ruler. "Our gracious lord's people were all born in one country and are bound to a single principality," declared the councillors of the Prince-Bishop of Bamberg in response to some grievances submitted by the bishopric's estates in 1534, and went on to admonish their petitioners that

> they should ask themselves whether or not what they demand, no matter how right and fair [*recht und pillich*] it may be, will help country and people, promote the common good, and create good will among all subjects [*untertanen*]. In this spirit it is our gracious lord's kindly wish that they should desist from their demands, to the end that good policy, order, and uniformity [*gleichheit*] may prosper.[4]

Good policy, order, and uniformity would have been the ideals of political organization if the ruling circles of the time had thought in ideal terms. Instead they served them as operational targets. That they were more often missed than scored, despite such formidable weapons aimed at them as Roman law and its agents, owes to the vigor, and the sheer copiousness, of the institutional and legal diversity of traditional German society. To princes, magistrates, and jurists, this variety was a wilderness to be cleared. To their subjects it was a hospitable milieu, one that provided protection for their autonomy and helped preserve the richness (as they saw it) and distinctiveness of their lives. The present chapter attempts to chart a way through this lush terrain.

Alternatives to the feudal structure of society were advanced from two directions in sixteenth-century Germany. In the following pages we shall only briefly touch on one of these—the aggressive state (whose actions are the subject of Chapter Five); in a concluding section, we shall consider the second, the "radical" attack. In its main body, the present chapter is concerned with the existing order and the problems of survival it faced. As has been indicated in passing in a number of places, political centralization was aggressively promoted from the seats of intellectual and administrative power in German territories

[3] This point is made by Kaspar von Greyerz in *The Late City Reformation in Germany. The Case of Colmar 1522-1628* (Wiesbaden, 1980), 48-49.

[4] From the records of *Rittertage* in the Bishopric of Bamberg. StA Bamb B28 No. 2, 93v-94r; No. 3, 72r.

and cities. Roman law and lawyers played a major role in advocating this cause, and it is not claiming too much to say that the early modern state was the product of their labors. Peter Blickle's characterization of the "power" state as a body dominating a defined geographical space, governed by a cadre of bureaucrats, and monopolizing the processes of law making, sounds excessively modern until one thinks of it in contrast to what it was replacing: a loose-jointed structure held together by a complex network of feudal ties.[5] The disappearance of this "medieval" arrangement in favor of a much more tautly built "modern" system was a major transition in European history. Its contemporary critics were clearly in awe of the new state as they denounced its "Spanish practices"[6] and blamed lawyers for their participation in its machinations. It was generally agreed that law furnished both the ideas and the instruments of political aggrandizement. "There is not a potentate and lord around," said Luther, "who doesn't let himself be controlled by a jurist or a theologian."[7] The menacing combination of statism and legalism—even in the relatively underdeveloped and inefficient forms it took in the early modern centuries—posed the threat against which established social groups acted. They recognized the state's reach for uniformity and coordination for what it was: a peril to the very survival of their corporate lives.

This fear was not unjustified. What looks to the historian like the end of an era was to those who lived through it the end of a world. The impending changes, more or less clearly perceived by all, were profoundly unsettling to a traditional society so passionately conservative and so deeply entrenched in its localism as was Germany in the early sixteenth century. This is why the constant appeals to ancient rights, immemorial customs, vital privileges, cherished freedoms, and common interests were much more than a rhetorical strategy. At the time, they were the closest thing one could find to a political ideology. As such, they were projected in deliberate opposition to the statist posture on legal and administrative centralization. As we shall see, the face-off between "good policy, order, and uniformity" and "ancient customs, freedoms, and traditions" defined and shaped all internal political debates.

Tradition (*Herkommen*) and fair dealing were linked by the fiction of common consent. According to the lawyers, the force of custom rested on the principle of tacit approval among people over time.[8] To

[5] Peter Blickle, *Landschaften im alten Reich. Die staatliche Funktion des gemeinen Mannes in Oberdeutschland* (Munich, 1973), 36.

[6] Luther, WA TR 5, No. 5635.

[7] *Ibid.*, No. 5252.

[8] For examples from Italian jurisprudence on this point see Donald R. Kelley, "Clio and the Lawyers. Forms of Historical Consciousness in Medieval Jurisprudence," *Medi-*

all who appealed to custom as the foundation of their rights, consent ensured the fairness of the resulting arrangements. The agreement on which it was based was taken as historical fact and presumed to have been both voluntary and informed. No custom once accepted as legitimate could in theory be altered except with the explicit approval of those to whom it applied. "Tacit consent" was, of course, a two-edged sword, capable of being used as an offensive weapon by governments anxious to demonstrate support for unpopular decisions. Like all political myths, it cut both ways. Yet, throughout the later middle ages and the early modern period, the claim made on behalf of custom and tradition, that they are, in effect, the authentic voice of the people was the only legitimate counterthrust to the growing power of the written law, its ideologues, and its operatives.

The strength of this claim depended largely on the assumption that what all had approved, and what had passed the test of time, must be better than what had been "invented" by a few. In one of Ulrich von Hutten's patriotic dialogues, a travelling party of classical deities on a journey of inspection through ancient Germany observe among the natives' other sound practices (they do not consult physicians, therefore they don't get sick) the absence of jurists. But how do these people pronounce justice? "By their old customs, and therefore wisely. Nowhere else in the world do people suffer so little oppression and injustice. For instead of written laws, they use their ancient traditions [alt härkommen]."[9] This equation of tradition and freedom was often made and firmly believed. By contrast, written statutes—Satzungen—expressed arbitrary authority. They stood against custom, which implies common approbation. Hence the emphasis given by many reform writers to the need to know and, when necessary, recite, customs. Johann Eberlin's insistence that each householder be familiar with his land's "common customs and rights" has already been mentioned. "We have abolished the imperial and canon law," Eberlin reports of the utopian community Wolfaria; instead, "each shall know his rights and what is fair and what is unfair."[10] Eberlin's admonition was anything but a utopian suggestion in his time. Citations of "our enduring ancient just rights and praiseworthy customs passed on to us in unbroken line by our forefathers" became a universal practice; the period's vast litera-

---

evalia et Humanistica N.S., No. 5 (1974), 35-37. On custom law generally see Walter Ullmann, Law and Politics in the Middle Ages. An Introduction to the Sources of Medieval Political Ideas (Ithaca, N.Y., 1975), Chapter 6.

[9] Ulrich von Hutten, Inspicientes/Die Anschawenden in Deutsche Schriften, ed. Heinz Mettke I (Leipzig, 1972), 167.

[10] Johann Eberlin von Günzdorf, Wolfaria (Buntsgnosz XI, 1521) in Neudrucke deutscher Litteraturwerke des XVI. und XVII. Jahrhunderts No. 141, 127.

ture of political conflict bears witness to it. "Law arises not from innovation but from custom," declared German peasants in 1525.[11] Even the jurists had good things to say about the roots of customs in the better impulses of mankind and the rarer processes of nature. Although no German legal writer went so far as to cite the classical simile of the silkworm—a people makes its own laws as a silkworm forms a web out of itself, with nothing borrowed or imposed—the indigenous origin of customs was always acclaimed. God governs the world by means of "ancient, honorable, fair, and praiseworthy customs," says Justin Gobler, "which have their origin in mankind's good reason and right understanding."[12] This was a powerful political image. The Justinian corpus itself gave its authority to the force of custom as binding law; it was affirmed there that "ancient customs, when approved by consent of those who follow them, are like statute" (*Institutes* 1.2.9).

This was the theory of custom and tradition in the sixteenth century. In actual practice the situation was much more ambiguous. Custom was closely integrated with the chief repositories of written law: imperial law and statutory law. In the form of regional codes, custom was, of course, itself written law, although as a kind of law that could not, by definition, be "invented," it always counted as *ius non scriptum*, whether codified or not. All types of law interpenetrated and interacted with one another, and many legal writers endeavored to clarify this relationship in a practical, useful way. Here is Gobler's explanation:

"Long usage" is a kind of law, largely unwritten but practiced and accepted through time in the form of handed-down customs. It has its authority from the silent consent of the people, though at some point in its history it has to be committed to writing. . . . That is to say, it is a necessary part of a custom that it be properly approved and accepted; and this happens either when a prince or magistrate issues a written declaration that such a custom has been accepted and confirmed, or when such a custom is substantiated from charters, records of litigation, or other public instruments, or from the testimony of a distinguished man of learning.

If none of these proofs of "long usage" is available, "let it be corroborated by the majority of the people, or else by ten witnesses."

These witnesses must testify to the truth of three things. First, that the custom in question is actually in use; second, that it has been acted on more than once; and third that the time of practice has been

[11] Quoted in Peter Blickle, *The Revolution of 1525* (Baltimore, 1981), 34.
[12] Justin Gobler, *Der Rechten Spiegel* (Frankfurt am Main, 1550), aʳ.

long. And this long time shall be as long as people can remember, or at least it shall be about ten years during which the said custom must have been practiced and used whenever the occasion has arisen. And this use and practice must have been voluntary, unforced, and uncoerced. The contrary would be a decree or statute, but not a custom.[13]

Popular consent, long practice, current use, voluntary performance, approbation by constituted authority, time out of mind: these were the criteria of legitimacy in custom law. Upon each of these points existed doubt and contention. On length of time, for example, Melchior Kling wrote:

I ask, what is a custom? I answer that custom is ancient mores or usages [*sitten*]. How old shall a usage be before it becomes a custom? Some say ten years . . . ; others say forty . . . ; and several hold that it should be so old that no one can think of a time when it was not observed. . . .[14]

The ten-year rule was given in the imperial law (which could be applied in this case, as in many others, to judge the validity of custom); the more stringent forty-year provision came from canon law and was said to apply "whenever a custom is in conflict with the common laws."[15] Definitions of the exact meaning of "longer than human memory can reach back" varied considerably, although it was usually taken to imply the absence of contrary indications to a local custom in the memories of people living thereabouts.[16] On the matter of consent there was more room for argument. Melchior Kling again: "Is it enough that a custom has been tacitly accepted? Or must it have been proven upon being challenged? Or must proof be given that it has been practiced two or more times?"[17] Each of these tests was employed as occasion demanded. Demonstration might also be required that a custom's origin

---

[13] Justin Gobler, *Spiegel der Rechten* (Frankfurt am Main, 1573), 20ʳ. Cf. *Digest* 1.3.32-35.

[14] Melchior Kling, *Das gantze Sechssisch Landrecht*, vʳ.

[15] Ulrich Tengler, *Layenspiegel* (Strasbourg, 1510), Giiiᵛ.

[16] Andreas Perneder, *Institutiones. Auszug und Anzeigung etlicher geschriehen . . . Rechte* (Ingolstadt, 1573), viᵛ. M. T. Clanchy, "Remembering the Past and the Good Old Law," *History* 55 (1970), 165-76, points out that in illiterate or semi-literate societies, where tradition is remembered rather than written down, a short time often seems like "time immemorial" or "age-old" (p. 172). Fritz Kern, *Kingship and Law in the Middle Ages* (New York, 1956), 160 remarks that "when law is called 'old,' it is rather a description of its high quality than a strict determination of its age."

[17] Melchior Kling, *Sechssisch Landrecht*, vʳ and ᵛ.

was purposeful, not the result of accident, chance, or error.[18] Purpose
involved a rational decision. If a custom was "reasonable" (*vernünf-
tig*), it had the force of law; if it was not, it lacked this power. Ulrich
Tengler stressed this point in his *Layman's Mirror*:

> Although a long or ancient usage has great force and is accorded
> great respect, it is not so powerful that it can detract from the com-
> mon [i.e., written] law, unless it is grounded in reason. . . . For if it
> lacks reason, it has no force, seeing that custom is like law [which
> also must be based on reason]. . . .

When should a custom be called rational or reasonable? Tengler continues: "Whenever a custom tends to benefit the general welfare [*gemeinen nutz*], it must be regarded as rational," adding, however, the
proviso that "it must be found to be so by knowledgeable judges."[19]

"Knowledgeable judges" (*verständige richter*) were active at all critical points of contact between customary and written law. In every particular case a decision had to be made about the two laws' compatibil-
ity or mutual contradiction. In some instances written law favored
custom. "Where custom agrees with the law, it strengthens the law. . . .
Where the law is not clear, it shall be interpreted by following custom."[20] In other cases, custom must defer to statute. According to
Kling,

> The general principle is that custom suppresses law. But the follow-
> ing distinctions must be made: If the custom is universal, existing all
> over the world, it breaks all laws. . . . If it is particular, it only breaks
> the law in places where the custom has been in use. However, if a
> written law covers a custom, the custom must give way. Custom has
> the same relation to natural law: the rule is that a custom cannot go

---

[18] Ulrich Tengler, *Layenspiegel*, Giii^v. A much clearer and more concise definition of
custom is given by Sir John Davies in the Dedication of his *Irish Reports* of 1612. It is
quoted in J.G.A. Pocock, *The Ancient Constitution and the Feudal Law. A Study of English Historical Thought in the Seventeenth Century* (Cambridge, 1957), 33: "For a Custome taketh beginning and groweth to perfection in this manner: When a reasonable act
once done is found to be good and beneficiall to the people, and agreeable to their nature
and disposition, then do they use it and practise it again and again, and so by often iter-
ation and multiplication of the act it becometh a *Custome*; and being continued without
interruption time out of mind, it obtaineth the force of a *Law*. And this *Customary Law*
is the most perfect and most excellent, and without comparison the best, to make and
preserve a Commonwealth."

[19] Ulrich Tengler, *Layenspiegel*, Giii^v.

[20] Melchior Kling, *Sechssisch Landrecht*, v^v.

either against natural law or against written law. If it does, you cannot excuse yourself by pleading custom.[21]

As we have already seen (in Chapter Two), a large number of legal proverbs were in circulation to make it appear that folk wisdom supported one or the other of the two colliding sides. "Where there is custom, there is law." "Custom cancels common law." On the other hand: "Truth and law strike out usage and custom" and "Custom gives way to written law."[22] With truth and law in each of the opposing camps, the fate of a given custom depended on a judge's decision in every instance, not only when usage and statute were in conflict, but also when larger issues were, or seemed to be, at stake. Gobler writes: "In many instances custom is rejected when it goes against God's word and law, or against the common good, or when it conflicts with religious freedom or is inimical to the salvation of our souls, or when it has been introduced by an error."[23] Litigation and arguments were ceaselessly waged about large and small—usually small—matters, each case necessitating judgments on all disputed points. Custom, and those who grounded their rights in it, were therefore obliged always to be on guard against judicial attempts to restrict and reduce its effectiveness as a position from which to argue for local and corporate particularism. Although "evident utility" had to be demonstrated before an old right or usage could be disallowed (*Digest* 1.4.2), jurists were strongly disposed to favor recent laws over older ones (*Digest* 1.4.4). This tilt in favor of new legislation, introduced from canon and Roman law and of obvious advantage to political modernizers, sought to reverse the longstanding preference for older traditions.[24] Thus, despite the philosophical respect (which also came from Roman law) given to custom as the most honorable matrix of a country's legal culture, defenders of the ancient tradition were hard-pressed to shield their heritage from detractors and despoilers. "Saving clauses" added to new law codes and purporting to guarantee the inviolability of "ancient, properly handed-down, rightful and fair customs" (the most famous example of such a clause is the prefatory statement to the imperial criminal code, the *Carolina*, of 1532) had little effect on the ultimate defeat of these rearguard skirmishes.

[21] *Ibid.*
[22] "Wo Gewohnheit ist, da ist Recht." "Sitte und Brauch hebt gemeines Recht auf." "Wahrheit und Recht hebt Sitte und Brauch auf." "Der Brauch muss dem Gesetz weichen." Quoted in Eduard Graf and Mathias Dietherr eds., *Deutsche Rechtssprichwörter* (Nördlingen, 1864), 10-14.
[23] Justin Gobler, *Spiegel der Rechten*, 20ʳ.
[24] Hermann Krause, *Kaiserrecht und Rezeption* (Heidelberg, 1952), 237-38.

The high stakes in this fight are evident in the repetitive formulas punctuating the grievances, petitions, appeals, and protests of which most of the political dialogue of the age consists. A disputed right dates back "ten, twenty, thirty, forty, fifty, sixty, seventy, eighty, ninety, a hundred years, or more years than people's memory can encompass."[25] An endangered practice is "older than anyone can remember, . . . it has been in use everywhere in this district since olden times and beyond human memory."[26] In 1569 the estates of Württemberg defended themselves against demands for higher contributions, made by their duke's privy council, by protesting that they had "from the days of yore, and longer than human memory can recollect, been free of such assessments and burdens, and have enjoyed their *possessio libertatis* in peace and continuity as an essential part of their ancient traditions."[27] Sanctity of ancient customs was claimed in the caucuses of every estate and corporate group. Saxon nobles appealed to *uralte gebrauch* in their fight against the Lutheran church's attempt to set aside the *ius patronatus* they enjoyed over the churches in their domains.[28] Townsmen disputed the right of neighboring villages to brew beer because they had not been exercising this privilege "since ancient days."[29] Village elders requested that fishing and foraging rights be restored because "this is how it has ever and always been done here and handed down to us from olden times."[30] Knights asked to be treated "in accordance with the old, well-preserved custom and order."[31] Peasants rejected a landlord's demand as *ungebreuchlich*—uncustomary.[32] The imperial city of Nuremberg based its claim to full independence from the emperor on the position that its government "had been making laws, ordinances, and statutes for more years than can be held in human memory."[33] Jurisconsults used "origin in time out of mind" as a criterion for deciding among competing jurisdictions.[34] When length of usage had to be ascertained,

[25] From gravamina of *Ritterschaft* of Bamberg, 1570, StA Bamb, B28, No. 3, 104r.
[26] From grievances submitted by eight towns and *Ämter* in Württemberg, 1535. HStA St A34, Bü 13b, *passim*.
[27] HStA St *Tomi actorum provincialium Wirtembergicarum* 7, 23v-24r.
[28] *Extract der gravaminum Anno 1609* . . ., StA Dr, Loc 9362, 27r.
[29] StA Dr, Loc 8830, 70r (1548).
[30] *Landgebrechen und Berichte* . . . (1556), StA Dr, Loc 9356, 3r.
[31] StA Bamb, B28, No. 3, 108v.
[32] Quoted in Winfried Schulze, *Bäuerlicher Widerstand und feudale Herrschaft in der frühen Neuzeit* (Stuttgart, 1980), 120.
[33] Quoted in Wolfgang Leiser, " 'Kein Doctor soll ohn ein solch Libell sein' . . . ," *Mitteilungen des Vereins für Geschichte der Stadt Nürnberg* 67 (1980), 7.
[34] From a memorandum by Nuremberg *Ratskonsulenten* on a dispute between city and Margrave Casimir of Brandenburg. StA Nbg *Ratschlagbücher* No. 5, 177r.

they devised lists of questions to be answered by townspeople and villagers: "Have they possessed this right from 5 to 10, from 10 to 15, 20, 25, 30, 35, to 40 years and beyond human memory?"[35] When the estates of Württemberg reconvened in 1551 after sixteen years of autocratic rule by the controversial Duke Ulrich, they organized themselves on the basis of "traditions . . . handed down . . . from ancient days . . . and existing from time immemorial."[36]

That these were formulaic phrases takes nothing from their ideological force. It was not that old was always good. From the stock of legal proverbs, "A hundred years of wrongdoing do not make a right" was quoted as readily as "Keep hold of the old" (*Das Alte behalte*) and "Custom does more than experts' lore" (*Gebrauch tut mehr als aller Meister Lehr*). "A bad custom doesn't make a thing good" cancelled "Where there is custom, there is justice" (*Wo Gewohnheit ist, da ist Recht*).[37] Moreover, the history of political debate in the sixteenth century provides many examples of rulers claiming "ancient customs and traditional usages" on their own side of a dispute with restive estates.[38] Custom did not always favor the underdog. Rural people, especially, found themselves entrapped in a net of "ancient customs" giving the advantage to landlords by empowering them to keep peasants tied to the soil. In such cases the struggle was directed *against* usage and tradition.[39]

Nonetheless, the twin principles of antiquity and continuity held firm. The only proviso was that customs be "good" and "right" as well as "old" and "long." "Do not be fooled by your lords' protestations," the peasant revolutionaries of 1525 were cautioned by their leaders: "Everybody cries 'old customs' nowadays! But we do not say only 'according to old custom.' We say 'according to *right* custom.' A thousand years of doing wrong do not amount to a single hour of doing right!"[40] To determine what *was* right in a given situation, protesters usually fell back on ancient customs. Objecting to certain unfair burdens, a groundlord's subjects complained that these old practices, although long in use, are harmful and insufferable to them, and "are contrary to

[35] StA Wei Reg Q, No. 87, no page numbers.

[36] HStA St *Tomi actorum* No. 1, 14ᵛ, 16ʳ, etc.

[37] All these given in Eduard Graf and Mathias Dietherr, *Deutsche Rechtssprichwörter*, 10-14.

[38] For example, see Peter Blickle, *Landschaften im alten Reich. Die staatliche Funktion des gemeinen Mannes in Oberdeutschland* (Munich, 1973), 204-05.

[39] Peter Blickle et al., *Aufruhr und Empörung? Studien zum bäuerlichen Widerstand im alten Reich* (Munich, 1980), 301-02.

[40] From *An die Versammlung gemeiner Bauernschaft* ed. Siegfried Hoyer (Leipzig, 1975), 113.

the common customs of our land as well as against the [imperial] laws."[41] In thus referring to their common customs, the petitioners assumed that these "handed-down usages," being based upon "rules prescribed by natural reason for all men" (*Institutes* 1.2.1), had stood the test of time and of repeated challenges to their fairness. It was agreed, in any case, that universal usage breaks particular custom, and this was the principle invoked whenever a local tradition, though old, was felt to be unjust.

Legitimation was the chief problem of all who had complaints or protests to make. As Peter Blickle has remarked, speaking of German peasants at the beginning of the sixteenth century, without a basis in law, their grievance lists were at best petitions, never demands. "Without legitimation no demands were possible, and legitimation was ancient custom, the key concept of all medieval legal thought."[42] Where custom could be supported by documentary proof, it had all the force of written law. Where this proof went against the petitioners, there was nothing to do but appeal to a written law beyond charters and codes: the law of God as revealed in Scripture. This recourse was taken, as we shall see, with considerable effect, but only as a last resort, when all other tests of legitimacy had failed.

Normally, each side in a dispute claimed legitimate right on its side, accusing the other of having introduced a *neuigkeit*, a departure from established practice. To deny the charge of innovation, documentary proof had to be offered of the custom's actual existence in time. The business of scriveners boomed throughout the sixteenth century as records of "ancient rights" were copied, transmitted, registered and recorded, confirmed, answered, refuted, and deposited in archives.[43] A "right" or "freedom" had no standing unless it was *verbrieft*, confirmed by someone with authority to accept it in a legal act and in the form of a specific instrument. Protests were useless if not buttressed by true copies of such documents. Often, demands were made for the originals of disputed charters. "Concerning the requested confirmation of their [the Tyrolean estates'] freedoms, . . . they will receive word of our action when they have submitted to us the *originalia* of their old privileges."[44] Estates, for their part, kept *Landschaftbücher*, records of

---

[41] Subjects of Monastery of Ochsenhausen in 1502, in Günther Franz ed., *Quellen zur Geschichte des Bauernkrieges* (Munich, 1963), No. 5, p. 29.

[42] Peter Blickle, *Die Revolution von 1525* (Munich, 1975), 80, 136.

[43] For a keen impression of this documentary aspect of the struggle over "ancient rights," see, e.g., LA Tir, *Tiroler Landtagsakten* Fasz. 8, relating to the 1560s through 1590s.

[44] Response by Tyrolean government under Maximilian III to estates grievances. LA Tir, *Tiroler Landtagsakten* Fasz. 10 for year 1603.

rights and privileges issued, confirmed and reconfirmed by successive rulers.[45] These were needed for accurate citation. Merely verbal pretensions to the possession of a right were pointless. Weighty matters—estate freedoms—were indistinguishable from petty affairs—a privilege to brew beer—in this regard. One example for many: the Saxon city of Belzig tried to prohibit a neighboring knight from brewing beer in the tavern of a village under his jurisdiction. According to the knight, the place was a true *Erbkrug*, a "hereditary" tavern, where beer had been brewed long before the present plaintiffs became councillors in Belzig. Let him prove it, rejoined the townsmen. "We agree to nothing in his unsubstantiated claims unless he can show that the said tavern in [the village of] Roggosen is in fact a true hereditary brewing tavern":

> It is not enough, and of no consequence, that a few living persons can be quoted as saying that they have drunk beer brewed on the premises. It may well be (and unfortunately it happens often) that his ancestors have brewed in secret at times, and without the city's knowledge. This does not make it a brewing tavern. We for our part know for certain that neither we nor our forefathers have ever granted brewing rights to the Roggosen tavern keeper. If we are wrong, let this be shown by proof of document.[46]

In another case, when the "dynasts"—counts and barons—of Saxony refused to be taxed, arguing that they and their subjects had traditionally been freed from all taxation, the duchy's cities and knights asked Elector Moritz to have a search made to see if such a privilege could be found among the tax registers of Leipzig or Wittenberg.[47] Normally the submission of documentary proof settled the matter. Respect for legitimacy was deep-seated, and acquiescence was not refused where it could be demonstrated. "We have requested several times," villagers belonging to the monastery of Sonnenfeld complained just before the rebellion of 1525, "that we be shown the letters in which it is recorded how our forefathers came to be transferred from the Bishopric of Bamberg to the monastery of Sonnenfeld. If such a letter exists," the villagers continue, "and if it is read to us, we will do and keep all that we owe to the said monastery, in accordance with the charter."[48] Their re-

---

[45] E.g., BHStA Mu Altbayerische Landschaft Lit 1172 for year 1588, *passim*. E.g., also a record of successive confirmations of the *Tübingen Vertrag* of 1514 kept by the Württemberg estates: HStA St A34, Bü lb, No. 4.

[46] StA Wei Reg Q, No. 82, 108ʳ-109ᵛ.

[47] Cited in Johannes Falke, "Zur Geschichte der sächsischen Landstände. Die Regierungszeit des Kurfürsten Moritz 1547-54," *Mitteilungen des königlich-sächsischen Alterthumsvereins* 22 (1872), 102.

[48] Günther Franz, "Beschwerden der Hintersassen des Klosters Sonnenfeld am Vor-

quest was made three years ago, the villagers add, and they still have not seen the document in question: hence their refusal to oblige. Had it been produced, they would in all likelihood have fulfilled their duties. Protesting against a patently unjust and outdated inheritance law, a group of peasant jurors from Münstertal admitted that they were powerless to do more than complain. "It is unfair," they said, "but seeing that it is an old handed-down custom [*von alter herkommen*], we cannot do anything to change it."[49]

Such readiness (to the discontented it was gullibility) to allow written proof to clinch a dispute led to a spate of forgeries, such as that of the abbot of Kempten, who produced a fake Carolingian charter imposing duties and fees on his peasants.[50] Spurious *uralte Rechte* turned up all over Europe.[51] They are a tribute to the respect paid to written contracts as denominators of political, social, and economic relations. The conservative society sought to preserve the inviolability of these contracts. Great weight was given to original charters spelling out the reciprocal rights and obligations of rulers and ruled. No political negotiation was complete without reference to these agreements. Often such attention took the form of phrase-by-phrase comparison of copies held by disputing parties. In 1523 representatives of the citizens of Coburg and deputies of the town council went over their municipal constitution, the *Vertragsbrief* (letter of contract) sentence by sentence in order to test the legality of a new tax: this was done by reading the document aloud, each party holding its own copy, "to show that each text is a true copy of the other. And then those of the people who had been in the Council Chamber during the reading went outside to make report to the assembled commune."[52] In Württemberg, the diet pressed ducal officials to swear an oath of loyalty to the Tübingen Contract of 1514, the duchy's fundamental charter of liberties. If this were not done, the estates argued, "officers [*amptleutte*] would act against the contract (as they have been doing in many cases) and then make easy excuses for themselves, saying that this or that doesn't concern them or had not come to their attention." The duke, for his part, resisted such an oath,

abend des Bauernkrieges," *Zeitschrift des Vereins für Thüringische Geschichte und Altertumskunde* NF 31 (1935), 46-63.

[49] Quoted by Karl Heinz Burmeister, "Genossenschaftliche Rechtsfindung und herrschaftliche Rechtssetzung. Auf dem Weg zum Territorialstaat," *HZ* Beiheft 4 NF (1975), 175.

[50] Cited in Wilhelm Zimmermann, *Geschichte des grossen Bauernkrieges* (1856; reprint Naunhof and Leipzig, 1939) I, 6.

[51] See the amusing comments on Coke in Howard Nenner, *By Colour of the Law. Legal Culture and Constitutional Politics in England, 1660-1689* (Chicago, 1977), 7.

[52] StA Wei Reg Q, No. 20, 336ʳ and ᵛ.

agreeing only that he would punish such infractions committed by his servants as were brought to his attention.[53] As we shall see in greater detail in the final chapter, central governments were always eager to bend the terms of such agreements, while estates, and the social groups constituting them, generally had everything to gain from strict adherence. Lawyers proved marvelously adept at devising strategies for an escape from restrictive provisions in social contracts, and this cleverness contributed greatly to their reputation as unprincipled manipulators.

On the other hand, no argument was made against the sanctity itself of contracts. Even Roman emperors, enjoying plenitude of power, could not deprive a man of what was legally his due, says Melchior von Osse, quoting Baldus on the point. "For the jurists say that consent, agreement, contract, and other obligations are like the natural elements as far as emperors and popes are concerned, not to mention lesser rulers. They do not control contracts and agreements any more than they can command the elements and the stars."[54] An all-embracing, close-meshed net of legal conventions offered in its intrinsic resistance to sudden change the best protection for those who saw the preservation of the existing social order as the only guarantee of their autonomy. The compelling power of *alt herkommen*—tradition—had its source in this determination to keep to the past. As long as its social position was sound, each group wished to remain in its accustomed place. This is why opponents of innovation—whether in religion, in politics, or in social arrangements—always built their cases on the mass of accumulated customs.[55] As a body of precedents, the legal heritage severely limited the possibility of discretionary action by a willful prince or a rash magistrate. We shall see in Chapter Eight how the outpouring of political grievances analyzed there demonstrates in its expressions of sympathy and antipathy the comfort offered to members of territorial and urban assemblies by their emplacement in a tangled legal structure whose parts offset, neutralized, and reinforced each other in a complex system

[53] The incident described happened at the Landtag of Böblingen, 1552. HStA St *Tomi actorum* 2a, 29^r. The estates won in the end, and the oath was required.

[54] Melchior von Osse, "Welchergestalt ein christliche obrikeit . . . ein rechtmessige justicien erhalten kan" in Oswald Arthur Hecker, ed., *Schriften Dr. Melchiors von Osse* (Leipzig and Berlin, 1922), 335.

[55] A good illustration: Konrad Peutinger's advice to the City Council of Augsburg in 1534 against *Änderungen* in religion. His brief traces the legal relations of church and state back to antiquity and brings it up to the recent diets of Speyer, Augsburg, and Nuremberg. All past legislation, Peutinger contends, argues against changing religion, and the weight of this body of precedents limits the council's freedom to act arbitrarily. The brief is in Stadtarchiv Augsburg *Literalien* 1534, *Nachtrag* I, No. 15.

of constitutional checks and balances. With space left for maneuvering toward the small adjustments made necessary by shifting social and economic currents, this conglomerate network provided stability and, through this, a chance for survival.

NONETHELESS, this structure was a fragile inheritance. If it was to escape extinction, its traditions needed constantly to be reaffirmed. "Privilege being a private and particular kind of law," commented the seventeenth-century Bavarian jurist Caspar Schmid, "it is valid only as long as it is used and observed. Standing, as they do, against legal reason [*wider die rechtliche vernunft*], privileges are lost when not used":[56] hence the ceaseless attempts by every regional and local estate to have its liberties and privileges reconfirmed at every suitable occasion. This was one way of preventing them from creeping into desuetude. In 1552, Duke Christoph of Württemberg invited every member of the duchy's estates to submit a copy of its *freyheiten*. The resulting mass of documents may still be inspected in the Württemberg state archive and the *Landesbibliothek* in Stuttgart: handsomely written and stoutly bound volumes, obviously produced with great care, exhibiting above all the bewilderingly rich profusion of particular arrangements made—centuries earlier in most cases—for the special local, historical, and personal circumstances defining each place and body.[57] The very prolificacy of these singular arrangements[58]—targets for the exasperation and derision of jurists—made them relatively safe from tampering. Remote from the theoretical constructs and tidy categorizations of bureaucratic innovators, and deeply rooted in the everyday lives of real people, this world of petty rules and time-bound conventions was historical actuality to nearly everyone in the Holy Roman Empire.

[56] Caspar Schmid, *Commentarius oder Auslegung des Chur-Bayerischen Land-Rechts* . . . (Augsburg, 1747) II, 804.

[57] In HStA St A34, Bü 13b. (An earlier set of local customs, for 1514, is in A34, Bü 1b, No. 2.) A composite volume of local liberties was also made: *Consuetudinum variarum, quae in hoc ducatu Wurtembergensi . . . floruerunt: Der stätt, dörffer, flecken, auch ettlichen gottsheuser des fürstenthumbs Würtemberg Breuch, Recht . . . auch andere Statuten, zu Tübingen vor den . . . gelerten Räten, zwein Herrn Prelaten und dann vieren von der Landtschafft den 9.10.11. und 12. Februarii Anno 52 gelesen.* This is a beautiful copy: Cod. Jur 24 in the Württembergische Landesbibliothek in Stuttgart. The collection is arranged by type of law (inheritance, marriage, etc.) and by locality, so that variations can be easily spotted.

[58] An even more vivid impression of the enormous variegation of local customs and folkways—also in Württemberg—can be gained from the sources gathered by Friedrich Wintterlin in the two volumes of his *Württembergische ländliche Rechtsquellen* (Stuttgart, 1910-1922). These sources give the detailed arrangements and regulations by which people in villages related to each other and ran their private and communal affairs.

What most people wanted was to be confirmed in their place in this familiar world.

> In the commune of Sadisdorf [a market village in the mining country of Saxony] the poor and the rich have the following freedoms: to brew beer, to bake bread, to butcher meat, to keep a tavern, to pursue all handicrafts, and to operate a mine. Let no one interfere with them in these freedoms, which they have been enjoying since olden times.[59]

"Since olden times" was the phrase that secured the people of Sadisdorf in their rights: the antiquity of their freedoms shielded them from intervention. At the beginning of each new reign—and often more frequently than that—rulers staged public readings of basic rights as a *quid pro quo* for obtaining the loyalty oath from their subjects. To governments, these were perfunctory, largely symbolic, occasions: to subjects, however, they were rich with meaning. Shortly after his accession in 1551, Duke Christoph of Württemberg convoked in every town and market village "all our bailiffs, overseers, stewards, foresters, town secretaries, revenue collectors, councillors, also all our communes and other subjects" for a public reading of the 1514 Tübingen Contract, to be followed by declarations of loyalty to this constitution and to the duke. In accordance with bureaucratic procedures which, by mid-sixteenth century, had been instituted in most German territories, reports flowed back to Stuttgart of missions accomplished. Stacks of them repose in the archives. "In the town hall of Rosenfeld this day were assembled town secretary, schoolmaster, mayor, the officials of the local sub-office, and the entire community, including domestic servants and farm hands, also the inhabitants of the neighboring village of Isingen. All present pronounced the oath with forefingers raised."[60] These proceedings are not without their ritualistic aspects (these will be explored in Chapter Eight). But the constitutional debates of which—even at their most routinized—they are an intrinsic part leave no doubt about two vital features of the problem of political rights in the sixteenth century: that they were immediate and urgent to people in low as well as in high ranks of society, and that they were valued as substantive rights bearing at all times on real, tangible issues of survival in the world.

The tenaciously conservative temper of the time expressed itself in this determination to uphold established usage at all cost. Fundamental to this endeavor was a general acceptance of the stratified nature of so-

---

[59] StA Dr, Loc 9905: "Zu Sadisdorff gehaltene Ehegerichte . . . 1531," 1r.
[60] HStA St A34, Bü 12b, No. 14.

ciety, requiring from every member his assent to a fixed social place and to the accustomed degrees of super- and sub-ordination. Herbert Grundmann describes both the objective and the psychological character of this society in an illuminating way. To belong to it, he writes, meant

> to be fitted into, and to fit oneself in with, a God-ordained, hierarchically ranked order, one that is also a legal order that gives to each his proper due, including his liberty, but always in proportion to the liberty of others as a relative, conditioned, ranked liberty, never as an absolute freedom, because this [latter] kind of freedom is appropriate only to God and to the world beyond the present one.[61]

The relativity of each member's condition with respect to everyone else's is expressed in the legal proverb "Show me the man and I'll show you the law."[62] Law, according to this persuasion (the *conservative* persuasion in a century of runaway change), was particular; society consisted of particles distinguished from one another by the possession of privileges—not the major estates only, nobles, prelates, knights, burghers—but groups within groups within groups. The citizens of the tiny town of Hohenstein in Saxony, for example, were officially (on the occasion of their rendering of homage to a new prince) listed as follows: "Inhabitants who have the freedom to brew [*Braufreiheit*] in addition to neighbor's rights" (*Nachbar Recht* or *jura vicinorum*: preferential rights enjoyed by large property owners): 39; "those without the brewing right, having only neighbor's rights": 12; "old burghers in old houses" (*Bürger uff alten heusern*): 20; *Hauseler*, or owners of modest domiciles: 23; *Hausgenossen*, or dwellers in huts on tiny plots of land: 22.[63] Elsewhere, citizens are enumerated by trades.[64] Always they are designated by some concretely defined, locally recognized condition: the status to which rights, privileges, and obligations adhered. Each must owe obedience to someone. To have a *Herr*, a lord, was the normal and proper station for both high and low. *Herrenlos*—lordless and therefore lawless, flouting authority—was a strong pejorative used to brand drifters like gypsies or *Savoyer*—itinerant peddlers—and suspected Anabaptists. Each group was expected to display conduct appropriate to its condition. Complaints were heard throughout the century of nobles carrying on *bürgerliche handel*, selling for profit; of

---

[61] Herbert Grundmann, "Freiheit als religiöses, politisches und persönliches Postulat im Mittelalter," *HZ* 183 (1957), 26.

[62] Graf and Dietherr, *Deutsche Rechtssprichwörter*, 31.

[63] StA Dr, Loc 8719: "Ander Buch Erbhuldigung . . . 1601," 175ᵛ-189ᵛ.

[64] *Ibid.*, 235ʳ-244ʳ: Dippoldiswalde.

townsmen engaging in *rittermessige* activities such as the chase; of villagers illicitly selling cloth, brewing beer, or carrying on a trade. Such-and-such an action "is contrary to noble traditions"; another "is not permitted to peasants; it is a burgherly activity alone."[65] "Some of the nobility," complained the estates of Mecklenburg (in 1536), "buy pigs from their peasants when fodder is available, fatten them in their woods, and then drive them in their own persons out of the country to market. This," they add, "is behavior never yet heard of the nobility in any country, and it goes against God and all the written laws."[66]

Common laws and particular rights often stood opposed on this principle. During one of the interminable quarrels about brewing which kept people in litigation in Saxony, legal counsel retained by a group of knights contended that the common—i.e., imperial—laws gave everyone the right to make what use he would of whatever God had given him. Not so, responded the townsmen, who were the plaintiffs in this case:

Nobles are so set apart and made different from burghers and peasants, and burghers and peasants again so divided from nobles in their dignity, nature, station, kind, and title, that burghers are legally barred from undertaking knightly and noble actions, and nobles are forbidden for the sake of their nobility to engage in burgherly enterprises and lowly trades. . . . And all this is to a good purpose, namely that the nobility may increase and burghers prosper in wealth.

Woe to the country, the townsmen conclude, where social orders are mixed and ranks are confounded: "If ever the burgher went to war and those of the nobility became bakers and brewers, chaos and disruption would reign in the Holy Roman Empire."[67] Nobles used the same argument when their own special interests needed protection. "It is a regular practice now in villages that peasant sons want to learn a trade," they complained, deploring this practice, one that deprived them of agricultural workers and servants. "Peasants ought to remain peasants."[68] Things should be left as they are. A strong distaste for novelty was the most pronounced symptom of the conservatism of this traditional society. "As little innovation as possible" was the advice given

[65] StA Dr, Loc 9356: "Beratschlagung der Landgebrechen . . . 1554," 44ᵛ-45ʳ.
[66] Quoted in Karl von Hegel, *Geschichte der mecklenburgischen Landstände bis zum Jahre 1555* (Rostock, 1856; reprint Aalen, 1968), 197-98.
[67] StA Wei Reg Q, No. 82, 56ᵛ-57ʳ. This occurred in 1519.
[68] StA Dr, Loc 9359, 109ᵛ.

by Christoph Scheurl to the governing council of Nuremberg.[69] Philip
Melanchthon expressed this sentiment in an especially trenchant way,
in the account he gave of the Lutheran Reformation. "I know well," he
wrote, "that people who value civic discipline and order [*bürgerliche
zucht und ordnung*] hold innovations in great abhorrence. In this dismal and perplexing life," he went on, men cannot avoid doing wrong
whenever they undertake anything new, "no matter how fair their
cause may be."[70] Melanchthon's theologically induced pessimism was
matched by misanthropic assumptions in lay circles about the consequences of human intervention. Men's instincts and motives could not
be trusted. It was best, therefore, to abide by what was old and securely
established. "This is not how it was done in the old days," or "This is
not the way things used to be," was the constant refrain.

The great majority of protests and complaints touch the concrete
concerns of livelihood and status. Only rarely do they rise above matters of everyday life. Cities denounce rural artisans (weavers, for example), many of them installed by nobles in their villages, especially if
they take on apprentices. Direct sale of grain, malt, or wine by noble
land owners reduces urban profits, as do village taverns in the countryside beyond city walls. Town fathers plead for a ban on jobbing "and
other forms of usury," citing this practice as the cause of steep increase
in the cost of hops, wool, linen, cheese, and butter. Rising prices make
everyone uneasy, and administrative remedies are sought to curb them.
Nobles fight with cities about restrictive trade practices, about imposition on them of beer and wine excises ("against our ancient immunities"), and about the practice of luring domestic and farm servants
away from noble households. Both groups object vehemently to the increasingly heavyhanded presence of central administrations: the usurpation of functions of local self-government by princely *Amtleute*, the
imposition of new chancellery and secretarial fees for obtaining documents, "formerly unheard-of" but now required, the high cost of litigating in central courts, direct interference by territorial rulers in the
nobility's patrimonial courts, new forestry regulations limiting the age-
old freedom to fatten pigs by letting them run in the woods and preventing the poor from gathering their traditional armful of firewood,
intervention by newly established church councils in noble patronage
rights, and generally high-handed behavior by agents for central gov-

[69] In 1530, when the new Nuremberg-Brandenburg church constitution was under
consideration. Germanisches Nationalmuseum Nuremberg, *Merkel-Handschrift* 129,
20ʳ.

[70] Melanchthon, *Vita Lutheri. Von dem Leben und Sterben . . . D. Martini Lutheri*
(Eisleben, 1555), 23.

ernments. In the city of Rochlitz, in Saxony, "whenever the castle needs a craftsman or two for making repairs or for building something, they send the bailiff into town, who walks into a man's house, orders him to pick up his tools and report forthwith to the castle, and if he refuses or even hesitates, he is taken straight to the tower!" Such behavior "has not before been seen here. It was not heard of in the old days."[71] The fact that many functionaries were "foreigners"—that is to say, not stemming from the district where they exercised authority—reinforced the instinctive xenophobia with which localities tried to ward off intervention from outside. Pleas for the appointment of "good, honorable, well-informed fellow-countrymen [*landleute*]" to man the posts now held by *auslender*[72] were throughout the period heard in every German territory.

Such reproaches were always advanced in full confidence that they rested on the solid ground of right and justice. "It is common wisdom," declared spokesmen for the estates of Hesse, locked in a quarrel with their *Landgraf*, "that a man cannot do wrong when he makes use of his rights."[73] This principle encouraged and, to a point, safeguarded all those—and they were innumerable—who had rights to keep up. Those who failed to act on their rights courted the danger of losing them, not only because another might appropriate them, but, passively, through atrophy. This was the chief reason for the incessant debates over rights, privileges, customs, freedoms, and traditions in the constitutional deliberations of the age. All ranks and orders of society were embroiled in them, from rural laborer to dukes and electors. They were both the form and the substance of political dialectic and social conflict.

RIGHTS were "freedoms" (*freiheiten*), but freedom was more than rights. It is fascinating to observe how the concept of freedom swells with philosophical and moral content as the debates gather momentum in the early and mid-sixteenth century.[74] In the ordinary sense of the

[71] All these from Saxony in the 1550s and to the end of the century: StA Dr, Loc 9356: "Der Chur zu Sachssen Clage . . . 1555" and Loc 9359: "Vorrichtung der Landgebrechen im Churkreise . . . 1601."

[72] E.g., Tyrol: "Beschwerden der Gemeinden Taur und Rettenberg, 1525," LA Tir, *Tiroler Landtagsakten* Fasz. II.

[73] *Hessische Landtagsakten*, ed. Hans Glagau (Marburg, 1901) I, 64.

[74] For general discussion of the problem of freedom in relation to late medieval and early modern German politics, see Herbert Grundmann, "Freiheit als religiöses, politisches und persönliches Postulat . . ." in *loc. cit.*; Karl Bosl, "Die alte deutsche Freiheit. Geschichtliche Grundlagen des modernen deutschen Staates" in *id., Frühformen der Gesellschaft im mittelalterlichen Europa* (Munich, 1964), 204-19; *id.*, "Freiheit und Unfreiheit. Zur Entwicklung der Unterschichten in Deutschland und Frankreich während

term, and in the use most often made of it by ordinary people, "freedoms" were stated privileges granted to a group or an individual, spec-
ifying something that could be done or could not be done. One's freedom in this sense was to be held exactly to the stipulated terms, and to
no other. This was the crux of most political controversies at the time,
as is clear from the synonyms to which the term was regularly tied:
"privilegia, exceptionen und freyhaiten." Justin Gobler had this meaning in mind when he referred in his *Mirror of Laws* to "a special right,
called *ius singulare* or privilege or freedom, not included in the rules of
common law but possessing its own peculiarity and characteristics."[75]
It was therefore an exercise of their "freedom" for Tyrolean farmers
"to sell our cattle, cheese, and lard inside and outside our own country,
as long as there is no war in the land," and another—"awarded to our
forefathers in remote antiquity [*vor uralten zeiten*]"—to graze cattle on
high-lying meadows in the spring.[76] Most "freedoms" concerned such
petty matters—petty, that is, to the historian, looking back, but vital to
ordinary people never far from the margins of subsistence. For this reason, villagers near the town of Kufstein were moved to make "most serious remonstrance" (*höchste beschwerung*) to their territorial diet
when townsmen attempted to put a stop to their selling "lean cattle" in
the city market; a duly notarized true copy of the ancient *freyhait* giving
them this right in perpetuity was included with the protest.[77] Among
the freedoms enjoyed by the city of Meran was a ban on "open inns and
taverns" within half a mile's circumference of the town. Holders of
other freedoms possessed rights to mint coins, try criminal cases, or
make free use of peasant labor. In each such transaction someone was
put at an advantage and someone else at a disadvantage: this was the
nature of "privileges, exemptions, freedoms, graces, and rights" as particular law. In an imperfect world they achieved a rough kind of balance among forces competing within the hierarchic social universe. No
wonder radical reformers like Michael Gaismair proposed to abolish
"all freedoms going against the word of God and violating the Law that

---

des Mittelalters" in *ibid.*, 180-203; Jürgen Schlumbohm, *Freiheitsbegriff und Emanzi-
pationsprozess. Zur Geschichte des politischen Wortes* (Göttingen, 1973), 14-20. The
most recent discussion, with excellent bibliography, is Klaus Arnold, "Freiheit im Mittelalter," *Historisches Jahrbuch* 104:1 (1984), 1-21.

[75] Justin Gobler, *Spiegel der Rechten* (Frankfurt am Main, 1573), 20v.

[76] From "Beschwerden Gerichts Ehrenberg, 1563," LA Tir, *Tiroler Landtagsakten*
Fasz. 8, 355r.

[77] Grievances of *Gericht* (i.e., district government) Kufstein addressed to Tyrol *Landtag* of 1563, *ibid.*, 371r and v, 377v.

says: no one shall be preferred over another."[78] The moment one stepped outside the system and looked at it from a moral perspective—as Gaismair and a number of other visionaries did—its inequities became glaringly obvious.

But "freedom" and "free" also signified something broader than the guarding of one's privileges. "In the County of Nellenburg it is the custom for women and men to marry as they please. We hope that we will be permitted the same freedom."[79] Here "freedom" clearly implies a measure of independent action and choice. Social crisis and agitation tended to bring out the libertarian strain running in the word, a trend strongly reinforced by classical allusions brought in by way of the near-universal admiration for the Swiss struggle for autonomy, as in the allegation that peasants uniting in the association of the *Bundschuh* were fighting "to win every kind of freedom in the manner of the Swiss: by force of arms" (*omnimodam libertatem more Helvetiorum armis vendicarent*).[80] In the 1520s many peasant groups asked for "freedom" from labor and transport service: in this case, "free" stood for the right to be quit of burdensome obligations.[81] "All game, fish, and birds shall be free" meant "let them be free for the taking."[82] For small tenants to be "free" to trap the rabbits and boars destroying their crops was an even more enabling kind of freedom from conventions they considered restrictive.[83] "Altogether free and without burden of menial servitude"[84] approaches a shift in status far beyond the merely "practical freedom," as it has been called,[85] solicited in most of the documents generated by the peasant war. "Although by rights all men originally were born free [*frei geporn*], . . . we have been taken into servitude without any fault of ours or of our forefathers," protested the peasants of Stühlingen and Lupfen in 1525, at the beginning of the conflict;[86] their declaration contained an apt (but selective) quote from *In-*

---

[78] Michael Gaismair, "Landesordnung" (1526) in Günther Franz, ed., *Quellen*, No. 92, p. 286.

[79] From grievances of village of Mühlhausen in the Black Forest, 1524 in *ibid.*, No. 23, p. 98.

[80] From articles of the *Bundschuh* in Untergrombach, Bishopric of Speyer, 1502 in *ibid.*, No. 16b, p. 73.

[81] E.g., *ibid.*, No. 19, p. 85; No. 25, p. 111.

[82] E.g., *ibid.*, No. 22, p. 96; No. 25, p. 116; No. 35, p. 164; No. 71, p. 239; No. 91, p. 277; and many others.

[83] E.g., *ibid.*, No. 25, p. 117.

[84] *Ibid.*, No. 64, p. 224.

[85] Winfried Schulze, *Bäuerlicher Widerstand und feudale Herrschaft in der frühen Neuzeit* (Stuttgart, 1980), 122.

[86] Günther Franz, *Quellen*, No. 25, p. 121.

stitutes 1.2.2. In the same vein, a complaint against the Prince-Abbot of Kempten deplored the severe harm done to his people's "liberty and freedom [*libertet und Freihait*] accepted and respected by all godly, common, papal, and imperial laws."[87] From such phrases it was a short step to explicitly political uses of the term, as in the common adage "to be free like the Swiss,"[88] or to its employment as a slogan, for instance in the patriotic writings of Ulrich von Hutten, who reminded Germans of their "long-lost freedom"[89] and opened his first letter to Martin Luther in 1520 with the motto *Vive libertas!*[90] Pithy proverbs were at hand to enhance this rhetorical appeal: "Freedom is dearer than eyesight and life"; "Freedom: a small thing, but an excellent thing"; "Better a free bird than a caged king."[91]

Appeals to liberty in this—in their own time quite extravagant—sense were not, however, representative. Much more characteristic was the cautious formulation given in the "Twelve Articles of All the Peasantry and Tenants of Spiritual and Temporal Powers by Whom They Think Themselves Oppressed" composed in 1525. The third article of this most famous and influential of all the documents produced during the peasant war touches the—by then—acutely inflamed issue of freedom:

> We find in Scripture that we are free and want to be so. Not that we wish to be wholly free, to have no ruling authority over us: God does not teach us that. We are taught to live by commandments, not in free fleshly license, but to love God, to recognize him as our lord in our neighbor, and to do all things as we would like them done to us, as God commanded us at the Last Supper.[92]

The careful distinctions being drawn here between the state of personal freedom and actions taken in consequence of it, between legitimate and illegitimate uses of freedom, reflect the contemporary legal and political context of all discourse on the subject. The article acknowledges subservience to authority and to rules; this is in accord with traditional

[87] *Ibid.*, No. 27, p. 128.
[88] Cf. Luther, "Man sagt, die Schweizer haben vor zeiten auch ire oberherrn erschlagen und sich selber frey gemacht. . . ." *Ob Kriegsleute auch in seligem Stande sein können* (1526), WA 19, 635.
[89] From the German translation, by Martin Bucer and himself, of his *Conquestiones* (1520), Preface, and *Ein Klagschrift . . . an gemein teutsche Nation . . . ,*" *passim*. Both in Ulrich von Hutten, *Deutsche Schriften* ed. Peter Ukena (Munich, 1970), 164; 176-86.
[90] Hutten to Luther, June 4, 1520, WA Br II, No. 295.
[91] Quoted in Graf and Dietherr, *Rechtssprichwörter*, 40-42.
[92] The German text of the Twelve Articles is printed in Adolf Laube and Hans Werner Seiffert eds., *Flugschriften der Bauernkriegszeit* (Berlin, 1975), 28.

notions of freedom, as we have seen: freedom was the acceptance of one's assigned place in the divinely appointed order in which everyone possesses stated rights and obligations. At the same time, an appeal is made to freedom as an essential condition of the individual—human beings cannot be appropriated or owned, like chattel—although in its actualization this condition is limited to doing what is explicitly allowed. The German word translated as "license" in the passage quoted above is *Mutwille*, a word with a precise legal meaning. It stood for action opposed to what the law demands: arbitrary, willful, capricious action. Such action is always illicit. But even while this is affirmed, the article's rhetoric apostrophizes a much more sweeping sense of personal freedom, and an attack on the restraints placed upon it by repressive social and political forces.[93]

Read in these terms, the classic peasant manifesto of 1525 (it was actually drafted by an urban artisan and evangelical pamphleteer, and by a preacher with Zwinglian sympathies, both residents of the imperial city of Memmingen) can be seen as part of the debate about rights, privileges, traditions, and innovations discussed earlier in this chapter. With a few changes of reference it could have spoken for any of the German estates engaged in the struggle to protect what each called its own. Although raised as a battle cry from time to time, freedom as idea and as legal title was too intricately interwoven with the medieval system of divided and reciprocal obligations to be developed into a "modern" political concept. As Karl Bosl has noted, in its actual historical setting freedom was never separable from its counterpart, which was lordship and authority. Where the one existed, the other also was found.[94] Justin Gobler's description catches this reciprocal relation: "Freedom is a man's natural power to do what he pleases, unless the law or another's power forbid it."[95] The time was not yet ripe for

[93] For an extended exploration of the matter of freedom, with special reference to the Reformation, see my article "Three Kinds of 'Christian Freedom': Law, Liberty, and License in the German Reformation" in *Michigan Germanic Studies* X:1-2 (1984), 291-306.

[94] Karl Bosl, "Die alte deutsche Freiheit" in *loc. cit.*, 205. One must, however, be cautious in evaluating such associations of freedom and authority. Adolf Waas, *Die alte deutsche Freiheit* makes much of this, but the fact that Waas's book was originally published in Berlin in 1939 (again in Munich, 1967), may explain such passages as this: "Dem bäuerlichen Menschen des Mittelalters erschien es als Selbstverständlichkeit, dass nur der, der sich einer machtvollen schützenden Hand anschloss, und sich ihr unterstellte, Freiheit haben konnte . . ." (p. 44).

[95] "Die freyhait ist ein natürlich macht und gewalt, was einem jeden zuthun gliebet, es verbiete es ihm dann das recht oder die gewalt." From Justin Gobler's translation of Constantine Hermenopoulos's *Handbuch und Auszug kayserlicher und Bürgerlicher Rechten* (Frankfurt am Main, 1564), xlvir.

breaking this symbiosis. Beginning in the 1520s, the Reformation did inject a new urgency into the debate over personal freedom (echoes of it sound in the peasant protests just referred to); but, as we shall see later, it did nothing to remove the discussion from its conventional frame, within which the protection of "rights" and the defense of "customs" and "traditions" were paramount concerns. The interest common to all groups in preserving this system of balanced thrusts and counterthrusts was great enough to contain, for the time being, even the most aggressive forces of dissension.[96]

The legal machinery available for litigating disputes in Germany was well fitted to a society of such varied political complexion and such contentious habits. Courts were estate-specific and locally based. They reflected the privileges of status groups and the needs and peculiarities of the country's diverse regions and cultures. At the beginning of the early modern period, a German territory (*Land*) was typically (and only a schematic picture need be given here) divided into a number of judicial districts, each headed by an urban or rural bench, some of them dating back to the tenth century, on which amateur jurors (*Schöffen*) pronounced justice on the basis of regional law, such as that given in the *Sachsenspiegel* or *Schwabenspiegel*, as well as in accordance with local statutes and their own more or less sound judgment. It was this system that, as we saw in the last chapter, was, from the late fifteenth century onward, being undermined and circumvented by ideas and procedures associated with Roman law and issuing from centers of territorial government and from several parallel court systems competing with the *Schöffenstühle*: ecclesiastical courts, princely superior courts (*Hofgerichte*), arbitration courts, and, intermittently after 1495, the empire-wide Imperial Chamber Court.[97]

Within each princely territory, a ruler's endeavor to control justice in his realm brought him into conflict with noble landowners who, in the course of the medieval centuries, had acquired extensive judicial privileges giving them authority over civil and non-capital criminal cases of local origin (as well as political jurisdictions, on the principle that "he who judges you is your lord"). In Bavaria, for example, every *Landgericht*—the bench of lowest instance in the duke's system of courts—competed with patrimonial courts under the jurisdiction of nobles

---

[96] See the interesting distinctions developed between resistance (*Widerstand*) and revolution (*seditio, rebellio, Aufruhr*) within the medieval political order by Karl Griewank, *Der neuzeitliche Revolutionsbegriff. Entstehung und Entwicklung* (2nd ed. Frankfurt am Main, 1969), 25-26.

[97] Adolf Stölzel, *Die Entwicklung des gelehrten Richtertums* I, 25-30; Otto Stobbe, *Geschichte der deutschen Rechtsquellen* I, 274-343.

whose privileges included judicial rights.[98] In Saxony, landlords' courts called *Ehegerichte* (from the middle high German word for law) functioned in rural districts as mainstays of social discipline.[99] More than the power to direct judicial affairs was at stake in this competition. Justice was a costly, and therefore a profitable, business: apart from fines, there were fees to be paid, and pocketed, at every stage and to every member of the judicial process.[100] More important, rural courts functioned locally as *Rügegerichte* with police authority; control over these tribunals was as vital to a private lord trying to maintain status among "his" people as it was to a regional ruler making good his claim to territorial sovereignty.[101] Within the patrimonial court, tension often divided its constituent parties: each such bench had "mixed jurisdiction," a locally produced blend of shared authority between landlord and village or small-town community.[102]

In the countryside, additional variety was provided by independent peasant courts surviving from a still older time. These met in village taverns, presided over by a "court elder" appointed by the groundlord upon election by the commune. In other variations they comprised the whole village summoned with the pealing of church bells by a *Bauermeister*, a head peasant. Judicial and government business were inseparable in the sessions of these bodies. The practice of *rügen*, which was the chief responsibility of these rural courts, touched all conceivable matters of local import, from a broken fence post to cutting grain beyond the edge of one's row, to theft, manslaughter, and blasphemy.[103] Communal life was closely tied to these courts, whose officers took their responsibility with great seriousness, though one would expect to see normal village and small-town tensions brought to the surface by the courts' dependence on denunciation and informers. Records were

[98] See Volkmar Wittmütz, *Die Gravamina der bayerischen Stände im 16. und 17. Jahrhundert . . . (Miscellanea Bavarica Monacensia* 26, Munich, 1970), 44-53.

[99] Karlheinz Blaschke, "Frühkapitalismus und Verfassungsgeschichte," *Wissenschaftliche Zeitschrift der Karl-Marx-Universität Leipzig* 14. Jahrgang (1965), 440.

[100] Volkmar Wittmütz, *op. cit.*, 46-47 for Bavaria.

[101] For a fascinating—though ultimately monotonous—picture of village conditions in Saxony, see the records of *Ehegerichte* for the entire sixteenth century in StA Dr, Loc 8832 and Loc 9905, organized by courts. For a very detailed account of one patrimonial court, see Hans Tütken, *Geschichte des Dorfes und Patrimonialgerichtes Geismar bis zur Gerichtsauflösung im Jahre 1839 (Studien zur Geschichte der Stadt Göttingen* 7, Göttingen, 1967), 246-75.

[102] *Ibid.*, 257; Karlheinz Blaschke in *loc. cit.*, 440.

[103] For a description of *rügen*, see Hermann Knapp, *Alt-Regensburgs Gerichtsverfassung, Strafverfahren und Strafrecht bis zur Carolina* (Berlin, 1914), 86-87; also Götz Landwehr, "Gogericht und Rügegericht," *ZRG* 83 (1966), *Germ.Abt.*, 127-43.

kept, many of which have survived. The village of Schwimbach, in the domain of the city of Nuremberg, for instance, kept a full chronicle of its court meetings from 1475 to the eighteenth century.[104] As for the larger cities, by the late fifteenth century they had gained—usually by purchase—virtually complete jurisdiction over all cases, including capital ones, within their walls.[105] As we have seen, cities were among the first authorities in Germany to codify and publish their law books around 1500. On the other hand, municipal courts were no more all-embracing than territorial ones. Guilds judged their own members, as did the clergy. In every city, the relations of laws and legal conditions to one another, and of all to the magistracy, were matters for negotiation.

This proliferation of courts[106] was a natural consequence of the many kinds of law operating in Germany in the late middle ages: imperial (going back to the Carolingian capitularies), territorial, feudal, urban, as well as special laws and statutes for Jews, clerics, knights, guilds, and so on.[107] In the early thirteenth century, these laws began to be collected and formalized. From that time on jurors and judges could consult written codes: the great *Rechtsbücher* containing the laws of the Saxons and Swabians, city codes, *Landrechte* issued by territorial rulers for their principalities, and collections of *Weistümer*, local laws regulating the relations of landlords and peasants in rural areas. Further decisions were then needed to determine how these overlapping and competing laws should be reconciled in court practice. "Courts in this territory shall keep Saxon law as it has been practiced in this land from ancient times. Although this may conflict with the common written law on some points, we declare by our princely might and authority that the law of our own land and people shall be preferred to the com-

---

[104] Georg Barth, "Das nürnbergische Ehehaftgericht in Schwimbach," *Mitteilungen des Vereins für Geschichte der Stadt Nürnberg 59* (1972), 1-39. See also the records referred to in note 101 above.

[105] Karlheinz Blaschke in *loc. cit.*, 438.

[106] The older literature found it deplorable. According to Adolf Gasser it represented a "heillose Staatsauflockerung, die in der Feudalzeit fast jedes Dorf . . . zu einem selbständigen Herrschaftsgebilde hatte werden lassen." "Die landständische Staatsidee und der schweizerische Bundesgedanke" in Commission internationale pour l'histoire des assemblées d'États, *L'organisation corporative du Moyen Age à la fin de l'Ancien Régime* III (Louvain, 1939), 121.

[107] See Otto Stobbe, *op. cit.* I, and Heinrich Mitteis, *Deutsche Rechtsgeschichte*, 184-91; Gerhard Köbler, *Das Recht im frühen Mittelalter. Untersuchungen zu Herkunft und Inhalt frühmittelalterlicher Rechtsbegriffe im deutschen Sprachgebiet* (Cologne and Vienna, 1971), Chapter 3.

mon written law."[108] A mass of such declarations came into being, but still the contiguity of so many types of law of different origins and objectives created friction and, to laymen, confusion. "There are three ways of pursuing this case," advised a legal consultant to the city of Nuremberg about 1470. "One way is through the common written law, another through privileges, a third through ancient customs." Any of these courses might be chosen, and if all three failed, one could resort to arguing from "the divine natural and biblical law."[109]

In criminal law, long-standing legal traditions were disoriented in the late middle ages by the introduction nearly everywhere in Europe of the inquisitorial procedure. Roman and canon law had much to do with this innovation, though the roots for trial by inquisition—in which crimes were from the moment of their occurrence regarded as public business and pretrial investigations were conducted on the initiative of the courts themselves—existed in German law as well.[110] The new method reached its full development in Germany in the publication of two comprehensive criminal codes, the *Constitutio Criminalis Bambergensis*, written in 1507 by Johann von Schwarzenberg, an appeals court judge in the service of the Prince-Bishop of Bamberg, and the *Constitutio Criminalis Carolina*, published, as we have seen, in 1532 over the seal of the Emperor Charles V and closely modeled on the *Bambergensis*, especially in its attempt to safeguard by means of rigorous rules of evidence the rights of the innocent, which inquisitorial methods had put into jeopardy. Although it never became a binding code applicable to all in the empire (the "liberties" of German princes and cities did not permit such broadside extensions of authority), the *Carolina* standardized criminal procedures to a considerable extent.[111]

[108] *Oberhofgerichtsordnung* issued in 1529 by Dukes Georg and Johann for Albertine and Ernestine Saxony. Quoted in Christian Gottfried Kretschmann, *Geschichte des churfürstlich Sächsischen Oberhofgerichts zu Leipzig* (Leipzig, 1804), 83.

[109] From an unsigned *Ratschlag* written about 1470. StA Nbg, *Ratschlagbücher* 2*, 80v-81r, 172v.

[110] On the *Inquisitionsprozess* in Germany, see, in general, Heinrich Mitteis, *op. cit.*, 192-93; Paul Flade, *Das römische Inquisitionsverfahren in Deutschland bis zu den Hexenprozessen* (*Studien zur Geschichte der Theologie und der Kirche* IX: 1, Leipzig, 1902; reprint Aalen, 1972)—an informative book marred, however, by rampant anti-Catholicism; Alfons Vogt, "Die Anfänge des Inquisitionsprozesses in Frankfurt am Main, *ZRG* 69 (1951), *Germ.Abt.*, 234-307. Enormous amounts of fascinating information on all aspects of criminal law and procedure are contained in two books by Hermann Knapp, *Das alte Nürnberger Kriminalverfahren* (Berlin, 1891), 258-545 and *Alt-Regensburgs Gerichtsverfassung.* . . . The two books are identical in arrangement of material.

[111] For evidence for this see Gerhard Schmidt, "Sinn und Bedeutung der Constitutio Criminalis Carolina als Ordnung des materiellen und prozessualen Rechts," *ZRG* 83 (1966), *Germ.Abt.*, 239-57.

More important, the trend represented by the *Bambergensis* and the *Carolina* strengthened the legal and political positions of central governments and introduced methods of investigation ever since considered typical of governments firmly placed and confident in their authority. Where Schwarzenberg's evidentiary rules were adopted, inquisitorial methods, including torture, were held to strict rules of propriety.[112] Elsewhere, the *erforschliches Gericht*, as the inquisitorial court was called in the vernacular, was often guilty of excesses. On the other hand, it was never unpopular with ordinary people, for whom it made legal action possible when lack of funds for going to court would otherwise have prevented them.[113] The landed nobility, too, was not disinclined to see governments play a larger role in criminal trials: an inherited distaste for "blood justice" made them reluctant to stain their escutcheons with the cruel physical penalties usually visited upon convicted felons.[114] Meanwhile the havoc created by *turbatores pacis* and *schädliche Leute*—criminal elements—in the land had to be dealt with.[115] The state was the largest beneficiary of this transfer of responsibility. "As criminal law became an aspect of state authority," writes Michael R. Weisser in his study of *Crime and Punishment in Early Modern Europe*, "one immediate result was a dramatic increase in the number of statutes, a revision of criminal definitions, and a general increase in the severity of punishments."[116] Unlike civil practice, criminal justice came to be part of the prerogative of the state.

[112] For a vivid contemporary picture in popular language of how the system operated, see Heinrich Rauchdorn, *Practica und Process peinlicher Halssgerichts Ordnung aus Keyserlichen, Geistlichen, Weltlichen und Sechsischen Rechten . . .* (Budissin, 1564). On Inquisitions: Ciiii[v]; on torture: Diiii[v]-Fiiii[r]. For an earlier impression, see Ulrich Tengler, *Layenspiegel* (Strasbourg, 1510), Qi[v]-ii[r].

[113] See the description of the functions of the *fiscal und sindicus* of Hessen given in a promulgation by Landgraf Philip, quoted in Franz Gundlach, *Die hessischen Zentralbehörden von 1247 bis 1604 (Veröffentlichungen der historischen Kommission für Hessen und Waldeck* XVI, Marburg, 1930-32) II, 82-83. As *fiscal*, the official was the prince's trial initiator; as *sindicus* he initiated legal action on behalf of the poor, "da die ire gerechtigkeit armuts halber nicht erfordern mochten, denselben auch ir wort gegen menniglich on belonung ze tun."

[114] Cf. Eduard Rosenthal, *Geschichte des Gerichtswesens und der Verwaltungsorganisation Baierns* (Würzburg, 1889-1906) I, 56-57.

[115] See the interesting revisionist arguments about early modern criminality by Michael R. Weisser, *Crime and Punishment in Early Modern Europe* (Atlantic Highlands, N.J., 1979). See statement of book's theme on pp. 3 and 171.

[116] *Ibid.*, 100. Weisser continues: "This last development was in many respects the most significant change in criminal procedure during the early modern period for, as we have seen, the personalised nature of medieval criminal law was exemplified most clearly in the lack of harsh punishments. The relative mildness of feudal punishment followed

During all this time, legal procedure changed in the direction of greater formality, as we have noted in passing in other chapters. The *processus ordinarius*—a lengthy, circumstantial undertaking—could be abbreviated by mutual consent of the parties into a *processus summarius*; but even this mode of civil litigation was a time-consuming and costly business generating masses of paper and involving officials and specialists at every stage. In obedience to the principle of *Schriftlichkeit*, everything had to be put in writing. This made an end of earlier less formal methods of conducting trials.[117] *Quod non est in actis non est in mundo*, it was said: what is not in the documents does not exist. Even small towns and rural courts recorded their fixed rules of procedure in trial manuals for the use of judges and jurors.[118] Many of these manuscript books are adorned with colored drawings depicting actions in progress: a territorial court in the Prince-Bishopric of Würzburg, for example, shows its presiding judge, the *Landrichter*, enthroned above a long table around three sides of which are positioned a recorder leaning over a bulky volume, seven jurors, and, standing at the bar, the two parties with their advocates.[119] As judges and jurors on these lower benches were always amateurs while law was becoming increasingly professional, the expert adviser grew indispensable, not only to the litigating parties, but to the courts as well.[120] He, in turn, was blamed for the corruption, notably the financial abuses, endemic in so ramified and overlapping a structure as the German court system.[121] On the other hand, it does not appear that the system allowed the rights of the innocent to go unprotected. Arbitrariness was generally considered the worst of the sins of which justice could be guilty. This, at least, was the principle to which professional jurists tried to convert the many laymen engaged in examining and judging. Even God, writes Melchior von

from the fact that the system had been designed to settle disputes between equals, rather than simply to punish the guilty party. But as criminal law moved into the public domain, punishment would take on a different meaning. The primary purpose of criminal law would be to punish the criminal, while retribution to the plaintiff would ultimately become obsolete."

[117] For a description of earlier medieval German court procedures characterized by orality, see J. W. Planck, *Das deutsche Gerichtsverfahren im Mittelalter* I, 133-37.

[118] E.g., the manuscript *Rechtsbuch* of the town of Markberg in Franconia, dated 1585. Copy in Germanisches Nationalmuseum Nuremberg Hs. 34.075ª.

[119] A reproduction of this drawing is in Franz Heinemann, *Der Richter* (Leipzig, 1900), Plate 11.

[120] Dirk Olzen, "Richter und Sachverständige in der neueren Rechtsgeschichte," *ZRG* 97 (1980), Germ.Abt., 164-231.

[121] Eduard Rosenthal gives a description of such abuses by court personnel in Bavaria based on the instructions issued to *Rentmeister* before their annual *Umritte. Op. cit.* I, 313.

Osse, does not practice arbitrary justice. When Adam broke the law in the Garden of Eden, he points out, God, like the good judge he is, "summoned Adam, charged him, and listened to his reply." In so acting, God recognized "that one must not act in any matter without due process."[122] And the Nuremberg jurist Dr. Christoph Scheurl advised his government repeatedly that it is better by far "to let the guilty go unpunished than to punish an innocent person." He added: "All the doctors agree on this principle."[123]

A cumbersome apparatus full of exasperating self-contradictions,[124] the German legal system accommodated a host of diverse status and interest groups whose coexistence it reinforced by being responsive to their distinct and jealously guarded particular concerns. Though undergoing rapid and far-reaching change, it was still, in the late fifteenth and deep into the sixteenth centuries, animated by traces of an ancient faith in a preexisting fixed legal order and in the normative sway of this order over everything touched by the hand of the law.[125] Anachronistic though this belief must have seemed to many contemporaries, no one would have impugned its intrinsic nobility or denied its relevance to people struggling against the changing odds in their daily lives. Attacks on the system were directed, instead, against its complex diversity and its internal inconsistencies. Advocates of the rational, written law suggested, as we have seen, a better—because more uniform and efficient—alternative to the prevailing clutter. But theirs was not the only option for change. From the opposite side of the political spectrum there was advanced a drastic solution powered by a faith rooted in a very different ideology. We turn now, briefly, to a consideration of this second, radical, alternative to the existing order.

THE extent to which people in all social ranks of late medieval and early modern society accepted law as a major presence in their lives is astonishing to the modern observer. But willing acceptance did not mean

---

[122] Melchior von Osse, *An Hertzog Augusten . . . Ein unterthäniges Bedencken* in *Schriften Dr. Melchiors von Osse*, 337.

[123] StA Nbg, *Ratschlagbuch* No. 1, 167ᵛ. The point is often repeated by Nuremberg legal advisers, e.g., *ibid*. No. 3, 20ʳ and ᵛ.

[124] The best description of how the German system actually operated is found in contemporary popular books on the subject, especially Andreas Perneder, *Gerichtlicher Process . . .* (Ingolstadt, 1573), and Heinrich Rauchdorn, *Practica und Process . . .* (Budissin, 1564).

[125] J. W. Planck, *Das deutsche Gerichtsverfahren . . .* I, 87; Dietrich Gerhard, "Regionalismus und ständisches Wesen als ein Grundthema europäischer Geschichte," *HZ* 174 (1952), 307-37, also in Hellmut Kämpf, ed., *Herrschaft und Staat im Mittelalter* (*Wege der Forschung* II, Darmstadt, 1974), 332-64. The reference is to page 343.

that they were wedded to a mystical view of the nature and origin of the laws that governed their world. An observation by Howard Nenner is apropos here:

> To speak [in the early modern period] of men being ruled by the law is rhetorically the same as saying, in the nineteenth century, that men are governed by machines or in the twentieth century, that their lives are directed by the computer. In each case the putative ruler is nothing more than an effective tool offering great benefits to any who can use and control it.[126]

By experience as well as by using their common sense people knew that, whatever might be said about it in a philosophical way, the law they lived by was the product of men, reflected existing power relations, and was intended to perpetuate these arrangements in the interest of those who profited from them. Any attack on the wielders of power would therefore have to strike at the laws that upheld them. This is why reformers and rebels always placed Roman law and its agents foremost among the targets of their assaults. They were mainstays of the structures of domination. They would have to go before life could return to that cohesive ethos from which "innovations" had torn it, and to which it could only be reattached by restoring law to—in the words of Georg Dahm—"the community's possession."[127]

This repossession was the aim of the most far-reaching proposals made on the occasion of the greatest upheaval in early modern Germany, the failed social revolution of 1525. Only a time of broad uproar could generate such truly radical departures. In normal circumstances the common belief that all good things lay in the past was too great an obstacle to iconoclastic thinking;[128] but the revolution of 1525 created enough external excitement to make the contemplation of radical solutions a matter of practical possibility. Our discussion of these radical plans for a new social order will be drawn from four publications produced during the revolutionary years: Wendel Hipler's and Friedrich Weygandt's so-called Heilbronn program—a draft proposal based on earlier German reform writings and intended for deliberation by an assembly of peasants in 1525; a statement of grievances prepared by mostly rural communes in the County of Tyrol for a diet held in the city

[126] Howard Nenner, *By Colour of the Law* . . . , 106-07.
[127] Georg Dahm, "On the Reception of Roman and Italian Law in Germany" in *Pre-Reformation Germany*, ed. Gerald Strauss (London, 1972), 314.
[128] This difficulty has been often noted. See, e.g., Karl Bosl, *Mensch und Gesellschaft in der Geschichte* (Munich, 1972), 184-85; Ferdinand Seibt, *Utopica, Modelle totaler Sozialplanung* (Düsseldorf, 1972), 50.

of Meran, also in 1525; the draft of a new territorial constitution for Tyrol proposed in 1526 by Michael Gaismair, a peasant leader with pronounced Zwinglian sympathies; and a stirring vision of a possible future written in the war's aftermath by the Nuremberg printer and evangelical publicist Hans Hergot shortly before his execution in 1527. Where appropriate, I shall note the correspondence of these proposals with grass roots sentiments recorded in lists of grievances submitted to the Prince-Bishop of Bamberg in the year of the revolution, as well as other such documents.[129]

As schemes for a communitarian alternative to the existing feudal society, these proposals were certainly radical—no more so, however, than the *other* alternative that was issuing piecemeal during these same decades from the superior courts and central chancelleries of early modern German state builders (it will be considered in the next chapter). Because it was the latter that gained the victory in the end, and because historians normally take their stand with the winning side, the early modern state (or, more accurately, this state as it was conceived and planned by its ideologues and bureaucrats) has most often been presented as the all but inevitable result of the natural flow of European history. At the time, however, although the currents of this flow were palpable and, as we have seen, much talked and written about, its ultimate issue could by no means be predicted. In this troubled, confused, and indeterminate setting, the vision of a restored communal past seemed neither futile nor whimsical. To its opponents, certainly, it was anything but a "utopian" dream. They took it most seriously as a real and present threat to their own preponderance.

All manifestoes speak for and to "the common man," the *arme* or *gemeine mann*. "To increase the honor of God and the public weal, I, an ordinary man [*ich arm man*], make known that which shall be," writes Hans Hergot at the opening of his prophetic *New Transformation of*

---

[129] For the "Heilbronn Program" of Wendel Hipler and Friedrich Weygandt I use the text printed by Klaus Arnold, " 'Damit der arm man unnd gemeiner nutz iren furgang haben. . . .' Zum deutschen Bauernkrieg als politischer Bewegung . . . ," *Zeitschrift für historische Forschung* 9:3 (1982), 296-307. The Articles of Grievances prepared for the Diet of Meran are in Günther Franz, ed., *Quellen* No. 91, pp. 272-85. Michael Gaismair's *Landesordnung* for Tyrol of 1526 in *ibid.*, No. 92, pp. 285-90. Hans Hergot's *Von der newen Wandlung eynes Christlichen lebens* of 1526 or 1527 is printed in Adolf Laube et al., eds., *Flugschriften der Bauernkriegszeit*, 547-57. The references below are to these editions. The Bamberg articles are in StA Bamb, B48, No. 12, 1r-248r. These texts (among many others, but not the Bamberg articles) have recently been systematically interpreted by Frank Ganseuer, *Der Staat des "gemeinen Mannes." Gattungstypologie und Programmatik des politischen Schrifttums von Reformation und Bauernkrieg* (*Europäische Hochschulschriften*, Reihe III, vol. 228, Frankfurt am Main, 1984).

Christian Life.[130] Friedrich Weygandt, conveying his draft program to his collaborator Wendel Hipler, writes:

I am sending you some articles that are useful, needful, and helpful to the poor common people [*dem armen gemeinen volck*], that is to say, to burghers and peasants, for abolishing constraints and oppressions newly introduced and invented by selfish men, and to help them toward their Christian brotherly freedom.[131]

Weygandt's and Hipler's articles score the political and economic exploitation to which princes, nobles, and *grosse hanssen* subject the *arm man*, whose birthright of Christian freedom should long ago have released him from such tyranny.[132] Gaismair proposed the elimination of all "who oppress the common man,"[133] and Hergot shows marked preference in his scheme for "small villages" and obscure people "who do not think they are so clever" and, for this reason, have always been Christ's favorites.[134] A lively controversy stirs scholars in early modern German history on the referential significance of the term, *arme mann*. Who was the "common man"?[135] Most often he was the man without power (given the preconceptions of the time, it would make no sense to expect the inclusion of women in contemporary definitions), a subject who acted less than he was acted upon, member of a village commune where he might play a local political role as part of a small collective or resident of a town where important civic posts were out of his reach

[130] Hergot, p. 547. For the most recent analysis of the question of the authorship of Hergot's *Von der newen Wandlung*, see Frank Ganseuer, *Der Staat des "gemeinen Mannes"*, 465-508, and Siegfried Hoyer, "Zu den gesellschaftlichen Hintergründen der Hinrichtung Hans Hergots (1527)," *Zeitschrift für Geschichtswissenschaft* 27:2 (1979), 125-39. Ganseuer thinks that Hergot wrote only one of the four parts of the text. Hoyer eliminates Hergot as author, supposing the tract's anonymous creator to have stood closer than the Nuremberg printer and bookseller to the lower orders of society.

[131] In Arnold (as in note 129), 307.

[132] Hipler and Weygandt, 297, 306.

[133] Gaismair, article 2. Also Meran Articles Nos. 20, 40.

[134] Hergot, pp. 552, 554.

[135] This is the title of a book by Robert Hermann Lutz, *Wer war der gemeine Mann? Der dritte Stand in der Krise des Spätmittelalters* (Munich and Vienna, 1979), which is the best introduction to the controversy. I follow the views of Peter Blickle, *Die Revolution von 1525* (Munich, 1975), 178-79 (English translation: *The Revolution of 1525* [Baltimore, 1981], 122-24) as modified by Heinz Schilling, "Aufstandsbewegungen in der stadtbürgerlichen Gesellschaft des alten Reiches" in *Der deutsche Bauernkrieg 1524-1526*, ed. Hans-Ulrich Wehler (*Geschichte und Gesellschaft*, Sonderheft 1, Göttingen, 1975), 237. Also interesting: Karl Bosl, "Der kleine Mann—Die kleinen Leute," *Dona Ethnologica. Beiträge zur vergleichenden Volkskunde* (Munich, 1973), 97-111, and Horst Buszello, "Die Staatsvorstellung des 'gemeinen Mannes' im deutschen Bauernkrieg," *HZ* Beiheft 4 N.F. (1975), 273-95, especially 274.

because they were reserved to the wealthy. The vast majority of common people were peasants, but the reformers of the 1500s speak also for urban artisans and workers in the eastern mines. Depending on their particular aim, different spokesmen attached the tag to different social groups, and the term became rather blurred in the polemical and propagandistic use made of it.[136] Of the personal grievance statements handed to the Bishop of Bamberg by his subjects in 1525, many begin with a ritualistic invocation of *ich armer man*,[137] and nobles indiscriminately refer to all under their jurisdiction as *arm* or *gemein*.[138]

The common feature of all these allusions to the common man is lack of power, usually coupled with lack of status. Common folk were those who had a hard time fending for themselves in the feudal order by whose principles of organization a weak man needed a stronger as his protector. Their rights and freedoms were inferior. They were, or in any case regarded themselves as being, the victims of political and economic "innovations" which had, or were thought to have, eroded the fixed contours of their familiar world. Against these they clung to their real or imagined traditions. "Let the common man not be oppressed by any innovation against ancient tradition" was a constant refrain in grievance lists.[139] But in many cases these traditions were a feeble reed, as we have seen. A far stronger support came from a more ancient charter of freedoms, one that, like venerable traditions, was understood in the 1500s to have been corrupted by illicit *neuerungen*: the word of God revealed in the gospel. From this rich source flowed a vast increase in the emotional force of the label *armer mann*. The poor man was the *pauper*, the suffering Christian standing against the *potentes*, holders and wielders of might in the world.[140] Underdog in this life, his ultimate triumph was assured. The late medieval reform movement in all its tumultuous vehemence formed the backdrop to the scene that was now being acted out in this-worldly, not in other-worldly, terms.

While evangelical in inspiration, the reform plans of the 1520s were

---

[136] As pointed out by Heinz Schilling in *loc. cit.*, 237.

[137] Bamberg, as in note 129, *passim*.

[138] Cf. Herbert Obenaus, *Recht und Verfassung der Gesellschaften mit St. Jörgenschild in Schwaben* (Göttingen, 1961), *passim*, especially 29-38.

[139] E.g., grievances of peasant *Gerichte* in Tyrol, 1525 in Fritz Steinegger and Richard Schober eds., "Die durch den Landtag 1525 . . . erledigten 'Partikularbeschwerden' der Tiroler Bauern . . . ," *Tiroler Geschichtsquellen* No. 3 (1976), *passim*.

[140] See the interesting remarks on this by Karl Bosl, "Das Problem der Armut in der hochmittelalterlichen Gesellschaft," *Österreichische Akademie der Wissenschaften, philosophisch-historische Klasse*, Sitzungsberichte 294, Abhandlung 5 (Vienna, 1974), 5-6, and *id.*, "Kasten, Stände, Klassen im mittelalterlichen Deutschland," in *id., Die Gesellschaft in der Geschichte des Mittelalters* (2nd ed., Göttingen, 1966), 76-77.

explicitly secular in their objectives. The "new order and reformation for the benefit and advantage of all Christian brothers"[141] was to be implemented here below, not awaited in the beyond. "O God, how wretched things are in your Christian sheep-fold!" laments Hergot.[142] The only way to mend this state of wretchedness was to Christianize society. Most reformers seem to have assumed that people's attitudes and behavior would respond favorably to an improvement in the security and comfort of their circumstances.[143] The imposition on society of a new law grounded solely in the word of God,[144] humbling the proud and raising the lowly,[145] imbuing every Christian of position and property with the truth of Matthew 25:40, "as you did it to one of the least of these my brethren you did it to me"[146]—such a law would restore the communal union considered by radical reformers to be the only adequate earthly counterpart of the heavenly city. This is the perspective from which we must view the prominence given in nearly every reform program to the request for freely elected pastors "to preach to us"— that is, to every community or congregation—"the holy gospel purely and clearly without human addition, human doctrines, or human precepts."[147] "Pure" and freed from "human additions," the gospel taught people how to act as Christians. Hans Hergot finds an emblem for the resulting egalitarian association in a powerful image with which he concludes his *New Transformation*:

> There are three tables in the world, the first laid sumptuously with great abundance of good things to eat; the second set modestly, neither too much nor too little; the third meagerly, providing only scraps. And those feasting at the bountiful table came intending to take the bread from the poorest table. From this arose the struggle, and now God will smash the table of surfeit and the table of privation and make broad the table of moderation.[148]

Hergot's prophetic language[149] should not be allowed to cloud the social relevance of his vision. Apocalyptic was the style of much of the

[141] Hipler and Weygandt, p. 296.

[142] Hergot, p. 548.

[143] E.g., Hergot, p. 548, lines 8-16.

[144] Gaismair, article 3.

[145] Hergot, p. 548.

[146] Meran Articles, p. 274.

[147] From the first of the *Twelve Articles . . . of All the Peasantry* (1525) translated in Peter Blickle, *The Revolution of 1525*, 196.

[148] Hergot, p. 557.

[149] See especially the opening paragraphs of *Von der newen Wandlung*, p. 547, lines 3-4 and 11-12.

social criticism of the time. But its suggestions for reconstituting Christian society were solidly grounded in contemporary expectations. This assertion can be easily tested by scanning the hundreds of grievance statements, protests, and reform proposals generated by the revolutionary movements of the 1520s.[150]

On secular no less than on religious grounds, the hoped-for Christian society must be essentially egalitarian in its values and organization. "Christian" had a pragmatically self-serving as well as idealistic meaning in this connection. It was not only an evocative term for a brotherly, loving union among men; it also stood very practically for equal access to the necessities of life. Streams, woods, pasture, birds, fish, and game will belong to the community; what people find on or in the soil is theirs; there can be no tax or interest on what God has given to all.[151] Hergot expects that, following the great transformation, no one will ever again be able to say "this is mine."[152] Once this principle has been recognized, all trades and crafts will "again" come into the right condition, returning from the search for narrow *eigen nutz* to a generous solicitude for the common good.[153] Then, writes Hergot, "Our Lord's Prayer will at last be fulfilled and people will understand the sense of that word he used so often when he prayed to Our Father: us, us, us."[154] Individuals are humbled as the community is raised: this is preached by all reformers as a liberating message. Privileges will be abolished, for they offend the rule by which no Christian may be advantaged above his fellows.[155] City walls will be torn down and all fortified castles destroyed. (Scores of them had already fallen victim to the fury of peasant armies in 1525.) As the great cities dissolve, all will live in villages "so that distinctions shall cease among people and complete equality [*gantze glaichaitt*] exist in the land."[156] Hergot wished people to live in intimate association with their neighbors "in the manner of the Carthusians. . . . And all will work, each according to his skill and what he can do. And all things will be in common use, so that no one will be better

---

[150] See the collections by Günther Franz and by Adolf Laube *et al.*, cited in notes 41 and 92, respectively. An analysis of the many sets of articles resulting from the "Peasant War" is given by Peter Blickle, *The Revolution of 1525*, Chapters 2-3.

[151] Hergot, pp. 547, 548, 552; Meran Articles, 277; Hipler and Weygandt, 303; Bamberg, 54ʳ. The references to this point in the collections of Franz and Laube *et al.* are too numerous to be cited.

[152] Hergot, p. 547.

[153] Bamberg, 49ᵛ.

[154] Hergot, p. 549.

[155] Gaismair, Article 4.

[156] *Ibid.*, Article 5.

off than the next."[157] If anyone makes a profit, he will lend it, give it away, or "offer Christian help to his neighbor."[158] Those who have little to offer, or have suffered misfortune, will be cared for: the sick nursed, the old housed and fed, orphans trained in useful occupations, the needy supported.[159]

The minimum mandated by the Christian conscience was a fair distribution of the wealth and a redirection of social effort toward supportive caring. There may well have been grass-roots sympathy for this position. But the maximum demanded by the radical reformers was the disappearance of all distinctions between mine and thine, and in raising this egalitarian end as their goal they must have realized how far they stood in advance of their followers. It is difficult to imagine the hardpressed peasants and frugal burghers of Bamberg, to take them as an example, giving up what little they had gained in the way of rights and possessions so as to share them with others still less fortunate. But this reluctance, or resistance, could not have fatally discouraged visionaries like Hergot who knew that only a God impelled transformation—a *Wandlung*—could make a reality of his scheme.[160] "Wicked abuses," rampant now in society, were preventing people from showing each other the loving generosity demanded by the gospel.[161] Short of a miracle, only a modest change of heart could be expected, and that only after concrete improvements had been made in the external conditions of life.

If this was less than the *Wandlung* for which Hergot was waiting, it was nonetheless an ambitious and, in its own time, not unrealistic plan for creating the outward circumstances for a Christian communal association. General agreement existed on the main steps to be taken. Mercantile life needed to be controlled above all, not only to bring prices down again, but also to encourage moderation in consumption, perhaps even to encourage a gradual return to the ancient system of barter. Hergot wrote of the members of his new society that

> they will wear simple clothing, white in color, or dyed grey, black, or blue. They will eat and drink only what they are able to raise from

[157] Hergot, p. 548.

[158] Hipler and Weygandt, 306.

[159] Hergot, p. 549. See also the sermons of Johann Schwanhausen, a Lutheran preacher active in territories under the Bishop of Bamberg from 1523. Rudolf Endres, "Probleme des Bauernkriegs im Hochstift Bamberg," *Jahrbuch für fränkische Landesgeschichte* 31 (1971), 108.

[160] *Ibid.*, p. 547, lines 4-8.

[161] Meran Articles, 272.

the soil. . . . And what a man has produced from the ground, he will exchange with another man for other products.[162]

Gesellschaften—monopolistic trading companies like the firms of Fugger, Welser, Hochstetter—must be abolished altogether.[163] Strict regulations will keep merchants honest.[164] Lending at interest and jobbing will be outlawed because "the common man is everywhere grievously burdened now with jobbers and middle men who force him to buy what he needs from a third or fourth hand. This is how each man looks first to his own special interest."[165] Production will be standardized and the sale of manufactured goods controlled regionally.[166] The ideal, concludes Justus Maurer, a historian who has studied the sermons of over two hundred evangelical preachers active in towns and countryside during the years leading up to the revolution of 1525, "was agrarian and artisanal, opposed to any and all long-distance trade, and, in general against luxury in the life of the individual."[167] A simpler political organization was to bring government closer to the ordinary person.[168] In keeping with the conservative preferences of most of its members, local society would close in upon itself and keep out foreigners (*auslender*) and alien people (*fremd volck*).[169] Most proposals also show a strong animus against men of academic learning, especially lawyers, and against the enlarged authority lately given them and their bookish wisdom in the councils of state and church. As we saw in Chapter Two, the populist backlash against these unwelcome outsiders resulted in proposals for everything from total abolition of all worldly laws[170] to the drastic simplification of the legal system to make it easily and cheaply accessible to simple folk.[171] Above all, lawyers and theologians were to be kept out of princes' councils and courts[172] because, as Hergot exclaims, "learned expounders of texts have succeeded in making

[162] Hergot, p. 549.

[163] Hipler and Weygandt, 305; Meran Articles, 278.

[164] Hipler and Weygandt, 298; Meran Articles, 283. The Bamberg articles support all these measures against traders and merchants.

[165] LA Tir, *Tiroler Landtagsakten* Fasz. 375. Also Gaismair, Article 13; Meran Articles, 278.

[166] Gaismair, Article 13.

[167] Justus Maurer, *Prediger im Bauernkrieg* (Stuttgart, 1979), 71.

[168] Meran Articles, 277; Hergot, pp. 550, 552.

[169] Meran Articles, 283, 278.

[170] Hipler and Weygandt, 301; Hergot, pp. 552-53; Gaismair, Article 7.

[171] Meran Articles, 275-76, 279; Gaismair, Articles 7-12; Bamberg, *passim*.

[172] Hipler and Weygandt, 299. The authors are inconsistent and ambivalent on this point, as they approve of the retention of three doctors of law in each university for the purpose of giving legal advice to governments: *ibid.*, 299.

the whole world blind."[173] Universities should confine themselves largely to teaching God's law, for the lesson of Scripture was, to all reformers, the only worthy guide for human striving: to advance "the honor of God and the common good."[174]

The divine law as the single rule for leveling and simplifying the whole of society was the most radical reform principle to surface in the revolutionary decades of the sixteenth century. Its ubiquity and prominence reflect both the frustrations of "common" folk and the revulsion of evangelicals and Christian reformers. The former felt increasingly disenfranchised in a culture of status and privilege; the latter abhorred a world so grossly at variance with the spirit and letter of the gospel. Both were troubled by the quickening pace of society's drift toward autocratic domination. Had it succeeded in its aims, this radical ideology would have abolished the feudal system as ruthlessly as the territorial sovereign state did in fact destroy it. As a "formative, if not yet clearly formulated, principle of a new society,"[175] the argument from God's law proposed to make reality match the ideal. It set out to accomplish this goal by replacing existing structures with the Christian commune, whose ethos matched the evangelical's understanding of the New Testament, and whose imagined place in history as the oldest social organization pointed to that reversal of the direction of historical change which all reformers considered a necessary precondition of reformation. The "peasant revolution" gave it a brief moment of prominence in the manifestoes of Gaismair, Hergot, and a few others. But that revolution's swift and conclusive defeat killed any chance of altering society along the lines suggested by the visionaries of 1525. Their elimination left the territorial state as the only transforming agent in a position to undertake the final dissolution of feudal society.

[173] Hergot, p. 555.
[174] Hergot, pp. 549, 550, 551; Gaismair, Article 13.
[175] Peter Blickle, *Die Revolution von 1525*, 181.

CHAPTER FIVE

Law and Politics: The New State

IN THE first quarter of the sixteenth century, the German territorial principality stood ready to complete the dismantling of the feudal system. Roman law was foremost among the tools available for the work of demolition, helping convert medieval structures marked by personalism and fragmentation into the politics of a modern state based on territorial integrity, permanent institutions, a standing bureaucracy, and the resolute exercise of sovereign prerogatives.[1] Ideologically, this transformation rested on the state's insistence that it spoke for justice (*Recht*), equality (*gleichheit, aequitas*), and the common good (*gemeiner nutz*):[2] hence the emphasis on "common" laws over privilege and particular "rights" and the boast, often heard from rulers and their agents—especially in the decades of the early Reformation, when religion was included among the requisites of *salus publica*[3]—that they alone stood high enough above *eigennutz* to govern in the interest of general and long-term goals. Jurists gave this claim the ring of legal authority. "Laws and statutes, no matter how useful to the common good, bear no fruit unless an executive power [*obrigkeit*] enforces them," declared Andreas Perneder at the opening of his *Institutiones*. "Thus we may say with good reason that responsibility for the common good and the general welfare rests entirely and solely with these executive powers."[4] Common good and general welfare demanded

[1] Theodor Mayer, "Die Ausbildung der Grundlagen des modernen deutschen Staates im hohen Mittelalter" in Hellmut Kämpf ed., *Herrschaft und Staat im Mittelalter* (*Wege der Forschung* 11 Darmstadt, 1974), 284-331; *id., Fürsten und Staat. Studien zur Verfassungsgeschichte des deutschen Mittelalters* (Weimar, 1950), 310; Otto Brunner, "Vom Gottesgnadentum zum monarchischen Prinzip" in *id., Neue Wege der Verfassungs- und Sozialgeschichte* (Göttingen, 1968), 170.

[2] See the interesting interpretation of the evidence from coins and medals by Guido Kisch, *Recht und Gerechtigkeit in der deutschen Medaillenkunst* (*Abhandlungen der Heidelberger Akademie der Wissenschaften, philosophisch-historische Klasse,* Jahrgang 1955-1956 (1956), 65-66, 93-105.

[3] Walther Merk, *Der Gedanke des gemeinen Besten in der deutschen Staats- und Rechtsentwicklung* (originally published 1934; Darmstadt, 1968), 62.

[4] Andreas Perneder, *Institutiones. Auszug und Anzeigung etlicher geschrieben kayserlichen . . . Rechte . . .* (Ingolstadt, 1573), 1ʳ.

above all other things the protective shield of "good government" (*gute policey*) and a sound "order" (*ordnung*). Rulers therefore pleaded "the maintenance of good administration and good order"[5] as justification for any and all aggrandizing actions. *Policey* was broadened in its meaning to denote, as well as the form or constitution of a government (*politia*), the "rules and regulations laid down for a city or a territory and binding on all their subjects for the purpose of securing peace and order in society."[6] Immensely wordy *Policey-Ordnungen*, issued everywhere in the later sixteenth and the seventeenth centuries, attempted to reach this objective by conforming the entire body public to common standards of approved conduct.

By the middle of the century, the image of a body public had become concrete enough to be hypostatized and given an identifying label. *Wesen* (being, or entity, but also meaning "establishment") was used with increasing frequency in political and legal documents to refer to the structure of a state, now meaning the collectivity of subjects, now indicating the administrative apparatus governing them.[7] Together with estates meeting in their diets—medieval survivals into the new age—this apparatus, headed by its sovereign, constituted the early modern state. Every contemporary observer recognized in the uneasy coexistence of these two forces the distinguishing quality of the sixteenth-century constitution. "God confirms and upholds worldly governments [*Regiment*] as part of his creation and ordained order," wrote Justin Gobler in a passage already quoted in another context, "including the estates, which are a necessary part of these governments."[8] Gobler's abstract language mirrors his academic detachment. Others, especially if they were directly embroiled in the tug of war between estates and princes, viewed the mutual antagonism of the two powers with less equanimity. A voice from the next century, when the issue had been resolved in most territories, evokes the spirit of rivalry more vividly. In 1651, near the end of his long reign, Duke Maximilian I of Ba-

---

[5] "... zu erhaltung guter policey und ordnung. ...." From response by the Bishop of Bamberg to grievances voiced at a *Rittertag* in 1534. StA Bamb B28, no pagination.

[6] Johann Heinrich Zedler ed., *Grosses Universal-Lexicon* ... vol. 28 (Leipzig and Halle, 1741), 1503.

[7] E.g., explanation of a new forest constitution for Tyrol, as "... dem ganzen wesen zu segen gemaint." LA Tir *Tiroler Landtagsakten*, Fasz. 10 for year 1603. For the rapidly spreading use of the term "state" in southern and western Europe, see Quentin Skinner, *The Foundations of Modern Political Thought* (Cambridge, 1978) II, 352-57.

[8] Justin Gobler, *Der Rechten Spiegel* (Frankfurt am Main, 1550), quoted in Hans Hattenhauer, *Geschichte des Beamtentums* (*Handbuch des öffentlichen Dienstes* I, Cologne, 1980), 45.

varia composed a memorandum of instructions for his wife. Commenting on the duchy's estates, he wrote:

> There exist in nearly all states a contrariety and opposition between territorial princes and estates [*Landtschafften*] arising from their special interests. In pursuing these interests, the estates attempt at all times to increase and extend their liberties [*Libertet*], privileges, and freedoms and to evade the burdens, taxes, and contributions for which people are rightfully in debt to their territorial ruler; or they try to lessen these obligations by every sort of device. . . . Thus the gain of one party in the state is always the loss of the other. For this reason I think it prudent to convoke no diets unless pressing grounds exist for doing so, as most diets will produce little more than expressions of grievances and submission of new propositions from the estates, and although these occasionally yield grants of money and lead to assumptions of debts, they also extract from us additional privileges and concessions, which contribute to the prince's enduring impairment, harm, and injury.[9]

In his own time, Maximilian's simple prescription for keeping estates on a short leash was no longer unrealistic. This is because the delicate balance (called "dualism" in historical literature) between *Regiment* and *Stände* shifted in the course of the sixteenth century in favor of the former as more and more of the instruments of real power came into the ruler's hands. "Among the spiritual as among the secular," the same Maximilian had written to his father, Wilhelm V, in 1596, "what counts nowadays is *ragion di stato*. Only he is respected who has much land or a great deal of money."[10] With the criteria of political survival stripped to such basic elements, the way was clear for the absorption of particular into general interests and for the reduction, ultimately the annihilation, of private and corporate rights by *raison d'état* embodied in a princely ruler.[11]

---

[9] Text of Maximilian's *Information* in Christian Ruepprecht, "Die Information des Kurfürsten Maximilian I von Bayern für seine Gemahlin vom 13. März 1651," *Oberbayerisches Archiv für vaterländische Geschichte* 49 (1895-1896), 311-20. Reference is to 317-18. See also F. L. Carsten, *Princes and Parliaments in Germany from the Fifteenth to the Eighteenth Centuries* (Oxford, 1959), 404.

[10] BHStA Mu *Fürstensachen* 427, 38ʳ.

[11] Peter Blickle describes the transition from *Ständestaat* to *Fürstenstaat* as follows: "Der Ständestaat hebt sich von seinem Vorgänger, dem mittelalterlichen Staat ab durch seine grössere Perfektibilität, seine Rationalität, seine stärkere Herrschaftsintensität, durch funktionierende, vom Beamtentum getragene Institutionen, durch die Einheitlichkeit des Rechts. Der Staat . . . ist gekennzeichnet . . . durch eine ungemeine Steigerung der politischen Intensität und des staatlichen Bewusstseins, die zu einem erhöhten Macht-

Territorial sovereignty (*Landeshoheit*), the legal and political center of gravity of reason of state in its German variety, was the end product of a slow process of piecemeal conquest and acquisition in the course of which hereditary heads of the empire's larger duchies and counties brought significant accretions of lands, resources, and jurisdictions into their own hands. In doing so, they created the semblance of unitary states in which legally established authority was exercised by stable institutions on behalf of a dynastically secure prince upon the subjects of an integrated territory—a *territorium clausum*.[12] Aiming at complete domination of a limited geographical space (without, however, actually possessing the capacity for reaching this goal), the successful territorial prince fused the proliferation of rights, immunities, and prerogatives held or acquired by him into a single source of sovereign authority that, in theory if not quite in reality, gave him preponderance of power, *superioritas territorialis* (a legal and political concept later—in the seventeenth century—inflated into *summa potestas* and *maiestas*).[13] Legal and administrative jurisdictions were inseparable in the exercise of this greatly enlarged authority. As *Landesherr, dominus* or *princeps terrae, Landesfürst*, the prince considered himself responsible for high (i.e., capital) justice, taxation, the preservation of peace internally and the conduct of a more or less wide-ranging policy in the empire and with other European states, the stimulation of profitable (i.e., taxable) economic activities and the promotion of agriculture, the founding and

---

willen führen. Daneben und demgegenüber steht das Ständewesen, das sich in den Landtagen organisiert und sich seine eigenen Institutionen schafft und zwar in einem Umfang, der die Geschichtsschreibung veranlasst hat, nicht nur vom Ständestaat, sondern vom dualistischen Ständestaat zu sprechen. Dieser Staat findet seine höchste Entfaltung im 15./16. Jahrhundert. . . . Bald jedoch wird die Zweiheit zum Antagonismus, denn das Fürstentum ist seit dem 17. Jahrhundert . . . das entwicklungsfähigere Element des Staates. Gelegentlich gelingt es dem Fürsten allein den Staat zu verkörpern." *Landschaften im alten Reich* (Munich, 1973), 33-34.

[12] *Territorium clausum* refers to the inclusion in the territory of lesser authorities such as knights and monasteries. Theoretically, every subject is *in territorio incluso*, but this was rarely true in actuality. For an excellent brief survey of the problems and literature relating to the creation of the sovereign territorial state in medieval Germany, see Heinrich Mitteis, *Deutsche Rechtsgeschichte* (11th ed. by Heinz Lieberich, Munich, 1969), 167-76, 216-21; also the books by Theodor Mayer and Otto Brunner given in note 1 above. See also Gerhard Oestreich, "Ständetum und Staatsbildung in Deutschland" in *id., Geist und Gestalt des frühmodernen Staates* (Berlin, 1969), 279-89.

[13] On this and all other points concerning the legal basis of politics in early modern Germany, see the excellent and profusely documented book by Dietmar Willoweit, *Rechtsgrundlagen der Territorialgewalt. Landesobrigkeit, Herrschaftsrechte und Territorium in der Rechtswissenschaft der Neuzeit* (Cologne and Vienna, 1975). Passages referred to are on 126-51.

funding of universities and schools, close supervision of church administration and the direction of religious policy, the maintenance of an armed force adequate at least for defense, and the upkeep of a court whose greater or lesser splendor depended, like every other aspect of his rule, on the prince's ability to raise or borrow money. We shall see in a later chapter how rulers proposed to achieve these self-assigned tasks, and what organizational means they favored in their attempt to change the order of politics. Among the more prominent of the states undergoing this transmogrification in the late middle ages (when the absence of a strong monarchical presence at the center of the empire created favorable conditions for concentrations of regional power) were the electorate and duchy of Saxony, the duchies of Bavaria, Württemberg, Brunswick, Austria and Carinthia, the Palatine electorate, the Landgraviate of Hessen, the County of Tyrol, and the Prince-Bishoprics of Münster, Bamberg, Magdeburg, Trier, and Würzburg. Together with populous and wealthy city states like Nuremberg, Augsburg, Ulm, Strasbourg, and Frankfurt, these sovereign principalities formed the political arenas in which nearly all of the sixteenth century's memorable constitutional, social, and ecclesiastical events were staged.

To a very large extent, these developments turned on legal questions, and this explains the highly visible part played by lawyers in the expansion of sovereign authority—everywhere in Europe, and in the Holy Roman Empire in particular. Their training and experience, and the attitudes toward politics and society they gained in consequence of these, made lawyers into effective "technicians of politics and administration," as they have been called.[14] They became indispensable to rulers whose internal as well as external affairs were, in an age of aggressive power politics, conducted as exercises in adversary relations. A dynamic strategy was essential to all states in their effort to absorb remaining enclaves of feudal independence and incorporate hitherto immune ecclesiastical jurisdictions. Lawyers were needed for the preparation and presentation of the legal arguments in which this endeavor had to be grounded. They also served as emissaries and diplomats, acting for their principals with a confidence of bearing born of their mastery of a legal science then gaining universal recognition. They lectured to princes on the *corpus iuris*, hoping to instill in them the Roman law's admirable principles of justice and fairness along with its pronounced sense of authority and majesty. Heirs to princely thrones attended university, where they sat at the feet of renowned teachers of

[14] Carlo M. Cipolla, "The Professions: The Long View," *The Journal of European Economic History* 2 (1973), 49.

law.[15] The jurist's model of a sound political jurisprudence was the leg-islation of late medieval Italian city states whose *freyhait* (in this case meaning self-determination) was such that—in words written by a counsel to the city of Nuremberg in 1516—"they recognize neither em-peror nor pope as their superior."[16] This view of the city republic as a sovereign entity whose independence was codified in positive law[17] proved formative for German jurists, who not only cited the Italian ex-ample as prototype and precedent,[18] but also adopted as their own po-sition the Italian lawyers' activist approach to statecraft[19]—all under the aegis of a broad concept of *salus publica* closely identified with the autonomous state personified by a dynastic ruler or a magistral elite.[20] The use of Roman and Italian terms to describe German conditions be-gan to shape the self-perception, and therefore the actions, of princes and magistrates. When *Landeshoheit* was declared to be *merum et mixtum imperium*, and decisions of municipal councillors (*senatores*) were labelled a *senatus consulta* to be executed by a *praetor* (né *Schultheiss*), more than terminology was being altered.[21]

[15] See the preface dated 1544 by Wolfgang Hunger to Andreas Perneder's *Institu-tiones*,)(iii^v. Hunger a *doctor iuris* and law professor at the University of Ingolstadt, was commissioned by Duke Wilhelm IV of Bavaria to read Justinian's *corpus iuris* "in offener schul" to his son, the future Albrecht V. This tradition was continued in Bavaria. Wil-helm V was educated by the humanist-jurists Dr. Michael Volckhamer and Dr. Michael Heumair. Wilhelm's son, Maximilian, studied in Ingolstadt in 1589-1590 where his teacher was the doctor of both laws Johann Baptist Fickler. See Helmut Dotterweich, *Der junge Maximilian* (Munich, 1962), 28, 113-18. Dotterweich gives an interesting descrip-tion of the course of studies followed by Maximilian and his tutor.

[16] StA Nbg *Ratschlaghücher* No. 1, 87^r.

[17] Cf. Lauro Martines, *Lawyers and Statecraft in Renaissance Florence* (Princeton, 1968), 436-37. Also Otto Brunner, *Land und Herrschaft. Grundfragen der territorialen Verfassungsgeschichte Österreichs im Mittelalter* (5th ed., Vienna, 1965), 392-93.

[18] This assertion is based on my examination of the memoranda of legal and political advice written throughout the sixteenth century by Nuremberg *Ratskonsulenten*, legal advisers—seven to nine in number—who gave solicited opinions on all matters, public and private, coming before the Council. The *Ratschlagbücher* contain fair copies of memoranda submitted by the individual *Konsulenten*. The opinions are written in lay-man's language and are held to practical terms. From the mid-1520s on, requests for opinions were also made of the city's theologians, and the *Ratschlagbücher* contain their views also. Many of the jurists' opinions make reference to how things were done "in welschen landen": e.g., StA Nbg, *Ratschlagbücher* No. 3, 22^r, 24^v.

[19] Lauro Martines, *op. cit.*, 412.

[20] Gerhard Oestreich, "Ständetum und Staatsbildung" in *loc. cit.* and in Heinz Rausch ed., *Die geschichtlichen Grundlagen der modernen Volksvertretung* II: *Reichsstände und Landstände* (Darmstadt, 1974), 52.

[21] This point is made, with examples by Otto Stobbe, *Geschichte der deutschen Rechtsquellen* II (Braunschweig, 1864; reprint Aalen, 1965), 123-24. For a lengthy *con-*

In more concrete ways centralization was advanced by the jurists' partiality for an administrative system of regular channels of competence leading to superior organs of authority situated at the ruler's court. An orderly and standardized network of legal and administrative jurisdictions was the heart of the sixteenth-century state. It represented the bureaucratic ideal of enduring institutions independent of the more or less fortuitous presence of a strong head of state.[22] This system also gave best assurance of the permanence of changes made, for—as Max Weber has pointed out—once it is firmly in place, bureaucracy is the hardest of all social structures to destroy.[23] To the extent that political ties permitted it, governmental processes were depersonalized. In the new state in the making, the objective legal order mattered more than its citizens' subjective rights.[24] A later chapter will show how administrative reorganization encouraged, and was in turn reinforced by, the state's involvement with the Reformation. We shall also gain some impressions of the new bureaucracy in action, and of the ambivalent, more often hostile, reaction to it by those with traditions and rights to protect. At this point in the argument it needs only to be reaffirmed that Roman law and its learned jurists and lesser attendants were important, probably essential, agents at the center of the momentum gathered by the new state. When the eighteenth-century constitutional lawyer Johann Jacob Moser described such professional boosters of the strong state (whom he disliked in his own time) as "a guild of sovereignty mongers"[25] he coined an apt epithet. It was not that lawyers were inevitably on the side of central power. We shall meet some who were active in opposing it. But by and large professional men trained in the principles of Roman law and Italian jurisprudence saw greatest merit in the case for a strong, centralized, tightly administrated, aggressively directed state. Whether arguing for primogeniture as the basis of territory-wide political stability[26] or defending taxation as the ex-

---

silium on a late-fifteenth-century government's use of the imperium, see StA Nbg *Ratschlagbücher* 2*, 174r

[22] Jürgen Bücking, *Frühabsolutismus und Kirchenreform in Tirol (1565-1665)* (Wiesbaden, 1972), 4.

[23] From Chapter 6 of Part II of Weber's *Wirtschaft und Gesellschaft* in *From Max Weber*, eds. H. H. Gerth and C. Wright Mills (New York, 1946), 228. See also G. E. Aylmer, "Bureaucracy" in Peter Burke, ed., *The New Cambridge Modern History* 13: "Companion Volume" (Cambridge, 1979).

[24] Max Weber in *loc. cit.*, 239.

[25] "Souveränitätsmacherzunft." Johann Jacob Moser, *Neues Teutsches Staatsrecht* (Frankfurt and Leipzig, 1766-1775) XIII, 1187.

[26] Cf. Joan Thirsk, "The European Debate on Custom of Inheritance, 1500-1700" in

clusive prerogative of the central power,[27] lawyers devoted their sharpest arguments and their most persuasive rhetoric to the material growth and ideological reinforcement of state power.

THE union of lawyers and the state was several centuries in the making,[28] but by the 1500s it had become the distinctive feature of political life. Their theoretical learning in a science considered crucial to the governing process, and their practical judicial and administrative know-how, gave jurists enormous influence in state affairs as rulers turned to them for assistance on all matters touching law, justice, and public policy. This growing involvement was of the greatest consequence to the unfolding of modern political society. To the day-by-day operation of the new judicial and administrative councils, which—from about the middle of the century—also included organs of church government, they became virtually indispensable as both thinkers and doers. Having drafted "reformed" law codes for their employers, "distinguished legal experts and experienced members of our central and provincial councils also serving on our law faculties and superior courts"[29] stayed on to perform sensitive and confidential governmental duties. In many places their growing number and prominence can be traced in lists of "*doctores* attached to our court" given in the house constitutions (*Hofordnungen*) of German principalities.[30] Crowding "non-learned" (*ungelert*) councillors from their accustomed posts, lawyers came to dom-

---

Jack Goody, Joan Thirsk, E. P. Thompson, eds., *Family and Inheritance* (Cambridge, 1976), 177-91, especially 183.

[27] Leonhard von Eck, the Bavarian chancellor, engaged the Bavarian estates in a confrontational argument over this prerogative in 1535. See Stefan Weinfurter, "Herzog, Adel und Reformation," *Zeitschrift für historische Forschung* 10:1 (1983), 17. The first time the Roman law argument was used in Bavaria to claim exclusive taxing rights for the prince was in 1488 when Dr. Johann Neuhauser, acting for Albrecht IV at a *Landtag* in Munich, denied the validity of nobles' *Freiheitsbriefe* granting freedom from taxation. See Hans Spangenberg, *Vom Lehnstaat zum Ständestaat* (Munich, 1912; reprint Aalen, 1964), 171-72.

[28] E. H. Kantorowicz, "Kingship under the Impact of Scientific Jurisprudence" in *id., Selected Studies* (Locust Valley, N.Y., 1965), 154-59. For an early example in Germany of the replacement of lay by learned councillors, see Hermann Heimpel on Job Vener's activity as chancellery secretary and council member in the administration of King Rupprecht in Heidelberg in the early years of the fifteenth century. *Die Vener von Gmünd und Strassburg 1162-1447* (Göttingen, 1982), 189-91.

[29] From the Electoral Saxon *Reformation* of 1572 printed in Franz Beyerle, et al., *Quellen zur neueren Privatrechtsgeschichte Deutschlands* I² (Weimar, 1938), 257. The quoted phrase recurs often in the introductions to other "reformations."

[30] As in the Archbishopric of Mainz, where the *Hofordnung* of 1541 shows an increase in the number of *doctores* employed as *Räte*. See Hans Goldschmidt, *Zentralbehörden und Beamtentum im Kurfürstentum Mainz vom 16. bis zum 18. Jahrhundert* (Berlin and

inate governmental operations while inevitably making bitter enemies of those whom they replaced. In Tyrol, for example, where a small number of *Landherren*—noble land owners—and *Gelehrte*—men with law doctorates, generally of burgher background—coexisted uneasily, and clashed frequently, in the archduke's privy council, representatives of the nobility complained formally in the early 1570s that "if more attention is not paid to the old usages and customs in matters touching our country, we, who have no experience in the written law, will in time become useless to the state [*Wesen*]. For," they continue,

> we are now regularly outvoted by the learned of whom there are twice as many in the council as there are of us, and who are always the first to vote, through which practice our territorial constitution, as well as our old customs and liberties, are being brought to a very great decline.[31]

The distaste of nobles for sitting on appellate courts and serving on central administrative councils—often mentioned and much criticized at the time, and frequently used as justification for removing them altogether—and their dismal record of absenteeism from the offices they did accept were a direct result of frustrations suffered in trying to keep up with professional men much more competent in meeting the demands of an increasingly complex job.[32] Territorial rulers like Ferdinand II of Tyrol, who saw in hereditary nobilities the chief obstacles to the well-governed state, did little to alleviate their chagrin.[33] Nor was it reasonable to expect laymen, no matter how well born, to match the

Leipzig, 1908), 25-37. The close connection between law faculties and high politics is illustrated, for Bavaria, by an interesting set of records showing appointments to state office in the seventeenth century: BHStA Mu G.L.446. Almost every man named is a *doctor*, and many move back and forth between Ingolstadt and the *Hofrat* in Munich.

[31] From a set of memoranda addressed to Ferdinand II in 1571, quoted in Tullius von Sartori-Montecroce, *Über die Reception der fremden Rechte in Tirol und die Tiroler Landesordnungen (Beiträge zur österreichischen Reichs- und Rechtsgeschichte* I, Innsbruck, 1895), 66. For the political background to this altercation, see Joseph Hirn, *Erzherzog Ferdinand II von Tirol. Geschichte seiner Regierung und seiner Länder* (Innsbruck, 1885-1888) I, 463-68.

[32] E.g., the reply by Elector August of Saxony in 1555 to knights and cities who had complained of the lack of lay persons on the electorate's *Hofrat* and other bodies: "His Electoral Grace would like nothing better than to have nobles on his court. It is well known, however, that those who serve become objects of their fellow nobles' contempt. For this reason most members of the nobility do not wish to be appointed, and His Electoral Grace has had to find good people elsewhere. If any noble is found who does not refuse to serve, and if he is competent, His Grace will appoint him before anyone else." StA Dr, Loc 9350 No. 10, 3r and v.

[33] Joseph Hirn, *op. cit.* II, 17.

jurist's skills. In the course of the sixteenth century the prerequisites for top-level posts in state service became ever more exacting. The just-mentioned Archduke Ferdinand of Tyrol, for instance, saw fit to reject a candidate who, though he had studied law in Italy, France, and Germany, had a year's experience at the Imperial Chamber Court, and spoke French, did not possess a degree. High administrative positions, the duke said, should go to none but holders of the doctorate, with several years' practical experience working for other princes and lords, and with good proficiency in Latin and at least one modern foreign tongue.[34] This was the ideal type of a "good administrator." A sufficient number of men of such accomplishment in a prince's service made his state a "good government." Immediate practical problems, however, nearly always interfered with the realization of this ideal. The chronic need for money often put offices on the auction block, as when Albrecht V of Bavaria, ordinarily a "good administrator" himself, approved the appointment to a councillorship of a nobleman willing to pay the handsome sum of two thousand gulden for the post in 1572. "As there is no money to be had from any other source," wrote Albrecht, "we have no choice but to make do with this man."[35] Although this happened with distressing frequency, many court and administrative posts did come into the hands of qualified and motivated officials in the later decades of the sixteenth century. Against such competitors, laymen—particularly rural people—stood little chance of advancing their own interests. Not until they themselves were represented, and their assemblies spoken for, by advocates of comparable skill was the distance between them and their antagonists narrowed. Even then, the professional man's natural facility at networking (*freundt und verwandtschafft* in sixteenth-century parlance)[36] put laymen at a distinct disadvantage.

The Austrian duchies under their Habsburg rulers provided German territories with the model of an "improved" political system. Under Archduke, later Emperor, Ferdinand, who was able to build on organizational foundations laid down by his predecessor Maximilian, Austria was given governmental organs that became typical for the empire's principalities: a central aulic council (*Hofrat*) supported by a chancellery divided into several secretariats, a central financial organization, a central war office, and, in the outlying regions, "governments" (*Regierungen*) presided over by appointed councillors who

[34] Mentioned in Tullius von Sartori-Montecroce, *op. cit.*, 70.
[35] BHStA Mu *Fürstensachen* 352, 52ʳ.
[36] E.g., HStA St A34, Bü 1c, No. 1.

were supported by a "chamber procurator"—always a *iuris doctor*—
to look out for the sovereign's fiscal and legal interests.[37] The chief aims
served by these institutions became the organizing principles of other
states as well: to centralize the territory's administration on the constitutional basis of a uniform law, to effect collegiality in the operation of
all important administrative bodies as the best guarantee of fair and
uniform procedures, and to increase the efficiency of financial organs
by making them semi-autonomous.[38] As such organizational objectives
encouraged a high level of specialization in the assigning of official responsibilities, and as traditional office holders were not ordinarily fully
adequate to these new tasks, it is not surprising that responsible positions fell into the hands of jurists who, by the 1550s, became pervasive
in the administration of the Austrian duchies.

A similar development occurred in the Landgraviate of Hessen. From
the 1520s "learned" councillors were distinguished there from "non-
learned" ones in the official job lists. The predominance of the former
under Landgrave Philip was owing to a prominent group of doctors of
civil and canon law who sat on the central appellate court in Marburg.
They, in turn, moved the appointment of jurists also to other government positions. On this foundation a professional bureaucracy was
built,[39] and law degrees were made essential for aspirants to its higher
echelons. In Germany as in the south, the Italian proverb "Chi non ha
Azzo, non vada in palazzo"[40] (referring to a seminal thirteenth-century
figure who had helped establish the modern profession of jurisprudence) epitomized the indispensability of legal expertise in politics. A
roll of "learned" aulic councillors employed in the Duchy of Bavaria
shows a marked rise in the number of doctors of law and licentiates between 1490 and 1517; many of these men had degrees from Bologna,
Padua, or Siena.[41] Among the varieties of learning brought by Bavarian
councillors to their office, jurisprudence was by far the most widely

[37] Eduard Rosenthal, "Die Behördenorganisation Kaiser Ferdinand I. Das Vorbild der
Verwaltungsorganisation in den deutschen Territorien," *Archiv für österreichische Geschichte* 69 (1887), 53-315.

[38] *Ibid.*, 57-58.

[39] Franz Gundlach, *Die hessischen Zentralbehörden von 1247 bis 1604* (*Veröffentlichungen der historischen Kommission für Hessen und Waldeck* XVI Marburg, 1930) I,
106-292.

[40] Quoted in Heinrich Mitteis, *Deutsche Rechtsgeschichte*, 201.

[41] The names and vital statistics of these men are given by Heinz Lieberich, "Die gelehrten Räte. Staat und Juristen in der Frühzeit der Rezeption," *Zeitschrift für bayerische
Landesgeschichte* 27 (1964), 147-89. Even before 1490, a significant number of canon
lawyers joined the duke's *Hofrat*, thus increasing the number of clerics relative to the
number of lay councillors. Italian degrees were in evidence elsewhere as well. In Würt-

represented discipline, even among clerical members.[42] As we have noted before, the study of law was becoming the surest path for men of modest origins to high position in the world of great affairs, usually by way of attachment to a prince or to magistrates of a major city. The founding of the University of Ingolstadt in 1472 enabled young Bavarians to gain their legal training at home instead of seeking it abroad; from then on the dukes could fill their need for trained administrators without violating the constitutional demand that preference be given to men of regional origin.[43]

Men prepared in this fashion staffed key posts in the Bavarian central and provincial administration, the creation of which around the middle of the sixteenth century marked the duchy's transition from its medieval to its modern condition.[44] After the 1550s, the Bavarian aulic council (*Hofrat*), until then the sole organ of political direction at the center of the duchy's affairs, split into specialized sections attending to finance, judicial affairs, church and religion, and war. Each division acquired a professional staff, as did agencies supervising the new direct and indirect taxes developed to meet the steeply rising cost of big government. In each of the five *Rentämter* forming the government of Bavarian regions, a *Rentmeister*, assisted locally by *Pfleger* and *Amtmänner*, had supervision of law and order, trade and commerce, coinage and finance, education and religious affairs. Only the ducal court could overrule the decisions of this official, whose annual month-long *Umritt*, a journey of inspection through his district, protocolled huge masses of data on every aspect of public and private life. This kind of information, about which more will be said later in this chapter, was second only to money as the vital nerve of the well-governed state. The coercive uses to which it could be put helped rulers in their undertaking to weaken private customs in favor of common and normative standards. A code of written laws was always the first step in this course of action, and men whose minds had been shaped by the study of this kind

temberg—a Protestant state—ten of the *gelehrte Räte* employed by the duke at the end of the sixteenth century had studied in Italy. See James A. Vann, *The Making of a State. Württemberg 1593-1793* (Ithaca, N.Y., 1984), 82.

[42] Heinz Lieberich in *loc. cit.*, 133-35.

[43] The Bavarian *Landesordnung* of 1501 stipulated that more "natives" than *doctores* were to sit on the duchy's superior court. See Eduard Rosenthal, *Geschichte des Gerichtswesens und der Verwaltungsorganisation Baierns* (Würzburg, 1889-1906) II, 145-47.

[44] For the details of what follows on Bavaria, see *ibid.* I (to the end of the reign of Wilhelm V) and II (beginning with Maximilian I); also Max Spindler, ed., *Handbuch der bayerischen Geschichte* (Munich, 1967-1975) II, 545-51; Hans Hornung, *Beiträge zur inneren Geschichte Bayerns vom 16.-18. Jahrhundert aus den Umrittsprotokollen der Rentmeister des Rentamtes Burghausen* (Munich, 1915), 7-25.

of law made the ablest and most willing agents. As office holders (*Amt-leute*) by vocation and training, their primary loyalty was to their principal. In the words of Archduke Ferdinand of Austria, they acted not as representatives of private interests but "only as our own councillors and servants."[45]

In Württemberg, where the fifteenth-century administration of Count (later Duke) Eberhard the Bearded had been largely dominated by nobles,[46] jurists were appointed by his sixteenth-century successors to help with their—ultimately unsuccessful—attempts to consolidate administration in a series of interlocking councils, chancelleries, and *Balleien*, and to curtail the role of the territorial estates in the making of policy.[47] Walter Bernhardt's prosopography of the duchy's governmental personnel shows for the later sixteenth century a steady rise in the number of jurists and men with judicial experience, especially during the reigns of Duke Christoph, 1550-1568, and Duke Friedrich, 1593-1608.[48] Because the central administrative organ, the *Oberrat*, was also the country's high court of justice, jurists played from the beginning a prominent part in this body's deliberations. Most members of its expanding staff of rapporteurs, assistants, and secretaries also had enjoyed legal training,[49] as had the officers of financial organs which, as in the case of Bavaria, proliferated in proportion to Württemberg's growing need for revenue. Roman law was from early in the century the government's law of choice. Even the Tübingen contract of 1514, the duchy's basic law, negotiated during an earlier time of estates ascendancy, while affirming "justice" and "due process" as guarantees of judicial fairness, qualified this concession to indigenous liberties by exempting "cases in which the imperial law permits us [i.e., the dukes] to do otherwise."[50] In Saxony, too, territory-wide legislation sought with the aid of jurist-bureaucrats to elaborate and solidify a bureau-

[45] Quoted in Eduard Rosenthal, "Die Behördenorganisation Kaiser Ferdinand I . . ." in *loc. cit.*, 68. On the development of officialdom in Germany, particularly in Prussia, see Erich Wyluda, *Lehnrecht und Beamtentum. Studien zur Entstehung des preussischen Beamtentums* (Berlin, 1969).

[46] Fritz Ernst, *Eberhard im Bart. Die Politik eines deutschen Landesherrn am Ende des Mittelalters* (Stuttgart, 1933; reprint Darmstadt, 1970), 16-20, 65-77, 102-06.

[47] Irmgard Kothe, *Der fürstliche Rat in Württemberg im 15. und 16. Jahrhundert* (Stuttgart, 1938); Walter Bernhardt, *Die Zentralbehörden des Herzogtums Württemberg und ihre Beamten 1520-1629* (Veröffentlichungen der Kommission für geschichtliche Landeskunde in Baden-Württemberg) 70-71 (Stuttgart, 1972-1973) I, 16-64.

[48] See the tabulation in *ibid.* II, 746-804.

[49] *Ibid.* I, 16-31.

[50] *Württembergische Landtagsakten* 1. Reihe I (ed. Wilhelm Ohr and Erich Kober, Stuttgart, 1913), 230.

cratic structure. A *Landesordnung* promulgated by the Elector August in 1555 touched most aspects of political, social, and religious life in the land and created supervisory organs to ensure compliance.[51] A stream of subsequent decrees kept up the pressure on the population.

Lawyers proved no less helpful to the magistrates of independent cities whose far-flung commercial contacts and involvement with the courts and governments of princely territories and the empire enmeshed them in ceaseless litigation. Although entrusted with important administrative positions,[52] jurists were generally confined to advisory functions in municipal government. According to a Nuremberg decree of 1497, *doctores* were allowed "solely to give advice, never to be a judge, never to vote, and never to make up a majority on any body."[53] The old distrust of the legal personality was at work when graduate jurists were permanently banned from membership in the city's governing council.[54] Nonetheless, the Nuremberg situation shows clearly how essential lawyers had become to the operations of so sophisticated a political apparatus as the government of an independent city. Jurists had advised Nuremberg councillors since the thirteen hundreds.[55] A century later the team of judicial advisers had risen from six to twenty-one.[56] The records of these legal consultants bear witness to their intimate involvement as policy experts on both large and small affairs. Their counsel ranged from the question of Nuremberg's acceptance of the Lutheran Reformation and her delicate relations with Catholic and Protestant states in consequence of this step, to trivial instances of public drunkenness and a cow injured by the collapse of a neighbor's wall. The common factor in all these cases, the weighty and the petty ones, was the need to protect and, where possible, to enlarge the state's sovereignty, judicial independence, and freedom of action. Possessing the *merum et mixtum imperium* of an autonomous power, as the jurists assured the councillors,[57] the latter must never "unbuckle their sword

[51] Woldemar Goerlitz, *Staat und Stände unter den Herzögen Albrecht und Georg 1485-1539 (Sächsische Landtagsakten* I, Leipzig and Berlin, 1928), 193-228.

[52] E.g., Gerd Wunder, *Die Bürger von Hall. Sozialgeschichte einer Reichsstadt 1216-1802* (Sigmaringen, 1980), 123-25.

[53] Friedrich Wolfgang Ellinger, *Die Juristen der Reichsstadt Nürnberg vom 15. bis zum 17. Jahrhundert* (Erlangen dissertation, 1950), 35.

[54] Helmut Wachauf, however, argues that the Nuremberg ban was primarily owing to the fact that jurists ranked socially as nobles and the Nuremberg council restricted membership to burghers. *Nürnberger Bürger als Juristen* (Erlangen, 1972), 74-76.

[55] All the Nuremberg legal advisers are listed, with their degrees and dates, in Friedrich Wolfgang Ellinger, *op. cit.,* 55-58.

[56] Helmut Wachauf, *op. cit.,* 65-75.

[57] StA Nbg *Ratschlagbücher* No. 2*, 177ᵛ.

and give it into the hands of others." This was the opinion of Dr. Christoph Scheurl, a jurisconsult with much carefully considered advice to give at the time of the rearrangement of Nuremberg's church organization in the late 1520s.[58] So important to the city fathers was the linkage of law to politics that, late in the century, they appropriated a large sum of money (never an easy decision for burgher-rulers to make) to establish a law faculty at the newly founded "Academy" in nearby Altdorf.[59] Wherever feasible, legal training was provided locally so as to furnish it as cheaply as possible to the greatest number of aspirants and to minimize the effect of "foreign" influences upon native sons who were to be entrusted with vital and sensitive political tasks. This pattern was repeated, if only modestly, in each of the German cities and princely states.

DISCUSSING the slow emergence of a *legibus solutus* concept in medieval political attitudes, Otto Brunner notes that, whereas medieval rulers tended to hold themselves bound by principles of legal justice of which they were considered guardians but not the authors, the sixteenth-century territorial prince in Germany was much more likely to take a self-determining, and therefore absolutist, view of his position. "For this transition to take place," comments Brunner, "no constitutional change in the modern sense was required. No more was needed than an objective increase in the prince's real power and the creation of a standing administrative apparatus subservient to him and ready to subdue resistance."[60]

By the middle of the sixteenth century such an enlargement of princely power supported by a permanent state bureaucracy was well on the way to becoming a reality in Germany. But one must not exaggerate the extent and scope of this aggregation. Political omnipotence by any late modern measure was beyond the capacities of the rulers of the time. Not that it was entirely out of the range of their imagination. Their plans for a "well-ordered police state"[61] envisaged a politically passive role for their hard-working, disciplined, and submissive subjects. In close coordination with the leaders of the reorganized Refor-

---

[58] From a series of memoranda by Scheurl and others on the proposed Nuremberg-Brandenburg *Kirchenordnung*, 1530, Germanisches Nationalmuseum Nuremberg, *Merkel-Handschrift* 129, 34ʳ.

[59] Hans Liermann, "Die Altdorfer Juristen," *Festschrift für Karl Siegfried Bader* (Zurich, etc., 1965), 267-80.

[60] Otto Brunner, *Land und Herrschaft*, 393.

[61] Marc Raeff, *The Well-Ordered Police State* (New Haven, 1983). See especially 2-3, 167-79.

mation and Counter-Reformation churches, they labored diligently to centralize politics and concentrate initiative and control.[62] And in a purely formal way they succeeded. The flood of edicts, mandates, decrees, territorial laws, and police ordinances inundating every princely and urban domain in the later sixteenth and throughout the seventeenth centuries created (as they were intended to do) an impression of dynamic direction and irresistible force at the hub of affairs. Accomplishment in real political terms is another matter, however. It is highly unlikely that state and church authorities were successful in their attempts to bring everyone into line, or that, at the local level, the structure and temper of society responded as readily to the enactments issuing from the top as rationalizing ideologues and reforming churchmen expected they would. On this grass-roots scene—that is to say, in parishes, villages, municipal councils, estates committees, and assembly meetings across the land—rights, customs, immunities, freedoms, and traditions waged a tenacious battle of resistance against creeping death by state regulation. This opposition was anything but a negligible factor, as we shall see. Considering the might brought to bear on them, however, the survival of rights and freedoms in the face of the princely march toward absolutism was anything but a predictable outcome.

The proliferation of rules and legislation, which is the characteristic self-expression of the early modern bureaucratic state, aimed at three objectives. It undertook to replace false or undetermined with correct and certain standards of social, political, religious, and moral behavior; it sought to level diversity and achieve something close to uniformity in the public's adherence to these standards; and it tried to counteract the danger arising from men's incorrigible frailties of mind and character by enforcing adherence through supervision, suppression, and, where necessary, punitive force. Formulated in less negative terms, the state's political activity, assuming the malleability of human behavior through habit formation,[63] saw in a fine-meshed network of regulatory commands the best chance of improving men's performance of public duties and private obligations. Estates were coopted into working with rulers in the construction of these legislative nets: throughout the sixteenth century territorial assemblies collaborated in issuing ordinances and edicts.[64] But despite their joint authorship, the laws of the early

[62] For an elaboration of this argument, see my *Luther's House of Learning* (Baltimore, 1978).

[63] See *ibid.*, Chapters 4, 8, 9.

[64] Peter Blickle, *Landschaften im alten Reich*, 547; Herbert Helbig, "Königtum und Ständeversammlung in Deutschland am Ende des Mittelalters" in Heinz Rausch ed., *Die*

modern state revealed in both letter and spirit the distinctive cast of the period's governing mind: a deep-seated suspicion of human nature and an abiding distrust of individual motives. Hence the mass of statutes, regulating everything and linked to frequent inquisitions to ascertain that the rules were being observed.

No one was exempt from surveillance. High councillors of state were no less subject to interrogation than were obscure villagers in their parishes. "Are his grace's [Duke Maximilian I of Bavaria] rightful interests obediently and diligently attended to by the Spiritual Councillors?" was not considered an inappropriate question to put once a year to members of the governing body of the Bavarian church.[65] Having interrogated their subjects by reading from printed questionnaires furnished them by their governments, officials had to record their answers in writing, following a fixed scheme. After receiving due scrutiny, these responses were stored in the state archives. It is not clear what future use they were to serve, but where no one could be trusted, the written word offered at least a small measure of security; hence "put everything down on paper" (alles auf papier bringen) and "make a careful record of everything" (alles fleissig protocollieren) as Wilhelm V of Bavaria instructed his son and heir Maximilian.[66] When joined to the state's penchant for collecting data of every kind, the piles of records thus brought together expressed the compulsive punctiliousness ever since associated with the bureaucratic mentality. Surveillance was a standing duty of public servants at all administrative echelons. Governments seem to have been terrified to think that something might be going on beyond their ability to discover it. "No private quarrel may be settled without giving due notification to the Amt" (the district administrative office), warned a Saxon ordinance often reissued in the 1550s and 1570s.[67] "When quarreling or discord occur in a household, the head shall report them, and not fail to do so in any instance whatsoever on pain of being fined one gulden for each offense."[68] No homeowner was allowed to accept a new member or boarder (Hausgenosse) under his roof "without the knowledge and approval of the Amt."[69] Strangers

---

geschichtlichen Grundlagen der modernen Volksvertretung II: Reichsstände und Landstände (Darmstadt, 1974), 119.

[65] BHStA Mu Staatsverwaltung 1,142.

[66] Ibid. Fürstensachen 427, 26ʳ.

[67] From Artickel der Geboth und Vorboth for Amt Stollberg, Saxony, 1579, StA Dr Loc 8832 Ambt Stolbergks Acta, 73ʳ.

[68] Ibid. Artickel der Geboth und Vorboth uff der von Schönbergk . . . ehe gerichten Anno 1556, 4ʳ.

[69] Ibid., 7ʳ.

could not be lodged longer than one night (in plague years no one could be lodged at all) without official permission.[70] Bailiffs and beadles made routine inspections "of inns and taverns in villages and the open country to ensure that strangers and people of unknown origin are not allowed to remain longer than one night." Suspicious behavior by such "unknowns" was to be reported to the prince's council directly.[71] When a pair of questionable Jewish travelers turned up at a public house in Pirna, in Saxony, in the year 1567, their movements and contacts were immediately noted, reported, and—as the surviving record shows—protocolled by responsible officials and interested citizens.[72]

Certain aspects of this bureaucratic passion for exhaustive information make some sense when seen as a reaction to the insecurity bred by the crises of the age. Religious turmoil, the periodic recurrence of epidemic disease, painful recollections of the social upheaval of the 1520s, severe economic dislocations, warfare, including civil war, and the apparently insuppressible spread of lawless elements put everyone on edge. Given the common, theologically based, presuppositions about the causes of human malefaction, those with responsibility for guarding the peace could think of no other remedy for social turmoil than effective (i.e. repressive) surveillance and control. Plenitude of information was the essential first step toward enforced social discipline; the state's big ears were therefore open to news of private lives and petty concerns as much as of weighty public matters. In Saxony, where citizens were expected to act as government informers, everyone was obliged to be on the lookout for fellow parishioners absent from divine service, for a neighbor uttering a blasphemy, for a fishmonger keeping stinking fish on his stall.[73] Bavarian law obliged barbers and surgeons to notify authorities of all suspicious-looking wounds and injuries they were called to dress.[74] Ideally, every subject would have been accounted for at every instant of his life. On the occasion of the periodic swearing of the loyalty oath in Saxony (briefly described in another connection in the preceding chapter), local officials compiled lists of the whereabouts of individuals not present at the ceremony:

[70] Ibid., 76ᵛ.
[71] From instructions to Amtleute in Jülich-Berg, 1568 in Georg von Below ed., Landtagsakten von Jülich-Berg 1400-1600 (Düsseldorf, 1895-1907), II, 125.
[72] On this incident see Gerald Strauss, "Staying Out of Trouble In the Sixteenth Century. A German Charm to Ward off Evil," Folklore Forum 14:2 (1981), 73-76.
[73] From Schrifften aus der Rentterei . . . de Anno 1569-77, StA Dr Loc 8830, 32ʳ and passim.
[74] From the Malefizordnung of Maximilian I, BHStA Mu Staatsverwaltung 1982, 6ᵛ.

Michel Lehman, a miner, away in the saltmines in Dedig. Hans Feuler, ropemaker, has gone to Hungary. Melchior Frenckner, carpenter, is in Dresden on a construction job. Jacob Loss, pastor, has moved to a village near Borna. Hans Legler, brickmaker, is working in Bohemia. Adrian Albinus Guttman has, with permission, left for Breslau. Nikolaus Hufstein, shoemaker, is old and sick. Wolf Gobel, butcher, has lost his citizenship after causing a young girl to be with child. Georg Lose, baker, is mortally ill. Tobias Jordan, textile worker, is abroad on his journey.[75]

These registers, when added to the long catalogues of oath takers in electoral Saxony, must have constituted by the 1580s a virtual census of male citizens with some property to their names.[76] But the state wanted to know more than names. The Bavarian government under Maximilian I had, at the end of the sixteenth century, attained a condition of such obsessive centralization that news of trifling infractions committed by obscure subjects in out-of-the-way villages travelled straight from the regional intendant, the *Rentmeister*, to the duke's chancellery in Munich. One *Rentmeister*, at the conclusion of his annual circuit ride through his district for purposes of fact-gathering (*auskundschaften*), reported for the year 1598, among innumerable similar trivial misdemeanors, a peasant who had entertained more than fifty guests at his daughter's wedding, "Wolf Kramer in Hohenwart, a married man [who] is said to have got an unmarried female drifter with child," an innkeeper who allowed dancing on Sunday, several householders rumored to have committed adultery with their maid servants, a man "who has twice blasphemed by invoking the holy sacrament," and several instances of alleged fast breaking, including

one Blaser, a burgher in Friedberg, who was reported to have eaten a piece of stewed liver on a Friday. When it became clear during interrogation that the said Blaser had taken only one bite of this liver and spat it out of his mouth as soon as he remembered what day of the week it was, a strong admonition [*starcker verweis*] was dealt him by the princely *Rentmeister* to be more careful in the future.[77]

The official mind allowed no distinction between the important and the trivial. Every human act was potentially calamitous. The Bavarian

---

[75] StA Dr Loc 8719: *Ander Buch Erbhandlung 1601*, 230ʳ-231ʳ, Dippoldiswalde.

[76] A comparison of *Erbhuldigung* lists ʟor the 1540s (*ibid*. Loc 8715) with those for the 1580s (*ibid*. Loc 8716) indicates the aim of officials in the reign of Elector August to make their lists as complete as possible. Only propertied men could swear the oath. Widows of householders had the oath pronounced for them by a son or other male relative.

[77] BHStA Mu G.R.1262, No. 4.

dukes' annual instructions to their *Rentmeister* cover the entire spectrum of public life in listing the topics on which precise data had to be gathered:[78] religious observance and belief (on this point the *Rentmeister*'s investigations overlapped with the work of ecclesiastical visitation commissions, which operated, as in most territories, under secular authority), the performance in office of all regional and local judicial and administrative functionaries, the condition of roads, bridges, and waterways, the number and value of domestic and foreign coins circulating in the duchy, customs and import duties, the administration of justice, especially the disposition of fines. Next to enforcing true religion, the instructions say, the *Rentmeister*'s most important duty is to ensure that all *Commertien*—wealth-producing activities—are carried on with sufficient vigor to increase the prosperity of the country and the wellbeing of the people. No self-serving tradesman must sit on a town council. No craft or business should be allowed to fall into the hands of "foreign, especially sectarian, persons." All traces of corruption must be investigated, every alleged violation of sumptuary rules looked into (excessive eating and drinking at a funeral, wedding, or guild meal was a waste of resources and a major offense). A special questionnaire was given to everyone with a political task to perform, down to underbailiffs, beadles, assistant foresters, and schoolmaster's helpers. Appended to each *Rentmeister*'s instructions was a list of twenty-seven documents he had to examine in the central town or village of every *Amt*, copies of which he then had to transmit to Munich. The list included protocols of all judicial trials with receipts of fines collected; the log of court cases heard and of crimes committed; a register of all correspondence received and sent; the roll of obligatory labor service (who must do what? who has actually done it?); the guardianship book with its record of financial transactions on behalf of wards; the names of all adulterers accused and convicted and the list of all persons who had fled or moved out of the country; the names of all legitimate children born during the year; the ledger showing money owned by foreigners living in the district; the *Rentmeister*'s recess to local officials following his last visit and the check list of actions taken by these officials in response to his instructions; all tax registers; all parish account books; and, finally, the master register of all inventories compiled in the district during the last twelve months.

The stupendous organizational effort represented and typified by the Bavarian *Rentmeister* documents gives some substance to allusions in the historical literature to the early modern state's "extraordinary

---

[78] *Ibid.* for instructions from 1581 to 1801.

growth of political intensity and self-awareness."[79] Of course, not every state in the Holy Roman Empire was an "early modern state" in this sense. But, in addition to the ones mentioned in these pages, Brandenburg, Tyrol, Austria, the Bishoprics of Mainz, Bamberg, Brixen, and Münster were among the princely states both large and small undergoing transformation in this direction.[80] As their princes became sovereigns in action as well as in pretension, their residents became *Untertanen*, a word beginning to acquire its pejorative associations as a result of official preference for politically inert citizens without the resolve to act on their rights or other claims.[81] Toward such "subjects," rulers adopted a form of address alternating between the condescending or paternalistic and the censorious and disparaging. Expressing their "vexed astonishment" over their estates' "most obedient supplication," princes communicated via learned privy councillors their "fatherly admonition to be spared such demands" in the future.[82] Again, this turn of affairs did not occur everywhere. But wherever a centralizing authority enfeebled, if only for a time, the autonomy of traditional corporations, the tone of politics became tougher.

Such centralization was the crux of politics in the sixteenth century, as we have seen. Even the less grandiose principalities undertook the exercise in judicial consolidation that was the *sine qua non* of central administrative control. The Bishop of Brixen set his own judges over courts in outlying districts and, wherever the law of procedure allowed, transferred cases to his capital.[83] His colleague in Mainz used the long recesses between quarter sessions as a pretext for moving trials from lay tribunals to the bench of learned councillors at court.[84] In Tyrol, the region's higher judicial benches routinely set aside the verdicts given by

[79] Peter Blickle, *The Revolution of 1525*, 122, quoting Gerhard Oestreich.

[80] For Brandenburg, Hans Hattenhauer, *Geschichte des Beamtentums*, 57-79; for Tyrol, Peter Blickle, *Landschaften im alten Reich*; Jürgen Bücking, *Frühkapitalismus und Kirchenreform in Tirol 1565-1665* (Wiesbaden, 1972); for Mainz, Hans Goldschmidt, *Zentralbehörden und Beamtentum im Kurfürstentum Mainz*; for Münster, R. Po-chia Hsia, *Society and Religion in Münster, 1535-1618* (New Haven, 1984), 110-11.

[81] While still referring in a neutral way to those "under" the jurisdiction of some authority, *untertan* came to mean, both in the rhetoric of government and in the grievances of those obedient to them, a passive "subject" without rights. E.g., LA Tir *Landtagsakten* Fasz. 8, 370^r; Cod. 48, 182^v.

[82] These quotations from reply by Ferdinand II of Tyrol to a plea by Tyrolean estates to be permitted to retain their liberties and rights, 1590. LA Tir Cod. 48, 182^r-183^v.

[83] "Die durch den Landtag 1525 ... erledigten 'Partikularbeschwerden' der Tiroler Bauern (Tiroler Landesarchiv Hs. Nr., 2,889)" ed. Fritz Steinegger and Richard Schober, *Tiroler Geschichtsquellen* No. 3 (1976), 46.

[84] Hans Goldschmidt, *Zentralbehörden und Beamtentum im Kurfürstentum Mainz*, 164-65.

amateur assessors at lower courts.[85] Patrimonial and seigneurial courts in Bavaria lost most of their ancient functions as tribunals of "lower justice" when the dukes' legal officers proceeded systematically to infringe on nobles' judicial rights.[86] In the Bishopric of Münster lower courts were greatly reduced in their competences as a result of the bishops' installation of a judicial bureaucracy.[87] The legal historian Georg Dahm has summarized these developments for the empire as a whole. "The strengthening of territorial sovereignty," he writes, "and the concentration of public authority in the cities—in other words, the emergence of the state in the modern sense—

had the consequence of replacing older popular courts by the administrative organs of sovereign rulers or municipal governments, or at least of placing these organs in a position of rivalry with the traditional institutions. Courts came to be supplemented or replaced by the ruler's chancellery, the privy councillor, or by ordinary councillors. Municipal courts existed side by side with the city's Governing Council or its individual councillors, magistrates, bailiffs, or city advocates. Rural courts coexisted with the *Amt* in its capacity as a country court. . . . There must have been an initial period of indecision during which the competence of traditional popular courts was at first complemented, then increasingly undermined, by newly created competences of extrajudicial bodies. This, of course, gradually dislodged the popular courts or at least narrowed their scope. It goes without saying that a court tied to tradition-bound procedures and encumbered by ancient conventions must inevitably lose out in competition with a modern administration which is more or less free to develop its own operations. In this way, then, governments increasingly took over the functions of the courts and produced, as time went on, a new judicial system staffed and developed by academically trained officials.[88]

Thus empowered, the state proceeded to enfeeble its corporative constituents by draining them—to an extent and in ways that varied from region to region and place to place—of self-rule and self-administration. Volkmar Wittmütz has shown how this happened in Bavaria. From the 1550s the towns and larger villages of that duchy lost most of

[85] Peter Blickle, *Landschaften im alten Reich*, 232-33.

[86] Volkmar Wittmütz, *Die Gravamina der bayerischen Stände im 16. und 17. Jahrhundert* (Munich, 1970), 21.

[87] R. Po-chia Hsia, *op. cit.*, 110.

[88] Georg Dahm, "On the Reception of Roman and Italian Law in Germany" in Gerald Strauss, ed., *Pre-Reformation Germany* (London, 1972), 285-86.

their autonomy to ducal officials, who often acted on their own authority but clearly reflected the political priorities of their princely master. Grievances voiced at territorial diets by these towns compiled a detailed record of official violations of urban prerogatives. Ducal *Amtleute* it was charged, usurped the punishment of malefactors whose trials were delayed longer than three days. They took over voluntary justice by naming themselves arbitrators. They notarized documents. In search of evidence, their beadles—*Schergen* (a title soon to acquire an opprobrious ring in German)—invaded private houses. They made their presence felt in urban self-government, taking over administrative responsibilities, gaining control of revenues. Demoralized from the start by this show of force, urban leaders offered only frail resistance. Municipal office was drained of its substance and became unattractive to men of ability. The result was the virtual incorporation of Bavarian towns into the prince's administrative domain.[89] This dénouement was not inevitable. In some parts of the country small and middle-sized communities managed to hold on to a measure of self-government.[90] And the large, free, "imperial" cities remained wholly impervious to princely depredations. They possessed the resources, the legal expertise, and if necessary the military strength to protect their vital interests. States themselves in political weight and energy, the imperial cities centralized judicial and administrative authority in their own domains no less aggressively than did the larger principalities.[91] But against weaker opponents than these, the concentrated might of princely power usually prevailed. Pleading "fiscal privilege" on the strength of passages in the Roman law asserting priority for the state's claim (e.g., *Digest* 49.14.46; *Code* 10.10.4), rulers pushed the demands of their *Fiscus*,[92] and with them the competence of their fiscal agents, into areas formerly immune to interference. Protests by estates that "neither *Fiscus* nor fiscal law have any standing in traditional rights"[93] were of no avail, and

[89] Volkmar Wittmütz, *op. cit.*, 34-38.

[90] For a searching study of these in the seventeenth and eighteenth centuries, see Mack Walker, *German Home Towns. Community, State, and General Estate 1648-1871* (Ithaca, N.Y., 1971).

[91] E.g., Paul Hofer, "Amtsleute im Ulmer Territorium zur Zeit der Reformation," *Ulm und Oberschwaben* 42-43 (1978), 313-15.

[92] Fiscus, originally basket, specifically money basket, was the term for the fortune of Roman emperors as distinct from the *aerarium*, the fortune belonging to the empire. In medieval times the word came to refer to the emperors' domain. In the terminology of European absolutism of the eighteenth century *Fiscus* referred to the state's role as the bearer of the country's financial and economic power. In the sixteenth century the term was in transition to this meaning.

[93] Quoted in Eduard Rosenthal, "Die Behördenorganisation Kaiser Ferdinand I" in *loc. cit.*, 217-18.

fiscal officials came to represent in the public mind the most relentless, exploitive, and heavy-handed of princely bureaucrats.

Though in principle only the dutiful emissaries of their rulers, such agents were in practice all-powerful. Subjects quickly discover, says Justin Gobler, "that when these officials [*Amptleut*] make a request it is not really a request at all but a command and injunction harder and more pitiless than that of the princes themselves."[94] Protests from all over Germany accused *Amtleute, Vögte, Pfleger, Keller, Schergen, Schosser, Schreiber, Landsknechte, Knechte, Unterknechte* of high-handed behavior. They were charged with willy-nilly transferring legal actions to distant courts.[95] They commandeered passers-by for labor service, "something that has not happened in living memory."[96] They made up new registers of taxes and dues, arbitrarily raising everyone's contributions.[97] They intervened in a private dispute between nuns and their mother abbess.[98] They entered houses uninvited to compel residents to perform service for the castle, threatening prison, "as the *Schosser* did the other day when he sent the *Landsknecht* after Bertold, frightening his wife so badly that she has since become ill."[99] They banished common people from the forest where, from time immemorial, they had been allowed to gather wood.[100] They demanded payment in money or kind for what had always been free services.[101] During their periodic visitations of town and village parishes they had to be expensively housed and fed.[102] The rough administrative justice meted out by them mocked the due process written so carefully into "reformed" law codes. "Our people and we ourselves," complained the knights of Albertine Saxony in 1517

> are attacked and assaulted by Your Grace's *Amptleute* acting in ignorance of the circumstances of the deed [they are charged with investigating]. In a manner never before witnessed in these lands, they thrash our people, throw them in prison, and confiscate everything

[94] Justin Gobler, *Spiegel der Rechten* (Frankfurt am Main, 1573), 5ʳ.

[95] C.A.H. Burckhardt, ed., *Ernestinische Landtagsakten* I: *Die Landtage von 1487-1532*, Nos. 38, 41, 68.

[96] *Ibid.*

[97] *Ibid.* No. 88.

[98] Günther Franz, "Beschwerden der Hintersassen des Klosters Sonnefeld am Vorabend des Bauernkrieges," *Zeitschrift des Vereins für Thüringische Geschichte und Altertumskunde* N.F. 31 (1935), 48.

[99] StA Dr, Loc 9356, *Der Chur zu Sachssen clage . . . 1555*, 271ʳ.

[100] LA Tir, Cod. 45, 756ʳ and ᵛ.

[101] Volkmar Wittmütz, *op. cit.*, 41-42.

[102] *Ibid.*, 40.

they own. And when we would defend these poor wretches, we are not permitted to do so.[103]

Against all law, tradition, and chartered liberties, even nobles were put to the torture. "If one of us persists in denying [the charge] they put him to the painful question and torture him like a criminal."[104] The usual response of rulers to these accusations was: specify the details of the charge and it will be investigated. Sweeping accusations made in general terms were nearly always denied or ignored.[105] Rulers were no doubt aware of bureaucracy's tendency to abuse the power bestowed on it, no matter how carefully duties and competences were specified and circumscribed. Duke Maximilian I of Bavaria, one of the shrewdest of German prince-adminstrators, saw his subjects' best protection against exploitive officials in the payment of adequate salaries. He knew that the blame for rapacious, cruel, and corrupt servants fell ultimately on the master who employed them, thereby undermining his standing with his people.[106] As we shall see in the next chapter, territorial and urban office holders, particularly if they were graduate lawyers, commanded excellent salaries. The price of their services was a weighty factor in the steeply rising cost of government. Approaching his estates for grants of money in the late 1550s, Duke Christoph of Württemberg, a vigorous secular and ecclesiastical modernizer, explained that the expense of maintaining his corps of officials and servants had risen to an annual sum of 50,000 gulden compared to 12,000 to 15,000 in the preceding reign. This piece of information produced demands for economy from the Württemberg diet, as similar revelations did in every other state where proliferating bureaucracies and the mounting cost of supporting them were resented.[107]

On the other hand, people—including estate deputies even as they protested loudly against the price of government—were quick to lean on their rulers for help with or against whatever troubled or displeased them in the world. State bureaucracy was resented, but its support was

[103] StA Dr, Loc 9353, *Landtags-Acta 1517*, 23ʳ and ᵛ.

[104] Franz von Krenner, ed., *Baierische Landtags-Handlungen in den Jahren 1429 bis 1513* XIII (Munich, 1805), 30.

[105] For elaboration of this point, see Chapter Eight.

[106] From Maximilian's instructions for his son Ferdinand Maria in Christian von Aretin ed., *Maximilian I . . . : Anleitung zur Regierungskunst* (Bamberg, 1822), 62. "Ain ziemlichen besoldung" for officials was also suggested by territorial estates as a means of combatting exploitation. See Württemberg estates' grievances 1514: HStA St A34, Bü 1c, No. 1, unpaginated.

[107] See the comments on the Bavarian court of the 1580s and 90s in F. L. Carsten, *Princes and Parliaments in Germany*, 387-91.

almost as often requested, even demanded, as its presence was deplored. Some documents from Tyrol illustrate this ambivalence. Throughout the 1580s and 1590s, rural communes in Tyrol complained to the archduke about grasping landlords; the restrictive economic policies of towns; borders wide open to Italian merchants, peddlers, gypsies, and loan sharks; the high price of this and the low price of that. They wanted their government to deal with each of these nuisances. Vintners of Meran face ruin from the flood waters of mountain streams; villagers are denied traditional grazing rights by the owners of Alpine meadows; a blight falls on crops; pigs or deer damage an orchard—in these and a thousand similar matters intervention by the central administration is sought.[108] The butchers of Bozen petition the archduke for help in their quarrel with the butchers of Trent who had bought up all available cattle in the countryside at a time when the sessions of the Council of Trent were driving up the demand for meat; they want the government not only to issue a mandate against this practice, but also to enforce it. This request, along with innumerable others, was carefully considered by the ruler's learned councillors, who drafted a long memorandum advising arbitration between the two towns.[109] But subjects want action more than advice. Several communities protest against the cornering of barley by big brewers. Mandates are not enough, they say; no one pays them any heed. What is needed is enforcement.[110] This inclination to rely on government for alleviation of hardships is the reverse side of the constant complaints—often made in the very same petition or protest—about intervention by big government. In 1573, a long list of charges against the growing autocracy of Ferdinand II also includes demands of swift and resolute steps against the importation of French and Italian wine, for investigation of the habit of Tyrolean *Postmeister* to open and destroy or misplace letters, for police measures to keep bands of foreign soldiers from marauding in the country, for help against local officials who have banned export of agricultural exports, and for prosecution of tax dodgers who refuse to pay their fair share of the common levy.[111] In Saxony, Lutheran pastors, normally wary of secular meddling in church affairs, appeal to the elector's government to put a stop to the activities of "false preachers whose doctrines are steeped in error and go against the Word of God."[112] When flood waters from the Elbe damage the low-

---

[108] The documents referred to here are in LA Tir *Landtagsakten* Fasz. 9-10.

[109] *Ibid.* Fasz. 375 (1546), unpaginated.

[110] *Ibid.*

[111] *Ibid.* Cod. 45, 182^r-183^v.

[112] StA Wei, Reg. Q, No. 19, 15^r.

lying parts of the city of Meissen—as happened regularly in the spring—the town fathers apply to their territorial government for aid even as they asked to be left in full possession of their municipal autonomy.[113] Every government received requests of this sort whenever assemblies met to address common problems.

But this tendency of subjects to turn to government for help does not seem to have lessened their resentment of their rulers' sprawling officialdom. The proverb "Order rules the world as the cudgel rules the dog"[114] epitomized the attitude of ordinary folk to the legal and administrative character of the early modern state. "Order," in early modern Germany, meant social discipline above all else, and *Amtleute* wielded the ruler's disciplinary cudgels.[115] Popular sayings about official posts and the men who occupied them express what must have been a widespread sense of skepticism (or perhaps resignation) concerning the qualities of honesty and humanity likely to be found in public servants. *Amt macht verdammt* is the most succinct of them.[116] Others are: "An office feeds you well, but it doesn't make you wise." "Public office allows what the law forbids." "Whoever takes public office is made worse by it." "Office is of God, but officials are the devil's." "The great and common complaint about them," wrote Justin Gobler of *Amtleute*,

> is that they scrape, skin, and coerce the poor, misrepresent the law, give preference to the rich and to those who can offer bribes, and hold ordinary people and the intelligent in contempt. Let such a hungry louse come into an official post and it will bite and suck there until it is full.

The official's watchword, Gobler adds, is "Grease the wheel and you will get a smooth ride. They learned this saying in school," he comments, "and none of them ever forgets it."[117] A satirical "Grammar for Office Seekers" reveals the routes of access encouraged by the system: some get their office by use of the nominative (they have great names); others get it by the genitive (because of their families) or by the dative

---

[113] StA Dr, Loc. 9362, *Erledigung der Gravaminum . . . 1609*, 65ᵛ.

[114] "Ordnung regiert die Welt und der Knüppel den Hund." Günter Grandmann *et al.*, *Rechtssprichwörter* (Leipzig, 1980), 18.

[115] On the office and role of the Amtmann in local administration in Germany, see Adolf Stölzel, *Die Entwicklung der gelehrten Rechtssprechung* I (Berlin, 1901), 408-13; Rudolf Wilhelm, *Rechtspflege und Dorfverfassung nach nieder-bayerischen Ehehafts-ordnungen vom 15. bis zum 18. Jahrhundert* (University of Munich dissertation, 1953), 98-99.

[116] For these and the following, see Eduard Graf and Mathias Dietherr, *Deutsche Rechtssprichwörter* (Nördlingen, 1864), 418; 515-18

[117] Justin Gobler, *Spiegel der Rechten*, 5ʳ.

(they make gifts in the right places) or by the accusative (they slander someone) or by the ablative (they take from one and give to another). Only very few get it by the vocative—because they are called to it.[118] A few laudatory proverbs intended to increase respect for incumbents tend to ambiguity: "Every man is wise in his office." "What a man can do depends on the office he holds."[119] There can be no doubt that office holders—including churchmen—aroused far more ill will than good and that angry feelings grew in proportion to the threat these men were seen to pose to traditional autonomies. Ordinarily, resentment smouldered out of sight of the mighty, who had to infer it from protests expressed in lists of grievances. But the parliamentary history of every German state has its moments of fury, when the stored-up outrage against these willing tools of a prince's ambition to power turned into ferocious vengeance after a crisis or change of ruler had left a formerly almighty councillor suddenly exposed to his enemies.[120]

To those who were antagonistic to it, the early modern state was far from what it claimed to be: a government by law and by legal process. With its self-aggrandizing prince, its exalted juristic decision makers, and its interfering officialdom, it bordered on the condition of lawlessness. According to the political wisdom of the time, law and arbitrary power were polar opposites. In the new state the willfulness of unchecked personal supremacy was joined to the concentrated force of political organization. Such a state could make no claim to either lawfulness or legality.

Needless to say, this was not the image conveyed by the lawyers' books. They described the normative and implied that it was actuality. The duty of emperors, kings, princes, lords, and magistrates, declares Gobler,

> is to govern and act in accordance with what is right, fair, useful, and in keeping with the letter and spirit of laws and the principles of justice. For justice and law are above the ruling power as the ruling power is above the people. That is to say: statutes and written law shall rule over holders of power, and the holders of power shall rule the commons.

[118] In Georg Philipp Harsdörfer, *Ars apophthegmatica* (Nuremberg, 1655), No. 3155.
[119] Graf and Dietherr, *op. cit.*, 33, 515.
[120] In 1613 Mathias Enzlin was tried and executed by the Württemberg estates for "intriguing." Enzlin had been the legal architect of Duke Friedrich's attempt to set aside provisions of the Treaty of Tübingen limiting the dukes' authority. When Friedrich died, his less headstrong successor could not control the Württemberg estates, which took their anger out on Enzlin.

"This is why princes and magistrates are called 'the living law,' " he adds, "and why we speak of laws as 'the voice of authority.' "[121] Laws, agrees Heinrich Rauchdorn, "are a plumbline and yardstick for rulers and magistrates. They keep them from doing too much or too little in their governance of affairs, and they also teach them how to keep good measure in all things and aim always at the right end."[122] No one denied that these admirable principles defined the political order as it ought to be. But that they described the actual operation of any system then in existence or likely to come into being was, in the age of the new prince and the sovereign state, open to serious doubt. The very "laws" so heartily commended by jurists as the surest guide and staunchest safeguard of princely policy-making were, to their opponents, destabilizing weapons threatening a precariously balanced political world. Far from curbing the exercise of power and checking its excesses, laws boosted it, honed its edge, and sanctioned its aggressive use.

As the priests of this law and the political theologians of the new state built on that foundation, jurists were compromised by their implication in a structure of force and intimidation. Upon the holders of power, their preachments had no more restraining influence than could be reconciled with immediate pragmatic objectives. And among those who knew themselves to be their victims, the jurists' gospel of the written law as the true voice and warranty of justice fell on unbelieving ears. Having been made indispensable to the operation of the organized society, lawyers attracted to themselves the distaste and suspicion due to a clergy whose intercession could not be avoided even as it created a nagging sense of dependence. Max Weber's assertion that "everywhere the revolution of political management in the direction of the evolving rational state has been borne by trained jurists"[123] was an everyday fact of life to contemporary observers of the political scene. But another fact was just as evident to them. The "rational" goal toward which the jurists labored was the aim of a ruthless levelling program directed against all the "irrational," "outmoded" features of their familiar social landscape. Serving as the advance troop of the new state, the legal establishment became its symbol and, as such, a lightning rod drawing upon itself all the apprehensions, the misgivings, and the anger aroused by a deeply disturbing phenomenon. We shall see in the next chapter how lawyers were positioned to bear up under the onslaught of this disapproval.

[121] Justin Gobler, *Spiegel der Rechten*, Aiii[v].

[122] *Ibid.* Heinrich Rauchdorn, *Practica und Process* (1564), Aiiii[r].

[123] Max Weber, "Politics as a Vocation" (1918) in *From Max Weber. Essays in Sociology*, translated and ed. by H. H. Gerth and C. W. Mills (New York, 1946), 93.

CHAPTER SIX

Careers and Social Place: Lawyers as a Class

THE political eminence achieved by lawyers in the sixteenth century was reflected in their social ascent as their calling won for them a place among old and new ruling groups commensurate with their growing importance. Reciprocity between law and elites was not a new phenomenon in Europe. Law and nobility had been closely allied in ancient Rome, where legal science was held to be among the most suitable occupations for men of gentle birth, joining them in the conduct of politics while affording a certain patrician distance.[1] In medieval Italy, too, lawyers tended to come from leading families of the old ruling groups.[2] But Bologna, Padua, and Florence also proved that new men from modest backgrounds could aim beyond fame and fortune to enter the great circles of influence and power, ultimately to found juristic dynasties of spreading wealth and prestige.[3] A long tradition thus associated jurisprudence with the highest achievements to which a man could aspire. Never disposed to reticence concerning their weight in the world of affairs, jurists explained their status by invoking the majesty of the law and the ideal of justice upheld by it. Azo, the thirteenth-century Bologna legist, writing in the preface to his *Summa Institutionum*, spoke unabashedly of the generous rewards awaiting him and his kind:

> Jurisprudence [he wrote] is an open-handed mistress. She ennobles her disciples, bestows high office on them, and doubles their estate and fortune. To say it honestly, everywhere in the world she has elevated her adepts into lords, gaining access for them to the court of the emperor himself. . . . Kings exercise their dominion by entrusting them with the reins of power. Through their efforts, Justice itself is preserved on earth.[4]

[1] Jan Kodrebski, "Der Rechtsunterricht am Ausgang der Republik und zu Beginn des Prinzipats," *Aufstieg und Niedergang der römischen Welt*, ed. H. Temporini and W. Haase II: *Prinzipat* 15 (Berlin and New York, 1976), 177-96.

[2] Lauro Martines, *Lawyers and Statecraft in Renaissance Florence* (Princeton, 1968), 76-77.

[3] E.g., Accursius, the great thirteenth-century glossator, three of whose four sons became jurists.

[4] Quoted in Hans Hattenhauer, *Geschichte des Beamtentums* (*Handbuch des öffentlichen Dienstes* I, Cologne, 1980), 25.

In an earlier chapter we saw how this encomium to the profession's ability to win honors was echoed by both admirers and detractors. No matter how observers felt about the presence of a powerful judicial elite in the courts and council halls of western Europe, no one could overlook the fact that—as Martin Luther wrote in 1530—"chancellors, syndics, and jurists are sitting on top."[5]

High social rank was the due of holders of such exalted positions. At a time when the accouterments of place and status were strictly regulated by convention and statute, the jurist's garb, the titles by which he was addressed, and his manner of self-presentation all proclaimed his standing among the distinguished and well-to-do. From medieval times, doctors of law possessed the right of being called *dominus* or *signore*.[6] In Germany their titles ranked them as the peers of knights and patricians. The *hochgelehrt* ("highly learned") of the doctor of both laws was fully equivalent to the *ehrenfest* (honorable, literally "constant in honor") of the knight and the *ehrenhaft* (honorific) of the urban burgher of ancient family.[7] Even the less illustrious master or licentiate of laws, properly addressed only as *gelehrt*, counted in official protocol among the lower nobles at least.[8] Titles were anything but empty formulas. They were observed punctiliously, as was the ranking order classifying men in their correct social relation to one another. Names of *doctores* were always placed among those of the nobility wherever ranking was called for—"princes, counts, doctors, knights, bishops, abbots. . . ."[9] In lists of personages attending council sessions, estate meetings, banquets, travel parties, or hunting sorties, jurists always stood with those *vom adel* (of the nobility),[10] their earned degrees distinguishing them from lesser men as others were set apart by birth and blood. Their distinctive doctor's cap, the purple *biretta*, corresponded as an outward sign of aristocracy to the knight's *cingulum militare*, the swordbelt. The medieval terminology of social classification, taken over almost unchanged into early modern usage, dubbed jurists

---

[5] Luther, *Eine Predigt, dass man Kinder zur Schule halten solle* (1530), WA 30[II], 567.

[6] Hans Hattenhauer, *op. cit.*, 24; E. H. Kantorowicz, "Kingship under the Impact of Scientific Jurisprudence" in *id., Selected Studies*, (Locust Valley, N.Y., 1965), 154.

[7] *Tyttelbuch* in Stadtarchiv Augsburg, Nachlässe.

[8] E.g., in the order of councillors who traveled with Count Eberhard of Württemberg to Mainz in 1488. Irmgard Kothe, *Der fürstliche Rat in Württemberg im 15. und 16. Jahrhundert* (Stuttgart, 1938), 28.

[9] For example, in the *Reformation* of the laws of the city of Worms, quoted in Otto Stobbe, *Geschichte der deutschen Rechtsquellen* II (Braunschweig, 1864; reprint Aalen, 1965), 54.

[10] E.g., in all the records of the meetings of Bavarian estates and their negotiations with the dukes of Bavaria.

as *milites legum,* distinct in function but equal in status to the *milites armorum.* "According to the sacred tradition of the laws," wrote the fifteenth-century canonist Peter von Andlau in his *Libellus de Caesarea Maiestate* of 1460, "there exists in addition to the knighthood of arms another order of knights . . . , namely that of the men who are learned in the law. These legal specialists, who bring complicated trials to a just conclusion, who defend righteous causes and thereby prevent injustice from triumphing in public and private matters benefit humankind as much as if they stood embattled in the defense of the fatherland." It is often asked, Peter continues, how one may decide which of these two knightly companies, the armed or the learned, exceeds the other in excellence. His considered answer is that

> in matters that are the proper business of a knight, the knight stands higher than the doctor, and in the opposite case the doctor counts for more than the knight. . . . All things being equal, however—and in this opinion we are in agreement with our predecessors—a doctor should have precedence over a knight. And we have reached this conclusion because we think that the state profits far more from laws than from arms, for laws are the cause of good things being done in the state, while arms merely see to their implementation and execution.[11]

In keeping with this hierarchy of social standing, learned jurists were in the city of Nuremberg regarded as the equals of the Seven Elders, the small band of patrician men in whose hands the city's government lay.[12] "They, their wives, and their children [are] by the express stipulation of the imperial law collectively and individually freed from all burdens placed upon other burghers touching their persons and their goods."[13] In Saxony, where sumptuary legislation strove to impose frugal habits throughout the century, holders of the law doctorate were permitted to take six-course meals and could entertain as many as one hundred twenty guests at a family wedding, with two servants attending each table.[14] Only the greatest among the nobility exceeded them in this outward sign of social distinction. Along with other "illustrious personages" (*erlauchte personen*) jurists had the right not to be put to

[11] Quoted in Josef Hürbin, *Peter von Andlau* (Strasbourg, 1897), 211-12.
[12] Wilhelm Fürst, "Der Prozess gegen Nikolaus von Gülchen . . . ," *Mitteilungen des Vereins für Geschichte der Stadt Nürnberg* 20 (1913), 133.
[13] StA Nbg *Ratschlagbücher* 2*, 83ᵛ.
[14] *Artickel etlicher nothwendiger Ordnung und Satzungen, zu Erhaltung guter Zucht und Disziplin* (Wittenberg, 1562) issued by Elector August.

the torture.[15] They could trim their doctor's gown and outer garments with fur, and they had the choice of costlier materials and a wider range of colors than merchants, artisans, and men in less respected professions. Nor was such ostentation merely for show. External trappings of a distinguished condition eased the judicial estate's passage into a titled and hereditary nobility later in the seventeenth and eighteenth centuries.[16] What had once been a characteristically bourgeois path to social ascent in Germany thus became an aristocratic profession, as lawyers—grandsons of artisans and innkeepers—took crested names and escutcheons, and—conversely—as scions of ancient noble and gentle lines chose careers in the law in order to hold on to what remained of their influence and power.[17]

To be sure, only the most accomplished of academic jurists belonged to the select group completing this climb to social eminence. Many of these men held the doctorate in both laws, the JUD, which, among Protestants no less than among Catholics, bestowed the supreme accolade of their discipline. But even a *iuris doctor* or *doctor legum* without the *utriusque* added to the title conferred a passport to nobility. The JUD, LLD, and JD formed the elite among lawyers. Licentiates and masters made up a respected but distinctly lesser stratum immediately below them. The profession's largest contingent, however, was composed of workers in the penumbra or on the fringes of law, men who used to be called condescendingly "semi-learned" by older German scholars who sympathized with the supercilious attitudes taken by contemporaries toward a group considered by many as parasitical on the legal establishment.[18] Recent interpreters tend to be more balanced[19] in their view of the activities of these para-judicials. Their work—as notaries, secretaries, procurators, advocates, attorneys, arbitrators, jurors, lay judges, purveyors of legal advice—responded to their society's call for assistance in the increasingly complex and bewildering business of legal affairs. But even as they met this demand they helped create an ever-increasing need for their services: this, at least, was the accusation

[15] Cited in Otto Stobbe, *op. cit.* II, 55.

[16] E.g., Heinz Durchhardt, "Die kurmainzischen Reichskammergerichtsassessoren," *ZRG* 94 (1977), *Germ. Abt.*, 89-128.

[17] Adolf Stölzel, *Die Entwicklung des gelehrten Richtertums in den deutschen Territorien* (Stuttgart, 1872; reprint Aalen, 1964) I, 126; II, 52-60.

[18] Roderich Stintzing, *Geschichte der populären Literatur des römisch-kanonischen Rechts in Deutschland* (Leipzig, 1867), xxix-xxxvii.

[19] E.g., Karl-Heinz Burmeister, *Das Studium der Rechte im Zeitalter des Humanismus in deutschen Rechtsbereich* (Wiesbaden, 1974), 21.

of contemporary critics, who blamed the greedy self-promotion of law-yers for the deepening entanglement of nearly everyone in litigation.[20]

The historical judgment has now reversed this supposed order of causation. Lawyers did not invent the work they were prepared to do. Early forms of capitalism in the cities brought about conditions nearly ideal for the proliferation of a legal profession, as did the concurrent breakup of the feudal system, which proceeded largely as a sequence of litigating thrusts and parries in matters of landed properties and the im-munities and privileges adhering to them.[21] A more dynamic society generated new legal problems. Enormous amounts of litigation pro-ceeded from bequests made to the Church and reclaimable as a result of the Protestant Reformation. Meanwhile the petty problems of quotidian existence in towns and villages continued unchanged for or-dinary people who worried about access to ovens and the right to brew and draw their own beer. As we have heard, local courts were fully oc-cupied with such business, sneeringly called *Bauernsachen* but not be-yond the reach of the more formal, lawyer-prone, procedures favored by the age. Tensions among people of all social ranks increased in pro-portion to the crises and dislocations for which the sixteenth century is notorious, and these, too, made work for lawyers. More important, the growth of municipal and state service enormously expanded the num-ber and range of positions to be filled by men with a flair for law and some legal training to go with it. In cities and territories going over to Protestantism, the founding of state churches further increased the need for lawyers. So much legal work needed to be done, in fact, that some leading members of the profession expressed alarm over the lack of qualified men "to lecture in universities, give verdicts and respond to the demand for learned opinions, sit on superior benches and appellate courts, . . . and be of service to princes and lords."[22] This particular la-ment, by Melchior von Osse, the Saxon jurist, refers to the availability only of graduate legists fully trained in at least one of the two bodies of written law. (Incidentally it also shows that the legal profession had by the 1550s begun to divide itself into the four specialist groups distin-

[20] Some modern observers agree. E.g., Keith Thomas, *Religion and the Decline of Magic* (London, 1971), 248. The example of lawyers shows, says Thomas, that "it is al-ways possible for a substantial social group to assert itself by proffering solutions to problems which they themselves have helped to manufacture."

[21] Karlheinz Blaschke, "Frühkapitalismus und Verfassungsgeschichte," *Wissenschaft-liche Zeitschrift der Karl-Marx-Universität Leipzig* 14. Jahrgang (1965), 435-41.

[22] Melchior von Osse, *An Hertzog Augustum . . . Ein unterthäniges Bedencken* in Os-wald Artur Hecker ed., *Schriften Dr. Melchiors von Osse* (Leipzig and Berlin, 1922), 385-86.

guished by the modern sociology of law: adjudicators, legal advisers, legal scholars, and advocates.)[23] Along with most lay critics of his day, Osse regarded the sprawling proletariat of semi- or unskilled hangers-on in the lower ranks of his discipline as a curse on the profession. But he also knew enough about the social snobbery prevailing among his fellow jurists to blame them for restricting access to their select group, which was far advanced by then toward stabilizing itself as a social, as well as a professional, elite. Entry into this chosen circle of future movers and shakers was no longer easy to gain. Family and money were becoming, if not an exclusive criterion, at least an increasingly restrictive test by which young men must pass into a juristic career. A few distinguished jurists active in the early decades of the sixteenth century were sons of poor folk: Melchior Kling and Johann Sichard among them, to name two individuals already mentioned in these pages. But even in their time the normal career paths were beginning to favor the rich. The long, arduous, and above all costly course of study required to prepare oneself for the highest degrees in law virtually shut out those candidates who did not enjoy the benefits of parental encouragement and support.

IN ROMAN antiquity, jurists had never been teachers or pupils in the formal sense.[24] It was in the later middle ages that legal education grew into a structured course of university study. This innovation in professional training is indicative of the intimate connection that linked law to other scholarly disciplines and to the system of interlocking institutional and social interests of which medieval universities formed a vital part.[25] Unlike Italian and French law schools, which enjoyed a significant measure of institutional autonomy, German law faculties were always closely integrated with their universities. In the sixteenth century about twenty institutions in the empire offered legal training. Among them Vienna, Heidelberg, Cologne, Erfurt, and Leipzig were regarded as leading centers of juridical learning. As mentioned before, Italian and, to a somewhat lesser extent, French legal education still exerted the greatest allure on ambitious students despite the gathering fame of native scholar-teachers. Italian and French law schools boasted the most renowned scholars among their teachers, and they offered supe-

---

[23] Cf. Max Weber, *Max Weber on Law in Economy and Society* ed. Max Rheinstein (Cambridge, Mass., 1954) *passim*, especially 96-97.

[24] Jan Kodrebski in *loc. cit.*, 184-96; Detlev Liebs, "Rechtsschulen und Rechtsunterricht im Prinzipat" in *ibid.*, 197-286.

[25] The following paragraphs on legal education are based on Karl-Heinz Burmeister, *op. cit.*, and Ferdinand Elsener, *Die Schweizer Rechtsschulen vom 16. bis zum 19. Jahrhundert* (Zurich, 1975).

rior conditions of study. Mostly, however, it was the reflected glory in naming Padua, Bologna, Ferrara, or Orléans, Bourges, or Poitiers as the source of one's degree that drew the steps of young Germans south of the Alps or west of the Rhine. At first merely an ancillary pursuit to gaining mastery in canon law, the study of the Justinian *corpus iuris civilis* became in the course of the fifteenth century, and for reasons that have been set out in an earlier chapter, a fully equal discipline. Decrees *in utroque iure* were awarded from the fourteenth century on. From about 1500 the number of university chairs in civil law matched that in canon law. By the late sixteenth century the unequal relationship of church and civil law in favor of the former had been reversed, and Roman jurisprudence emerged as the reigning discipline in terms of numbers of chairs, quantity and ability of students, and place of importance in the university's hierarchy of faculties.[26]

Most students began the advanced study of law with the MA in hand (though, in the absence of formal prerequisites, this was not always so). If they stayed the course, they were likely to take a full ten years beyond the MA to reach the highest decree, the JUD.[27] Although there were exceptions—Hieronymus Schürpff, for example, was only twenty-two when he received his JUD at Wittenberg[28]—most lawyers were in their late twenties or early thirties when they quit the schoolroom and, carrying a tall stack of expensive books, returned home with their sheepskin and doctor's cap. Lectures and training centered on Justinian's civil law. Two or three professors expounded the *corpus iuris*; the Institutist, the Pandecist (always the senior and most distinguished member of the faculty),[29] and the Codicist lectured on each of these chief divisions of the *corpus* successively. The basic teaching tool was the *Institutes*, a textbook that carried out Justinian's original pedagogical purpose well into the seventeenth century by introducing fledging lawyers to the rudiments of their subject. Lectures on the *Institutes* could take up to four years, for the principle was that "unless the *Institutes* are as familiar to you as the back of your own hand, you will never understand your professors when they quote Bartolus and Baldus."[30] But

[26] Details are given by Karl-Heinz Burmeister, *op. cit.*, 73-84.

[27] *Ibid.*, 200-04; Ferdinand Elsener, *op. cit.*, 110. See also the remarks about Job Vener's studies at Bologna from 1390 to 1397 in Hermann Heimpel, *Die Vener von Gmünd und Strassburg* . . . (Göttingen, 1982), 161-65.

[28] Theodor Muther, *Der Reformationsjurist D. Hieronymus Schürpf* (Erlangen, 1858), 11.

[29] Ferdinand Elsener, *op. cit.*, 114.

[30] From Johann Apel's *Dialogus de studio iuris recte instituende* of 1540, quoted in Franz Wieacker, "Einflüsse des Humanismus auf die Rezeption. Eine Studie zu Johannes

in view of the growing need for qualified lawyers, and with more students entering law in response to this demand, the trend in the sixteenth century was to reduce the introductory stage to two years, here and there even to a single one. An enormous number of editions of the *Institutes* came off German presses; one Basel printer alone published it in 1476, 1477, 1478, 1481, and 1486.[31] No other introductory handbook ever took its place.

The first two semesters were devoted almost entirely to a close reading of *Institutiones grammatice*, that is to say, of the plain text of the *Institutes*, without gloss or commentary. The following year, or years, repeated these procedures and amplified them by including the commentaries of the great law teachers and practicing jurists of past and present times.[32] Apart from inculcating a basic knowledge of text and principles of Roman law, this long immersion was intended to ease the student into methodical habits of thought, a mental posture of which the Justinian *corpus*, and the *Institutes* in particular, was thought to offer the most compelling example. The objective was to implant in him as a kind of second nature a rational approach (as it was thought to be) to all intellectual subjects. Close attention to the glosses of several outstanding masters also gave the student invaluable training in an essential skill, the sifting and balancing of contrary, or mutually antagonistic, opinions.[33] This habit of mind, it appears, was a difficult trait for neophytes to master, and students often went outside the lecture hall to seek the aid of private tutors or crammers to enable them to absorb the substance and method of the texts.[34] The difficulty seems to have been caused, not by unfamiliarity of ideas or intricacy of method, but by the sheer quantity of information to be absorbed before the process could work. This information had to be stored in the memory. Students therefore tended to make use of drilling aids and mnemonic devices, or of shortcuts such as the "Card Game" of Thomas Murner, the popular writer and Catholic controversialist, who was also a lawyer, which offered helpful bracketed outlines to the beginner and even reduced the entire contents of the *Institutes* to a set of picture emblems to help fix the book's essential material in the learner's mind.[35]

Apels Dialogus," *Zeitschrift für die gesammte Staatswissenschaft* 100 (1940), 423-56. Apel was a humanist critic of the *mos italicus*.

[31] Hans Rudolf Hagemann, "Rechtswissenschaft und Basler Buchdruck an der Wende vom Mittelalter zur Neuzeit," *ZRG* 77 (1960), *Germ. Abt.*, 248-49.

[32] For example, Melchior Kling's *In quatuor Institutionum Iuris principis Iustiniani libros Enarrationes* (Leiden, 1548), a favorite in Protestant Germany.

[33] Lauro Martines, *op. cit.*, 86-87; Franz Wieacker in *loc. cit.*, 432-33.

[34] Franz Wieacker, in *loc. cit.*, 429.

[35] Thomas Murner, *Chartiludium Institute summarie* . . . (Strasbourg, 1518). Murner was the first to use mnemotechnics in jurisprudential education. See Adalbert Erler,

Explication of the *Digest* and *Codex* followed the same pattern. Early morning "ordinary," or main, lectures delivered by the most distinguished teachers were supplemented by "extraordinary" readings later in the day, and "repetitions" given by adjunct staff, who also conducted *collegia*, private tutorials for individual students and small groups. Where canon law was part of the curriculum, the Professor of Decretals read on the *Decretum Gratiani* and the so-called *Liber extra* (published in 1234 by Pope Gregory IX). Additional lectures introduced German students to some of the constitutional texts of their own country: the Golden Bull, selected feudal laws, and, from the 1530s, criminal law as codified in the *Carolina*. But this "new" legislation was treated by nearly everyone as of a distinctly lesser order of importance than the civil and canon law, the foundations on which all written law was thought to rest. As for customary law, it was almost entirely absent from the curriculum. Most academic jurists deemed it "unknowable," a relic of an unenlightened age of chaos and confusion, and a vestigial remnant whose impending eclipse by the orderly, systematic written imperial law was long overdue.

The harsh value judgment behind this disparagement, and the arrogance supporting it, were perpetuated by the style of instruction prevailing in German law schools. Dominated by the "Italian manner," the teaching, and therefore the learning of law, and in consequence the professional bias of qualified jurists, eschewed historical perspective and critical discussion of the materials studied, treating them instead as texts to be analyzed, fixed in the memory, and grasped as a set of intellectual propositions. The Italian "case method," universally employed in lectures and training exercises, bred experts with a virtuoso command of the literature of law. But deeper questions about the relation of law to its social and cultural context were of slight interest to them. Alternative methods were not entirely missing from the academic legal scene. They were recommended by humanistically inclined scholars, most of whom operated from the arts faculty. In 1518, Melanchthon commenced his lectures on the *Institutes* in Wittenberg where, however, the entire law faculty was devoted to the *mos italicus*.[36] A few years after this, the humanist-jurist Johann Sichard taught the same text in Freiburg. Both men favored a French-oriented approach to the expounding of law, a method that aimed at reaching a much more discriminating understanding of legal texts by relating them to their linguistic, literary, and historical situations. Nor were Melanchthon and

---

Thomas Murner als Jurist (Frankfurt am Main, 1956), 57. Murner was also the first to translate the *Institutes* into German, in 1520.

[36] Guido Kisch, *Melanchthons Rechts- und Soziallehre* (Berlin, 1967), 127. Melanchthon himself later defended the glossators and commentators, *ibid.*, 156.

Sichard isolated figures in their own time.[37] For the moment, however, the much more limited, but immensely meticulous and, for immediate and practical purposes, effective, Italian manner won out. It proved itself to be highly successful in educating legal specialists distinguished above all by their exhaustive knowledge of texts, by the accuracy and swiftness of their recall, and by their deadly skill in forensic argument. The latter talent was sharpened in scores of obligatory disputations where law students gave public demonstrations of what they had learned and how spontaneously they could bring it to bear on a problem at hand. Academically qualified lawyers had "cases" at their finger tips to support or destroy any legal contention. They instantly found "parallel passages" enabling them to advance from single points to general principles. They debated brilliantly, aiming at total destruction of opposing opinions. Humanist critics likened this facility to the vacuous glibness of a man who knows the name of every leaf and fruit in a garden but has nothing to say about their beauty, taste, or utility.[38] But although a more reflective approach nourished by literary and historical studies was gaining some followers in Germany in the course of the sixteenth century, the established curriculum, and the profession as a whole, continued to adhere to the Italian style of legal thought.

Faculty regulations and study manuals, many of them written by famous law teachers, established the criteria for the mastery of law in German universities.[39] Knowledge by heart gained through repeated reading was the first rule. Some teachers regarded memory exercise as a tonic for tired minds exhausted by bouts of hard thinking. As in the case of other subjects, however, an ulterior belief underlay this insistence on rote learning: a good memory was taken as the surest measure of intellectual ability. Teachers therefore recommended daily exercise in committing to memory several titles from the *corpus*, until the entire arrangement of the twelve books of the *Codex*, the fifty books of the *Digest*, and the four books of the *Institutes* were clear and present to the student's mind. Much time was saved later, in legal practice, by the rapid reference through automatic recollection made possible by memorization. The most admired jurists could give stunning evidence of instantaneous and total recall of long passages. For the same practical reason it was also recommended that reading matter be stored up in books of commonplaces. Points of law with their glosses and commen-

---

[37] See the general picture of humanist reformers of the law curriculum given by Karl-Heinz Burmeister, *op. cit.*, 251-61. Franz Wieacker's article on Johann Apel, cited in note 30, gives the details of one such humanist reform program.

[38] From Johann Apel's criticisms, quoted in Franz Wieacker in *loc. cit.*, 438.

[39] For these see Burmeister, *op. cit.*, 226-33.

taries were entered verbatim into large tomes arranged by categories in alphabetical order and supplied with copious indices to facilitate speedy reference. Many scholars kept commonplace books as a record of their life's reading. Others used them to distill from years of diligent study what they took to be the essences and kernels of their art.[40] In any case, it was generally believed that copying itself was a powerful spur to learning by heart, and for this reason, too, it was encouraged. Without a more than ordinarily retentive and agile memory, no law student could hope to make a good career. Incessant repetition therefore stretched and stoked this all-important faculty and, as in all the other academic disciplines, frequent examinations tested the results.[41]

With his acquired store of law and legal opinion imprinted on his mind, and supported by a desk library of indispensable texts, interpretations, and books of reference, the fledgling lawyer was equipped to enter professional life. What he knew after years of intensive preparation was almost exclusively the product of his reading and of his attendance at lectures. The study of law involved preeminently the absorption of books and the internalization of the ideas and presuppositions contained in these. Now and then attempts were made to expose students to some experience in the world of legal affairs. The "case method" allowed instructors to introduce an occasional instance from contemporary life. If the professor was a writer of *consilia*, his students were able to profit from the master's brush with real-world situations, from which "cases" were taken to be exemplary. In some law faculties, modern *consilia* were part of the required curriculum.[42] With their often detailed, and usually very interesting, descriptions of circumstances that created a legal conundrum, these opinions must have conveyed the impression that the subject of law was more than a text to be mastered and a body of principles to be absorbed. Here and there law students even served a kind of apprenticeship by being attached for a time to the Imperial Chamber Court, where places were set aside for a

[40] From the middle of the century, ready-made commonplace books existed as models. E.g., Johannes Oldendorp's *Loci communes iuris civilis* (Lyons, 1551), which consists of alphabetized entries ("Consuetudo est optima interpres legum"; "Onus probandi incumbit ei, qui dicit, non qui negat"), each with citation of source.

[41] Karl-Heinz Burmeister, *op. cit.*, 234-40.

[42] Many anthologies of legal opinions existed, and these were used not only for the guidance of jurists and judges, but also for purposes of study, e.g., *Receptorum sententiarum sive, ut nunc loquuntur, Communium opinionum iureconsultorum utriusque iuris opus absolutum et perfectum . . . quin omnis in dubium vocata quaestio, hinc resolui possit* (Frankfurt am Main, 1568-1569) by several prominent sixteenth-century jurists, including Johann Fichard.

few journeyman lawyers.[43] Still, throughout the century, older jurists and many laymen criticized the legal profession for the academic manner in which it chose to pass on the sum of its knowledge. Critics pointed especially to the lack of experience and to the naive bookishness of young law graduates practicing at German courts. In the 1550s, for example, the estates of Saxony complained about "law students [who] are in a great hurry to gain their doctorate" and who think that "they have learned enough when they have satisfied the requirements for the degree." What the deputies had in mind was the common observation that these scholars, having had no practical instruction, could not function in a courtroom situation. "When they get into litigation and face opposing advocates they discover how ill prepared they really are." Incompetence was thus added to the other faults of which lawyers stood accused. Because of their inexperience, the Saxon estates concluded, "the university and the whole legal profession have acquired a bad name."[44]

Unaware of the *usus iuris*, of how legal business was transacted in real-life conditions, inept young lawyers contributed to the system's sluggish procedural pace and apparent insensitivity to the rights of the litigant. Their obtuseness to the demands of ethical standards of justice contrasted sharply with the lofty jurisprudential pronouncements made by the famous jurists who had taught them. Their ignorance of indigenous law and its basis in custom helped create the perception of them as creatures of a remote and abstract book learning alien to, and alienated from, the living native tradition. The stilted manner of their speech, formed by academic Latin and the stylized prose of their glosses, estranged them from the everyday language of the people among whom they worked. Prolixity they had developed into a fine art by making it a sign of their learning. Notarial handbooks taught them that half a dozen words were always better than one, because

> it is decorous, useful, and polite for a man who would speak or write German never to employ only one word, but always to use several different synonyms as well as some Latin words conveying the same meaning. For such synonyms act on the understanding like the rising or falling tone of the voice, and thus they sharpen or sweeten what is said, which is useful especially when weighty and important matters are discussed.[45]

[43] Karl-Heinz Burmeister, *op. cit.*, 238.

[44] StA Dr, Loc 9356, "Beratschlagung der Landgebrechen" (1554), 18ʳ.

[45] From Abraham Saur, *Formular und volkomlich Notariatsbuch* (Frankfurt am Main, 1582), 68.

As for the notorious tricks of his trade—incessantly observed and deplored by laymen—the beginning lawyer could learn these from several books of so-called cautels, the most famous being the *Tractatus cautelarum* of Bartholomaeus Cipolla, republished throughout the sixteenth century.[46] "Cautels" were cautionary clauses which, when incorporated or concealed in a contract, enabled one to reinterpret it at a later time. Cautels also gave instruction in how to spot loopholes and take advantage of vagueness and ambiguity in the wording of a law. Cipolla's *cautela prima*, for instance, showed ways of evading the death penalty after committing a capital crime.[47] For the young lawyer, these ruses put a fine edge on his legal cunning and made him a master of subtle points. They were the keys to his profession's secret wiles. To the public at large, they represented what legal practice was all about. Little exaggeration was needed to create the effigy of the lawyer as he appeared in shrovetide play and anecdote: obscure, verbose, false, sly, grasping, proud, scornful, and getting rich on the backs of a public trapped helplessly in his snares.

As FOR getting rich, there is good evidence to show that the suspicion was justified. Top jurists earned splendid salaries, and even on the lower rungs of the ladder of juristic success, an excellent living could be made. Most lawyers no doubt thought these rewards well deserved. Preparation for a legal career was expensive in the sixteenth century. A student might well spend a thousand gulden for books alone during his eight to ten years at university, not to mention matriculation fees, the price of maintaining himself in the style of a young man of good family, the fees asked for each of the advanced degrees (the University of Ingolstadt, for example, charged one hundred gulden for promotion to the doctorate in both laws, twenty-five gulden to the licentiate, and twenty gulden for a plain *doctor legum*)[48] and the large sums required for staging the ceremony marking one's ascent to the doctorate at the end of the long course.[49] These expenses had to be recovered. But the profits coming to able lawyers with a busy practice or in high positions did a great deal more than this. They transformed these costly outlays into a very good investment. Long, arduous, and expensive as it is, wrote Jacob Lersner in 1542 of the study of law, "those who persevere

---

[46] *Tractatus cautelarum* (Lyons, 1535, 1552, etc.).

[47] This was the first of more than 250 such cautels given by Cipolla.

[48] Helmut Wachauf, *Nürnberger Bürger als Juristen* (Erlangen, 1972), 80.

[49] On the cost of legal study in Italy in the fifteenth and sixteenth centuries, see Lauro Martines, *op. cit.*, 84. For Germany: Karl-Heinz Burmeister, *op. cit.*, 274-75.

in it are later amply compensated for their time, hard work, and money."[50] The sources show this assertion to be essentially correct.

Throughout the sixteenth century, the incomes of all grades of lawyers rose steadily, far above what would have been needed merely to keep up with the rise of prices. In step with lawyers' growing usefulness to potentates in state, city, and church, and responding to the seller's market for their services, earnings from official posts and private practice became very handsome. Foreigners continued to draw the largest sums,[51] and not until the early 1600s did native sons reach as high a level of compensation as Italians and Frenchmen. But Germans, too, profited from the sustained increase in fees and salaries over a fifty- or sixty-year period. In the early 1500s, Johann Zwick got sixty gulden annually as a law professor in Basel, Jacob Sturzel forty gulden in Freiburg, Christoph Scheurl eighty in Wittenberg, and Georg Schmotzer forty in Freiburg. By the middle of the century these salaries had gone up to two hundred gulden, and by the 1560s to three hundred.[52] Melchior von Osse noted that since the days when he had taught Roman law as a young man at Leipzig, the salary for the post of *ordinarius* had—he was writing in 1556—risen from sixty to three hundred gulden, and that for the extraordinary lecturer, who read the *Institutes*, had moved from thirty to one hundred gulden in the same span of time.[53] As jurists entered princely service, often combining the duties of this career with the responsibilities of their university posts, figures began to climb steeply (although salaries varied widely from place to place and among positions). In the Landgraviate of Hessen, the chancellor, Johann Engellender, a doctor of both laws and former *fiscal* at the Imperial Chamber Court, earned three hundred gulden a year as early as 1500, half of it paid directly by his prince, the other half taken from the revenues of his chancellery. About thirty years later, three resident members of the landgrave's council holding the doctorate got between seventy and one hundred gulden each for their part-time obligations, to which was added a quantity of expensive cloth for the obligatory court dress. Two licentiates got fifty gulden, some cloth, and an allowance of grain.[54] In the 1560s, mere assessors at the consistory

[50] Jacob Lersner, *Antwort . . . auf die Frage, ob es besser sey, nach . . . beschribenen . . . Rechten . . . oder nach aygener vernunfft . . . zu regiren* (Augsburg, 1542), Aiiiʳ.

[51] Karl-Heinz Burmeister, *op. cit.*, 64-65. François Hotman was offered 500 gulden to go to the University of Königsberg in the 1550s, an invitation he turned down.

[52] *Ibid.*, 164.

[53] Melchior von Osse, *op. cit.*, 411-13.

[54] Franz Gundlach, *Die hessischen Zentralbehörden von 1247 bis 1604* (*Veröffentlichungen der historischen Kommission für Hessen und Waldeck* XVI, Marburg, 1930-1932) I, 106; II, 41-42.

and the superior court in Saxony got forty and sixty gulden, respectively.[55] The post of syndic, or resident jurisconsult, of the imperial city of Hall, which had paid two hundred gulden in 1568, brought six hundred in 1620. In that same year, the advocate to the municipal council of Hall earned two hundred gulden, while the town secretary, a man with legal training, earned one hundred sixty gulden, a salary double the sum paid in 1568.[56] In the middle of the sixteenth century, the University of Leipzig gave its *ordinarius* for Roman law three hundred gulden annually (compared to a mere two hundred each for the "humanist," the *mathematicus*, the *philosophus*, and the professor of Hebrew), but attached the proviso that he must "stay in place at the university and not move about to carry on his practical business."[57]

But most academic jurists did just that: they carried on a lively trade in consulting. The register of lectures at the University of Wittenberg shows long hiatuses when no law was read at all while the professors were away from their posts, working for the elector or for private clients.[58] In 1576 the estates of Saxony lodged a protest against lawyers serving on the boards of consistories and other governmental bodies who, they charged, "look after their private practice instead of meeting the duties of their employment."[59] Such protests were made frequently. If a law faculty was an *Aktenfakultät*—a juristic group to whose judgment the records (*Akten*) of difficult cases were referred for written opinions—its members had a guarantee of high additional income and a reliable means of enhancing their professional reputations.[60] Having gained names as jurisconsults, these men then charged their clients high fees for providing them with opinions and counsel. Melchior von Osse, who wrote scathingly about judicial conditions in his own state of Saxony around the middle of the century, saw this insatiable quest for reputation and wealth as the chief source of his profession's decline into mediocrity. Though the elector had tripled the salaries of law professors, Osse charges, they still took on so much private work that they were bound to neglect their students over it. Those who sat on the *Schöffenstuhl*, the court of appeals in Leipzig "have, because of the fame of this court, the largest and best [private] practice in the whole

[55] StA Wei, Reg N, No. 480, 1ʳ.
[56] Gerd Wunder, *Die Bürger von Hall . . .* (Sigmaringen, 1980), 124.
[57] StA Dr, Loc 9349, No. 7, 20ʳ.
[58] Theodor Muther, "D. Johann Apel" in *Aus dem Universitäts- und Gelehrtenleben im Zeitalter der Reformation* (Erlangen, 1866), 238.
[59] StA Dr, Loc 9349, No. 7, 176ᵛ.
[60] Hans Liermann, "Die Altdorfer Juristen," *Festschrift für Karl Siegfried Bader* (Zurich, etc., 1965), 274.

land." For years now, he said (in 1556), one of the six places on this body has been vacant because the incumbents, eager "to make their personal share of the verdict fees as large as possible," were unwilling to fill it.[61] Prominent jurists often held multiple consultancies or accepted retainer fees from clients while holding a full-time position with a prince.[62] So great was the demand for legal experts of recognized distinction that governments entered into keen competition for their services. Johann Fichard recalls in his autobiography that, while he was studying in Italy for the advanced degree (he already had the *doctor iuris*), he received offers from the emperor's Aulic Council, from the cities of Memmingen and Frankfurt, from the Archbishop of Trier, and from the University of Vienna.[63] Nervous about its bargaining power for legal talent, the imperial city of Hall ordered the most gifted of the theology students among burgher sons away at university to change over to law.[64] It was a good time for lawyers to sell their services, and salaries rose to meet the demand.

The capacity of qualified jurists to earn large sums of money was common knowledge. "I have known several," wrote Argula von Grumbach, a well-connected Bavarian noblewoman, "who did not have enough to pay for a cup of wine when they were young. But after wearing the purple cap for four years or so, they could buy anything offered for sale."[65] Melchior Kling, the well-known Saxon jurist, though of poor parentage and unpromising origins, died a very rich man after making excellent matches for his children with the patrician families of his home town of Halle. Henning Göde, who taught canon law at Wittenberg, was able to endow stipends and scholarships before he died in 1521 and made munificent bequests to charity. Toward the end of the sixteenth century, the jurisconsults of the city of Nuremberg were on annual retainer for five hundred gulden,[66] and when Johann Thomas Freige, the controversial Ramist educator, was made professor of law and rector at Nuremberg's *Gymnasium* in Altdorf, in 1576, he got a salary of four hundred gulden, a magnificent sum compared to the mere one hundred forty gulden earned by teachers of other subjects.[67] Sala-

[61] Melchior von Osse in *loc. cit.*, 411, 453, 433.

[62] Helmut Wachauf, *op. cit.*, 90.

[63] Johann Fichard, *Descriptio brevis cursus vitae meae,* printed in *Frankfurtisches Archiv für ältere deutsche Litteratur und Geschichte,* Johann Carl von Fichard, ed., (Frankfurt am Main, 1812)II, 35-48.

[64] Gerd Wunder, *Die Bürger von Hall,* 126.

[65] Argula von Grumbach, *Ein christenlich schrifft einer erbarn frawen vom Adel . . .* (n.p., 1523), b^v.

[66] Wilhelm Fürst, "Der Prozess gegen Nikolaus von Gülchen" (as in note 12), 133-34.

[67] Hans Liermann in *loc. cit.*, 270.

ries for jurists occupying administrative positions in German territories were even higher. Ludwig Camerarius received six hundred and fifty gulden a year as a member of the Palatine elector's privy council around 1600.[68] The pay of a member of the Württemberg *Oberrat*, a body handling the duchy's legal business with the Imperial Chamber Court, rose between 1550 and 1620 from one hundred and fifty to eight hundred and fifty gulden.[69] Dr. Georg Esslinger, a councillor in Württemberg's *Kirchenrat* and other central bodies, got eight hundred and twenty-four gulden in 1604,[70] while Dr. Matthäus Enzlin, who rose to great fame and influence as privy councillor to Duke Friedrich I of Württemberg, made at about the same time, and by his own estimate, over three thousand gulden annually from the salaries of his various full- and part-time posts and from the fees he charged in his busy consulting practice, not counting free lodging, grain, wine, and cloth, the paid services of a secretary, and freedom from taxation. In 1593 Enzlin's fortune was estimated at over thirty thousand gulden.[71] A contemporary of his, a Dutch jurist on the faculty of the Altdorf Academy, left a fortune of twenty-five thousand ducats.[72] Johann Rehlinger, a jurist in Augsburg and member of an old patrician family there, had, earlier in the century, over sixty thousand gulden invested with various banking and merchant firms (Fugger, Baumgartner, Welser, Manlich) which he also represented before the Imperial Governing Council when they were accused of monopolistic practices.[73]

For less renowned jurists, and humbler practitioners in the lower reaches of the law, the taking was far less lucrative than this. But modest wealth could be acquired in all branches of the legal fraternity. Bartholomäus Sastrow, who served a long apprenticeship as secretary and notary, and later practiced independently as a lawyer, reports in his autobiography that as a humble *sollicitator*—little more than a scrivener—in the service of attorneys attached to the Imperial Chamber Court in Speyer (including one Dr. Simon Engelhard, whose practice brought him in more than two thousand gulden per year), he earned enough in the 1540s to lead a comfortable life. "This trade," he comments, "as long as it has been properly learned and is practiced skill-

---

[68] Hans Hattenhauer, *Geschichte des Beamtentums*, 76-79.

[69] Walter Bernhardt, *Die Zentralbehörden des Herzogtums Württemberg und ihre Beamten* (*Veröffentlichungen der Kommission für geschichtliche Landeskunde in Baden-Württemberg* 70-71, Stuttgart, 1972-1973) I, 20.

[70] *Ibid.* I, 275.

[71] *Ibid.* I, 264.

[72] Hans Liermann in *loc. cit.*, 271.

[73] Franz Josef Schönigh, *Die Rehlinger von Augsburg* (Paderborn, 1927), 16.

fully, allows no one to live in poverty." Many people hold the humble *Schreiber* in contempt, he adds, "but I can tell you that this despised calling has fetched me many a delicious morsel to eat and good mouthful to drink."[74] Generally, such secretaries did well. The post of municipal secretary in the city of Munich, nearly always occupied by a *doctor juris* in the sixteenth century, paid two hundred gulden in the century's last quarter.[75] In Nuremberg the *Stadtschreiber* earned the same sum.[76]

Those who lived entirely from the proceeds of their private practice could also prosper. In Saxony, near the end of the sixteenth century, the fee for preparing a case for trial was three gulden; it cost two gulden to reach settlement out of court.[77] Fee limits were set in many parts of the country in response to complaints about exorbitant charges, and lawyers themselves saw some profit in curbing the competition for clients and what they could pay. Even within the confines of a regulated fee structure, however, a very good living could be made, as comparisons of lawyers with other occupations show. About 1590 a schoolmaster at the Munich *Gymnasium* earned a mere twenty-four gulden per annum plus a free daily meal, but this last perquisite was cancelled a few years later when the post's wages were increased to thirty gulden.[78] Around the same time, the city of Munich's barber-surgeon, a municipal employee, received forty-eight gulden a year in salary (while three medical doctors, also employed by the city, got one hundred gulden each).[79] The post of prison warden in Nuremberg paid thirty-two gulden a year in the middle of the century; this was considered an excellent salary at the time.[80] For ordinary working people, of course, even such sums, poorly as they compare to a jurist's income, would have been princely rewards. In most parts of Germany around 1570 the wages for seasonal work in construction, laboring, hay cutting, and so on, ranged from twenty to forty-five pfennig per day. For about forty pfennig one could at that time buy a pound and a half of lard, or ten herrings, or eight pork sausages, or a pound and a half of beef, or enough turnips to eat

[74] Bartholomaeus Sastrow, *Bartholomaei Sastrowen Herkomen, Geburt und Lauff seines gantzen Lebens* . . . ed. Gottlob Friedrich Mohnike (Greifswald, 1823-1824) II, 610.

[75] M. J. Elsas, *Umriss einer Geschichte der Preise und Löhne in Deutschland* . . . (Leiden, 1936)I, 776.

[76] On the Stadtschreiber generally, see Gerhart Burger, *Die südwestdeutschen Stadtschreiber im Mittelalter* (Böblingen, 1960).

[77] StA Dr, Loc 9362, 139ᵛ.

[78] M. J. Elsas, *op. cit.* I, 755-57.

[79] *Ibid.*, 760, 768.

[80] Gerald Strauss, *Nuremberg in the Sixteenth Century* (New York, 1966), 206.

for a month.[81] Even assuming more or less steady work throughout the year, around twenty gulden was the most a plain worker could make, and no doubt many took home much less than that.[82] The steady rise of prices, particularly of food prices, throughout the decades of the later sixteenth century,[83] and the corresponding drop in real wages,[84] opened still further the huge divide between those who barely got by and those with wealth to spare. This gulf was no less a psychological than it was an economic one, raising resentment of the rich even among relatively comfortable segments of the producing population, and isolating the poor still further. Needless to say not all lawyers were well off; many, in fact, at the semi- or quarter-skilled end of the scale of competence struggled to keep their heads above water. But the high earning power of the famous names at the top of the guild created a stereotype with which the profession as a whole was stamped. Luther spoke for many of his contemporaries when he expressed the opinion that "the real reason why you people study law and become jurists is money. You want to be rich."[85] Wealth, status, and social distance thus tended to embitter still further the deep antipathy which the lawyer's perceived role as an innovator and intervener had aroused in society.

Conforming to the characteristic behavior of a social group solidifying itself as a class, jurists arranged suitable marriages for themselves and their children, founding families with the potential of gaining and holding on to dynastic as well as professional distinction. Some examples follow of this familiar pattern. Dr. Gregor Brück, a jurist in Saxony and an early Lutheran partisan, son of a well-off burgher in the town of Brück near Wittenberg, situated his family solidly in the Protestant establishment there. His son, Christian, became a *doctor iuris* and, eventually, chancellor to Duke Johann Friedrich; he married Ursula, the daughter of the elder Lucas Cranach, while his sister married Lucas

---

[81] M. J. Elsas, *op. cit.* I, 709-39, 248, 288, 294, 304-05, 354, 478.

[82] As a gold coin, the gulden was the currency of the rich, while ordinary people never rose above the silver system of *Pfennig, Kreuzer,* and *Schilling.* Although various coinage regulations among the estates entitled to issue money—emperor, princes, and cities—fixed the relationship between the silver and gold systems, the value of silver to gold continued to deteriorate in the sixteenth century, further favoring the rich who could afford to hoard gold.

[83] See the information and tables in Heinrich Bechtel, *Wirtschaftsgeschichte Deutschlands vom Beginn des 16. bis zum Ende des 18. Jahrhunderts* (Munich, 1952), 85-97; also the discussion there of possible causes of this phenomenon.

[84] See especially the tables in *ibid.,* 87, 384, based on the calculations of Wilhelm Abel and others, of wages in kilograms of rye flour and of the falling purchasing power of money.

[85] WA TR III, No. 2831 (1532).

Cranach the younger. Gregor himself took as his second wife the sister of Antonius Pestel, his duke's secretary. In another part of Germany, Johann Busenreuth, who taught law at the Altdorf Academy in 1580, married into the patrician Fürer family of Nuremberg. Two of his sons also became lawyers. Another Altdorf jurist, Hubertus van Giffen, took as his second wife Justine Ölhafen, who belonged to a leading family in the city.[86] One Melchior Jäger, private secretary to Duke Friedrich of Württemberg in the 1570s, married three times and in ascending social order: first the daughter of a scribe, second the daughter of a knight in the territory, and third Barbara von Haugsleben of old Swabian nobility.[87] As noted already, jurists tended to merge with the territorial aristocracy, but this generally happened through ennoblement. Marriage normally took place within the profession, or else jurists allied themselves with the families of prominent physicians.[88] The Württemberg councillor and advocate Dr. Philipp Lang, for example, joined his daughter to his sovereign's personal physician, Dr. Johann Kielmann, a fellow councillor. The couple's son, also Johann and also a physician, married the daughter of Dr. Kilian Vogler, a law professor in Strasbourg and Tübingen and a member of the duke's council as well. Vogler's other son-in-law was Dr. Johann Bratslager, a Württemberg councillor and judge, who later became chancellor. Kilian Vogler himself had married into the family of Dr. Jacob Königsbach, a council member and advocate, whose father, Johann, had served on the Württemberg superior court since 1521.[89] To take another instance from Württemberg, Dr. Hieronymus Gerhardt, a Tübingen JUD and a prominent council figure: his son, also named Hieronymus and also a councillor, married Anna Maria Varnbühler, whose father, Dr. Nicolaus Varnbühler was a patrician in Lindau, a professor of law at Tübingen, and a councillor serving the state of Württemberg. His two sons, Gerhardt's brothers-in-law, were both well-known jurists.[90]

Prosopographical studies like those of Irmgard Kothe and Walter Bernhardt for the Württemberg councillors, Helmut Wachauf for Nuremberg jurists, and Franz Gundlach for officials in the central admin-

---

[86] Hans Liermann in *loc. cit.*, 271.

[87] James A. Vann, *The Making of a State: Württemberg 1593-1793* (Ithaca, N.Y., 1984), 62.

[88] Irmgard Kothe, *Der fürstliche Rat in Württemberg*, 17, notes that in the late fifteenth and early sixteenth centuries, physicians often served in princes' councils and other bureaucratic posts, being gradually replaced by lawyers in the course of the sixteenth century.

[89] *Ibid.*, 155, 165-66, 182.

[90] *Ibid.*, 161, 168.

istration of Hessen show this pattern to be typical. Thus Dr. Alexander Dittrich, chancellery secretary to Landgrave Philip of Hessen in Marburg and then to Philip's son Ludwig from the 1550s to the 1580s, married the daughter of Konrad Zolner, the chancellery secretary in Kassel, who was a member of a family of similarly placed bureaucrats. Alexander's brother, Dr. Johann Dittrich, held the same post in Kassel under Wilhelm IV in the late 1560s, when Hessen was divided into four parts, as did his son, Alexander, Jr., in the early years of the seventeenth century.[91] Dr. Reinhard Scheffer, the son of a tailor in Homberg who had studied in Padua and, with a JUD gained in 1556, became Hessian chancellor, married the daughter of another Hessian chancellor, Johann Feige. His son, also Reinhard, a judge in the *Hofgericht* in Marburg, married the daughter of a JUD and chancellor Johann Heinzenberger. His wife's mother had been Katharina Lersner of a prestigious judicial family spread all over Germany.[92] Another Lersner, Elisabeth, was married to Dr. Heinrich Krug, JUD, a councillor and judge in Hessen.[93] One more example: that of Dr. Johann Walther, JUD, who was councillor and advocate in Hessen. His son, Dr. Christoph Walther, also a councillor and married to the daughter of a leading burgher in Eisenach, united his two daughters with prominent medical and legal families in the territory. The son of the lawyer family also became a lawyer; he was Dr. Christoph Paul, JUD, later a judge at the appellate court in Marburg.[94]

Toward the end of the sixteenth century, and in the centuries following, this trend in family linking and career making grew more pronounced. Typical is the case of the already noted Ludwig Camerarius (1573-1651), a JUD trained at Italian Universities and Basel, who served as privy councillor to the Elector Palatine and later went as ambassador into Swedish service. Camerarius's wife was the daughter of a JUD and fellow councillor; her brother was a *doctor iuris* who sat as assessor on the Electorate's superior court. His son, also a lawyer, became a secretary and administrator in Sweden. Each of his two daughters also married a *doctor iuris*.[95] Prominent Nuremberg jurists and administrators show the same planned management of family alliances: the Gugel, Ölhafen, Scheurl, Wölcker, Fetzer, Pfintzing, Paumgartner,

[91] Franz Gundlach, *Die hessischen Zentralbehörden von 1247 bis 1604 (Veröffentlichungen der historischen Kommission für Hessen und Waldeck* XVI, Marburg, 1930-1932)III, 46.

[92] *Ibid.* III, 227-28.

[93] *Ibid.* III, 141.

[94] *Ibid.* III, 286-87, 191.

[95] Hans Hattenhauer, *op. cit.*, 76-79.

Tucher, Löffelholz were and remained the prominent *Juristenfamilien* in the city.[96] Studies of individual family lines reveal an astonishing amount of what has been called "social and professional in-breeding" among legal families: the Carpzovs, for example, descendants of Benedict (called "The First"), 1565-1624, a law professor in Wittenberg and Saxon chancellor. Nearly every one of Benedict's children, grandchildren, and great grandchildren married into academic and administrative families, and most of the men were lawyers.[97]

Württemberg, as already indicated, offers us a particularly revealing case of the resulting social and professional network in operation. Thanks to an exemplary prosopographical study by Walter Bernhardt of the officials active in the duchy's central administration, we can trace marriage alliances in process of deliberate cultivation. Taking as an example the families of the twenty-one "learned councillors-in-chief" (*gelehrte Oberräte*) of Duke Christoph (1550-1568), Württemberg's most energetic religious and political organizer in the early modern era, one can observe in a few generations of marriages and consequent kinships the coming into being of a powerfully entrenched class of academic bureaucrats. Only a stemma chart spread over the wall of a room could adequately display the relationships and associations tying lawyers, theologians, statesmen, and—to a lesser extent—physicians into a compact social group whose members were linked not only to one another, but also to their common vested interests as an economically secure and politically prominent elite.

Taking shape soon after 1500, this new elite was firmly in place by the middle of the century. Its founding members were descended from ducal bureaucrats—*Amtmänner, Vögte, Landschreiber, Forstmeister,* and so on—and from municipal secretaries, mayors, judges.[98] With their degrees earned and their positions taken, they made suitable matches and succeeded in placing their sons in positions equal to or better than their own. Dr. Johann Cnoder, for instance, a Tübingen JUD (1523) and chancellor as well as an *Oberrat* at the ducal court in Stuttgart, twice married daughters of mayors of Württemberg cities, including the mayor of the capital, Stuttgart. His son, Dr. Johann Werner Cnoder, also a JUD from Tübingen, began as an advocate in Strasbourg, then joined Duke Ludwig's administration. Johann Werner's

---

[96] Helmut Wachauf, *Nürnberger Bürger als Juristen* (Erlangen, 1972), 78-80, and, especially, the prosopography on pp. 7-64.

[97] Harald Schiekel, "Benedict I. Carpzov (1565-1624) und die Juristen unter seinen Nachkommen," *ZRG* 83 (1966), *Germ. Abt.,* 310-22, especially the table on pp. 318-19.

[98] For this early generation see Irmgard Kothe, *op. cit.,* 131-54.

son, Dr. Georg Cnoder, became an advocate at the superior court in Tübingen. Related by marriage to the Cnoder were, among others, Dr. Johann Brastberger, a *Dr. iur.* from Tübingen and judge at the court there, *Oberrat* in Stuttgart, and later a chancellor under Duke Ludwig. He, in turn, was linked by marriage to the already mentioned Dr. Kilian Vogler, a law professor and councillor in Tübingen, whose daughter, Ursula, married Dr. Ulrich Broll, founder of a large family of lawyers in the late sixteenth and seventeenth centuries. The Cnoder were also related to the family of Dr. Hieronymus Gerhardt, Sr., who had married Johann Cnoder's daughter. Their son, Hieronymus, Jr., married the daughter of Dr. Nicolaus Varnbühler, the Tübingen jurist, which made him brother-in-law to Dr. Matthias Enzlin, who was first a law professor at Heidelberg and Tübingen and then—as mentioned in the preceding chapter—a powerful chancellor in the service of the would-be absolutist Friedrich I until he incurred the ill will of the Württemberg estates. Enzlin, in turn, was tied by blood and kin to the Württemberg councillor Dr. Martin Aichmann, to the theologian and court preacher Dr. Antonius Varenbühler, to Dr. Balthasar Eisengrein—one of the "political," i.e., lay, members of Württemberg's powerful *Kirchenrat,* the supreme administrative authority over the territory's church—and to Dr. Johann Engelhardt, JUD, an advocate attached to the central government's chancellery. One of Enzlin's brothers-in-law, Dr. Johann Christoph Zenger, was chancellor in the County of Mömpelgard (Montbéliard), the home territory of Enzlin's patron, Duke Friedrich. Through his mother's family, finally, Enzlin was tied to the descendants of Dr. Matthäus Alber, a well-known theologian and preacher in Tübingen whose grandchildren, all prominent in church, law, and medicine, included the later *Kirchenrat* member Johannes Alber.[99]

These ramifications could be pursued almost *ad infinitum.* Dr. Hieronymus Gerhardt, for instance, just mentioned as son-in-law to Dr. Johann Cnoder, took as his second wife the widow of another jurist, Dr. David Kachel. His daughter, Anna, was married to an official in the financial administration of the Margraviate of Baden-Durlach, Johann Wilhelm Breitschwerdt, whose half-brother, Dr. Veit Breitschwerdt, JUD from Basel, was a Württemberg councillor as well. Hieronymus's son, also Hieronymus, already mentioned as the son-in-law of Dr. Nicolaus Varnbühler, chose as his second wife a daughter of Dr. Christoph Grösser, a privy councillor in Brandenburg (this second wife, in turn, later became the wife of Dr. Johann Jacob Reinhardt, another

---

[99] For the Cnoder line, see Walter Bernhardt, *op. cit.*, 183-90, 213-16, 314-17; for Enzlin: 121, 249, 258, 270, 314, 686.

Stuttgart *Oberrat* and councillor). Hieronymus Gerhardt, Jr.'s three daughters by his first wife married Dr. Johann Faber, a syndic in Lübeck, Dr. Georg Fischer, a procurator in Speyer, and—almost incestuously—Dr. Johann Wolfgang Grösser, an assessor at the Imperial Chamber Court in Speyer.[100] One final case in point: Dr. Johann Jacob Reinhardt, just mentioned as the second husband of the widow of Dr. Hieronymus Gerhardt, Jr. Of Reinhardt's daughters, one married the son of Dr. Sebastian Mitschelin, JUD, counsel to the Württemberg estates and *Oberrat* for the duke; the other the son of an advocate of the Chamber Court, Dr. Sigmund Haffner. His sons were Dr. Christoph Jacob Reinhardt, married to a daughter of Dr. Simon Ayhin, who had JUD degrees from Siena and Tübingen and was a learned councillor in Stuttgart, and Johann Jacob Reinhardt, who married a daughter of the Tübingen law professor Dr. Zacharias Schäffer.

So tightly woven a net of kin and colleagues situated in high places of state and church could not fail to raise significantly the profession's status, prestige, wealth, and influence. To be a lawyer, certainly to be a doctor of laws, meant taking one's place among the mighty in the world. When Benedict Carpzov, named above as founder of a prolific juristic clan, was a young lawyer late in the 1580s, his profession and family—both his father and his maternal grandfather had been mayors—assured him of easy access to the circles of the well born and highly placed. The autograph book he carried with him on his travels attests to this fact. The names under the *sententiae*, quotations, and remembrances written on the book's crowded pages are those of dukes, counts, knights, patricians, theologians, humanist scholars, and, of course, jurists, all of them willing to give generously of their time and friendship to a promising young man soon to join their ranks.[101] Such connections not only eased an already upward bound course onto the shortest climb to a distinguished career. They did two things more. One was to bind the profession securely to the established elites in society. Everywhere jurists now joined the older ruling classes in positions of social and political eminence. In the city of Hamburg, for instance, lawyers held only two of the twenty places on the City Council in 1575. But by 1650 more than half of the memberships had come into their possession. By then, also, all four mayors were jurists.[102] This was the

[100] *Ibid.*, 188-92, 314-17.

[101] Harald Schiekel, "Der Freundes- und Bekanntenkreis eines deutschen Juristen im letzten Viertel des 16. Jahrhunderts," *ZRG* 87 (1970), *Germ. Abt.*, 290-305.

[102] Martin Reissmann, *Die Hamburgische Kaufmannschaft des 17. Jahrhunderts in sozialgeschichtlicher Sicht* (Hamburg, 1975), 344.

trend from the late fifteen hundreds onward.[103] In the seventeenth and eighteenth centuries, lawyers were mixing comfortably with urban patricians and landed nobles.[104]

A second consequence was that exclusive familial links helped guard the legal profession from infiltration by unwanted elements coming from outside the privileged class. Some observers blamed this closing of ranks for a decline in the creativity of legal thought. "No young lawyer," charges Melchior von Osse, speaking of Saxony in the 1550s, "is advanced nowadays to a university lectureship, or to a position on a central court or prince's council unless he is a member of a family of notables or belongs to their friends, alliances, or cliques [*freundschaften, verstendnusen oder Ketten*] as they are now called."

> If he is born into them, or has connections with them, or has somehow ingratiated himself so that they have taken a liking to him, he is slipped into a good post whether he is qualified for it or not. But whoever does not enjoy their favor, even if he has been to the right universities and excels above all others in intellect and achievements, is not only denied their help, he is also effectively obstructed and harrassed in every way until he takes the hint and goes away. I have often myself seen such things done. The upshot is that no one can get anywhere in this country unless he belongs to the right families or to their circles of friends and relations.[105]

Osse was thinking of widely diffused, interrelated, and powerful juristic families in Saxony like the Fachs, Kommerstadt, Mordeisen, and Pistoris. Ulrich Mordeisen, for example, member of a wealthy clan, with law degrees from Padua and Wittenberg, chancellor for Elector Maurice of Saxony, took as second wife Barbara, the widow of Dr. Modestinus Pistoris, son of the equally prominent jurist-administrator Simon Pistoris, whose other son, Dr. Hartmann Pistoris, was already Mordeisen's son-in-law. Barbara's father, in turn, was the late Dr. Ludwig Fachs, a law professor at the University of Leipzig in the early years of the century. By the 1550s this was a common family story among lawyers, and Osse could easily have found comparable cases elsewhere in Germany to support his charge.

It is no wonder, given this consolidation, that lawyers began to be-

---

[103] Another example: the city of Münster in the early seventeenth century. See R. Po-chia Hsia, *Society and Religion in Münster, 1535-1618* (New Haven, 1984), 111-24.

[104] E.g., Josef Sturm, *Johann Christoph von Preysing. Ein Kulturbild aus dem Anfang des 30 jährigen Krieg* (Munich, 1923), 138-39.

[105] Melchior von Osse in *loc. cit.*, 387-88.

have as a group in the sociological sense of the word,[106] jealously ranking and grading themselves within their profession,[107] blocking incursions from without by introducing educational restrictions and raising social barriers. The "learned" among them—holders of doctoral degrees and especially of the admired degree *utriusque*—dominated the innermost core of this exclusive guild. But influence, place, privilege, and wealth radiated outward from the center to include as well, though in attenuating ripples, the greater part of practitioners in the law. Even a struggling small-town procurator or village notary walked more self-importantly in the reflected glory shone upon his trade by the exalted figures who occupied positions of honor and influence in the high places of society.

But this gleam also made him more noticeable than his obscure station deserved. The general readiness to blame him for the many vexations of ordinary life was greatly intensified by the suspicion and antipathy aroused by celebrated jurist-bureaucrats in conspicuous public positions. One other factor in the rise of lawyers to their eminence remains to be considered if we are to gain a full appreciation of the emotional force of this resentment: the ambiguous role played by them, and by law itself, in the Protestant Reformation. To this subject we now turn.

[106] Heinz Durchhardt, "Die kurmainzischen Kammergerichtsassessoren" *ZRG* 94 (1977) *Germ.Abt.*, 89.

[107] See the convincing hierarchy of types of lawyers given by the French jurist Barthélemy de Chasseneuz in his *Catalogus gloriae mundi* (Lyons, 1529; Frankfurt, 1579, 1586, etc.), a work giving ranks and orders of precedence of the various professions. "Among all doctors of law, those are to be preferred first who teach, then those who have the larger salaries . . . , who compile or write books . . . , who are appointed by the Pope or Emperor . . . , who have several degrees . . . , who teach in the larger, more famous, and better universities. . . ." Quoted in Donald P. Kelley, "Vera Philosophia: the Philosophical Significance of Renaissance Jurisprudence," *Journal of the History of Philosophy* XIV:3 (1976), 269.

CHAPTER SEVEN

Law and Religion: The Reformation

To SUMMARIZE: law and lawyers were prominent features in the social and political landscape of early modern Germany. The high visibility of jurists and their "semi-learned" colleagues resulted from the centrality of law in public affairs, and this, in turn, was a product of new institutions and untraditional practices associated with the shift from a pre-modern to a modern organization of society. To the extent that this transition caused anxiety and distress, law and lawyers were objects of ill will. Held responsible for the disappearance of old ways and the imposition of unwanted new ones, they became targets for society's resentment, anger, fear, and suspicion. More than mere symptoms of what was viewed with alarm, law and lawyers were representative figures standing for an accelerated pace toward untried objectives and the seeming loss of control suffered by individuals over their own destinies.

Roman law was an especially vivid emblem of these menacing trends. As written law, it represented the intransigence of external constraint. As a code enacted by superior force, it stood for intrusion and the leveling efforts of centralizing authority. Above all, it represented power and the unflinching use of it to override all that stood in its way. Of the ideological weapons available for self-defense against this "new" and "strong" law, one—appeals to customs and traditions— had become a blunted tool. Easily circumvented or set aside by administrative fiat, it was often turned against those who tried to use it, thus further disadvantaging the already disadvantaged. This left defenders with one recourse only: to seek aid and comfort from the divine law. As the most radical of all critiques of the existing order of things, the appeal to the will of God in Scripture gave powerful impetus to the revolutionary momentum of the 1520s, and its reforming potential was not lost when the great insurrection went down to defeat. As hope, promise, and—at times—warning, the invocation of divine justice retained throughout the sixteenth century its power to inspire and guide.

These reactions to Roman law were immeasurably magnified by their coincidence with the events of the German Reformation. In an important sense—to be developed in the course of the present chapter— the Lutheran Reformation centered on problems of law: in this respect it was a characteristic event of its age and culture. For this reason, as well, society was prepared to respond to it, enthusiastically at first, more guardedly later. Theologians as much as jurists and statesmen occupied themselves with questions touching the nature of law and justice, the extent and limits of jurisdiction, rights, duties, license, and freedoms. Judged by the quantity of words written on pages and spoken from the pulpit, law counted among the reformers' most pressing religious concerns. To their followers, too, law posed issues considered central to the Reformation's message. No less than in the realm of politics, law functioned in religion as symbol and emblem. Persuaded by early Lutheran preaching, people came to believe that what they had in the past been taught to accept as given truths were, in fact, only statutes made by men. Rejection of these "human" laws was a way of ridding oneself of unwanted intervention. In its original impulse, therefore, the Reformation was driven by a strong antinomianism: hence the shock to public perceptions of the movement's direction when leading reformers appeared to change course in the mid and late 1520s. By sounding its call for a return to a primitive condition existing before written, man-made law, the Reformation at first held out hopes of emancipation from enforced obedience to artificial restraints. Separating salvation altogether from legal obligations, it encouraged during its initial free-wheeling phase, in a public well primed to act on this appeal, an almost irresistible sense of lost Christian freedoms restored. In interesting and significant ways, this expectation was analogous to the widely felt wish to shake the grasp of that other law of the Romans whose agents were seen everywhere now, ready to turn people into passive subjects. Awareness of this correspondence must have mightily reinforced the public readiness to respond to both forms of anti-Romanism. Chronologically and thematically concurrent, the movements of opposition to the two kinds of Roman law, the secular and the religious, seem so closely linked that they cannot have been discrete phenomena. Exploring the connections between them should throw some new light upon both.

In a Christian society—i.e., one more than perfunctorily attached to the gospel as its source of inspiration—law and justice could never be categories wholly temporal or purely religious. Any attempt at segregating them would have been precluded by the gospel itself, in which the interaction of political and theological concerns was established at the very beginning of the Christian era. Like the gentiles, who obey the same (Mosaic) law though they "do not possess [it] and carry out its precepts by the light of nature,"[1] Christians live in a secular world

---

[1] Rom. 2:14.

whose political and social structures represent God's purpose on earth. Paul's famous affirmation of the legitimacy of these external structures is the strongest defense given in the Bible of the authority of legal power over people's lives:

> Every person must submit to the supreme authorities. There is no authority but by act of God, and the existing authorities are instituted by him; consequently anyone who rebels against authority is resisting a divine institution, and those who so resist have themselves to thank for the punishment they will receive. For government, a terror to crime, has no terrors for good behavior.

> You wish to have no fear of the authorities? Then continue to do right and you will have their approval, for they are God's agents working for your good. But if you are doing wrong, then you will have cause to fear them; it is not for nothing that they hold the power of the sword, for they are God's agents of punishment, for retribution on the offender. That is why you are obliged to submit. It is an obligation not merely by fear of retribution but by conscience. That is also why you pay taxes. The authorities are in God's service and to these duties they devote their energies.[2]

Whatever distinctions may be permissible in theology, the "existing authorities" allowed in their own interpretation of "God's service" no differentiation between inner states and outer conduct. As the policies of Reformation churches were to demonstrate, religious and political realms interpenetrated seamlessly in the new Christian state. The Christian subject's correct relation to law was therefore a matter of special interest to both theologians and jurists. Questions about his place in the courtroom were raised explicitly by early Christian writers, and repeatedly throughout the Middle Ages. Sixteenth-century legists asked them again, always answering positively and with great self-assurance and emphasis. Paul himself approved of courts and litigation, notes Justin Gobler in an exegesis of the Apostle's apparent rejection of legal actions in I Corinthians 6:1-7 ("Why not rather suffer injury? Why not rather let yourself be robbed?"). The passage, Gobler argues, means to say only that Christians should settle their disputes among themselves because "Christians are clever enough to make decisions and resolve wrongdoing in worldly affairs." Gobler points out that Paul himself acknowledged the authority of Roman law when he appealed to the emperor. "In any case," he says, "justice and courts were not invented by men but established by God." Scripture speaks

---

[2] Rom. 13:1-6. The translation is taken from the New English Bible. Cf. Rolf Bernhard Huschke, *Melanchthons Lehre vom Ordo politicus* (Gütersloh, 1968), 38-40.

highly of judges, he adds, bringing his argument to a close, and we should do no less.[3]

Regardless of how political the context in which they were spoken, words like "judgment" and "court" (*gericht*), "judge" (*richter*), "law" (*ordenlich recht, gesetz*), and "appeal" (*appeliren*) could not fail to ring with the religious associations imparted to them in sermons and tracts. The reverse was equally true; mental cross references to the worldly judicial scene were deliberately encouraged by the concrete and vivid language favored by preachers and evangelical pamphleteers. For example:

> Christ steps into the courtroom, invites the sinner to approach him, lifts him on his shoulders and carries him to his father who sits in the judge's seat. First he turns to the sinner. "*Confide fili!*" he speaks, "be of good cheer! I shall make a plea to our father as earnestly and dedicatedly as if your case were my own." Next he turns to God. "Father," he says, "here is a poor sinner who has come to me prayerfully seeking counsel and succor. He has reminded me of the love I have shown the world by dying and rising again in obedience to your command. I beg you now to continue to help him, as you have helped him in the past and, when the time comes, to perfect him with your righteousness." And to this plea God the Father replies: "My dearest son, I am well pleased with you. You have paid for this sinner with your own obedience to me, having fully satisfied all my demands. I can refuse you nothing. Go, take him with you."[4]

This vivid little vignette was written in 1552 by the theologian Andreas Musculus as part of an attempt to popularize orthodox Lutheran doctrine at a time of controversy within the Protestant church. It dramatizes Philip Melanchthon's interpretation of justification as a "forensic act" in which God, presiding over the highest of all courts, pronounces the sinner innocent on account of Christ, whose total obedience has ac-

[3] Justin Gobler, *Spiegel der Rechten* (Frankfurt am Main, 1573), 100r and v. Melanchthon offered a rhetorical defense of actions in law in his *Oratio de legibus*, given 1523 or 1524, printed 1525, reprinted in Guido Kisch, *Melanchthons Rechts- und Soziallehre* (Berlin, 1967), 189-209; reference to 193. Attempting to reconcile evangelical values with actions in law, Kilian König, at the beginning of his treatise on procedure, points to this same passage in I Cor. 6 as establishing the legitimacy of litigation for Christians. He cites Deut. 19:15 as Old Testament support for his contention. *Practica und Prozess . . .* (Bautzen, 1555), preface.

[4] Andreas Musculus, *Gründliche Anzeygung, was die Theologen des Churfürstentums der Mark zu Brandenburg von der christlichen evangelischen Lehre halten . . .* (1552) quoted in C. W. Spieker, *Lebensgeschichte des Andreas Musculus* (Frankfurt an der Oder, 1858), 34-35.

complished the forgiveness of all sins.[5] Such metaphors rang true in an age of faith, which was also an age of judicial litigiousness and a time when ever-greater numbers of citizens were gaining first-hand knowledge of legal action. Mental associations shuttling between the heavenly judgment seat and the worldly courtroom with its jurors, advocates, witnesses, and bailiffs placed a solid frame of reference around religious instruction. *Vice versa*, they added a larger-than-life dimension to the ways of earthly justice. Care was taken that the divine guardianship of legal principles was not forgotten on either side of the judicial bar. God and his heavenly justice were more than implicitly present in court. Scenes of the Last Judgment showing God in his high seat adorned the walls of German courtrooms from the fourteenth century on. In the larger cities such paintings were a feature of market squares where the local court met in session.[6] "When the judge pronounces justice, God sits above him, judging judges and jurors. For this reason every judge on his bench shall keep as severe [*streng*] a court as that of our Lord Jesus Christ."[7] In his *Layman's Mirror* Ulrich Tengler admonishes the worldly judge to keep his eyes ever on this spectacle. "A righteously angry judge sits above him," he warns, "and below him yawns hellish torture, within him lies a nagging conscience, and all around him hovers the plaintive world." Facing his own judgment in the end, he will receive as much justice as he has given.[8] Some Judgment paintings made explicit reference to the bearing of true and false witness[9] (a major concern in the conduct of trials influenced by Roman procedure), and to the burden of obedience. Religion being total submission to God through adherence to his law, compliance was the Christian's first obligation. It was the primary duty also of the worldly

[5] On the theological principles involved in this position, and the controversy surrounding it, see Albrecht Ritschl, *The Christian Doctrine of Justification and Reconciliation* trans. H. R. Mackintosh and A. B. Macaulay (Edinburgh, 1900), 122-25.

[6] Adolf Weissler, *Geschichte der Rechtsanwaltschaft* (Leipzig, 1905; reprint Frankfurt am Main, 1967), 234.

[7] Quoted in Georg Troescher, "Weltgerichtsbilder in Ratshäusern und Gerichtsstätten," *Westdeutsches Jahrbuch für Kunstgeschichte* 11 (1939), 139-214. Troescher gives 122 examples of Last Judgment scenes painted on city hall and courtroom walls in German-speaking countries from 1340 into the eighteenth century. The pages on Last Judgment scenes in German town halls and courtrooms in Craig Harbison, *The Last Judgment in Sixteenth-Century Northern Europe* (New York, 1976), 51-64, are based mainly on Troescher's work. See also Samuel Y. Edgerton, Jr., *Pictures and Punishment. Art and Criminal Prosecution During the Florentine Renaissance* (Ithaca, 1985), 22-27.

[8] Ulrich Tengler, *Leyenspiegel*, ed. and expanded by Sebastian Brant (Strasbourg, 1514), 156r-170r. These pages draw an extended analogy between the Last Judgment and actual court trials.

[9] Georg Troescher in *loc. cit.*, 211.

citizen, who had to obey the law and honor the lawgiver—both of these without question or qualification. Each side of this double duty reinforces the other. This is the source of that mutually beneficial close association in which church and state coexisted for so long in the Christian era. The Reformation caused no disruption in this symbiosis.

As long as it is believed that laws originate in God's will, exist in harmony with his commandments, and endure as an expression of his purpose, no major reconstruction of existing arrangements could be justified. Medieval politics allowed for rectification and occasional reformation of conditions believed to be in a state of disorder, corruption, or decrepitude. But revolution was always illegitimate. With its aim of replacing the existing order, revolution usurped the divine prerogative. Only God creates and destroys. Men did not meddle in God's ordained order without the gravest danger to themselves.[10]

On the other hand, if it could be shown that the statutes and ordinances by which men lived failed to agree with God's laws, and for this reason could no longer be said to represent his design, sweeping changes were indicated. Indeed, effecting such a transformation was made obligatory on men by the command to honor and obey God above all other loyalties. Every commitment to drastic change therefore bound its proponents inevitably to the search for a religious justification. It was when things had reached this pass that "God's law" usually made its appearance. This had happened on numerous occasions in the middle ages; it happened again in the late fifteenth century when *reformatio* became a fixed revolutionary idea, growing overtly political in its objectives while leaving the roots of its emotional power buried deep in the ground of religion.[11] The *Reformation of the Emperor Sigismund*, for example, a comprehensive reform treatise written in the 1430s, first printed in 1476 and republished many times thereafter as late as the age of the Reformation, asserts that

> It is an unheard of situation that in Christendom today a man . . . may say to another, before God, "you belong to me!" as though we were pagans and God had not redeemed and emancipated us. God has relased us from all bonds, and no one should be so bold as to claim ownership of a fellow human being. . . . In heaven no one has greater freedom than the next man. For this reason we know that a man who says to another "you are my property" is not a Christian.[12]

---

[10] Karl Griewank, *Der neuzeitliche Revolutionsbegriff. Entstehung und Entwicklung* (2nd ed. Frankfurt am Main, 1969), Chapter 1.

[11] *Ibid.*, 49.

[12] *Reformation Kaiser Siegmunds*, ed. Heinrich Koller (*Monumenta Germaniae Historica. Staatsschriften des späteren Mittelalters* 6, Stuttgart, 1964), 276-78.

No arguments were needed to defend the proposition that human laws should conform to divine commandments. Nor was a distinction between religious and secular kinds of freedom allowed where God's ordinances were concerned. When the astrologer Johannes Lichtenberger announced in his immensely popular and trusted *Practica*, first issued in 1488, that "a new reformation, a new body of laws, a new order, and a new walk of life [*wandel*] will be undertaken, both among the spiritual kind and among ordinary people,"[13] no reader needed to have it explained that this *newe reformation* would first and foremost reestablish the right relationship between God's commandments and man's laws. It was this return of society's positive legislation to its divine source and standard that Zwingli seemed to be announcing in the thirty-ninth of his Sixty-Seven *Conclusiones* of 1523, certainly the most influential declaration made during the Reformation of the principle that "all . . . laws and statutes must conform to God's will."[14] The human individual's paramount duty of obedience to God made any neglect of this principle an act of willful insubordination.

Appeals and warnings of this kind were the recurrent theme of the reform literature of the late fifteenth century. Adopted by the early Reformation, they explain the request made so often in the protest and grievance writings of the 1525 revolution that communities be allowed to hear the word of God "purely and simply." What people wanted to hear above all other things was how the gospel related to their real world, what it entitled them to do in their lives, and what it forbade. This point has been made in an earlier chapter. As the truth of Scripture was not open to doubt, people were willing to accept its authority as long as they heard it proclaimed "purely," that is unmixed with "human interpretations." Justus Maurer notes in his study of evangelical preachers in the years just before and after the outbreak of the revolution that people seemed eager to hear the "pure gospel" applied to their concrete social and economic circumstances, that is to say, to their own reality as they experienced it in their daily existence.[15] A glance at the grievance writings produced during the peasant war shows this to be an accurate observation. What people desired most was a "reformation" of the conditions governing their lives, and they wanted it undertaken on principles taken from Scripture.[16] Secular and religious themes were

[13] Quoted in Klaus Arnold, "Damit der arm man unnd gemeiner nutz iren furgang haben . . . ," *Zeitschrift für historische Forschung* 9:3 (1982), 257.

[14] Article 39: "Darumb sollen all ire Gesetze dem göttlichen willen gleichförmig sein. . . ." *Zwingli Hauptschriften* 4 (ed. Oskar Frei, Zurich, 1952), 112-113.

[15] Justus Maurer, *Prediger im Bauernkrieg* (Stuttgart, 1979), 164-65.

[16] Cf. R. W. Scribner, "Practice and Principle in the German Towns: Preachers and

inseparable, in fact indistinguishable, in the formulation of these principles.

This fusion was not merely the fantasy of naive laymen untrained in the art of making distinctions.[17] Some highly accomplished academic figures, including the jurist Andreas Karlstadt of Wittenberg, agitated during these years—the first decade or so of the Lutheran Reformation—for the implementation of God's law on the human scene, even if this meant setting the civil law aside.[18] One who did draw what seemed to him the proper distinctions between Bible and worldly justice, among God's law, the law of nature, and positive law—Philip Melanchthon—attacked in an academic oration late in 1523 certain doctors who, he charged, planned to turn Scripture into a universal law book,[19] a confusion he found alarming. The practical difficulties standing in the way of achieving this revolutionary aim tended to confine the radical view of "God's law" to manifestoes, protests, and critiques. On the other hand, it became a common practice to justify or defend existing legal and institutional structures by attempting to demonstrate that they met scriptural criteria. In the Protestant state of the later sixteenth century this was routinely done. When the highest ecclesiastical court in Lutheran Saxony announced in 1569 that its president and assessors would henceforth judge cases "by the pure word of Christ, the teachings of the prophets and apostles, the constitutions of the Christian emperors, our common imperial laws (which are entirely compatible with God's Word), and our country's praiseworthy ancient customs," the implication was that all these laws, commandments, and conventions had been brought into agreement with one another, both in the letter and in the spirit.[20] No stronger argument could be advanced for the Protestant state as the executive agent of God's will on earth—although, by the 1560s, the Lutheran claim of having accomplished the long-awaited "reformation" through the territorial church had become too controversial and too partisan a contention to gain more than half-hearted acceptance.

People" in *Reformation Principle and Practice. Essays in Honour of A. G. Dickens*, ed. P. N. Brooks (London, 1980), 98.

[17] For some examples of attempts during the revolution of 1525 to settle legal disputes by reference to God's law, see Justus Maurer, *op. cit.*, 178-85.

[18] Ulrich Bubenheimer, *Consonantia Theologiae et Iurisprudentiae. Andreas Bodenstein von Karlstadt als Theologe und Jurist zwischen Scholastik und Reformation* (Tübingen, 1977), 236, 244-47.

[19] Melanchthon, *Oratio de legibus* (1525) in Guido Kisch, *op. cit.*, 190.

[20] *Ordnung und reformation ecclesiastici consistorii zu Jena . . . Anno 1569* in Emil Sehling, ed., *Die evangelischen Kirchenordnungen des 16. Jahrhunderts* I (Leipzig, 1902), 236.

The dense compound of secular and religious associations in the mental habits of the period made it futile to insist on observing in practical life the tidy discriminations deemed so important by theological and juristic theorists. Ideas and words current in each realm were enriched by meanings imported from the other. At the time of the Reformation, the lavishly orchestrated religious consonances surrounding the concept of law significantly affected the ways people understood and experienced their legal order and the institutions upholding it. Their perceptions of legal constraints, and of the ways in which these constraints bound them to their political and social world, were governed at least as much by religious expectations as by political awareness. The religious side of consciousness was in any case more highly developed, and much more pervasive, than the political side. Public responses to law and to the whole legal situation were therefore significantly more complex, ambivalent, and unstable in the age of the Reformation than the judicial context alone suggests. Martin Luther had much to do with this broadening of attitudes.

FOR obvious reasons, Luther's declarations on law were of great importance in shaping the opinions of his followers. The reformer had a great deal to say on the subject, and much of what he said was passionately expressed, often in strong and vivid language. But as was usual with him, his message was far from unambiguous to readers and hearers not qualified to go to the systematic core of his thought. Depending on the drift of one's selective reading of his many pronouncements, one can gain the conviction that good and honest people owe no obligation to the laws that govern their worldly lives and to the official functionaries who enforce them. Or one can conclude that obedience is the Christian's first and constant duty in temporal affairs. Both conclusions were, in fact, drawn, and in each case the consequences were serious for the Reformation. The point here is not to convict Luther of inconsistency, or to demonstrate lack of clarity or forthrightness in his writing and preaching. It is only to discover and gauge the direction his rousing words are likely to have given to public attitudes to law and the legal order.

As is well known, Luther tended to court extravagance in his declarations, particularly when engaged in polemic combat, which was often.[21] He felt free to assert, for example—in his provocatively rhetor-

---

[21] The best recent discussion of Luther's controversies, and the relationship of his language to the circumstances in which Luther used it, is found in two books (especially the second) by Mark U. Edwards: *Luther and the False Brethren* (Stanford, 1975) and *Luther's Last Battles* (Ithaca, 1983).

ical *Address to the Christian Nobility of the German Nation* of 1520—
that, if the job of reform were done thoroughly, ecclesiastical law
would be abolished altogether and the "long-winded and far-fetched"
imperial law sharply curtailed to make room for his country's "native,
simple, and concise laws." "They say," he writes, warming to his subject,

> that no finer worldly government is found anywhere than among the
> Turks, a nation without either church law or worldly law; they have
> only their Koran. But we, for our part, are forced to admit that, be-
> cause of our canon and imperial laws, there is no more disgraceful
> government on earth than ours, so that no estate nowadays behaves
> in accordance with natural reason, not to mention Holy Scripture.[22]

Far from making people peaceful, agreeable, and productive, laws actually contribute to their baseness. Society, Luther suggests, will be
much better off without them.

Throughout his life as a reformer, Luther gave hints that in his heart
he was at one with the protest against governance by written laws. "I
write more for the sake of conscience than for the sake of law":[23] this
declaration can stand as his motto. Drawing up statutes, or promulgat-
ing, interpreting, and enforcing them, were responsibilities in which he
never took much interest or pleasure, "for law is a temporal thing that
will come to a stop in the end, but conscience is forever; it never dies."[24]
Very often in his career, this disparaging bias led Luther into angry outbursts against lawyers and their profession, particularly when he felt
resisted, impeded, or contradicted by them.[25] At other times, he seemed
to find positive values in the written law. When making his plea for better schooling, for instance, he urged that young people be given an educational grounding from which they could later be trained for posts in
state and church. "As our government in these German lands shall and
must adhere to the Roman imperial law, which is the wisdom and reason inherent in all politics, and a gift of God," he wrote in 1530, "it
follows that such a government cannot survive, indeed it would go to

[22] WA 6, 459.

[23] *Von Ehesachen* (1530), WA 30ᴵᴵᴵ, 245.

[24] *Ibid.*, 246.

[25] Useful surveys of Luther's involvement with, and relationship to, lawyers are
K. Köhler, *Luther und die Juristen. Zur Frage nach dem gegenseitigen Verhältnis des
Rechtes und der Sittlichkeit* (Gotha, 1873); Herrmann Dörries, " 'Der Juristen Schwitz-
bad.' Das beirrte Gewissen als Grenze des Rechts" in *Festschrift für Erich Ruppel* (Hannover, 1968), 63-88; Hans Liermann, "Der unjuristische Luther," *Luther-Jahrbuch* 24
(1957), 69-85.

destruction, if the law were not upheld." Fists and weapons cannot protect our laws, Luther said, only brains and books can uphold them. "We must learn and understand what our worldly empire's laws are, and what their wisdom is." He is speaking not only of *doctores*, he added, "but of the entire judicial trade and profession, namely chancellors, secretaries, judges, advocates, notaries, and whoever else carries out the administration of justice and the government of the state, including the great councillors residing at princely courts." Without the work of these men, he says, peace cannot reign in society; "there will only be robbing, murder, wickedness, and naked power, as among the wild beasts."[26] Local customs and regional codes like the *Sachsenspiegel* do not offer adequate protection against the tendency of men to harm each other. Many of these, indeed, are as crude as the offenses they seek to subdue. "It would be best," he was heard to say, "if the common imperial laws were accepted and observed throughout the whole empire" (this was in 1538, and he had changed his mind by then about the preference to be given to local laws, which he had extolled in 1520).[27]

Such statements—on both sides of the issue of law in society—are found throughout Luther's writings and could be multiplied here at will. Their inconsistency might be embarrassing to a political or legal thinker. But Luther's pronouncements on law and related matters did not evolve from serious reflection on, or deep concern with, the management of temporal affairs. Quite the opposite: his legal views always proceeded from theology, a realm he took to be both preeminent and autonomous. Nonetheless, questions of justice and law occupied a central place in his thought. They were not questions of *justitia civilis* in the ordinary political and jurisprudential sense of the term, to be sure. Law, like everything else, was of primarily religious significance to Luther. But as such it permeated nearly everything he thought and wrote. "All [Luther's] major doctrines contain decisive judicial elements," writes the closest student of the place of law in Luther's theology, Johannes Heckel. "Think of his theology of law, or of his doctrine of the two realms, . . . or of what he has to say on the two ruling authorities, spiritual and worldly! . . . His terminology alone makes it apparent that in discussing these problems, Luther always raises questions of law

[26] *Eine Predigt, dass man Kinder zur Schulen halten solle* (1530) WA 30[II], 557, 559, 578.
[27] WA TR IV No. 4139 (1538). 1520: *An den christlichen Adel deutscher Nation*, WA 6, 459-60.

as well as of theology."[28] This basic affinity tends to be concealed from
us by Luther's habit of portraying jurists as the implacable enemies of
theologians. The reformer was often extreme in characterizing this reciprocal hostility. Jurisprudence and theology are as unlike each other
as heaven is different from earth, he said once, "because jurists will
have nothing to do with conscience."[29] The mutual aversion of lawyers
and theologians was not mere worldly rivalry (though it was this as
well); it represented a much deeper antagonism. "There is eternal strife
and conflict between jurists and theologians," Luther said. "Just as
Law and Grace cannot get along with each other, because they are adversaries, so jurists and theologians are locked in combat, each wanting
to be on top of the other. And the cause of this," he adds, "is that the
jurists insist on having their work acknowledged as the greatest."[30] As
we shall see, Luther was highly intemperate on occasion in castigating
the mental habits and attachments of lawyers of his acquaintance. Despite his antipathy to them, however, he himself saw law as a basic
component of the religious doctrines most closely identified with Protestantism, and this, in turn, shaped his views on the place and uses of
law and justice in temporal affairs. In specific terms, these views related
to three distinctions fundamental to his theology: between law and gospel, between the worldly and the spiritual realms, and between justice
in the world and justification in heaven.[31] Inevitably, temporal justice
and worldly laws got the worst of the associations engendered by this
polarization.

The starting point for all Luther's thoughts about law is the partition
of the world into two realms, one ruled by Satan, to whose empire we
are committed by birth, the other, governed by Christ, the realm of
grace to which admittance is gained through baptism.[32] Each part has

[28] Johannes Heckel, *Lex charitatis. Eine juristische Untersuchung über das Recht in
der Theologie Martin Luthers* (Bayerische Akademie der Wissenschaften, Abhandlung-
en, *philosophisch-historische Klasse* N.F. 36, Munich, 1953), 9. Unlike most other scholars of the question (see note 25), Heckel maintains that Luther was a serious legal
thinker, though, of course, as an aspect of theology. Heckel's assumption is that Luther's
legal thought is consistent and integrated and makes a seamless whole with his theology.
See especially pp. 296-97 for the extent of Luther's knowledge of law, especially canon
law.

[29] WA TR I, No. 320 (1532).

[30] WA TR VI, No. 7029.

[31] See H. W. Beyer, "Glaube und Recht im Denken Luthers," *Luther-Jahrbuch* 17
(1935), 56-86.

[32] For what follows see Johannes Heckel, *op. cit.* For an admirably clear examination
of the terms of Luther's *Zwei Reiche* doctrine, and of the exegetical and interpretive controversies surrounding them, see W.D.J. Cargill Thompson, "The 'Two Kingdoms' and
the 'Two Regiments': Some Problems of Luther's Zwei Reiche Lehre" in *id., Studies in*

its own laws, both natural and positive. Christ's realm is ruled by the divine law of nature situated in the hearts of men, its exemplar being the golden rule, and by certain positive laws through which God has established the right relationship between himself and his creatures. The earthly realm, for its part, is governed by a secular natural law. The code of this law is the second table of the decalogue, the rule to which all positive statutes must conform, although Luther argues that pagan peoples have had independent access to the natural wisdom of this law, and he devoted a page of a major treatise in 1535 to demonstrating that the laws of the ancient Romans should be taken as the model of such *heidnische weisheit*.[33] Positive law in the secular world consists of written codes in which the duties of the social estates to each other are set down. The basis of all these worldly arrangements is the family. The domestic polity headed by the *Hausvater* is the origin, the nucleus, and the model of every political organization.

In the full context of Luther's theology, however, law is never as neutral a force as this simple scheme suggests. Originating in the human being's fall from grace, law (both as *lex / Gesetz*—the words normally used in a theological context—and as *ius / Recht*—usually the jurisprudential terms) is preeminently a bulwark against the evil tendencies rooted in the human heart. Law insists upon complete obedience and subservience, but this is a posture man is neither willing nor able to assume: even the reborn Christian, while on earth, remains as much a sinner as the unregenerate. Both as the divine commandments given in the Bible, and as the natural law in man's conscience, law demands the impossible. Incapable of understanding God's purpose, man rebels, seeks to escape, feels and expresses anger and resentment against the law and its author. In truth, the law is a hard taskmaster. But, as Luther writes in commenting on Galatians 3:24, it does not only flog and frighten us. As *paedagogus*, law also leads us to Christ, and "for this reason the law is good, holy, useful, and necessary, so long as we use it in a legitimate way."[34]

Thus Luther on the spiritual law, the law relating to faith and salvation. As for the temporal law, it "is not a doctrine or law of grace, but of wrath."[35] Three varieties (*dreierley art*) of law exist, Luther explained in his preface to the German Old Testament of 1523. "One sort

the *Reformation: Luther to Hooker*, ed. C. W. Dugmore (London, 1980), 42-59, especially 48-53.

[33] *Auslegung des 101. Psalm* (1534-1535) WA 51, 200-64. Reference is to 242.

[34] *Lectures on Galatians*, ed. Jaroslav Pelikan, *Luther's Works*, vols. 26-27 (St. Louis, 1963), reference to 26, 346, 348.

[35] Sermon of 13 January, 1544, WA 49, 316.

deals only with temporal goods, our imperial laws, for instance. These were established by God mostly for the sake of the wicked, to keep them from doing worse harm. Such laws are intended to fend off rather than to instruct [*nur Wehrgesetz, mehr denn Leregesetz*]."[36] The two other kinds of law, those pertaining to divine service and to faith and love, are not only necessary and useful, but also "good" and "holy." Like the temporal sort, however, their principal purpose is to confront us with our inadequacy. All law reveals sin "and the arrogance of human effort." "For this reason Paul called Moses a minister of sin [*einen Amptmann der Sünde*] and his office an office of death. . . . For Moses could accomplish no more with his law than to show what we ought to do and ought not to do. The power and ability to do it or not to do it he cannot grant." This disparity—between ought to do and can do—is the cause of sin, and therefore of death. "So it is all the fault of Moses: he both creates and punishes sin through the law. And death follows perforce."[37]

This is the "killing function" of Moses the lawgiver. It stands opposed to Christ's life-giving mission. Both are necessary, the killing process initiated by the preaching of the law being a prerequisite of salvation.[38] But it is a task without saving grace. "Now, a minister of sin is nothing more than a legislator, a teacher and executor of the law."[39] Laws are made for the unregenerate:[40] this is as true of the "theological" use of laws (the *usus theologicus*) as of their "political" use (the *usus politicus* or *civilis*). "Law, sin, and death: these three are inseparable,"[41] so Luther concluded in his theses against the antinomians. The stirring passages in his *Lectures on Galatians* in which he portrays the psychological burden on a law-abiding individual who tries conscientiously, but vainly, to fulfill the demands of the law, are justly admired. "By the very act of trying to satisfy the law and to be set free

[36] From Preface to the Old Testament, 1523 and 1545. WA DB, 8, 16-17.

[37] *Ibid.*, 20-27.

[38] Heinrich Bornkamm, *Luther and the Old Testament*, ed. V. I. Gruhn, tr. E. W. and R. C. Gritsch (Philadelphia, 1969), 144-45.

[39] From *Lectures on Galatians*, WA 40¹, 256.

[40] The controversy within Lutheranism over the "third use" of the law—for the sake of the regenerate, as a fixed rule by which to direct their lives—did not erupt until after Luther's death. On this see Lauri Haikola, *Usus legis* (Uppsala and Wiesbaden, 1958) and Edward L. Long, *A Survey of Christian Ethics* (New York, 1967), 84-85. For Calvin on the "third use" of the law, see *Institutes* II, Chapter 7, paragraph 12.

[41] *Hae tria, lex, peccatum, mors sunt inseparabilia.* From Luther's theses against the antinomians (Fifth Disputation, thesis 7, 1538), WA 39¹, 354. Cf. Gerhard Ebeling, "Zur Lehre vom triplex usus legis in der reformatorischen Theologie," Theologische Literaturzeitung 75, No. 4/5 (1950), 243.

from it you have involved yourselves all the more completely in its yoke." This, Luther says, he has learned from his own experience. "The longer I tried to heal my uncertain, weak, and troubled conscience with human traditions, the more uncertain, weak, and troubled I continually made it." There can be no escape from this predicament. "The law was not even given with the purpose that it should justify, but that it should disclose sin, frighten, accuse, and condemn."[42] For this reason, law must be allowed to do its work before the possibility of grace is offered in the preaching of the gospel.

Luther sharpened this view in the late 1530s, in the course of a bitter controversy with antinomian opponents led by Johann Agricola.[43] He accused them of falling into an error opposite to, but just as grievous as, that of the papacy: of relying on grace and gospel to the exclusion of law. To Luther, both were indispensable, but only the gospel spoke of hope and happiness. On the law, Luther stood with Saint Paul in I Timothy 1:9-11:

> We all know that the law is an excellent thing, provided we treat it as law and recognize that it is not aimed at just men but at the lawless and disobedient, at the impious and at sinners, the irreligious and worldly, at parricides and matricides, murderers and fornicators, perverts, kidnappers, liars, perjurers—in fact at all whose behavior goes against sound doctrine.

In an earlier phase of his career, Luther acknowledged, he himself had preached and written against the law. But that was under the pope, when "the Christian church was utterly overwhelmed and burdened with superstitions and false beliefs and Christ was altogether obscured and buried." His object, then, was to liberate Christian hearts "from this incarceration of their consciences." Never had he rejected the law, he maintains, even then.[44] But now that the papacy's stranglehold has been broken, it is possible to see law and gospel in their mutual interdependence. This relationship assigns to the law a double function: the "civil" one of maintaining outward discipline, and the "theological" one of leading men to an acknowledgment of their sins. For Christians in whose hearts the gospel has taken root, the law further ensures (to cite the elaboration of this doctrine later in the Formula of Concord) "that the old Adam . . . may not employ his own will but may be sub-

---

[42] *Lectures on Galatians* (reference as note 34), vol. 27, 13-4.

[43] Mark U. Edwards, *Luther and the False Brethren*, Chapter 7.

[44] WA TR III, No. 3650d (1537). Cf. Mark U. Edwards, *Luther and the False Brethren*, 164.

dued against his will, not only by the admonition and threatening of the law, but also by punishments and blows."[45]

In their writings on the subject of law, Luther and his immediate successors made no formal distinctions between political and theological laws. Though Luther speaks of "varieties" or "kinds," there is but one law, differentiated only by its sundry guises—divine, Mosaic, natural, civil or statutory (i.e., imperial or regional)—and by the uses made of it.[46] All are God's law. The various forms and functions in which it expresses itself are identical in their essentially negative role and their restrictive use. Law always sets bounds, usually narrow ones. Law prevents, forestalls, impedes, and frustrates. Such is its objective. At times Luther presented this goal as a great blessing for humankind. In his 1523 German preface, for example, Luther introduces the Old Testament as "a book of laws that teaches what should be done and should not be done, and, in addition, shows by examples and stories from history how these laws have been observed or broken." All divine laws, Luther says, aim at two objectives: faith in God and love of neighbor. But before people can accept this lesson, they must be admonished and punished; and this is the purpose of all the legislation in the first four books of Moses. Why, Luther asks, the punctiliously detailed lawgiving in these books? His answer is:

> Let us notice in the first place that the laws instituted by Moses for the people are so precise that no room is left for reason to choose any work of its own or to invent any form of worship. For he not only teaches people to fear, trust, and love God, but he also establishes for them the ways of outward worship . . . so that no one needs to choose anything for himself. In addition, he teaches planting, tilling, marrying, litigating, how to govern children, servants, and the household, buying and selling, borrowing and repaying, in short everything that people need to do outwardly and inwardly.

But why such a huge number of statutes (satzungen), including many that seem to us trivial and useless, even foolish? Because, Luther explains, God wants his people to be certain of doing the right thing. In this quest they cannot be allowed to rely on their own devices. "So they are prevented in all things from following their own reason and free will." This also explains why Moses so often adopts a gruff tone and

---

[45] From the Formula of Concord (1577), *Concordia Triglotta* (St. Louis, Mo., 1921), 806.

[46] WA TR III, No. 3047. Cf. F. Edward Cranz, *An Essay on the Development of Luther's Thought on Justice, Law, and Society* (Harvard Theological Studies XIX, Cambridge, Mass., 1959), 104.

seems so repetitive in stating and restating his laws. On other occasions Luther agreed with the common saying that "the more severe the law, the greater the harm done."[47] Moses's mission, however, was not to make things easy for humankind. "This reveals the true nature of his office," Luther writes,

> for whosoever wishes to govern a people with laws must admonish without ceasing, he must constantly urge them on and struggle with them as though they are donkeys. For laws are never obeyed gladly and willingly. No, force and coercion must always be used. And since Moses is a law teacher, it is up to him to show through goading and driving that the work of the law is a work of compulsion. He must wear the people down until by unrelenting insistence he has made them see what is wrong with them and has brought them to an understanding of their hatred for God's laws and a longing for grace.[48]

Again, no essential distinction is allowed here between religious and civil laws, the laws declaring one's duty to God and the laws governing people's mutual obligations in society. All law condemns, all law restrains and thwarts. Law can never be completely fulfilled, but obedience to it is everyone's first duty. To Luther's contemporaries, these phrases could not have sounded—as they are apt to sound to us—like recondite theological dogmas or remote moral imperatives. The civil and criminal statutes of their own cities and states bore the distinguishing marks of this very kind of law. Distrust, suspicion, fear of human instincts were the motives underpinning all political and social legislation in Luther's day. Laws threw up restraining walls, leaving as little space as possible for people's natural inclinations to assert themselves. They were petty, repetitious, admitted no distinction between public duties and private concerns, and treated every deviation as a major infraction. Luther's pointed description of Moses as an *Amtmann*[49] could not have been lost on a public to which the ubiquitous officials bearing that title were—as we saw in earlier chapters—feared and resented intruders pressing peremptory demands. Nor was it accidental that Luther chose this charged political word as the German translation of Paul's *minister*.[50] The Mosaic code—harsh, insistent, hectoring—was the universal paradigm of political legislation. Its fearsome character-

[47] *Summum ius, summa iniuria.* WA TR IV, No. 4178; *Auslegung des 101.Psalm* (1535) WA 51, 204.
[48] WA DB 8, 12-21.
[49] *Amptmann der sünde*, in his preface to the Old Testament (1523 and 1545) WA DB 8, 20-21.
[50] Galatians 2:17.

istics were shared by all forms of law. Laws confine men and confront them with their weakness. They are a constant irritant. Luther's emotive terminology may have served to intensify common suspicions. On the other hand, he could count on the assent of his contemporaries to his theology of law, and he must have powerfully reinforced prevalent attitudes when he concluded that "where there is law, there is loathing."[51]

The impact of this assertion was, however, seriously undermined by two other postulates advanced by Luther, namely that Christians (that is to say true, as opposed to merely nominal, Christians) are freed from the grasp of the law; and, secondly, that to be valid, all laws must conform to the dictates of natural reason. In practice, these positions had the effect of mitigating the psychological burden of Luther's stern lessons, for they opened possibilities of escape from the sentence of condemnation inevitably pronounced by the law. It was this hope of deliverance, of course, and Luther's enormous effectiveness in addressing it to people's real religious and worldly needs, that explains the popular success of the Reformation movement in its early phase. There can be little doubt that Luther's initial appeal—the appeal that gained him the attention of millions whose awareness had been sharpened by decades of reform agitation—was heard as a denunciation of law. Unprepared to accept the distinctions drawn in his theology between their religious and their social selves, Luther's early adherents found in "law" a convenient bridge on which to cross from the spiritual to the worldly realm. Support for the evangelical cause grew in large part out of the period's general dissatisfaction with existing legislation. Luther rallied his followers by holding out the prospect that the fall of the old order would bring new and better laws.

Luther spoke so often and in so many different ways of the ambivalent ties joining Christians to the law that his audiences could not have failed to pay due heed to this fateful problem. The fixed point of departure is I Timothy 1:9: the law is not aimed at the just and law-abiding, but at the lawless and the unruly. The former require neither statutes nor political direction. If all the world were Christian, says Luther (in his 1523 treatise *On Secular Authority*), there would be no need for kings, lords, authority, or law:

> A good tree needs no instruction or law to bear good fruit. Its nature alone causes it to bear what is proper to its kind, without instruction or law. It would be a foolish man who wrote a law book for an apple tree, saying that it should bear apples and not thorns, when the tree

[51] WA TR V, No. 5391.

can do it so much better out of its own nature than if it were compelled by books of instruction and directives. In the same way are all Christians so natured by Spirit and faith that they do more good and right naturally than anyone could force them to do with books of law and instruction.[52]

"For themselves, they need neither statutes nor a code of laws," Luther concludes. But, alas, the world is far from such perfection. "Not one in a thousand is a right Christian," he suspected.[53] Instruction, law, and compulsion are therefore indispensable. The alternative to these is chaos. "The world and the crowd are and remain unchristian," Luther wrote, "though they are all baptized and call themselves Christians by name." Even now, when the gospel has risen again, there can be no talk of abolishing laws, not the Old Testament and not any of the other forms of law. Jesus did not abrogate them; what he accomplished was to remove his own people from its grip.[54] "You Christians," Jesus said to his followers, "must so conduct yourselves that you neither make use of, nor require, such a law. . . . You own the kingdom of heaven. Leave the kingdom of the earth to those who want it."[55] Christians, then, are released from the law, although nothing about their behavior in the world reveals this state of emancipation. Indeed, they are in everything they do the most punctilious abiders by the law. Once again, Luther permits no distinction here between religious and secular laws. Neither Christians nor "non-Christians" discriminate between them in their workaday lives. All law is one. In its overall purpose and in its objectives, it is indivisible.

One might wonder—and, in view of the massive response provoked by Luther in the 1520s, this would not be an idle speculation—where this doctrine left the individual follower with respect to the many external rules set for him by his society. Is it likely to have affected his attitude and demeanor toward laws, and if so, how? The answers given to these questions depend, in turn, on one's solution to a prior puzzle. As they listened to Luther and to his fellow preachers in the evangelical cause, did people tend to think of themselves as lost or saved? If "not one in a thousand" was a right Christian, on what grounds was an individual entitled to think that God in his mysterious way had selected him or her above the other nine hundred and ninety-nine?

No deep psychological insight is needed to doubt the supposition

---

[52] *Von weltlicher Oberkeit* (1523) WA 11, 250.
[53] *Ibid.*, 251.
[54] *Ibid.*, 260.
[55] *Ibid.*, 259-60.

that anyone did in fact perform such a tortured mental calculus. So great is the rhetorical force of Luther's words—particularly when he spoke and wrote in the popular vein—and so positive and optimistic, despite his constant disclaimers and qualifications, the sense he conveys of God's eager solicitude for perplexed humanity, that few men and women are likely to have been persuaded that they must exclude themselves from the ranks of the chosen. In fact, the exhilaration of election is sure to have contributed signally to the enticement of the early Reformation. While accepting, with equanimity or resignation, the unregenerate state of the great majority of his fellow citizens, the receptive individual must have been moved to see himself or herself as part of that special elite of whom Luther, speaking in the voice of Christ, writes so affectingly. This sense of participation placed Luther's followers in a highly privileged situation vis-à-vis the law—a favored position exactly opposite to the subordinate condition in which the greatest number of them actually found themselves in the world. Complying with the law out of a sense of *noblesse oblige* was a far better thing than obeying it because low birth and menial rank left one no choice. Minding commands as a member of a select small band was infinitely preferable to heeding them because it was one's station in life to submit. In these—explicitly political and social—terms, the Reformation's original message would seem to have contained a deeply—because psychologically based—and concretely—because socially understood—antinomian strain and a bracingly libertarian allure. The broadcasting of this appeal won Luther the massive acclaim that lifted his movement off the ground. The expectation of changing places with the privileged—those favored by the law—could not have been the least among the attractions of his cause.

One can only guess, of course, at the contribution made by this outlook to the individual Lutheran's sense of personal worth. But surely it gave a significant psychological and emotional boost to the Reformation movement. The triumph of the New over the Old Testament was in this context understood in concrete terms as the victory of the emancipator over the *Amtmann*.[56] Luther's most patiently explained and in-

[56] I agree with Steven Ozment's formulation of the original appeal of Lutheranism: "In an age when religion embraced far more than it does today, people were most sensitive to social change radiating from the religious sphere. The basic thing one needs to know in weighing the attraction of the Reformation is exactly what Protestants proposed to do to the religious life of cities and towns. How were communities to be altered, individually and socially, psychologically and institutionally, by the implementation of Protestant ideas?" *The Reformation in the Cities. The Appeal of Protestantism to Sixteenth-Century Germany and Switzerland* (New Haven, 1975), 47. I disagree, however, with Oz-

sistently reiterated distinctions between spiritual and secular realms[57] could not break down the penchant of his age for merging and confounding the two. This tendency to link and fuse[58] must be kept in mind if one is to understand the dismay, and consequent loss of fervor, shown by many groups in society when they witnessed the Reformation's later turn to a posture of law and order.

Early responses to the Reformation were reinforced also by the second of the two claims with which Luther in effect moderated his pronouncements on the restrictive character of laws. To deserve assent, he contended, laws must agree with natural reason. Like his declaration setting reborn Christians apart from the law, this doctrine of natural right created ambiguities on the question of the individual's responsibility to the law: when do the dictates of natural right apply, and who is to judge? Luther worked out no formal separations between natural law and divine law: he tended to treat them as equivalent or even as identical.[59] By God's dispensation, natural law is "implanted in all mankind," "in everyone's heart,"[60] enabling us to distinguish right from wrong. Pagans have it as well as Christians (Romans 2:15). Somewhat "dark" and "obscure," natural law calls upon reason to reduce it to intelligible propositions. Moses achieved this most excellently among human lawgivers,[61] but the imperial law, too, is "what human reason has concluded and established from the law of nature."[62] "Written laws" cannot extend the natural law to every single case. "I say this

---

ment's contention that religion is always the primary arena of experience. It seems to me that, then as now, mundane life is what matters. When Ozment, emphasizing the Reformation's conservatism, wonders why it was that when "so many religious concepts, values, practices, and institutions [were] shaken at their foundations, yet seemingly so few questions [were] raised about basic social attitudes and political structures . . ." (ibid., 116), he has neglected to ask how people below the ranks of evangelical leaders felt about these issues.

[57] E.g. Sermon on John 8:34-38 (1532): WA 33, 668. Cf. ibid., 659-60.

[58] For some telling examples of this tendency, see Justus Maurer, Prediger im Bauernkrieg, 178-85. Peter Blickle, The Revolution of 1525, 92, sums up the advantages, to the revolutionaries of the 1520s, of using the New Testament as a criterion: "Godly law was particularly dynamic in three senses. First, demands of any kind could be submitted, so long as they could be supported from the Bible. Secondly, corporate barriers, which had formerly divided peasants from townsmen, could be dissolved. And thirdly, the social and political order of the future now became an open question." See also ibid., Chapter 9: "Reformation Theology and Revolutionary Practice."

[59] WA TR II, Nos. 2151, 2243; III, No. 3650d. For a guide to the literature on Luther's view of natural law, see F. Edward Cranz, op. cit., 105, note 107.

[60] Wider die himmlischen Propheten (1525), Part I, WA 18, 80. Also, Eine Unterrichtung, wie sich die Christen in Mosen sollen schicken (1525) WA 16, 372, etc.

[61] WA TR III, No. 3650d.

[62] Ibid. VI, No. 7013.

212 — The Reformation

so that no one should imagine that it is enough and well done merely to follow the written law and the palavering of the jurists. More than this is needed."[63] What is needed, in addition, is *vernunft*, reason. Without this faculty to give it meaning and application, the written law is dead.

During the troublesome mid-1520s, this growing conviction that positive law must be animated by divinely authorized and rationally interpreted natural law led Luther to a thoroughgoing reexamination of the place of the Mosaic code in Christian life. In the face of spiritualists (*schwermergeister*) and other "sectarians" who, he said, "want to govern people by the letter of the Mosaic law,"[64] he now maintained that Moses "is of no concern to us" as a lawgiver.[65] Only as a religious teacher need Christians accept him; we turn to him "for the sake of the splendid examples he has given in his books of faith, love, and the cross," and for certain lessons which we cannot learn "by nature" concerning "God's promises and assurances about Christ."[66] For the rest, the Mosaic code is only "the Jews' *Sachsenspiegel*," in other words, a book of particular laws made for their special circumstances, "given to the people of Israel alone."[67] "If someone," says Luther, "holds Moses and his commandments up to you, urging you to obey them, say to him: 'Be off to the Jews with your Moses. I'm not a Jew. Don't bother me with your Moses.' "[68] Before Christians can agree to heed them, Moses' laws must meet one vital condition. Only when they coincide with the natural law are they to be taken as universally binding. "Thou shalt not kill," for instance, "is not Moses' law only . . . but also the *natürliche gesetz*, inscribed in everyone's heart." We are bound to obey it because it is a natural, universal law, not merely a law of Moses. We teach the Ten Commandments because "nowhere else are the natural laws so excellently and suitably indicated as by Moses. This is why we take our examples from him."[69] Luther concludes: "I do not observe the commandments given by Moses simply because Moses commanded them. I keep them because they were implanted in me by nature, and because Moses and nature are in agreement on them."[70]

This position marks a considerable change from the days when Lu-

[63] *Von weltlicher Oberkeit* (1523), WA 11, 272.

[64] *Eine Unterrichtung, wie sich die Christen in Mosen sollen schicken* (1525), WA 16, 372.

[65] *Ibid.*, 373.

[66] *Ibid.*, 391, 381.

[67] *Ibid.*, 378; *Eine Unterrichtung, wie sich die Christen in Mosen sollen schicken* (1527), WA 24, 6, 9.

[68] *Ibid.*, 7.

[69] *Wider die himmlischen Propheten* (1525), WA 18, 80-81.

[70] *Unterrichtung . . .* (1525), WA 16, 380.

ther praised the Old Testament as "a book of laws that instructs us on what we shall do and shall not do."[71] Actually, Luther often reverted to this older position. The words just quoted, from the 1523 preface to the German Old Testament, were repeated when the preface was published again in 1545. We hear his earlier voice also in his opinion on marriage in 1530[72] and in his advice to Philip of Hesse on the question of bigamy.[73] Attempts have been made to resolve the inconsistency.[74] But to find the explanation for Luther's shifts it is necessary only to remember how volatile the reformer was in his reactions to the events and problems crowding in upon him in the 1520s and 1530s. No law is so well drafted or so cogently worded, he found, that it does not lend itself to abuse by the wrong-headed, the ignorant, or the malevolent. Written law therefore offered no protection from human folly and vice. It is the interpreter's "heart and mind" that makes the law just or unjust in its application. "For this reason I do not write laws for a prince; instead I try to inform his heart so that he may be well disposed in all law-making and in his councils, judgments, and actions."[75] Only if those who make and use them fear and love God, can laws be good.[76] By themselves, laws are mute. No judge can give a sound verdict unless he be pious, wise, learned, and possessed of moral courage.[77] Matters of law are therefore always first and foremost questions of conscience.[78] This is why good men are so desperately needed at all times in government, and so sorely missed when they are wanting.

Working on his exegesis of Psalm 101 in the early 1530s while worried over political and moral conditions at the Saxon court, Luther made clear what he considered to be the correct relationship between law and reason, or conscience (not recognizing much of a distinction between the two).[79] God made "two kinds of people," he writes, who live on earth in their various estates. A few among them are especially favored with qualities of heart and mind. These gifted individuals need little instruction or learning. "Before one can teach them what they should do, they have already done it." Of such men it can be said that "they carry the natural law in their heads." Antiquity was full of such

[71] *Vorrede auff das Alte Testament* (1523 and 1545), WA DB 8, 12-13.
[72] *Von Ehesachen* (1530), WA 30[III], 208, 218, 241, etc.
[73] K. Köhler, *Luther und die Juristen*, 26-31.
[74] Heinrich Bornkamm, *Luther and the Old Testament*, 82-83, 120-79.
[75] *Von weltlicher Oberkeit* (1523), WA 11, 273.
[76] *Auslegung des 101. Psalm* (1535), WA 51, 204.
[77] *Der grosse Katechismus* (1529), WA 30[I], 169-74.
[78] *Von Ehesachen* (1530), WA 30[III], 246.
[79] *Auslegung des 101. Psalm*, WA 51, 200-64.

champions, and even in our time, an occasional political personage is found to be so endowed, the late Elector Frederick the Wise, for one. For the most part, however, we are bereft now of these "miracle men of God," though most of us still "imagine that we carry the natural law in our heads."

> If natural law and reason were crammed into all the heads that look like human skulls, even fools, children, and women could govern and make war as successfully as David, Augustus, and Hannibal. . . . Indeed all human beings would be the same, and no one could assume rule over the rest. . . . But this is not so, for God has created us in such a way that people are unequal . . . , the precious gem called natural law and reason being a rare thing among them.[80]

In the absence from the political scene of *Wundermänner* innately enlightened by the natural law our statutes lack that "force of nature" (*Kraft der Natur*) that would make them "healthy." Deprived of that strength, they are "feeble," mostly "patchwork and petty-fogging." Pending the appearance of new *Wundermänner*, it is best, therefore to stay with the imperial laws, at whose core lies that "pagan wisdom" captured by "the splendid old jurists" of ancient Rome, the like of whom we are not likely to see again. Such laws are no guarantee of justice in a sick world. But they will serve us better than anything else, says Luther, "while the Roman empire endures to the day of reckoning."[81]

Apart from clearing the way for new "miraculous men" to judge laws and pronounce them good or ill, this position reinforced the double standard intrinsic to Luther's religious thought: a few know, a few can act, but most cannot. Having first raised expectations that oppressive laws might be set aside in favor of more equitably distributed burdens, Luther then dashed these hopes by upholding existing statutes as the best that circumstances permitted in a corrupt world. Though he showed open contempt for the pretensions of princes and jurists who acted, he often said, as though they had "the law of nature in their heads," he was content to suffer their arrogance "while the Roman empire endures." He counselled respect and obedience for the law even as he excoriated, ridiculed, and condemned its practitioners. This was piling ambiguity upon uncertainty. But the upshot for those who read and

---

[80] *Ibid.*, 207-14.
[81] *Ibid.*, 242. These sentiments contrast somewhat with TR IV, No. 4734 (1539): "Die römischen Gesetz sind nu ab und todt weil Rom nicht mehr ist, sondern ist gewest." In any case, Luther believed that the last of the empires would not endure much longer: TR I, No. 349 (1532): "Der Perser und Griechen Gesetze haben aufgehört und sind abgetan. Die römischen oder kaiserlichen hangen noch gar ein wenig, gleichwie an einem seidenen Faden. . . ." On Luther and Roman law, see Johannes Heckel, *op. cit.*, 86-88.

heard Luther could not possibly have been the deferential and cooperative assent to the laws to which he admonished them.

No ambiguity, on the other hand, clouds Luther's view of lawyers. In this he remained constant throughout his career. He disliked them, sometimes with a passion, and it is not possible that his strong animus, copiously expressed, could have failed to inflame further his followers' already irritated opinions on the legal profession. Luther's antagonism arose from conflicts over fundamentals. But it also chafed against petty annoyances and chicancries. "They rule the world with opinions and suppositions, not with the principles of right and wrong,"[82] he charged, denying to jurisprudence any regard for truth, faith, and ideals. "Jurists say that it is hazardous to give definitions, to describe a thing as it really, rightly, and certainly is." What can an "anxious, perplexed conscience looking for help" do when offered their "shifting notions and presumptions"?[83] The root cause of Luther's distaste for the law was therefore his belief that it lacked a grounding in certainty. Jurists are like organists, he said; if one of their stops doesn't work, they pull another.[84] Unlike theology, which does not admit to exceptions or reservations, jurisprudence knows no rule or principle "that cannot in particular cases be bent or set aside."[85] For Luther, this was the ultimate in moral irresponsibility. "The simple truth," "right and wrong," "the ground or foundation of things"[86]—these are of no interest to jurists. "Lawyers are concerned only with what will work in practice [auf der Practica]."[87] What distinguishes them, then, from cobblers and tailors?[88] He has only known one pious jurist in his life, Luther said.[89] "If you distilled a jurist down to his quintessence, he would not be able to explain a single one of God's commandments."[90] Even if you found a jurist or two who believes like a Christian, you could be certain that "he has learned it from me and from Holy Scripture, not from his law books."[91] Hence the proverb *Juristen, böse Christen.*[92] "Many of them are enemies of Christ. As the saying goes, 'a good jurist is a wicked

82 WA TR III, No. 3622 (1537).
83 *Ibid.* I, No. 1043 (early 1530s).
84 *Ibid.* I, No. 134 (1532). Cf. I, No. 577.
85 *Ibid.* I, No. 349 (1532).
86 *Ibid.*
87 *Ibid.* III, No. 3872 (1538).
88 *Ibid.* VI, No. 7018.
89 *Ibid.* II, No. 1421. He meant Dr. Gregor Brück, a prominent Wittenberg jurist and strong Lutheran partisan in the 1520s and 1930s.
90 *Ibid.* IV, No. 4382 (1539).
91 *Ibid.* VI, No. 7014.
92 *Ibid.* III, No. 2809b; V, No. 5663 (1544). Or *omnis jurista est inimicus Christi, ibid.* I, No. 1217 (1532).

Christian,' for they all extol and praise justification by works as if through this we could gain righteousness and salvation before God."[93]

Preaching on Matthew 5 to 7, Luther identified jurists as fighting in the devil's vanguard against the Sermon on the Mount:

> The most zealous of those who have launched an attack on this fifth chapter [of Matthew] are those loutish pigs and asses, the jurists and sophists, . . . who have sucked poison from this lovely rose and spewed it upon the whole world. . . . And they cannot deny this sin, for their own books and glosses testify against them, not to mention the wicked and unrepentant lives they lead as they follow their own teachings, which are that the twelve counsels of the gospels need not be kept, namely, not to requite wickedness, not to avenge, to turn the other cheek, to resist not evil. . . . None of these, they sputter, is commanded. . . .[94]

Jurists can give you sharp advice on how to make a quick profit from money lent to a fellow Christian in need.[95] In such "filthy business" (*Dreckhändeln*) they are unrivalled experts,[96] and Luther is willing to leave them to it. Happily he can say that "I don't understand the laws [*die Rechte*], but I am an authority on what is right [*im Rechten*]," meaning in matters touching the human conscience.[97] But these charges do not go to the heart of his objections. The most serious accusation he hurled at jurists is that they intrude on God's domain and usurp powers not rightly in their earthly province. On this point—"that they invade the realm of Christ and make war on poor consciences"—he vented his fury in a sermon, in 1544, the tone of which reached what was, even for Luther, a climax of intemperance and abuse:

> . . . they have extended their reach into the Lord Christ's own spiritual government and want to have their hands in all things, forcing everyone to live by their law and thus make a ramshackle thing of people's conscience, which we have only recently begun to build up again by giving it a stable foundation to rest upon.

Even "in our own town of Wittenberg," he charges, we now have "arrogant jurists [who] don't read our books, who care nothing about our

---

[93] *Ibid.* I, No. 349 (1532).

[94] From the preface to *Das fünffte, Sechste und Siebent Capitel S. Matthei gepredigt und ausgelegt* (1532), WA 32, 299-300.

[95] *An die pfarrherrn, wider den Wucher zu predigen* (1540), WA 51, 334.

[96] WA TR VI, No. 7021.

[97] *Ibid.* I, No. 1043 (early 1530s).

Lord, and who never see the inside of our churches." Why should we take their advice on anything?

> If all the jurists in the world called a hundred thousand witnesses, but I knew in my conscience that an injustice was being done, I would not let the pope's law stand in the way of doing the right thing. [And if they say] "you are going against the law," [I ask] against what law? Against the imperial law? I shit on the imperial law, and on the pope's law too, and for good measure on the jurists' law as well.

And if their witnesses come to testify against you, say to them, "My dear jurists, I can name you many false witnesses from the beginning of the world." Law is a matter of conscience. A pious judge knows in his heart when an accused man is innocent, or which side is right in a particular case. "But a jurist doesn't concern himself with conscience."[98]

Several circumstantial factors combined with Luther's overall position on the law to cause this particular outburst and many similar ones in the 1530s and 1540s. Most galling to him was the judicial fraternity's refusal to abandon the canon law. Luther had long regarded the law of the Church as clear evidence of the papacy's usurping ambitions (in 1520 he had urged that it be "blotted out from A to Z").[99] Now he thought it deplorable that "the jurists [still] hold canon law in repute and give it authority."[100] Their stubborn adherence confirmed his suspicion that the greater part of them were open or clandestine papal loyalists.[101] "I could put up with you," he told lawyers, "if you kept to your imperial laws and let go of the papal laws. But all you doctors of both laws are partisans of the pope and his canons."[102] It enfuriated him that the ecclesiastical law continued to be taught at the universities:

> Jurists have the impudence to give public lectures to our young men on that papal filth, the canon law. So much for our efforts to banish it from our church! . . . We see them bloated with pride as they now

[98] Sermon of 6 January 1544, WA 49, 294-307. References to 298-304. Luther returned to the attack on jurists in several subsequent sermons in January and February 1544.

[99] *An den christlichen Adel deutscher Nation* (1520), WA 6, 459. On Luther's attitude toward canon law in the years before 1520, see Wilhelm Maurer, "Reste des kanonischen Rechtes im Frühprotestantismus," *ZRG* 51 (1965), *Kan. Abt.*, 146, reprinted in *id., Die Kirche und ihr Recht*, ed. Gerhard Müller and Gottfried Seebass (Tübingen, 1976), 145-207.

[100] WA TR VI, No. 7023.

[101] *Ibid.* VI, No. 7011.

[102] *Ibid.* II, No. 2496b.

reintroduce this stinking filth. . . . But don't provoke me! . . . We theologians are not going to be ruled and dominated by you. Authority and dominion belong to us.[103]

Luther vowed that "we will not let the jurists force us to go down on our knees before the papal dung and filth. If they want to keep their law for themselves, let them. . . ; but we must not permit them to put this godless doctrine into the heads of our young people."[104]

As many scholars have pointed out, Luther's attack on canon law was a particularly virulent episode in a long-standing bout between theologians and jurists. Fought in the medieval church, notably at the universities, this conflict between two professional groups touched not only the rival claims of divine and human justice, but also their members' competing responsibilities in the administration of the church.[105] This battle continued to be waged in the Reformation. To Luther the issue was clear-cut and simple. "The canonists' preeminent argument is the following," he asserted. "They say 'our teachings have been confirmed by emperors and kings. The Lutheran doctrine, on the other hand, has been neither accepted nor confirmed; on the contrary, it has been condemned.' I answer: God is above emperors and kings, and he is above jurists, too."[106] God's word and law are superior to all codes and statutes. As for the papal law, Luther said, take vanity, ambition, and greed away from it, and what is left but "a painted façade"?[107]

This was the theological view, and Luther proclaimed it with all his might. For academic lawyers the problem was a great deal more complex. As they saw it, canon law remained what it had been for centuries: an inseparable part of the legal tradition, civil and criminal, of Europe. It was interlinked so intricately with imperial, regional, and urban codes and, through these, with the procedures used in secular and church courts throughout the empire, that it was virtually impossible to pry it loose. Although a kind of visceral reaction against it accompanied the excitement of the early Reformation—Luther symbolically burned the canon law in 1520—it was back in the university

---

[103] *Ibid.* IV, No. 4382b (1543).

[104] *Ibid.* IV, No. 4743 (1539).

[105] See Heiko Oberman, *Werden und Wertung der Reformation. Vom Wegestreit zum Glaubenskampf* (Tübingen, 1977), 199-200; Ulrich Bubenheimer, *Consonantia Theologiae et Iurisprudentiae*, 218-20; Erich Genzmer, "Kleriker als Berufsjuristen im späten Mittelalter," *Études d'histoire du droit canonique dédiées à Gabriel LeBras* II (Paris, 1965), 217. Cf. Roderich Stintzing, *Geschichte der deutschen Rechtswissenschaft* (Munich, 1880-1884), 1. *Abteilung*: "Der Kampf um das kanonische Recht."

[106] WA TR IV, No. 4743.

[107] *Ibid.* IV, No. 4083.

curriculum by the 1530s, even in Wittenberg where, though reduced in importance (only one professor taught it, compared to four before 1517), it was as firmly established as a necessary discipline as it had ever been.[108] Lutheran jurists who could not accept this accommodation changed over to theology, as Justus Jonas did, for example. On the opposite side were legal scholars like Ulrich Zasius, Bonifacius Amerbach, and Christoph Scheurl, who abhorred the break with tradition represented by the Protestant movement and supported it only half-heartedly for this reason, or turned against it. As Zasius wrote to Luther, in 1520, "we think it is wrong to overturn an arrangement that has for so long a time been accepted as right."[109] Most Protestant jurists, following the example of Melanchthon, agreed with the latter position and suppressed their doubts. Whatever incongruity they sensed between the old papal law and their evangelical doctrines, they subordinated their scruples to the canon law's indispensability as the only available, universally recognized, comprehensive, and uniform code of laws with which to organize and operate the new territorial churches.[110]

Because it had long ago been received into the common law of Europe, and was closely meshed with it, the canon law thus retained its validity for Lutheran churches; the fact that it was also a papal law did not—at least from the jurist's point of view—jeopardize its legitimacy. Even Luther himself distinguished on occasion between the *Decretum*, the original twelfth-century core of the canon law composed by Gratian, and the additions later made to it by the popes.[111] It is not true, wrote Lazarus Spengler, the influential secretary to the government of the city of Nuremberg, in an—anonymously published—anthology of selected passages from canon law, that "like the spider, we suck, draw,

[108] Hans Liermann, "Das kanonische Recht als Gegenstand des gelehrten Unterrichts an den protestantischen Universitäten Deutschlands in den ersten Jahrhunderten nach der Reformation," *Studia Gratiana* III (Bologna, 1955), 541-66; K. Köhler, *Luther und die Juristen*, 110-23. On the interpenetration of canon and civil laws in the administration of a state, see Lauro Martines, *Lawyers and Statecraft in Renaissance Florence* (Princeton, 1968), 92-93.

[109] Zasius to Luther, 1 September 1520, WA Br II, No. 336, p. 182.

[110] Hans Liermann in *loc. cit.*, 542. For examples of the acknowledgment of canon law in Lutheran *Kirchenordnungen* in the sixteenth century, see Rudolf Schäfer, "Die Geltung des kanonischen Rechts in der evangelischen Kirche von Luther bis zur Gegenwart," *ZRG* 36 (1915), *Kan. Abt.*, 181-202.

[111] In a brief preface to a compilation of parts of the *Decretum* and *Decretals* that agreed with Scripture made by Lazarus Spengler in 1530, Luther seems to approve of the original, twelfth- and thirteenth-century core of the canon law, arguing that the popes themselves violated this law in their later declarations and actions. WA 30[II], 219.

and use from these books of church law only matter opposed and repugnant to divine and human truth, Scripture, virtue, and fairness." There is much in these books, he maintained, "that is godly, Christian, founded in Scripture, and conducive to an upright, honest, and pious life."[112] This eclectic acceptance became the Protestant position. The new school of canonistic jurisprudence founded in Wittenberg by the distinguished Lutheran jurist Melchior Kling became exemplary for other Lutheran universities in Germany.[113] As late as the eighteenth century, the *Decretum* and *Decretals* were cited by chapter and verse in the *consilia* of Protestant law faculties and in the legal opinions handed down by consistorial authorities of Lutheran state churches.[114] "As long as it is not abused and is kept within its proper limits," declared the juristic faculty of Leipzig, speaking of the canon law, "it cannot be regarded as godless, unchristian law, nor is it harmful or burdensome to our church."[115]

A particular bone of contention between Luther and his Protestant canonists was the law of betrothal. In the 1530s and 1540s the conflict over this issue—not a major legal point between Catholics and Lutherans, but a problem close to Luther's most heartfelt concerns as pastor and curator of troubled souls—surfaced in a number of disputes on the question of clandestine engagements.[116] Canon law, following Roman law on this point, recognized two kinds of betrothal as valid contracts leading to marriage. One was agreement for present marriage, called *sponsalia per verba de praesenti*, the other agreement for future marriage, *sponsalia per verba de futuro*. The couple's consent being mandatory in each case, the distinction lay in the tense of the words spoken by each to the other: "I take you" (present tense) or "I shall take you" (future). "Present" betrothal leading to immediate consumma-

---

[112] [Lazarus Spengler], *Eyn kurtzer ausszug aus dem pebstlichen rechten der Decret und Decretalen* (Wittenberg, 1530), Aiii^v-Aiv^r. The first edition of this work, also 1530, was printed in Nuremberg. For the controversy surrounding Spengler's selection—Johann Cochlaeus published three attacks and refutations of it—see WA 30^II, 215-18.

[113] Hans Liermann in *loc. cit.*, 548-49. For the interesting early view of Andreas Karlstadt on the grounds for a "consonance" of theology and jurisprudence, see Ulrich Bubenheimer, *op. cit.*, 222-32.

[114] Roland Kirstein, *Die Entwicklung der Sponsalienlehre und der Lehre vom Eheschluss in der deutschen protestantischen Eherechtslehre ... (Bonner rechtswissenschaftliche Abhandlungen* 72, Bonn, 1976), 48.

[115] Quoted in Rudolf Schäfer, *loc. cit.*, 209.

[116] Roland Kirstein, *op. cit.*, Rudolph Sohm, *Das Recht der Eheschliessung aus dem deutschen und kanonischen Recht geschichtlich entwickelt* (Weimar, 1875), 197-257. For the medieval canon law background, see Willibald M. Plöchl, *Geschichte des Kirchenrechts* II (Vienna, 1962), 305-37.

tion and, hence, to insoluble marriage encouraged private arrangements between groom and bride. These were recognized under canon
law (until the practice was struck down by the Council of Trent) but
Luther found them abhorrent, for, apart from abetting immorality,
they evaded the need for parental consent and public banns preceding
marriage and thus undermined the main pillar of the stable society, the
fourth commandment. Secret marriages also presented a grave problem
in legal practice, for contested private arrangements filled court dockets
with an unending succession of suits and actions.[117]

Luther took up this problem at some length in a treatise on marriage
written in 1530,[118] and he returned to it from time to time (joined by
other evangelical reformers such as Brenz and Bucer) with increasing
fury against lawyers, whom he presented as the chief stumblingblocks
to the dissolution of secret engagements. The height of his vehemence
came in a sermon of January 1544, already mentioned as one of his
most ferocious outbursts against the legal tribe.[119] Reason, natural law,
the imperial statutes, even the old canons of the Church, he declares,
support his own view of Christian marriage law. Only the "almighty
jurists" insist that once a secret arrangement has been entered into by
the couple, it remains binding forever. Try to explain the difference between "take" and "shall take" to a peasant. One cannot even make the
distinction in spoken German. Who has ever heard an ordinary person
say *Ich werde dich nehmen*—"I shall take you"? As a pastor, Luther
knows how often a foolishly given secret promise, later set aside for an
open agreement, leaves "woe and misery" in the heart of a poor girl or
boy because canon law tells them that only their first engagement is
valid, and that the second has led them into a life of adultery. Even in
Wittenberg, Luther says, cavilling *Schandjuristen* perplex poor souls
with this rigid interpretation which ignores circumstances and is blind
to what is right and fair. Proud and arrogant in their fur collars and
golden chains of office, upholding "the pope's justice and his jurists'
law," lawyers offer advice which, Luther tells his parishioners, will
send them straight to hell.

Luther's special grudge against the traditionalists among Protestant

[117] The legally and doctrinally complicated matter of clandestine marriages is treated
illuminatingly, and with excellent bibliography, by Beatrice Gottlieb, "The Meaning of
Clandestine Marriage" in *Family and Sexuality in French History*, eds. Robert Wheaton
and Tamara K. Hareven (Philadelphia, 1980), 49-83. A brief survey of the problem is
offered by Steven Ozment, *When Fathers Ruled. Family Life in Reformation Europe*
(Cambridge, Mass., 1983), 25-29.
[118] *Von Ehesachen* (1530), WA 30[III], 198-248.
[119] Sermon on Matthew 2:6 (1544), WA 49, 294-307.

jurists prompted him to direct his ire indiscriminately at all jurists. None of them will acknowledge a higher truth than what is written in their law books, he charged. They think they know everything:

> When a matter is brought before them, they respond at once, saying "we can deal with this," and never give a single thought to God. We poor theologians go down on our knees in church and pray before we mount the pulpit to give a sermon. But the jurists feel no need for prayer. . . . No wonder things stand so badly in worldly affairs.[120]

The scope of their influence over princes and magistrates is matched only by the enormity of their arrogance and their craven careerism. There is not a princely court in Christendom that does not now prostrate itself before its jurists, "bowing to their commands and obeying them to the letter. Whatever they call right, no matter how wrong it really is, is accepted there because the jurists say it is so."[121] Cunning toadies and flatterers, they ingratiate themselves with the mighty by telling them what they like to hear.[122] In this way they have made themselves indispensable. "We theologians," Luther said, "tell the truth; this is why we are regarded as enemies and are persecuted. If you jurists were to say to your noble clients to their faces just what virtuous Christians they are with their usury, their tyranny, and so on, they would deal with you as cruelly as they have been treating us."[123]

It was their easy access to power, combined with their moral indifference, that so outraged Luther. This was a subject he talked about almost obsessively. Law was sheer might and strength now, he thought; "truth, right, and justice have no place in this world."[124] Law is an instrument for those who want to dominate their fellow men. "In this life," Luther said, "jurists catch only gnats and flies with their laws. The big wasps and bumble bees crash through the net as through a spider web, and fly away unpunished."[125] Real justice—God's justice—requires no lawyers. "The gospel doesn't tell us to worship jurists. . . . When our Lord God sits in the judgment seat, what does he care about jurists?" Lawyers' statutes are fit only for this corrupt world,[126] a world in which their "vicious tongues" and their "sordid, gross, and repulsive trade" make the rich richer, the poor poorer, and stir each up against

[120] WA TR V, No. 5486 (1542).
[121] *Ibid.* I, No. 349 (1532).
[122] *Ibid.* III, No. 3038b (1533).
[123] *Ibid.* II, No. 1364 (1532).
[124] *Ibid.* III, No. 3793 (1538).
[125] *Ibid.* I, No. 2.
[126] *Ibid.* II, No. 1241 (1531); III, No. 3793 (1538).

the other, while they gain for themselves enormous wealth.[127] They are a curse on humanity and will remain one until, like the theologians, they "get a Luther to change them."[128] Luther knew that his anger carried him too far at times. "You must forgive me, good people, my outrage against the jurists," he interrupted himself once while preaching to his congregation in 1544. "It's more a zeal for God," he explained, "and to do honor and give support to God's teachings."[129] "I don't hate the profession," he said; "it's what they do to confuse and befuddle the Christian conscience that I cannot bear."[130]

Everyone, of course, agreed with Luther that the honor due to God should be humankind's overriding concern. At the same time, no one reading or hearing him could have been left unaffected by his unremitting denigration of law and his ceaselessly reiterated words of contempt for lawyers. Luther's pronouncements on law are highly complex and tinged with ambivalence, and it is hazardous to conjecture how they were received in his time. At least one thing seems certain, however. What he said on the subject could not possibly have fortified people's respect for law and persuaded them to assent and submit to it. The contrary is more likely to have been the case. Indeed, his words must have exacerbated the already intense distaste for law and lawyers. His constant admonitions to observe the law in letter and in spirit were therefore undercut by his jaundiced opinion of law generally and by his fierce denunciation of lawyers in particular. *Juristerey*, he said in a sermon in 1544, "is a doctrine not of grace but of wrath."[131] The possibility, held out by him, of an escape from this ugly doctrine must have opened a tempting prospect to his auditors who, though their points of reference were vastly different from the reformer's own spiritual signposts, were more than ready to accept his censorious judgment on the profession and on the mischief it had brought to their lives.

WHATEVER the expectations encouraged by Luther's mixed signals, the Reformation brought its followers no release from restrictive laws, nor did it lift the heavy hands of judicial bureaucrats from their lives. In any case, Luther's declarations ceased to set the tone as the evangelical

---

[127] *Ibid.* VI, No. 6908; III, Nos. 2831 (1532), 3575 (1537), 3584 (1537); II, No. 1528 (1532). On Luther's charge that jurists choose their profession for money, some table companions talked back to the reformer, denying the accusations. But Luther persisted in his view: *Ibid.* III, Nos. 2831 (1532) and 3496 (1536).

[128] *Ibid.* III, No. 3584 (1537).

[129] Sermon of 6 January, 1544, WA 49, 299.

[130] Sermon of 13 January, 1544, WA 49, 316.

[131] *Ibid.*

movement transformed itself into established churches, and as more conventional voices than his gave the tenor for the era following the decades he dominated. This shift was not hidden from the reformer. Luther often warned that, though he might hold jurists at bay while he lived, "as soon as I have laid down my head to die, you will see how things go!"[132] "As long as I'm alive," he told lawyers, "I shall keep the church safe from you. Or should I see all my hard work undone by your dirty tricks?"[133] He observed jurists making common cause with the nobility and other notables in a move to take over the operation of the church, in order, so he suspected, to gain control of people's consciences along with the governance of their lives.[134] Twenty years after Luther's death, the editor of his *Table Talk*, Johann Aurifaber, a loyal partisan of what he took to be orthodox Lutheran doctrine, noted sadly that this aim appeared to have succeeded. "Politicians, lawyers, and courtiers" run the church now, he wrote, "directing religion like worldly affairs."[135] He was referring to the government of state churches, in the daily administration of which jurists played an important and—as we have seen—steadily expanding role.

By then Luther's ambivalence on the place of written law in the society reorganized by the Reformation had given way to Melanchthon's strongly affirmative posture. In promoting this shift, Melanchthon was, of course, in step with processes long underway in European politics, to the historical momentum of which was now added the ideological force of religious sanction. Owing to Melanchthon's personal influence within the Lutheran academic establishment in the critical second quarter of the century, his emphatic approval of the uses of law, and the weight he gave to the interpretive and administrative functions of jurists, powerfully encouraged the fraternity of Lutheran lawyers, and further magnified their prominence and authority in church and state.

As a systematic theologian with philosophical and some legal training (at Tübingen and Wittenberg)[136] Melanchthon worked out a consistent theory of law showing how established codes had been legiti-

[132] WA TR VI, No. 7022.

[133] Sermon on II Cor 6:1 (1539), WA 47, 671; also TR VI, No. 4382 (1539).

[134] WA TR III, No. 3496 (1536); VI, No. 7029.

[135] From the preface to Aurifaber's edition of Luther's *Tischreden* (1566) printed in Johann Georg Walch, ed., *Dr. Martin Luthers sämmtliche Schriften* 22 (Halle, 1743), 49.

[136] On Melanchthon's competence as a jurist, see Albert Haenel, "Melanchthon der Jurist," *ZRG* 8 (1869), 249-51, 267-69. Guido Kisch, *Melanchthons Rechts- und Soziallehre*, 62-67, explores Melanchthon's connections in Wittenberg with the distinguished Roman jurist Hieronymus Schürpf.

mately drawn from divine purpose and natural law and were linked by their common origin in the will of God to biblical commandments.[137] As "the unchangeable wisdom of God proclaimed in the decalogue," natural law resides in every human being as an innate idea, one that "remains in man even after he sins."[138]

> Paul teaches in Romans 2:15 that there is a law of nature. He concludes that Gentiles have a conscience which either defends or accuses their acts, and for this reason it is law. . . . Thus the law of nature is a common judgment to which all men give the same consent. This law, engraved by God in the mind of each one of us, is suitable for the shaping of morals.[139]

Commanding the worship of God, a caring sympathy for neighbors, and respect for property, this natural law declares in a general way "the ground rules for all human activity." When made in accordance with these rules, positive law may be called just. More than that, it may be called beneficial, for its goal is to instruct and train men in morality, upright behavior, discipline, and *pietas*.[140] In establishing codes of written laws, political rulers are therefore doing God's good work. Obedience to them is part of men's duty to the creator,[141] not merely because God has so commanded, but also because the laws properly enacted by governments are in accord with reason.[142]

Reason alone, however, does not suffice to make corrupt mankind do what is reasonable. Only by following the rules laid out in Scripture can fallen men be certain of doing what God wishes them to do. Natural human reason cannot know what is right except by observing God's law as given in Scripture.[143] Of the parts of this divine law revealed in the Bible, only the moral injunctions, prescribed succinctly in the two tables of the Decalogue, are binding on Christians, for whom

[137] Philip Melanchthon, *Loci communes theologici* (1521) tr. L. J. Satre in Wilhelm Pauck, ed., *Melanchthon and Bucer* (*Library of Christian Classics* XIX, London, 1969); *Loci communes* (1555) tr. C. Manschreck, *Melanchthon on Christian Doctrine* (New York, 1965); *Oratio de legum fontibus et causis* (1550) in *Corpus reformatorum* XI and Guido Kisch, *Melanchthons Rechts- und Soziallehre*, 260-68; *Oratio de legibus* (1525) in *Corpus reformatorum* XI, and Guido Kisch, *op. cit.*, 189-209. See also Wilhelm Maurer, *Der junge Melanchthon* (Göttingen, 1967-1969) II, 230-489, and K. Köhler, *Luther und die Juristen*, 54-55, 100-05.
[138] *Loci communes* (1555) in Manschreck, *op. cit.*, 128.
[139] *Loci communes theologici* in Pauck, *op. cit.*, 50. Translation slightly altered.
[140] *Ibid.*, 50, 53.
[141] *Oratio de legibus* in Kisch, *op. cit.*, 196.
[142] *Loci communes* (1555) in Manschreck, *op. cit.*, 333.
[143] Wilhelm Maurer, *op. cit.* II, 288-90.

they are peremptory commands, not merely good advice and sage counsel. The remaining parts of the Mosaic law, judicial and ceremonial, are the Jews' special statutes, and Christians need not observe them, although they may find in them helpful allegories and examples.[144] The moral imperatives themselves rest on such high expectations and make such severe demands that no one can fulfill them. "Paul teaches the right understanding of the law, which is that it is a terrible judgment on the inner and outer sinfulness of all mankind."[145] Those Christians whose hearts are open to this correct understanding know that "God reveals to them the law, shows them their hearts, and terrifies and confuses them with a realization of their own sins."[146] Thus the law does two things. It teaches the fear of God to the sinful, and this is a terror so great that they will want to subject themselves to external discipline. Secondly, it points those who are reborn in the Holy Spirit to the works they should still do in order to please God, for the "saints," too, are human, and therefore sinners, dominated by passions and self-love.[147] They need the law as much as the unregenerate.[148] No one, in fact, is released from obedience to the law. "With regard to justification and perdition," Melanchthon wrote in his *loci communes*, "we are free of it, [but] not with regard to obedience."[149]

It is commonly said that Melanchthon's insistence on subjection to laws was born in his unhappy experience of the mid-1520s in Germany. Before these events took place he may indeed have speculated on the possibility of governing Christian society with no law other than the non-coercive evangelical rule.[150] This would explain his outrage at the rebellions of 1525, and his extreme reaction to the manifestoes of

[144] *Loci communes theologici* (1521) in Pauck, *op. cit.*, 53-69.

[145] Melanchthon, *Unterscheid des alten und newen Testaments* (1544) in Robert Stupperich, ed., *Der unbekannte Melanchthon* (Stuttgart, 1961), 192-209.

[146] *Loci communes theologici* (1521) in Pauck, *op. cit.*, 79.

[147] Heinrich Bornkamm, "Melanchthons Menschenbild" in Walter Elliger, ed., *Philipp Melanchthon: Forschungsbeiträge* (Göttingen, 1961), 76-90.

[148] *Loci communes* (1555) in Manschreck, *op. cit.*, 123-27. See the statement of the developed Melanchthonian position in the 1577 Formula of Concord: ". . . the law was given to men for three reasons: first that thereby outward discipline might be maintained against wild, disobedient men . . . ; secondly, that men thereby may be led to the knowledge of their sins; thirdly, that after they are regenerate and the flesh notwithstanding cleaves to them, they might on this account have a fixed rule according to which they are to regulate and direct their whole life. . . ." *Concordia Triglotta* (St. Louis, 1921), 805. On the "third use" of the law, see note 40 above.

[149] *Loci communes* (1555) in Manschreck, *op. cit.*, 200.

[150] Guido Kisch, *op. cit.*, 114, 120-23. This supposition is suggested by a letter to Melanchthon by Luther of 13 July, 1521, WA Br II, 356-59.

that revolution.[151] As Guido Kisch has noted in his study of Melanchthon as a legal and political thinker, Melanchthon's preoccupation with law and jurisprudence was in large part the product of the leading position he occupied in the Lutheran movement in the 1520s and 1530s. His duties made it necessary for him to develop responses to the many immediate problems of the day, some of them theoretical—for instance the question of the applicability of Mosaic law—others practical and organizational—such as church administration and usury.[152] The outcome, for Melanchthon, of these experiences was an emphatic and permanent turn toward the law, especially the Roman law, which he now saw as the only weapon within human reach to ward off moral and social anarchy.[153]

Guido Kisch points out that it could not have been an accident that Melanchthon's first public statement of this theme should have been printed in the year of the revolution.[154] *De legibus*, an academic oration first given late in 1523 but published in 1525, defends the written law of pagan origin against the "calumnies" of modern "cyclopes and centaurs" who would replace it with unwritten principles of right and fairness drawn from Scripture.[155] Melanchthon acknowledges the existence of widespread feelings of hostility against Roman law and lawyers. His apologia seeks to prove by means of biblical citation that law, litigation, and jurisprudence are godly and expressly recommended by God for mankind's own good. He also shows by means of extended argument and historical example that written law offers the only practically workable safeguard against the exercise of arbitrary power. Of all specimens of written laws available to us, that of the Romans is the best that history has to offer. It is God's gift to humanity, to Germany in particular, its recovery in that country having been a great

[151] See *Eyn schrifft Philippi Melanchthon widder die artickel der Bawrschafft* (1525) in Robert Stupperich, ed., *Melanchthons Werke in Auswahl* I (Gütersloh, 1951), 190-214.

[152] Guido Kisch, *op. cit.*, 48-49. Wilhelm Maurer, *Der junge Melanchthon* II, 415-16 shows how Melanchthon's religious and secular thought developed in response particularly to the disturbances in Wittenberg 1521-1522. He concludes: "Drei Jahre lang war er ihr [i.e., academic youth] zugehörig gewesen, an Jahren ihr gleichstehend, an Kenntnissen ihr voranschreitend. Jetzt war er aus der Reihe der Kommilitonen auf die Seite der herrschenden Ordnungsgewalten getreten."

[153] On Melanchthon's commitment to order and discipline in the aftermath of 1525, see Wilhelm Maurer, "Über den Zusammenhang zwischen kirchlicher Ordnung und christlicher Erziehung in den Anfängen Lutherischer Reformation" in *id.*, *Die Kirche und ihr Recht. Gesammelte Aufsätze zum evangelischen Kirchenrecht* (Tübingen, 1976), 254-59.

[154] Guido Kisch, *op. cit.*, 82.

[155] *Oratio de legibus* in *ibid.*, 189-209. References to 190, 234, 243-44.

blessing for the nation.[156] Today, says Melanchthon, Roman law is indispensable not only to judges and lawyers, but to statesmen as well, for the only suitable theoretical preparation for high political office is the study of law books and jurisprudence.

Melanchthon returned frequently to these subjects: in his brief commentary on Aristotle's *Politics* (1530), in his contributions to the polemical pamphlet literature of his time, and in several academic addresses on the dignity and the sources of the law.[157] His two chief tenets remain unchanged. There can be no well-ordered society without written laws, as is shown by the confusion and turmoil that inevitably follow upon any attempt to abolish or curtail laws.[158] Secondly, the law does much more than place restraints on human instincts. It is an instrument of civilization, the word *paedagogus* in the famous passage in Galatians 3:24 being capable of far more generous interpretation than Luther's.[159] Melanchthon offers this broader interpretation.[160]

One or the other of these complementary themes emerges constantly in the rhetoric of Melanchthon's time, the former at moments of stress or times of crisis, the latter when things seemed to go well. All reformers believed—as Melanchthon put it in 1524—that the *impii*, the great mass of unbelievers, must be kept under the rod of the law and thereby under the discipline of "human justice." But this same law is part of a *paedagogia politica* capable of mending public mores.[161] It is not a taskmaster only, but a teacher as well. Of these great benefits God himself is the author. His wisdom illuminates the Roman law, which, with its concern for principles of fairness and justice, is the best of all legal systems, at once the most rational and the most reasonable.[162]

---

[156] *Ibid.*, 201-02.

[157] *Commentarii in aliquot politicos libros Aristoteli* (1530) in *opera* ed. C. G. Bretschneider (*Corpus reformatorum*) XVI, 417-52. See especially cols. 440, 443-49; *De dignitate legum oratio* (1538) in Guido Kisch, *op. cit.*, 221-27; *De legum fontibus et causis* (1550) in *ibid.*, 260-68. See *ibid.*, 99, for a list of Melanchthon's academic speeches.

[158] *De dignitate legum* in Guido Kisch, *op. cit.*, 227. See also Wolfgang Günther, *Martin Luthers Vorstellung von der Reichsverfassung* (*Reformationsgeschichtliche Studien und Texte* No. 114, Münster, 1976), 132.

[159] But see Heckel's argument that Luther did endow politics and political authority with ethical value and positive function. Johannes Heckel, "Recht und Gesetz, Kirche und Obrigkeit in Luthers Lehre vor dem Thesenanschlag von 1517. Eine juristische Untersuchung," *ZRG 57* (1937), *Kan. Abt.*, 285-375.

[160] *De legibus* in Guido Kisch, *op. cit.*, 244.

[161] *Epitome renovatae ecclesiasticae doctrinae* (1524), written for Philip of Hesse, in Robert Stupperich, ed., *Melanchthons Werke in Auswahl* I (Gütersloh, 1951), 179-89. Also in *Corpus reformatorum* I, 703-11. Reference to 707.

[162] *Oratio de dignitate legum* (1543), in Guido Kisch, *op. cit.*, 234-40; *De legum fontibus et causis* in *ibid.*, 265.

Melanchthon urges all who heard him to cherish it, to give due honor to its learned interpreters, the jurists, and to revere the exalted lawgivers who have been called to turn its admirable principles into political legislation.[163]

Melanchthon's standing in the world of learning assured the wide dissemination of these sentiments within the Protestant academic community. But he took care also that they should reach a much wider audience. In a basic guide to evangelical doctrine he wrote in 1528 for pastors of all the churches in Saxony, he underlined the legitimacy of existing laws, explaining that "God approves and confirms these [Saxon and Roman] codes as long as they do not go against God and reason."[164] And in the vernacular chronicle he edited and published in 1532 from a draft by Johann Carion, he spoke of Roman law in glowing terms—as we heard in an earlier chapter. "Thus was this wonderful treasure returned to the light of day," he writes of the reception, "and much good followed from it, namely that Europe once again had a reasonable law, . . . and many other blessings [followed], too, for we have no better guide than this law to good morals and good manners."[165]

This positive vision of law as a force for good in earthly things was more than a slight shift of emphasis in the emerging Protestant creed. It was part of the redirection of the movement's basic thrust. Combined with a systematic pedagogical program launched during these decades,[166] the Lutheran establishment's new stress on law as "teacher" as well as "taskmaster" and "disciplinarian" significantly increased both the readiness and the power of public authorities to exercise control over private lives. In this new activist role, Lutheran governments leaned heavily on Roman law and its technicians. They inclined with equal weight to forceful indoctrination. They ordered laws inscribed on tablets and displayed in school rooms "for the benefit of the schoolmaster and his young people, so that they can know themselves in these *leges* and be made mindful of their duties."[167] The objective, recollect-

---

[163] *Oratio de scripto iure* (1539), in *ibid.*, 231.

[164] *Unterricht der Visitatorn an die Pfarhern ym Kurfürstentum zu Sachssen* in Robert Stupperich, ed., *op. cit.* I, 254-55.

[165] Quoted in Guido Kisch, *op. cit.*, 158.

[166] This program is examined at length in my *Luther's House of Learning. Indoctrination of the Young in the German Reformation* (Baltimore, 1978). The best study of Melanchthon's part in it, and of the intellectual and empirical sources of Melanchthon's thought, is Wilhelm Maurer, *Der junge Melanchthon*, volume II. See especially 462-63 for a statement of the long-range impact of Melanchthon's ideas and work on education in Germany.

[167] From the visitation report on schools in the countryside around the city of Ulm, 1626: Stadtarchiv Ulm A [1836], 43ᵛ.

ing 1525, was internalization of rules, a move from enforcement by threat and punishment to inner acceptance and voluntary compliance. For this reason Melanchthon devoted a disproportionately long section of his *Instruction of the Visitors to the Pastors*—instructions which pastors were expected to pass on to their parishioners—to the Christian's divinely imposed duty not only to honor and obey, but also to respect and love his *Obrigkeit*.[168] Far from being "a calamity [*verhengnis*] sent by God to punish us," Melanchthon writes in this programmatic guide, political authority ensures peace in society and makes possible a productive life. He who recognizes God's work in the actions of his superiors will love them in his heart.

> If you know that someone has rescued your child from certain death, will you not thank him with all your heart? Why, then, are you not grateful to your government, which daily saves you, your children, your wife from murder? . . . When you look at your wife and children, say to yourself, "These are gifts of God whom I may keep thanks to the good work of my government." And as you love your children, so you must love the magistrates.[169]

Presented—as was customary by then in Lutheran didactic literature—in the context of the fourth commandment to honor your father and your mother, Melanchthon's admonition was intended to encourage the political subject to display an obedience at once unquestioning and willing. This complicitous subjection was specifically required to direct itself to the laws of the state. "Some wonder whether . . . Christians are permitted to use laws that were made by emperors or heathens," Melanchthon writes in the *Instruction of the Visitors*. His answer: "Let it be made clear that we may, indeed, keep the emperors' laws. . . . No existing laws must be nullified, it does not matter how burdensome they are. Our forefathers who made these laws knew that our wild and unruly people must be subjected to harsh commands. Let everyone therefore accept and use the laws of his state . . . [for] Paul himself endorses pagan laws when he says in Romans 13:1 that all authority is of God."[170] Civil and criminal laws, Melanchthon wrote in a vernacular pamphlet, "are clear evidence that government, civic life [*bürgerlich leben*], judicial trials, penalties, just wars, buying and selling are good works and God's own ordinances."[171] All are parts of the

---

[168] Reference as in note 164, 228-35.

[169] *Ibid.*, 230-32.

[170] *Ibid.*, 233-34.

[171] *Unterscheid des Alten und Newen Testaments* (1543) in Robert Stupperich, ed., *Der unbekannte Melanchthon*, 202-03. For Melanchthon's developed position on the

political order, the *ordo politicus*, which is Melanchthon's term for (to use a succinct definition by Rolf Bernhard Huschke) "everything in public life that is legally constituted, all laws being understood as 'the voice of God.' "[172] Attempts to "dream up" new laws always fail. Melanchthon compares the vain endeavor to do so to a family of monkeys attempting to organize themselves into a political society.[173] "People who value burgherly discipline and good order abhor innovation," Melanchthon wrote,[174] concluding that "there is nothing worthier and nothing more useful than the established order."[175] Those who reject it, he thought, "are truly possessed by the devil."[176] For such destroyers of civic order Melanchthon found no pity in his heart, as he demonstrated in 1525 when, following the disastrous events of that year, he urged reliance on the punitive, rather than the educative, powers of the law.[177] Facing a "crude," "licentious," "wild," and "bloodthirsty" people like the Germans, who, he said, "deserve even less freedom than they now have," he portrayed worldly government as God's sacred sword. "But a sword," he says, "must cut, as the wicked deed demands it, whether the punishment is exacted upon possessions, on the body, or on life. . . . We know how severely God punished his own people in the desert. And in his law he commanded that 'You shall show no mercy.' "[178]

To avoid a repetition of 1525, all Lutheran states incorporated the correct definition of Christian freedom in their ecclesiastical constitutions (*Kirchenordnungen*), the charters in which the organizational structure and doctrinal orthodoxy of German territorial churches were established under the ruler's or magistrate's name.[179] The conviction

Stände and *Werke* in civic life, see *Loci communes* (1555) in C. Manschreck, tr., *Melanchthon on Christian Doctrine* (New York, 1965), 323.

[172] Rolf Bernhard Huschke, *Melanchthons Lehre vom Ordo politicus*, 68. Huschke points out that the German word *Oberkeit*, or *Obrigkeit*, is much more sweeping than its supposed Latin equivalent, *magistratus*, the latter meaning only "more power," rather than "supreme" power, because in theory every Roman citizen could be a magistrate. Melanchthon emphasizes the contrast between *Obrigkeit* and *Untertan* or *subditus*, whose duty it was to obey. *Ibid.*, 121.

[173] *Oratio de legibus* (1550) in Guido Kisch, *op. cit.*, 249.

[174] "Nun weiss ich wol, das leuth, so burgerliche zucht und ordnung lieb haben, gross abschewen haben für allen newerungen. . . ." *Vita Lutheri. Von dem Leben und Sterben . . . D. Martini Lutheri* (Eisleben, 1555), 23.

[175] *Nihil ordine neque honestius neque utilius* (quoting Xenophon). *De dialectica* (1528) in *Corpus reformatorum* XI, 160.

[176] *Loci communes* (1555) in C. Manschreck, *op. cit.*, 100.

[177] *Eyn schrifft . . . widder die artickel der Bawrschafft* (1525) in Robert Stupperich, ed., *Werke in Auswahl* I, 206.

[178] *Ibid.*, 208.

[179] These are printed in Emil Sehling, ed., *Die evangelischen Kirchenordnungen des 16.*

behind the inclusion of this definition was that false preaching in the years before the revolution had caused much, if not all, of the harm. The nature of Christian freedom had therefore to be made clear, authoritatively and in plain, explicit language. When the Alsatian estates met in August 1525 to deliberate on how best to prevent peasant unrest in the future, they resolved that "good preachers, presenting the gospel without rebellion [on uffrur]" should from now on "preach with the highest earnestness and vigor about the freedom of the subjects' [untertanen] spirit and, at the same time, the submission of their bodies to their government."[180] Luther's original distinction between the inner and the outer kind of freedom was made unmistakable now, and all correct inferences to be drawn from it were spelled out. Stated positively, Christian freedom was said to include, first, forgiveness of sins without our own merits; secondly, release from the ceremonial laws of Moses; and, thirdly, the irrelevance of ceremonial rules to our salvation. A consequence of the second freedom was "that Christians are at liberty to use the legal order of their respective countries, the English, English law, the French, French law, the Romans, Roman law. As long as this legal order does not offend God or reason it is approved and confirmed by God. . . ."[181] Explained negatively, Christian freedom was now linked directly to the subject's obligation to accept the institutions of the world as he found them. As the Margraves of Brandenburg declared:

> Christian freedom has nothing to do with being quit of rents, interest, tribute, tithe, tax, service, or similar outward burdens and grievances (as subjects now call them), but it is solely and exclusively . . . an inner, spiritual thing. In all external, temporal concerns, laws, and other matters, subjects owe their government full obedience, and all preachers shall explain and point this out to their congregations

Jahrhunderts, vols. 1-5 (Leipzig, 1902-1913); vols. 6ff. continued by the Institut für evangelisches Kirchenrecht der evangelischen Kirche in Deutschland zu Göttingen (Tübingen, 1955ff.). A systematic overview of Kirchenordnungen in relation to each other and to canon law is offered by Johann Friedrich von Schulte, Die Geschichte der Quellen und Literatur des canonischen Rechts . . . III, parts 2-3: "Das evangelische Recht . . ." (Stuttgart, 1880), 3-21. Ibid., 22-39, gives a list of Protestant jurists in Germany with biographical sketches and the titles of their chief works.

[180] Quoted in F. W. Müller, Die elsässischen Landstände (Strasbourg, 1907), 120-21.

[181] Kirchenordnung. In meiner gnedigen herrn der marggraven zu Brandenburg und eines Erbern Rats der Stadt Nürnberg Oberkeyt und gepieten . . . (1533) in Sehling XI, 170. This is taken nearly verbatim from Melanchthon's Unterricht der Visitatorn of 1528 (ibid. I, 166-67), where the Saxon law is specifically mentioned. Melanchthon's "positive" formulation of Christian freedom was taken over by several other Kirchenordnungen as well.

whenever they preach about Christian freedom, so that people may not be lured away from the right, true Christian freedom of the spirit to the Satanic and unchristian freedom of the flesh.[182]

Or, more curtly, in the church constitution of 1559 of the city of Rothenburg:

Christian freedom does not relate to the external order. . . . On the contrary, it confirms this order and commands that it be observed, respected, and obeyed by all. Subjects may not under the cloak of Christian freedom withdraw their obedience from their lawful government, which has power over them. They must submit to it with gladness in their hearts and in the full knowledge that in this they are obeying their Lord.[183]

"Whoever preaches in this way about Christian freedom," wrote the Nuremberg theologian Veit Dietrich in his *Agenda for Pastors in the Country* of 1545—incorporated in his city's ecclesiastical constitution—"will never encourage rebellion but will admonish people most diligently to obey worldly authority. . . . For Scripture is our witness," he concluded, "that God himself has appointed all the worldly powers and commanded us to obey them in everything that touches worldly things."[184] Thus was the law-making authority of government, and the laws themselves, declared to be holy and good.

That this legislative and disciplinary authority embraced religion and included it within the purview of political authority was, for practical if not for doctrinal reasons, a foregone conclusion. It could not have been otherwise, given the long history of encroachment of state upon church, and given the aid and comfort bestowed on the ambitions of sixteenth-century rulers by the Reformation's elimination of an autonomous church. In a late edition of his *loci communes* Melanchthon himself posed the critical question about political direction of religious affairs, and answered it emphatically in the affirmative. Should government be limited to abolishing idolatry, he asked, or is it obliged also "to establish right doctrine and true divine services"? After more than thirty years of reformation in Germany, the question was academic. "In our time," Melanchthon declared, "those worldly princes and lords

---

[182] *Der . . . Hochgebornen Fürsten . . . Casimir und . . . Georgen . . . Anzeygen, wie die gewesen empörung . . . nit den wenigsten tail auss ungeschickten predigen entstanden sind . . .* (1525) in Sehling XI, 86.

[183] *Ordnung der Kirchen in eines Erbarn Raths der Stat Rothenburg uf der Tauber Oberkeit und Gebiet gelegen* (1559) in Sehling XI, 575-76.

[184] Veit Dietrich, *Agendbüchlein für die Pfarrherrn auff dem Land* (1545) in Sehling XI, 552.

who have abolished idolatry and false doctrine and have established
the pure teachings of the gospel and true worship of God have acted
correctly. All rulers are obliged to do this . . . : to believe, to confess,
and to direct others to true divine service."[185] By the middle of the sixteenth century, this was no more than a description of what was actually being done. "As 'emergency bishop,' the territorial ruler had
originally been intended to serve only as a temporary substitute for the
missing episcopal jurisdiction. But while undertaking the necessary re-
forms in his land, he steadily gained organizational power over the
church in his state."[186] De facto possession of the ius reformandi, an
essential precondition of state building in the modern style, led naturally to political domination, not of the institutions of religion only, but
of all of religious life. Luther was not happy with this development but
had to resign himself to an accomplished fact.[187] Melanchthon, after
1525, seems to have regarded it as not only an inevitable, but also as a
rightful, solution.

Interestingly enough, jurists tended to much greater caution on this
constitutional point than did the reformers. Most advised their governments to move slowly in dismantling the remaining legal barriers between church and state. In Saxony, Hieronymus Schürpf argued
against confiscation of ecclesiastical properties.[188] A legal counsel for
the city of Nuremberg, studying a draft of the ecclesiastical constitution
to be issued jointly by Nuremberg and Brandenburg, advised care "lest
the spiritual sword be mixed with the secular," although a few pages on
in his memorandum this writer extols the public usefulness of preaching, which, he says, is conducive to social peace. "Through frequent
preaching subjects can be effectively persuaded to obey their government," he explained, "and the common people, always impertinent and
uncouth, will thereby be made more mannerly and docile."[189] More
consistently, the well-known Nuremberg jurist Dr. Christoph Scheurl
warned his government against doing anything that would cause "dissension [Zerrüttung] in the body politic." "Innovate as little as possi-

[185] Loci communes (1555) in C. Manschreck, op. cit., 335-37. The German text is in
Corpus reformatorum XXII, 616-17.
[186] Wolfgang Günther, Martin Luthers Vorstellung von der Reichsverfassung, 151-52.
[187] Hans Walter Krummwiede, Zur Entstehung des landesherrlichen Kirchenregiments
in Kursachsen und Braunschweig-Wolfenbüttel (Göttingen, 1967), 120-45; Karl Trüdi-
ger, Luthers Briefe und Gutachten an weltliche Oberkeiten zur Durchführung der Reformation (Münster, 1975), 68-108.
[188] Gisela Becker, Deutsche Juristen und ihre Schriften auf den römischen Indices des
16. Jahrhunderts (Berlin, 1970), 121.
[189] From a memorandum by Johannes Müller to the Nuremberg city council, 1530.
Germanisches Nationalmuseum Nuremberg, Merkel-Handschrift 129, 87ᵛ.

ble," he cautioned, pointing out to the city fathers the inappropriateness of their issuing articles on such disputed theological points as free will "which are held by many learned men to be a dreadful error." Those "to whom God has entrusted worldly government" should not meddle in such "sophistries," he said. "No one will be persuaded or forced to believe by these articles [and they] will remain a piece of paper." Moreover, the "daily changes" necessitated by the proposed course will cause general confusion.[190] But Scheurl's magistrates disregarded his advice, establishing what they considered sound doctrine and correct religious conduct as an act of political fiat.

In the 1530s, the pros and cons of state involvement in the making of religious doctrine were argued heatedly in chancelleries and judicial chambers. The record of one such debate in the imperial city of Augsburg shows how fateful the decision was known to be in each case, and how clearly the participants in it read the danger signals.[191] Facing demands for religious change from a restive populace fanned by evangelical preachers, the city's magistrates, having chosen a committee to deal with the issue on an emergency basis, requested that legal advisers supply memoranda on the question "Whether the Honorable Council, as the temporal government of the City of Augsburg, has the authority to undertake, institute, and maintain actions, alterations, and new ordinances in matters concerning religion and the holy faith, or not."[192] Split largely along confessional lines, several jurists, notably Zwinglian sympathizers, answered in the affirmative. Others, led by stalwart Catholics, said no. Those opposed to religious change by government decree stressed the importance of keeping to the separation of authority.[193] The power of secular law should not be used to compel belief, they said. Governments are ill equipped to make and enforce such legislation. Secular and religious lawmaking are fundamentally different enterprises. "Every doctor of jurisprudence has the power to interpret and explain [secular] laws" and should be believed in the absence of contrary interpretations argued more convincingly. But in religion such "opinions" carry little weight "if contradicted by authorities who by

[190] Memorandum by Dr. Christoph Scheurl (1530), *ibid.*, 4r-41v. Quoted phrases are from 11v, 20r, 5v-6r, 8r, 10v.

[191] The documents are in Stadtarchiv Augsburg *Literalien* 1534. For a brief account of the debate in the context of Augsburg's social history in the Reformation period, see Philip Broadhead, "Politics and Expediency in the Augsburg Reformation" in *Reformation Principle and Practice. Essays in Honour of Arthur Geoffrey Dickens*, ed. P. N. Brooks (London, 1980), 53-70.

[192] Stadtarchiv Augsburg *Literalien* 1534, *Nachtrag* 2, No. 56.

[193] See especially the memoranda by Konrad Peutinger and Johann Rehlinger, both in *ibid.*, Nos. 15 and 21.

ancient Christian tradition have been empowered to pronounce and declare on matters of faith." In law, moreover, a lay person is obliged to obey a single judge. In religion, by contrast, we are bound to accept "what is commonly held in Christendom, and no person may be forced to believe and observe merely because some other individual believes and observes it."[194] Only "the whole of Christendom, acting through a General Christian Council," can declare the faith.[195]

Equally weighty was the argument for preserving the established balance between greater and lesser authorities in the empire. Although possessing full power to make laws and statutes, the City of Augsburg as a government is not entitled to override a superior authority. Such contravention is forbidden by the common law of the empire, which enjoins lesser powers from abrogating what higher powers have decreed:

> If every inferior government of a prince, a count, or a city were permitted to make its own particular laws respecting religion and faith, it would follow that not only towns and villages, but also sectarian parties within cities and villages could separate themselves, go their own ways, and practice their own religions. This is a course that would bring us nothing but tumult, rebellion, and mutual hatred.[196]

As an estate in the Holy Roman Empire, Augsburg is a member of a *corpus*, the jurists argued. There should be as little discord in this political body as possible. It is the wisdom and strength of the common law that it seeks to prevent such *Widerwärtigkeiten*.[197] Accepting limitations to one's authority offers the only safeguard against total chaos in the imperial ranks. Arguing fervently, and at great length, jurists opposed to disregarding such limits cited existing laws, precedent, tradition, and common sense in warning against "mixing the two swords."

Memoranda by jurists favoring intervention echoed Melanchthon's position. Scripture will tell you that political power has been divinely instituted for one purpose only: "to be God's tool for removing whatever stands in the way of his divine decrees and holy word."[198] Mindful of this mission, can we say that it is legitimate for us to transgress against the decrees of Worms and Speyer which forbid religious change? Yes, because when an imperial law "stands against truth and the word of God," we are not bound by it. We are taught by Justinian's

---

[194] *Ibid.*, No. 21, 4ᵛ-5ᵛ (Rehlinger).
[195] *Ibid.*, 6ʳ.
[196] *Ibid.*, No. 15, 32ʳ (Peutinger).
[197] *Ibid.*, 54ʳ.
[198] *Ibid.*, No. 22, 3ʳ (Balthasar Langnauer).

Institutes that "the emperor's law is inferior to the divine law, and [that] the former, if it goes counter to the latter, need not be obeyed." This opinion "is based on, and evident in, the common written law."[199] Nor need we fear that religious change will lead to social turmoil. "Let the appropriate laws be published with a preamble, and let this preamble be preached from every pulpit, and let it explain that the new laws are in complete agreement with what God has ordained for us in the Bible."[200]

In Augsburg, as elsewhere, the opposition to the advance of politics upon religion lost out to those who favored it. And the older distinctions between greater and lesser authorities disappeared as every political enclave, large and small, professed sovereign power to determine its own affairs, including the governance of religion. Augsburg's magistrates were an *Obrigkeit*, as were the rulers of every other autonomous entity in the empire. The Roman law gave compelling ideological support to their claims of authority, and furnished an arsenal of legal instruments in support of the exercise of it. F. W. Maitland's remark that "there was pleasant reading in the Byzantine Code for [a ruler] who wished to be monarch in church as well as state"[201] explains why political leaders listened to those among their legal advisers who, brushing aside traditionalist cautions, counseled aggressive lawmaking as a means of bringing about and perpetuating religious change. *Rex in regno suo est imperator* might have seemed an incongruous pose for a German prince or urban magistrate to strike.[202] But in practice every government possessed of the means of doing so acted out the role of *imperator in regno suo*.

This was as true of the empire's Catholic states as it was of its Protestant principalities, for Counter-Reformation rulers were no less energetic than their Lutheran colleagues in constructing the *landesherr-*

---

[199] *Ibid.*, No. 20. 10ᵛ, 17ᵛ (Hieronymus Rott). The reference to the *Institutes* is probably to 1.2.11.

[200] Stadtarchiv Augsburg *Literalien* 1534, 28. Juli, 6ᵛ (Dr. Franciscus Frosch). Later in the sixteenth century, when Augsburg had been recatholicized, the local Protestants argued differently, now claiming that the—Catholic—government lacked all powers over religion except to offer "external protection and sustenance to the church." *Bericht, warumb die Diener der evangelischen Kirche . . . nit verwilligen kunden, in die Newerung des Beruffs der evangelischen Kirchen Diener, welcher auss dem Gaistlichen gewalt in die politisch solte verwendett werden.* 1585. Stadtarchiv Augsburg *Nachlässe, Einzelstück* No. 10.

[201] F. W. Maitland, *English Law and the Renaissance* (Cambridge, 1901), 14.

[202] See Walter Ullmann, "This Realm of England Is an Empire," *Journal of Ecclesiastical History* 30:2 (April, 1979), 175-203, for the use throughout the later middle ages of *Rex in regno suo est imperator* as a means of gaining control over church and religion.

liche Kirchenregiment, the sovereign church government through which—to quote the historian of Bavaria's governmental system in the early modern period—"the power of the state, single-mindedly pursuing the goal of preserving the old faith, intervened legislatively and administratively in the duchy's internal religious life."[203] Everywhere in Protestant and Catholic Germany the prince's bureaucratic apparatus, having formulated church policy with the collaboration of "political" advisers, turned to the enforcement of religious discipline as a responsibility of state power. Church visitations—the favored procedure for gathering information and implementing laws at the local level—were planned and supervised by lawyers in collaboration with churchmen. The superintendent of Jena, Johann Wigand, assured the Elector of Saxony that a questionnaire (*Fragstück*) to be placed before every pastor during the visitation planned for 1569 had been drawn up in "discussion and deliberation between politicals [*politischen*] and theologians."[204] Among the jurists who wrote the questions on doctrine in this document was Dr. Peter Brehm, who sat not only on the duchy's ecclesiastical consistory, but also on the elector's appellate court.[205] When the elector suggested that additional interrogations on matters of belief be included, the superintendent advised limiting the printed questionnaire to the salient points. For, he wrote, "all other articles can be taken up in each locality by the bailiffs and tax collectors."[206] In such documentary glimpses of the routine operation of government—and they are offered, massively, by nearly every territorial and city archive—we can see the merger of church and state taking place. From the perspective of the humble parishioner, certainly, the two powers, and what they represented and seemed to be doing, were indistinguishable.

From the highest policy-making bodies where fateful matters such as resistance,[207] new consistorial constitutions, or the legal status of cler-

[203] Eduard Rosenthal, *Geschichte des Gerichtswesens und der Verwaltungsorganisation Baierns* (Würzburg, 1889-1906) II, 42, 48.

[204] StA Wei Reg N, No. 475, 1ʳ and ᵛ. The questionnaire is in *ibid.*, No. 472.

[205] See letter from Brehm to Duke Johann Wilkhelm complaining about the pressure of time on his double duty: *ibid.*, No. 480.

[206] *Ibid.*, No. 475.

[207] Ekkehart Fabian, *Die Entstehung des Schmalkaldischen Bundes und seiner Verfassung . . .* (Tübingen, 1962), 117-24, discusses the memoranda submitted in 1530 on this question by Lutheran jurists Gregor Brück, Hieronymus Schürpf, Sebald Münsterer, Caspar von Teutleben, and Benedict Pauli. For an excellent survey of theories of resistance 1529-1546 see Quentin Skinner, *The Foundations of Modern Political Thought* (Cambridge, 1978) II, 189-224. On this point alone Luther agreed with the Saxon jurists, who furnished him with grounds on which resistance might be offered: K. Köhler, *op. cit.*, 63-70.

ics were debated, down to the villages and parishes where directives were, or were attempted to be, put into action, the agents of state and church worked jointly to fashion a legislative and regulatory net with which to cover the whole of society.[208] This was a far cry from what had been the Lutheran Reformation's promise to its first followers. Release from intrusive laws was not to be its outcome. More clearly than ever before, the trend now ran in the opposite direction. The disappointment suffered by all those who had shared the original expectations counted heavily in shaping that embittered attitude toward the written law which, after the middle of the sixteenth century, was so noticeable a feature of the German political and religious scene.

[208] For a discussion of the activities of some leading Lutheran jurists in the sixteenth century, see Gisela Becker, *Deutsche Juristen* ... , 115-57.

CHAPTER EIGHT

Estates: The Heart of Resistance

THE many legal, political, and religious questions raised by the German encounter with Roman law were most heatedly debated in the forum of estate assemblies, whose negotiations with their respective rulers turned on all the salient points at issue: uniform law versus diversity of customs, central versus distributed power, authority versus freedoms. In their vigor, and no less in their immense verbosity, these exchanges reflect the gravity of the problems as seen by participants. In their rhetorical vehemence they echo, as well, the excitement of the historical moment: the agitation leading up to, and later fueled by, the Reformation with its fusion of secular and religious concerns compounded under the pressure of a relentless rush of events. This unprecedented stimulus had a determining influence on the conduct of the debate. A brief look at it will be useful before we turn to the estate deliberations themselves.

"Reformation" was a word with broad and non-specific meanings at the opening of the sixteenth century. This point has been made in an earlier chapter. Luther's uncharacteristically triumphant exclamation "Ich hab eine reformation gemacht": "I have . . . made a reformation to set the popes' ears ringing and hearts bursting with fury"[1] exulted in progress achieved in the religious realm: church and university reform, education, above all the decisive turn to Scripture. But in common usage the word meant much more than this. Ulrich von Hutten's polemical "what this country needs is a reformation and an improvement in the general situation"[2] more nearly catches its holistic ring. "Reformation" was correction, or attempted correction, of all that seemed wrong or corrupt, and around 1500, as the preceding chapters have surely shown, this aim covered a huge expanse of religious, social, and political ground. In his own catalogue of things to be done "for improving the condition of Christians" Luther, in 1520, listed the most

---

[1] Preface to *Von Priesterehe des wirdigen herrn . . . Stephan Klingebeil* (1528), WA 26, 530-33; reference to p. 530.

[2] Ulrich von Hutten, *Die Anschawenden* (1521) in *Deutsche Schriften* ed. Heinz Mettke I (Leipzig, 1972), 179. The Latin version of the dialogue, *Inspicientes*, was published in 1520.

outstanding questions to be confronted, among them the problem newly posed by the "imperial laws." He also sounded the patriotic note and the theme of national victimization that had for at least half a century given the driving impulses to the literature of reform: "the misery and oppression bearing down on all parts of Christendom, and most grievously on our German lands."[3] This conviction—that Germany epitomized the Christian condition and had taken upon herself the largest share of its wretchedness—had by then been absorbed into the country's national folklore. "German lands are the heart of Christendom," declared Eberlin von Günzburg in the first pamphlet of his "Fifteen Confederates" of 1521,[4] in which he also confessed pride in the fact that both Luther and Hutten were "native Germans."[5] Hutten himself said that in his German poems he had "cried out to the fatherland in its own tongue and exhorted it to take revenge" on the papacy for the injury done to country and people.[6] This theme of national outrage and betrayal, which also runs through the catalogues of grievances pressed by the "German Nation" against Rome,[7] was a constant strain in the century's reform literature. It added the stridency of patriotic passion to the sometimes plaintive, sometimes angry, tones of protest that filled the air around 1500 in each of the empire's regions.

The sense of approaching a turning point was especially acute in the 1520s. Older tendencies to look for concrete signs of an imminent transformation had by then been consolidated by the emergence of Luther as an exemplary figure, and by his movement's propensity for conflating reform impulses with eschatological anticipations and apocalyptic prediction. For the impending general "reformation," every

---

[3] *An den christlichen Adel deutscher Nation von des christlichen Standes besserung* (1520), WA 6, 404-05; reference to imperial laws: 459-60. On the image of Germany as victim in sixteenth-century Protestant literature, see Gerald Strauss, "The Course of German History, the Lutheran Interpretation" in *Renaissance Studies in Honor of Hans Baron*, eds. Anthony Molho and John A. Tedeschi (Florence, 1971), 663-86.

[4] Johann Eberlin von Günzburg, *Ein klaegliche klag an den christlichen Römischen kayser . . . (Der erst bundtsgnoss*, 1521. *Neudrucke deutscher Litteraturwerke des 16. und 17. Jahrhunderts*, No. 139, Halle, 1896), 2.

[5] *Ibid.*, 4.

[6] *Klag und Vermahnung gegen dem übermässigen . . . Gewalt des Papsts zu Rom* in *Deutsche Schriften*, ed. Peter Ukena (Munich, 1970), 207.

[7] *Die Beschwerden deutscher Nation* (1521) in *Deutsche Reichstagsakten*, Jüngere Reihe II (1896; reprint, 1962), 661-718, in part translated in Gerald Strauss, *Manifestations of Discontent in Germany on the Eve of the Reformation* (Bloomington, Ind., 1971), 52-63; *Die Beschwerden deutscher Nation* (1523) in *Reichstagsakten*, Jüngere Reihe III (1901; reprint 1963), 645-88. See also Hans Christoph Rublack, "Gravamina und Reformation" in Ingrid Bàtori, ed., *Städtische Gesellschaft und Reformation* (Stuttgart, 1980), 292-313.

interested party had its special agenda. Reform scenarios ranged from the elimination of illegitimate restraints in both religion and secular life—probably the chief source of Luther's original appeal and of the common understanding of "evangelical liberty"—to the concentration of governing powers in the hands of a Christian prince or magistrate. To some, Melanchthon for instance, this latter alternative was the only effective prescription for holding things together in the time remaining before Judgment Day.[8] To others the drift toward concentrated rule and the curtailment of freedoms was itself a sign of the running down of time.

Even in the meetings of territorial assemblies, the discussion often resounded with the exceptional ardor generated by the German predicament. This intensity was ascribed most often to the special qualities said to be possessed by the German people. Eberlin von Günzburg spoke proudly of the "ancient honesty of the German nation"[9] and praised "our plainness and uprightness," explaining that "we are endowed by nature with so much openness and simplicity of heart that we think others are as unlikely to deceive us as we are unwilling to defraud them." Eberlin contrasted this natural integrity and preference for straight dealing with "the trickery and fickleness of Italians."[10] In the same vein Luther asserted that it was the Germans' greatest asset that they were recognized as "faithful, truthful, steadfast people who, when they say 'yes' mean yes, and when they say 'no' mean no," as enjoined by Matthew 5:37. "We Germans," he added,

> still have a spark (may God fan it into a great fire) of that old-time virtue that enables us to feel a touch of shame and makes us dislike being called liars and not laugh and make a joke of it, as the Latins and Greeks do.[11]

In the opinion of writers most instrumental in shaping the country's self-image, this innate gravity of character combined with a child-like simplicity of heart and trusting openness of mind was the chief reason for the centrality of the German experience. It endowed affairs in Germany with a breadth of significance unattainable by other modern nations.[12] In the diffusion of this vision of German history, the Reforma-

---

[8] On Melanchthon's Doomsday expectations see O. Albrecht, "Eine handschriftliche Notiz Melanchthons aus dem Jahre 1559," *Theologische Studien und Kritiken* 70 (1897), 797-99; also Johann Carion, *Chronica . . .* (Wittenberg, 1532), Aviiʳ.

[9] Johann Eberlin von Günzburg, *Ein klaegliche klag . . .* (1521), 8.

[10] *Id., Der VIII. bundtsgnosz* (1521) in *Neudrucke* (reference as in note 4), 80.

[11] *Auslegung des 101. Psalms* (1534-1535), WA 51, 259.

[12] This notion of Germany and Germans as having a more solid and profound substance than other peoples endures into the twentieth century. For some examples of this

tion was a vital agent: it raised that history to the stature of a national myth. In this way the figure of a Christ-like Germany beset by cunning enemies served to magnify the disputes on which the domestic debate turned. That great issues were at stake was clear enough from the political events themselves. But the larger themes of reformation and national struggle set these events in a universal frame and imbued them with world-historic importance.

THE arena for state building in the empire was the territorial principality. It was there that the segmenting and parcelling process, which is the most characteristic feature of the political economy of feudalism, was reversed. Roman law was the ambitious ruler's most reliable device for bringing this turnabout to its intended conclusion: the transfer of territorial sovereignty into the prince's hands. "Only a forceful ruling personality supported by a new type of official, the learned jurist," comments a recent historian of Bavaria, could accomplish this goal, and this team could do it only "by ruthlessly utilizing the newly created territorial law, by running a taut administration, and by combining the ruler's several prerogatives into a single concept of sovereignty."[13] The outlines of this development have been suggested in an earlier chapter, where the intended victim of the would-be sovereign prince was identified as the late feudal society itself, as represented by its *Stände*. Needless to say, spokesmen for these estates differed dramatically from princely strategists in their understanding of the prevailing constitutional reality and in their sense of what was allowed and what was illicit in the conduct of politics. These issues, and a host of related ones, were the subjects of discussions carried on among the member groups of regional estates in the empire's *Länder*, and between leaders of these estates and agents of territorial princes. As is to be expected, the records

idea among historians, see Karl Holl, "Was verstand Luther unter Religion?" *Gesammelte Aufsätze zur Kirchengeschichte* I (Tübingen, 1932), 110; Ludwig Zimmermann, "Motive und Grundformen moderner Staatsbildung in Deutschland" (1939), reprinted in Hellmut Kämpff, ed., *Herrschaft und Staat im Mittelalter* (*Wege der Forschung* II, Darmstadt, 1974), 378; Heinrich Mitteis reviewing Otto Brunner's *Land und Herrschaft* in *HZ* 163 (1941), 256, reprinted in Hellmut Kämpf, *op. cit.*, 21. Georg Troescher, wondering why it was only in Germany that paintings of the Last Judgment adorned the west walls of town halls and courtrooms, finds the explanation in the "tiefen ethischen Anschauungen unserer germanischen Vorfahren." "Weltgerichtsbilder in Ratshäusern und Gerichtsstätten," *Westdeutsches Jahrbuch für Kunstgeschichte* XI (1939), 213-14. Johannes Heckel, who emphasizes Luther's "deutsche Eigenart" and the German-ness of his legal thought, ascribes to the German people inspired by the Reformation a "tendency to personalize and subjectivize legal relations." "Recht und Gesetz, Kirche und Obrigkeit in Luthers Lehre vor dem Thesenanschlag von 1517. Eine juristische Untersuchung," *ZRG* 57 (1937), *Kanon. Abt.*, 301-15, 323-24.
[13] Max Spindler, *Handbuch der bayerischen Geschichte* II (Munich, 1966), 273.

244 — The Heart of Resistance

of these debates plunge us into the thick of arguments and counter-arguments traded by the contending parties. Roman law and all that it stood for played a leading role in their exchanges.

Two rival concepts of law defined the respective positions of the opposing sides. One, the "modern" concept, taken from Roman law and its political use, equated law with the will of the state: law was what the state declared. The other, "medieval," view insisted on preserving the agreement between law and the principles of righteousness and equity that governed the world: to be legitimate, law must accord with God's justice and the dictates of fairness.[14] To the individual—at least to individuals in places of responsibility—belonged the ultimate right of judging whether this accord was intact or had been broken. The victory of the former position, and with it the ascendancy of the sovereign principality, was very much in the cards at the beginning of the sixteenth century. But obvious as this outcome is to the historian tracing lines of development leading to the modern state, it did not appear inevitable to contemporary observers. They, too, could see which way the signs pointed. But the powerful central state with its penchant for legal absolutism and its encroaching bureaucracy was still, in the early 1500s, seen as a menace to be warded off rather than as a foregone conclusion to be acknowledged. As such, the threat it posed to established constitutional and social relations was most sharply perceived in the deliberative assemblies of regional estates.

Estates were privileged corporations exercising certain governing functions within a principality, notably taxation.[15] What powers they held rested on their character as associations of individuals, each of

[14] For a development of this distinction, and a discussion of its implications, see Otto Brunner, *Land und Herrschaft. Grundfragen der territorialen Verfassungsgeschichte Österreichs im Mittelalter* (5th ed. Vienna, 1965), 133-46.

[15] For some definitions of "estates," see Robert Folz, "Ständeversammlungen in den deutschen Fürstentümern" in Heinz Rausch, ed., *Die geschichtlichen Grundlagen der modernen Volksvertretung* II: *Reichsstände und Landstände* (Darmstadt, 1974), 187-88; *id.*, "Les assemblées d'états dans les principautés allemandes (Fin XIIIe—début XVIe siècle)," *Schweizer Beiträge zur allgemeinen Geschichte* 20 (1962-1963), 171-72; Wilhelm Schwer, *Stand und Ständeordnung im Weltbild des Mittelalters* (2nd ed. Paderborn, 1952); Siegfried Bachmann, *Die Landstände des Hochstifts Bamberg (98. Bericht des historischen Vereins für die Pflege der Geschichte des ehemaligen Fürstbistums Bamberg*, Bamberg, 1962), 31; Johanna Maria van Winter, *Rittertum, Ideal und Wirklichkeit* (Munich, 1969), 80; Karl Bosl, *Die Geschichte der Repräsentation in Bayern* (Munich, 1974), 47; Peter Blickle, *Landschaften im alten Reich. Die staatliche Funktion des gemeinen Mannes in Oberdeutschland* (Munich, 1973), 3-23. A plain-spoken political definition of "estates" in the German context is offered, along with a concise discussion of their role vis-à-vis the ruler in the *Ständestaat*, by Gianfranco Poggi, *The Development of the Modern State: A Sociological Introduction* (Stanford, 1978), 43-56.

whom possessed a defined legal status in the ranked order of society: prelates, nobles, knights, burghers, even peasants. The often-quoted definition by the eighteenth-century constitutional lawyer Johann Jacob Moser, "estates are the body of those subjects who, in accordance with territorial privileges and tradition, must be consulted by the territorial ruler for their advice or consent on certain points touching the territory, and who in other ways are involved in administrating or taking part in matters concerning the welfare of the country,"[16] reflects a late phase in the history of estates, when initiative had passed out of their hands and their "involvement" in affairs of state had become more or less perfunctory. In the sixteenth century, though the situation then was extraordinarily fluid and differed from region to region in the empire,[17] it is more accurate to describe ruler and estates as "cobearers of central power" in a state.[18] Considerable scholarly controversy exists as to the quality of the estates' contribution to statecraft in the early modern period.[19] But this question is of little consequence for our purposes here. Estates deputies knew their rights and freedoms, and they fought for them tenaciously and with resourceful ingenuity. In their understanding of the rough and hazardous game of politics, defense of the *status quo* was the chief purpose and the best justification of their participation in affairs of state. Older German historians tended to see this goal as largely nugatory. They judged it petty, unworthy of the grand goals of national politics. "Their objective remained more negative than positive," the constitutional historian Fritz Hartung wrote of sixteenth-century estates. "They were out to restrict the territorial ruler, to prevent him from taking measures that could have damaged their own interests; . . . the principle of all their actions was autonomy in the medieval style."[20] Other scholars have been willing to give the estates

[16] *Von der teutschen Reichsstände Landen* (1769), 322, quoted in Otto Brunner, *op. cit.*, 415.

[17] For the great manifoldness of characteristics and development of estates in the Holy Roman Empire, see the general picture drawn by Herbert Helbig, "Fürsten und Landstände im Westen des Reiches im Übergang vom Mittelalter zur Neuzeit" in Heinz Rausch, ed., *op. cit.*, 123-80. For a warning against generalizing from single instances, see Fritz Hartung, "Herrschaftsverträge und ständischer Dualismus in deutschen Territorien" in *ibid.*, 31-33.

[18] Robert M. Berdahl, "The *Stände* and the Origins of Conservatism in Prussia," *Eighteenth-Century Studies* 6:3 (1973), 299.

[19] For a good guide to this debate, see F. L. Carsten, *Princes and Parliaments in Germany from the Fifteenth to the Eighteenth Century* (Oxford, 1959).

[20] Fritz Hartung, *Deutsche Verfassungsgeschichte* (8th ed. Stuttgart, 1950), 55-56. Hartung's book was first published in 1914. His argument is developed in "Herrschaftsverträge" (as in note 17), 28-46.

good marks for helping to limit arbitrary rule pursued by the rulers of the time in the manner of the patrimonial kind of politics so congenial to them. "But their insistence on special rights, their frequent refusal to acknowledge the obligation to be taxed, and, in general, their wish to evade all co-responsibility in the state—these," so charges Herbert Helbig, "are evidence of a reactionary element in the political concepts of the estates . . . , and this impeded the process of the formation of the modern state."[21] "Locked in the conservatism of their mental habits," Helbig continues, the estates "rarely advanced to higher political undertakings than to insist on the right to vote taxes."[22]

In our present-day view, such judgments[23] seem badly out of focus. "Medieval autonomy," "conservatism," "reactionary" or "special rights" "impeding the formation of the modern state" were not, in the sixteenth century, understood as qualities deserving of the kind of heavy disapprobation that some modern historians, approaching the age with very different political values in mind, have pronounced upon them. We are much more sympathetic now to the partisans of the endangered *status quo*.

As indicated, estates (*Stände*) developed gradually in the course of the late thirteenth and the early fourteenth centuries out of unions formed by established social groups at their periodic meetings: knights and other nobles, ecclesiastics, burghers, and in a few places—especially in the southwest of Germany, near Switzerland—peasants.[24] Called into session by rulers who needed them to relieve their financial straits and help out with other common problems (severe economic setbacks, dynastic divisions of the territory, succession crises, regencies for minor heirs, assumptions of debts, territorial defense), these associations (*Einungen*) eventually—by the late fourteenth century in most places—aspired to joint government with the territorial ruler in a polit-

[21] Herbert Helbig in *loc. cit.*, 180. See notes 1, 6-15, of this article for bibliography on the debate concerning the achievements of territorial estates in European politics.

[22] *Id.*, "Königtum und Ständeversammlung" in *ibid.*, 117-18.

[23] As Gerhard Oestreich points out, only since the late 1940s has scholarly attention been directed to the importance of German estates in the constitutional history of Europe. Until then, they were treated from the monarchistic point of view as "impediments." "Ständetum und Staatsbildung in Deutschland" in *id., Geist und Gestalt des frühmodernen Staates* (Berlin, 1969), 277-78. For an example of the attitude thus characterized by Oestreich, see Hans Spangenberg, *Vom Lehnstaat zum Ständestaat* (Munich, 1912), *passim*, e.g., p. 116: "Eine Gesundung des öffentlichen Lebens war nur von oben her zu erwarten."

[24] For the historical development of estates in Germany see Friedrich Wilhelm Unger, *Geschichte der deutschen Landstände* (Hannover, 1844); Hans Spangenberg, *op. cit.*; Robert Folz, "Ständeversammlungen" (as in note 15); Karl Bosl, *op. cit.*, 1-237.

ical arrangement usually described as "dualism." Where this system came into being (and this, too, is a subject of controversy among regional historians), the ruler recognized the associated groups as bodies assembled for the purpose of guarding corporate freedoms and privileges, while the estates, for their part, affirmed their loyalty to the prince and agreed to assume a share of the government's burdens. Even as they so affirmed, however, they did not fail to reserve the right to revoke this agreement and, if compelled by circumstances to do so, rise to armed resistance in order to defend themselves. In this way, as the Bavarian historian Karl Bosl has put it, the old feudal obligation to render "advice and aid" to one's lord became a stated right, on the basis of which the body of estates acted as an organ representing the country as a whole.[25] Owing to the ruling princes' need for ever larger sums to help them out of their mounting debts, estates met more or less regularly from the mid-fifteenth century on. They assembled in *Landtage*, territorial diets, with whose speakers the rulers or their agents negotiated the most pressing problems facing the country. The late fifteenth century and the early sixteenth were the high point of this development. Never again in the early modern era were estates to hold so influential a position.[26]

Membership in the *Landschaft*, the body of estates meeting in a diet, varied from region to region (as did procedure, competence, and responsibilities); the full complement of social orders ranging from "dynastic" aristocrats (counts and lords) through petty nobles and knights, prelates (bishops, abbots and abbesses, priors, cathedral chapters, university delegates), deputies of the urban bourgeoisie and artisanate, emissaries of administrative districts (*Ämter*), and peasant representatives[27] was never present in any single territory.[28] In most regions the

[25] Karl Bosl, *op. cit.*, 43-44. In Bavaria this happened at the very beginning of the fourteenth century; in other regions it came later. Bosl generalizes on the Bavarian model because our state of information about Bavarian estates in the late thirteenth and the fourteenth centuries is the best in Germany. For the process of development leading to dualism in this sense, see Otto Brunner, *op. cit.*, 426-40.

[26] See F. L. Carsten, *op. cit.*, 431-34 for a summary statement of his conclusions on the strong position of estates in the sixteenth century. *Ibid.*, 436-40, for symptoms and reasons of estates' decline in the seventeenth century.

[27] For the regions of the southwestern part of the Holy Roman Empire where peasants attended, sat in, or constituted the territorial estates, see Peter Blickle, *Landschaften im alten Reich*, 97-336. They were, chiefly, Austrian Swabia, Salzburg, Tyrol, Baden-Durlach, and the monastic domains of Kempten and Ochsenhausen.

[28] In ecclesiastical territories, the estates nearly always included the canons of the cathedral chapter. In Würzburg and Bamberg, for example, the estates consisted of the

burden of participation fell on knights and burghers. The former attended personally (if ownership of a manor or other property made them *landtagsfähig*, entitled to a seat in the diet)[29]; the latter sent elected deputies, usually a mayor accompanied by one or two councillors, sometimes by a learned *syndicus*. Representatives were given plenipotentiary power, which was conveyed by an enabling document, called *Gewalt* or *Vollmacht*, carried by each deputy.[30] In some regions, Württemberg, for example, even small country towns and market villages sent a deputy or two.[31] Where districts—*Ämter*—were represented, the procedure for choosing delegates was the same as in the towns.[32] Following the summoning of a *Landtag* by the ruler,[33] each group caucused separately on the prince's *Proposition* or the estates' *gravamina*, the two documents on which discussion usually centered.[34] Such caucuses often led to meetings of single estates to press special concerns. There were occasional *Rittertage*, *Städtetage*, and *Bauerntage*, and each of these divisions developed the tendency to regard itself as the entire *Landschaft*, or as its essential part.[35]

Following the *Correlation* of positions separately arrived at, the es-

---

chapter, the region's *Ritterschaft*, and representatives of towns and *Ämter* in the bishopric. For estates in the Bishopric of Bamberg, see Siegfried Bachmann, *Die Landstände des Hochstifts Bamberg* (reference as in note 15).

[29] In some regions—Mecklenburg, for instance—even widows and orphans of estate holders were *landtagsfähig*. They were represented by male relatives or neighbors. Hermann Krause, *System der landständischen Verfassung Mecklenburgs in der zweiten Hälfte des 16. Jahrhunderts* (Rostock, 1927), 8-9.

[30] On the membership of estate bodies see Johannes Gut, *Die Landschaft auf den Landtagen der markgräflich badischen Gebiete* (*Schriften zur Verfassungsgeschichte* 13, Berlin, 1970), 45-47; Gerhard Buchda, "Reichsstände und Landstände in Deutschland im 16. und 17. Jahrhundert" in Heinz Rausch, ed., *op. cit.* (reference as in note 15); Robert Folz, "Ständeversammlungen" (reference as in note 15), 188-209. In the HStA St, A34, Bü 16f. one can see a folder with a score or so of *Vollmachten* given to representatives of towns and *Ämter* in 1566.

[31] Walter Grube, "Dorfgemeinde und Amtsversammlung in Altwürttemberg," *Zeitschrift für württembergische Landesgeschichte* 13 (1954), 196-98.

[32] For example, LA Tir *Landtagsvollmachten*, Fasz. 1, 1484-1486.

[33] Normally estates were convoked by rulers. But in the course of the sixteenth century, estates increasingly insisted on the right to convoke themselves, a right exercised by the estates' executive committee. In theory every member was obliged to attend. But in practice excuses were often made, with "weakness of body" and "act of God" predominating as the reasons given. The real reason for non-attendance was the heavy cost of lodging, food, and fodder.

[34] On procedure, see Gerhard Buchda in *loc. cit.*, 235-37; Johannes Gut in *loc. cit.*, 47-49; and F. W. Unger, *op. cit.* II, *passim*.

[35] For example, the *Ritterschaft* in Jülich-Berg: Georg von Below, *Landtagsakten von Jülich-Berg 1400-1600* (Düsseldorf, 1895-1907) I, 23-25, 46.

tates, whose discussions were taken down in a mixture of German and Latin for later verbatim transcription,[36] proceeded to vote. Unlike the imperial diet, where, in principle at least, only unanimity counted,[37] territorial practice generally accepted the majority rule, although not all estates everywhere agreed to this. As we shall see, the actual mode of procedure was in every case a great deal more complicated, and infinitely more time-consuming, than the scheme given here suggests, and this is especially true of discussions taking place between estates and rulers following the voting. Rulers were expected to be personally present. Nothing, however, obliged them to conduct face-to-face negotiations, and most contacts between prince and estates were by written document. Extraordinary amounts of time and paper were expended. Repetition and reiteration abounded. The ceaseless trading of documents slowed the pace to a crawl, and verbosity was advanced to the state of a consummate skill. A Tyrolean noble covers three folio pages to explain to Ferdinand II that his place at the territorial diet of 1573 will be taken by his son.[38] A governmental proposition generates a response followed by the trading of *replica, duplica, triplica, quadruplica,* and *quintuplica* until at last a *Schlusschrift* or *Abschied* is reached.[39] These cumbersome exchanges had been imported into politics from courtroom procedure, where they had complicated litigation since the introduction of canon law in the fifteenth century.[40]

Making one's way through stacks of such documents in the regional archives, one begins to suspect that it was the main purpose of each side in the negotiations to gain victory through attrition. At their diet in Innsbruck in 1525, for example, the estates of Tyrol asked for a statement allowing litigating parties in the county's courts the free choice of oral or written trial procedures. Refusing, Count Ferdinand laid out his reasons in an *Antwort*, to which the estates then made *Gegenantwort*,

[36] Few protocol notes have survived. For a sample, see HStA St A34, Bü 16g, No. 35.

[37] This was also the case in the assembly of the Swiss Confederation. See Adolf Gasser, "Die landständische Staatsidee und der schweizerische Bundesgedanke" in Commission internationale pour l'histoire des assemblées d'États, *L'organisation corporative du moyen âge à la fin de l'Ancien Régime* III (Louvain, 1939), 123. On majority decisions in the imperial diet, see Helmut Neuhaus, *Reichsständische Repräsentationsformen im 16. Jahrhundert* (Berlin, 1982), 26-27.

[38] LA Tir, *Tiroler Landtagsakten,* Fasz. 9, unpaginated.

[39] For example, Tyrolean diet in Innsbruck, 1573, *ibid.,* Cod. 45, *passim.* The same scheme of operation prevailed in the imperial diet. For a personal description of how it worked, see Bartholomäus Sastrow, . . . *Herkomen, Geburt und Lauff seines gantzen Lebens* . . . , ed. G. F. Mohnike (Greifswald, 1823-1824) II, 100ff.

[40] Helmut Coing, *Die Rezeption des römischen Rechts in Frankfurt am Main* (Frankfurt am Main, 1939), 106-18.

accepting the count's reasoning but "begging submissively" to be restored to their old liberties, among which they enumerated the free choice of procedure in trials. Several stages later, the ruler finally granted this request but added the proviso that "his Princely Grace expects the honorable estates to agree in time that in insisting on written procedure, His Princely Grace has his honorable estates' best interests at heart." In this sense the final *Abschied* was drafted and recessed.[41] Most negotiations between estates and rulers took this form and rhythm. Propositions, grievances, replications, memoranda (*Bedenken*), protestations shuttled back and forth between estate leaders and their advisers on one side and the prince's councillors, most of them lawyers, on the other. For their part, the estates nearly always entrusted the negotiating to committees, and by the sixteenth century the importance of these smaller bodies had come to exceed that of the estate assemblies themselves. In some regions estates even had permanent representatives; in Lüneburg, for example, eight members of the estates' executive committee, called *Landräte*, negotiated with the duke's officials when the diet was not in session.[42]

Raising tax revenues was the estates' principal task from the territorial ruler's point of view, and diets tended to be called whenever a prince's income was depleted, or when a sudden need for funds arose or creditors were pounding on the door. Demands for taxation and debt assumption to help defray the runaway cost of government became ever more clamorous in the fifteenth and sixteenth centuries when rulers began to regard responsibility for these services as a self-evident obligation upon estates. Ferdinand II of Tyrol wrote in this vein to his duchy's diet in 1571. "Whereas our faithful lands and people have always granted, and will always grant, generous help for the maintenance of our person and the whole state [*gantzen wesens*]," he said, "as well as for the assumption of our debt burdens and the quittance of our pawned properties, we show ourselves generously aware of this assistance and express our good will and benevolent inclination to our faithful, willing, and obedient estates and subjects."[43] Estates usually agreed to appropriate the needed sums, if a need could be demonstrated. But they did not do so without obtaining a *quid pro quo*, one that was, from their perspective, the chief matter of assembly business: the confirmation, reconfirmation, and—whenever possible—extension of their liberties. If this favor was granted them, they were willing to swear

[41] I failed to note the location of this excerpt from the Innsbruck diet of 1525 in LA Tir.

[42] Christian von Arnswaldt, *Die Lüneburger Ritterschaft als Landstand im Spätmittelalter* (Göttingen, 1969), 17-19.

[43] LA Tir *Tiroler Landtagsakten*, Fasz. 8, unpaginated.

"fidelity, surety, and obedience to our natural territorial prince and rightful hereditary lord, as we are by rights obliged to do, but always reserving our freedoms,"[44] and to proceed to the discussion of amounts, proportions, and other details of the sum to be raised. Taxes and liberties were closely tied to each other throughout the fifteenth and for part of the sixteenth century. Thus the Württemberg estates pledged in 1514 to furnish twenty-two thousand gulden in each of the succeeding five years to help Duke Ulrich pay off his accumulated debts. In exchange they got the Tübingen Contract, a fundamental charter of their rights and the basis of negotiations between themselves and their dukes from then on.[45]

Decisions on revenue matters were greatly facilitated by the circumstance that those who voted taxes rarely paid them. Most taxes were collected from ordinary people, who were not present to object. In Würzburg, for example, a "knightly agreement" concluded in 1525 among bishop, chapter, and knights meeting in diet agreed that every townsman and peasant in the bishopric would pay eight and a half gulden over the following three years to compensate nobles and prelates who had suffered damage in the peasant war. "When the lords had finished bickering," a chronicler commented on this arrangement, "the common man gave them the shirt off his back."[46] On occasion participants showed themselves mindful of the severity of these burdens. The Württemberg estates, having agreed on one hundred thirty thousand gulden for their duke in 1551, worried that "such a sum will not be easy to raise from the poor, ruined [by war and inflation] common man."[47] Such references to penury and ravage were not hyperbole. In Bavaria, in the 1570s under Albrecht V, taxation took away one thirtieth of a man's assessed fortune every other year or so, and it has been estimated that in the three decades of Albrecht's reign, every Bavarian peasant paid out in taxes more than half of what his farmstead was worth. The duchy's estates objected to such excesses, but—as the tax was paid only by the peasants (who had no direct representation in the diet)—their protests were muted.[48] The estates' greatest problem after voting taxes, therefore, was the collection of them in the country. For that purpose

[44] Quoted in F. W. Unger, *op. cit.* II, 234.
[45] Walter Grube, "Dorfgemeinde und Amtsversammlung . . ." in *loc. cit.*, 83-85.
[46] Quoted in Ernst Schubert, *Die Landstände des Hochstifts Würzburg* (Würzburg, 1967), 116.
[47] HStA St *Tomi actorum* No. 1, 169[v].
[48] Siegmund Riezler, *Geschichte Baierns* IV (Gotha, 1899; reprint Aalen, 1964), 619-25.

they created special financial institutions under their own control,[49] and this action, in turn, strengthened their demands for participation in other governmental undertakings to the point that they at times declared to their rulers that "he who is not consulted does not cooperate" (*wer nicht mit räth, der nicht mit thät*).[50] This was not an empty threat. For much of the sixteenth century (but not in all territories equally) the estates' executive committees helped decide major questions such as war and peace, advised on legislation, and considered themselves competent in everything that touched the country's welfare. Most energetically—and for the historian most interestingly—estates availed themselves of the ancient custom of presenting *gravamina* or *Beschwerden*, complaints and grievances describing unsatisfactory conditions in the land and among its people (*Landgebrechen*), for the purpose of gaining remedy and redress. By means of these grievances, submitted in lengthy lists at diet after diet, estates sought to extend their influence to all the important affairs of state, society, and religion. Their political lever in attempting this move was their acknowledged right to vote taxes. But equally important was an ideological weapon: the claim that estates embodied not only the particular social orders convoked in the diet, but *land und leute* as well, the country as a whole and all the people in it.[51]

Grievance lists originated in submissions made by individual nobles and prelates, by town councils, village courts, and administrative organs (*Ämter*) in each territory in the empire.[52] Upon request, these lists were sent to the country's ruler. More often they made their way to one of the standing committees of a territorial assembly as it prepared for a meeting of the country's diet. Some examples from the huge bulk of grievance writings resting in German archives will show how this process worked. Local courts in Saxony, situated in market villages and staffed by six or more jurors (*Schöffen*) and an appointed "country judge" (*Landrichter*), served two principal purposes. They investigated, tried, and punished crimes and misdemeanors (by a primitive inquisitorial method called *rügen*, to indict and rebuke—hence the court's name, *Ruggericht*); and they voiced grievances, forwarding

---

[49] For the development of estate-controlled tax organizations in Bavaria, see Edmund Rosenthal, *Geschichte des Gerichtswesens und der Verwaltungsorganisation Baierns* I (Würzburg, 1889), 400-08.

[50] Quoted in F. W. Unger, *op. cit.* II, 390.

[51] On the question of the representative nature of estates, see Karl Bosl, "Das Problem der Repräsentation im spätmittelalterlichen Deutschland. Ständebewegung, Ständegesellschaft, Ständestaat" in *Bohemia. Jahrbuch des Collegium Carolinum* 15 (Munich and Vienna, 1974), 19-29. For an introduction to the extensive bibliography on this point, see Johannes Gut (reference as in note 30), note 20.

[52] Many examples of this procedure are contained in BHStA Mu *Altbayerische Landschaft* 1158-1207 for the years 1572-1612.

these to the central *Amt* of the district in which they were located. Records of these tribunals survive from the 1550s,[53] and they are full and detailed both for the courts' law-and-order function and for their role as formulator of complaints. Very little acquaintance with these materials is needed to make one realize that the salient concerns of ordinary people changed very little over time and from place to place. The same complaints are registered, and the same requests made, in ceaseless repetition. Pray leave our rightful entitlements unimpaired: this supplication heads every list. By "rightful entitlements" (*Gerechtigkeiten*) villagers meant such guarantees as free access to fishing streams, brewing privileges for property owners, traditional benefits such as the gift of firewood for newlyweds; the right—increasingly jeopardized—to employ a few artisans (a smith, a miller, a weaver, a tailor) in the village to lessen its dependence on towns; stable prices for milling, retailed beer, and other necessities; fair distribution of labor service in the community (to keep the *Landknecht* or bailiff from playing favorites in assigning tasks on behalf of the patrimonial noble); country-wide control of monopolists (*monopolirern*) and jobbers (*fürkäufer*) "who must not be allowed to buy up everything"; effective measures against "Savoyards" or itinerant peddlers without fixed abode;[54] and so on. These items are ritualistically recapitulated in village after village, year after year, which makes the reading of grievances a tedious enterprise.

Procedural formalism was encouraged also by the obligatory routines by which village courts operated. Each session opened with an unvarying *Danksagung*, a "rendering of thanks" to God, to the elector or duke, to regional and local officials, to the "preacher and curate of our souls," and to the judge and jurors sitting behind the bar; following which

> each neighbor then gives thanks to his neighbor, poor and rich, young and old, great and humble, from the highest to the lowest and from the lowest to the highest, praying that they might all be peaceful and amicable toward each other. May God help us all live in peace and unity.[55]

---

[53] StA Dr, Loc. 8832. In one case the records go back to 1531. The voluminous documents in this collection are organized by *Ämter*.

[54] Complaints about *Hausierer*—peddlers—and *Savoyer* were constant in the sixteenth century. For examples see LA Tir *Landtagsakten*, Fasz. 375 (1549), *passim*. On "Savoyards" in western Europe, see Peter Burke, *Popular Culture in Early Modern Europe* (New York, 1978), 99. On "monopolists" see the statement by Mecklenburg estates in Karl von Hegel, *Geschichte der mecklenburgischen Landstände bis zum Jahre 1555* (Rostock, 1856; reprint Aalen, 1968), 197.

[55] E.g., StA Dr, Loc. 8832, *Dorff Kemnitzer . . . Ehegericht* 1584, 14ʳ-16ʳ.

The session having been thus inaugurated, the village spokesman stepped up to the "judicial enclosure" (*gehegte bank*) to present the community's remonstrances.[56] Familiar though they were to all participants in this ritual, grievances were taken seriously by those to whom they were addressed. The archives of the County of Tyrol, for instance, contain detailed official responses to every item on each of the many local grievance lists sent in by the *Pfleger*, the head of the local government. In Württemberg, to take another example, the estates' executive committee went carefully over all the local submissions before incorporating the gist of them in the assembly's master list of *Landbeschwerden*.[57]

Given the glacial pace at which things moved in the countryside, the absence of much development, or even variety, in the voicing of complaints is not difficult to understand.[58] But among nobles, too, sameness prevailed. Although the grievances supplied by groups of knights often bear individual seals and signatures (so-and-so "in my own hand"),[59] the innumerable complaints about violations of jurisdictional claims and the requests to the prince for directives to "remove" (*abschaffen*) long-standing abuses are reiterated monotonously, very often without a single word having been altered. One gains the impression that the presentation itself of grievances was considered the vital part of the political process, a cherished right which, like all rights and freedoms, must be kept alive by regular demonstration: use it or lose it. But it may also be that all concerned acknowledged the essential im-

---

[56] The whole procedure is given verbatim in *Ehegerichts Ordnung oder Process Gericht zu hegen* in StA Dr, Loc. 8832, *Amt Stolbergks Acta*, 19ʳ-34ᵛ. For another set of examples from Saxony see StA Dr, Loc. 9356, "Der Chur zu Sachssen clage . . . 1555," a volume of over 600 pages of local grievances submitted in 1555 to the elector. Also StA Wei Reg. Q, Nos. 82-97, individual grievance statements by nobles, town councils, and village corporations (*Dorfschaften*) submitted to the executive committees of diets, and later incorporated in the *Landschaft*'s grievance documents.

[57] LA Tir *Landtagsakten*, Fasz. II; HStA St A34, Bü 18b, containing fifty sets of local complaints addressed to the estates and to Duke Ludwig in 1583.

[58] For the operation of comparable village courts in other territories, see the following. Bavaria: Edmund Rosenthal, *op. cit.* I, 204-11; Rudolf Wilhelm, *Rechtspflege und Dorfverfassung nach niederbayerischen Ehehaftsordnungen vom 15. bis zum 18. Jahrhundert* (University of Munich dissertation 1953); Württemberg: Walter Grube, "Dorfgemeinde und Amtsversammlung" in *loc. cit.*, 194-219; Würzburg: Walter Scherzer, "Die Dorfverfassung der Gemeinden im Bereich des ehemaligen Hochstifts Würzburg," *Jahrbuch für fränkische Landesforschung* 36 (1976), 37-64.

[59] For Saxony: e.g., StA Dr, Loc. 9359 "Gravamina und ander Gebrechen Anno 1602." For Bavaria: BHStA Mu, *Altbayerische Landschaft* Nos. 1158-1207 for the years 1572-1612. Individual noble submissions in StA Dr Loc. 9356 and StA Wei Reg. Q Nos. 82-97.

potence of government when it came to intervening in deeply rooted social conventions. The chorus of bitterly resentful complaints about the fearful damage done to crops by free-running game, for example, never abates. It is as loud, and sounds as exasperated, in the eighteenth century as it did in the sixteenth. Nothing, apparently, could be done.[60] If this was so, the registration of complaints about deep-seated *Missstände* and *Gebrechen* in the country was a kind of domestic political theater in which the power relations among the orders of the state were acted out, a drama without climax and without dénouement, but with much catharsis for everyone. On the territorial stage, the submission of grievances always coincided with the ruler's request for money. In this exchange the former—the free discussion of complaints—was expected to make the latter—the exaction of contributions—tolerable. Grievance writing was therefore encouraged by the state, particularly in times of financial need. As very little was ever done about the substance of the protests, their constant repetition must have had a largely formal function. On the other hand, there can be no doubt that—as I hope to show later in this chapter—most grievances arose from very real concerns in society, nor that, at the local and personal level—as evidenced by the mass of individual and local submissions—they mattered very seriously as to their substance, and not only as to their form.[61]

Following their formal presentation as itemized lists of *gravamina* or *Beschwerden*, the estates' documents were worked over by the territorial prince's advisers (their marginalia attest to this attention), a register or summary was made for handy reference by appropriate state organs,[62] and the documents themselves were then gathered into bundles or bound in volumes for deposition in the archives.[63] These procedures, and the lapidary official comments jotted in the margins, again suggest

[60] The best survey of this problem (but mostly for the seventeenth and eighteenth centuries) is Hans Wilhelm Eckardt, *Herrschaftliche Jagd, bäuerliche Not und bürgerliche Kritik. Zur Geschichte der fürstlichen und adligen Jagdprivilegien im südwestdeutschen Raum* (Göttingen, 1976). For the sixteenth century see Peter Blickle, *Landschaften im alten Reich*, 553, where the amount of damage owing to game is estimated.

[61] See for example the grievances of knights in the Upper Palatinate from the 1520s to the 1550s, as detailed in Klaus Köhle, *Landesherr und Landstände in der Oberpfalz von 1400-1583* (*Miscellanea Bavarica Monacensia*, Heft 16, Munich, 1969), 58-167.

[62] E.g., StA Dr, Loc. 9359, "Landtags-Sachen oder Verzeichnis aller Gravamina . . . 1601" (the register) and "Vorrichtung der Landgebrechen . . . 1601" (the summary).

[63] E.g., *ibid.*, "Gravamina und Landgebrechen Anno 1602." The Saxon estate records are remarkably full and well preserved. In StA Dr, see the following signatures: Loc. 9353-9357, 9359, 9362, covering the entire sixteenth century. 9356 and 9359 are especially rich in gravamina lists. In StA Wei, see the large mass of *Landschaftsbeschwerden* under the signature Reg. Q from the end of the fifteenth century on. In these, the parliamentary procedure of submission, response, *duplik, triplik*, etc. can be traced.

a certain perfunctory quality in the exchanges between estates and central governments. Formalistic rigor is even more evident in the rulers' response to the petitions submitted to them. Do not trouble us with vague allegations of defects and abuses, the estates are told, censoriously. Inform us instead by name, place, and occasion where an alleged offense is said to have occurred. It will then be duly investigated. This is asserted again and again in communications which, in intent, wording, and tone, are remarkably alike in all the empire's territories. "His Grace would be pleased to know who it was whose liberties were invaded in the manner suggested, also the name of the official or agent accused of doing him this injury. . . . In the absence of names of the *Amtleute* said to be guilty of these offenses, His Grace cannot understand what ancient customs and privileges have been disturbed."[64] This was in Saxony, in the 1520s. Later in the century the tone turns sharper while the nature of the response remains unchanged. "Let His Princely Grace henceforth be spared such accusations," wrote Ferdinand II of Tyrol in 1590, referring to alleged infringements of chartered liberties, "or let charges be presented *in specie* as to where, when, by whom, and in what manner such or such a man has been unlawfully aggrieved or injured in the possession of his freedoms."[65] In Bavaria, at the beginning of the seventeenth century, the duke's councillors still "repeat the resolution heretofore given by His Grace to his estates, namely that they must specify the cases, how, and by whom the said offenses were done."[66]

The uniformity of these responses over time is easily explained by the common training and sympathies of princely advisers and chancellery staff. But more substantive, and more sinister, reasons may also have been responsible. In the political ambiance of the late-sixteenth-century princely state, the insistence that remedial attention was possible only where names were named and offenses specified must have inhibited effective identification of abuses of authority. One can imagine aggrieved persons thinking twice before lodging complaints against powerful local officials and central agents whose ill will might spell long-lasting hardship for their hapless victims. Even more importantly: by shifting the government's responsibility from having to justify new administra-

---

[64] StA Wei Reg. Q, No. 19 (documents relating to Diet of Altenburg, 1523), 69ᵛ, 73ᵛ, 105ʳ.

[65] Response by Ferdinand II of Tyrol to *Beschwerden* of 1590. LA Tir *Landtagsakten* Cod. 48, 183ʳ. Almost identical: response of Archduke Leopold of Tyrol, 1619, *Landtagsakten* Cod. 2902, 96.

[66] Memorandum by councillors of Maximilian I of Bavaria, 1605. BHStA Mu *Staatsverwaltung* 1983, 9ᵛ.

tive practices to needing only to censure their abuse by over-zealous subordinates, the state was taking a long step toward the legitimation of the theory and practice of territorial absolutism. Professional counsel to princes on this point illuminates this shift. Ferdinand II of Tyrol was encouraged by his team of advisers to stand fast in his refusal to act on generalized complaints:

> It is our practice in such cases [the councillors wrote] that when a subject [*unterthan*] has been aggrieved or oppressed by tax assessors, district administrators, judges, court bailiffs, or other officials, he must report them by name and not merely complain about them in general terms. Once a concrete report has been made to us, we call for a description of the case, and then we request additional inquisition and investigation. And where we find that this or that official has indeed acted wrongly toward the subject, has harmed, oppressed, maltreated, or in other ways abused him, it is our practice to order the offending man to appear before the Chamber Procurator in Upper Austria, and there to have him examined as to his offending conduct.[67]

At about the same time—the 1570s—the elector of Saxony refused to act on a complaint about his church administrators on the ground that "general grievances and accusations" offer no justification for proceeding against anyone. This, the elector added, we learn from the trial of Paul in Acts 25, and also from the written law, where it is set down that

> if a man would accuse another of having committed a slight or injury, he must present definite and certain charges, and say specifically by whom the offense was committed.[68]

This being the political reality, it is unlikely that monotonously reiterative grievance statements performed the constitutional service with which some historians have credited them, namely that they enlightened governments about the real conditions in their lands, exercised the all-important function of political criticism, and in these ways contributed to an improvement of justice and administration in the state.[69] By

---

[67] LA Tir *Tiroler Landtagsakten*, Fasz. 9, unpaginated. The year was 1577.

[68] StA Wei Reg. Q, No. 65, 82ᵛ.

[69] These claims are made by Gerhard Oestreich, "Ständetum und Staatsbildung in Deutschland" in Heinz Rausch, ed., *op. cit.*, 51-52. Also Karl Bader, *Der deutsche Südwesten in seiner territorialgeschichtlichen Entwicklung* (Stuttgart, 1950), 19. On the informational function of grievances, Peter Blickle, *Landschaften*, 233. The decline of grievance procedures into formalism is noted by Volkmar Wittmütz, *Die Gravamina der bayerischen Stände im 16. und 17. Jahrhundert als Quelle für die wirtschaftliche Situa-*

the second half of the sixteenth century, if not before then, the grievance procedure had become far too routinized to have been capable of producing this beneficial effect.

The grievances themselves, on the other hand, were real enough. Even at their most trivial, they touched concerns both actual and portentous. This will become plain as we proceed to a closer look at what was actually said and written by those who felt themselves sorely aggrieved by the political trends of their time.

THE protest—to put it first in general, and therefore anachronistic, terms—was against the early modern state in the making. More precisely, it was against the accelerating efforts of its rulers to substitute their own agencies of power for functions traditionally exercised by estates, and to intervene at will in the performance of time-honored conventions. Although only a small number of princes were able by the end of the sixteenth century to complete the construction of a comprehensive judicial and administrative sovereignty in their lands, the legal and political changes occurring in all territories were signs pointing in that direction. Rightly interpreted, these signs had been causing alarm for many decades. In the constitutional confrontations of the sixteenth century, sharpened by the Lutheran Reformation, they indicated open conflict. In each case, the villain—as seen by the estates—was the sovereign state in process of formation.

Bavaria is a case in point. Around the middle of the sixteenth century, governing organs in that duchy were being brought under central control and the country's laws and court system "reformed" to that same purpose. Utilizing components from a loose-jointed administration with origins in the eleventh and twelfth centuries and irresistibly centrifugal tendencies, the Bavarian dukes and their agents had, beginning in the 1480s, assembled the basic structure of a solid political system firmly controlled from the capital.[70] In each of the duchy's four

_____

tion und Entwicklung Bayerns (Miscellanea Bavarica Monacensia Heft 26, Munich, 1970), 3-7. It may be that my generalization about the routinization of estate procedures holds less for Tyrol than for other regions in the empire. Peter Blickle, Landschaften, 189-227, finds that, at least in the early part of the sixteenth century, estate grievances by and large were "crystallized" in the country's Landesordnungen. Something of the contemporary flavor of grievance presentations is reflected in the fanciful etymology of "parliament" given by William Lambarde in his Archaeion, or a Discourse upon the High Courts of Justice in England, written 1591, printed 1635. He derives the word from parium and lamentum, explaining that "the peeres of the countrie did at these meetings lament and complain each to other of the enormities of their countrey, and thereupon provided redresse for the same." (Ed. Charles H. McIlwain and Paul L. Ward, Cambridge, Mass., 1957), 123-24.

[70] Eduard Rosenthal, op. cit. I, 236-581; Max Spindler, ed., Handbuch der bayer-

provinces, the sovereign power was represented by an exalted minister, the *Rentmeister*, who—as we saw in an earlier chapter—exercised sweeping jurisdiction over justice, administration, peace, and security, trades, commerce and finance (the latter his original area of competence, hence his title), religion, civic morality, and that fussy supervision of public and private activities to which the newly fashionable label of "police" was given. The *Rentmeister* moved about his province from his seat in Munich or Landshut or Straubing or Burghausen, inspecting his districts (*Pflegegerichte*), subdistricts (*Ämter, Obmannschaften*), towns and communities (*Gemain*), and compiling massive protocols on the results of his efforts to integrate and standardize all the important processes of public life.[71] He and his assistants, the *Pfleger, Landrichter*, and various degrees of *Amtmänner*, represented not so much the personal position of his hereditary prince as the legal and political sway of the state itself. A swarm of lesser functionaries carried their authority into every town and village. *Schergen* and *Fronboten* executed the *Rentmeister's* judicial powers, with bailiffs and sub-bailiffs to back them up. Forest masters, game and fish wardens, and border inspectors helped him protect the ruler's regalian rights—each attended by a staff of scribes and record keepers. Minting masters, mine inspectors, sworn money changers, assayers and their scriveners looked after the duke's monopolies. Custom officials (*Mautner, Zollner*), *Ungelter* and other revenue agents gathered tolls and indirect taxes. Auditors checked and rechecked the books. And a host of *Knechte* and *Diener* in the lowest grade of public service did the donkey work of running the state's errands. Toward the end of the sixteenth century, the reign of Maximilian I saw the addition to this bureaucratic apparatus of a network of secret information gatherers who filed reports four times a year and were paid by the quantity and quality of the data supplied. The need to root out religious deviance in the Catholic duchy seemed at the time to justify this covert force of paid informants. Seen

---

ischen Geschichte II (Munich, 1966), 545-85; Hans Hornung, *Beiträge zur inneren Geschichte Bayerns vom 16.-18. Jahrhundert aus den Umrittsprotokollen der Rentmeister des Rentamtes Burghausen* (Munich, 1915), 7-25. For evidence of "modern" administration in the part of Bavaria ruled by Albrecht IV at the end of the fifteenth century, see Pankraz Fried, " 'Modernstaatliche' Entwicklungstendenzen im Bayerischen Ständestaat des Spätmittelalters" in Heinz Rausch, ed., *Die geschichtlichen Grundlagen der Volksvertretung* II: *Reichsstände und Landstände* (Darmstadt, 1974), 349.

[71] On the protocols of the yearly *Umritt*—circuit ride—of the Bavarian *Rentmeister*, and the duke's instructions given them (*Umrittsordnungen*) annually to guide them in their inspections, see Edmund Rosenthal, *op. cit.* I, 297-321. Instructions for the annual *Umritte* are gathered in BHStA Mu G.R. 1262 (from 1584). These *Umritte* continued in Bavaria well into the nineteenth century.

in another light, it appears as the capstone to a process of political "rationalization" that had been under way since the fifteenth century.

Friction developed at every point of contact between this teeming officialdom and the country's population as the former carried out its chief mission, which was to expand the scope of public power at the expense of private rights and local peculiarities. In a transitional age of slipping feudal institutions passing into not yet fully articulated modern forms of social organization, state prerogatives clashed with private freedoms wherever jurisdictions overlapped. District courts collided with seigneurial tribunals, ecclesiastical reorganization with patrimonial churches, *Ämter* with urban and village communes. Everywhere central sovereignty was in conflict with *Herrschaft*, particular rights, and local autonomy. At the hub of Bavarian politics, the *Hofrat*, or aulic council, an organ formed out of the traditional offices of medieval courtiers, was transformed into a central government in Munich. Along with the duke, this council exercised ultimate authority in judicial, administrative, financial, military, and ecclesiastical affairs. Its gradual professionalization as a standing collegiate body is also the history of the gathering of political authority in Bavaria. Academically trained administrators replaced old-time nobles and prelates in the ranks of trusted councillors, and casual procedures gave way to formal routines laid down in *Landesordnungen*. Under a chancellor (originally a learned cleric, later an academic lawyer) to lead it in policy matters, and a president to oversee its routine operations, the Bavarian *Hofrat* functioned, from the middle of the sixteenth century on, as an effective source of direction and control. At about the same time, a *Hofkammer* staffed by a college of "chamber councillors" emerged as the office of central financial supervision. It raised the excises (mostly on beer and wine) and the monies from the duke's regalia which made up, in addition to the ever-increasing loans, the ruler's most reliable revenues, and its officers negotiated at territorial diets the assessment and collection of auxiliary taxes (*Beisteuern*) voted by the estates.[72]

Meanwhile the dukes also strengthened their hand in the operation of the Bavarian church and the exercise of religion. With the approval of Rome, on the shared assumption that no more effective way was available to prevent the spread of heresy, the government expanded its surveilling authority over parish and monastery, consolidating this su-

---

[72] Max Spindler, ed., *op. cit.* II, 588-90. See Edmund Rosenthal, *op. cit.* I, 400-09, for a description of how the estates' levying system worked. Also Ludwig Hoffmann, *Geschichte der direkten Steuer in Baiern vom Ende des 13. bis zum Beginn des 19. Jahrhunderts* (Leipzig, 1883).

pervisory power in a special committee of *Hofräte* who, in 1570, were constituted, most likely on the Protestant territorial model, into a Council for Spiritual Affairs (*Geistliche Rat*). From then on this body had charge of "all religious matters in our land,"[73] including, eventually, the appointing of bishops and the administration of the university. In law, finally, the dukes had for some time been solidifying their symbolic medieval title of *princeps et iudex* into a position of judicial preeminence. For their central court, the *Hofgericht* (originally formed out of the aulic council) they had won acceptance as the highest appellate bench in the land.[74] By the beginning of the sixteenth century most of this court's assessors were academic jurists whose influence became pervasive in the land, extending through provincial courts (*Landgerichte*) and urban courts under centrally appointed *Stadtrichter*, to the country at large.[75] It was this central court system that was embroiled in unending conflicts with the one thousand or more private tribunals and jurisdictions of the Bavarian nobility whose "ancient immunities and privileges" assured its members of the right to "ordinary" (i.e., non-capital) justice, a right constantly under attack now as a result of the dukes' effort to standardize, by means of new codifications, the law in their realm.[76]

In Bavaria, the newly gained dominance of Roman law and lawyers was in no small measure owing to the territorial university of Ingolstadt, where Justinian jurisprudence had been taught since its foundation in 1472 and whence many legal experts had moved to posts in the central administration. The role of these *doctores* in government was established by a constitution issued in 1551 by Albrecht V, which declared that

---

[73] "sie [members of *Geistliche Rat*] sollen alle Religionssachen unseres Lands anstellen." From 1573 constitution of *Geistliche Rat*, quoted in Eduard Rosenthal, *op. cit.* I, 518.

[74] Sigmund Riezler, *Geschichte Baierns* III (Gotha, 1889), 687-716; Edmund Rosenthal, *op. cit.* I, 52-181; Max Spindler, ed., *op. cit.* II, 528-44.

[75] On Roman law in Bavaria, see Heinz Lieberich, "Die gelehrten Räte. Staat und Juristen in Baiern in der Frühzeit der Rezeption," *Zeitschrift für bayerische Landesgeschichte* 27 (1964), 120-89, which tells the story of the reception in the form of a prosopography of learned councillors and other public servants.

[76] For a description of the operation of traditional justice in the *Hofmarken*, or patrimonial courts, see Edmund Rosenthal, *op. cit.* I, 191-235. On the role of Roman law in the struggles between central and patrimonial courts, see the general remarks by Karl Bosl, *Die Geschichte der Repräsentation in Bayern*, 74, 131-32. Actually, "reformed" Bavarian law contained little Roman material until the *Landrecht* of 1616. For an analysis of this in terms of its Roman contents, see Caspar Schmid, *Auslegung des Chur-Bayerischen Land-Rechts* (Augsburg, 1747), *passim*.

whereas . . . our learned councillors are called chiefly for this reason, that better than anyone else they know and understand what is right, and with this knowledge are able to expedite decisions on matters coming before the council, it is hereby ordered that council business, and above all items of great importance, subtlety, and difficulty, be submitted to these learned councillors before they are considered in council, so that they shall see them first and decide on the basis of their books what is right and proper for us to do about them in accordance with both law and equity, and that in due course they inform the other [i.e., lay] councillors of the legal ground, cause, and right reason of their opinions.[77]

"Their books" were, of course, the *Codex*, *Digest*, and *Institutes* of the *corpus iuris* and the learned commentaries upon it by Italian scholars.

From their strong positions in these decision-making bodies, jurists provided the drive for the intrusive political tendencies of the Bavarian state later in the century.[78] These tendencies coalesced into determined policy in the reign of Maximilian I. Claiming to stand for the Bavarian people's common good and the whole country's *publica utilitas*,[79] the state under this strong and determined ruler, in whom principles of Christian paternalism coexisted with the dictates of a pragmatic Machiavellism,[80] went a long way toward realizing the goal of a "police state" in the early modern sense of that term, that is to say, of a government bent—though not always successfully—on exerting effective control over its subjects' lives.[81] Against the massed strength of this aggregation of power, the country's *Landesfreiheiten*, its chartered lib-

[77] From the *Hofrats-Ordnung* of 1551, quoted in Eduard Rosenthal, *op. cit.* I, 446.

[78] A good example of this tendency, as expressed by a leading learned councillor in the Bavarian government, are the letters of Leonhard von Eck to Dukes Wilhelm IV and Ludwig X in the 1520s, in which Eck, a doctor of both laws who was Bavarian chancellor from 1519 to 1550, leaves no doubt of the determining value of his knowledge, experience, and expertise as he tells the young dukes how to interpret events and consider policy options. See Wilhelm Vogt, *Die bayrische Politik im Bauernkrieg und der Kanzler Dr. Leonhard von Eck* (Nördlingen, 1883).

[79] Walter Merk, *Der Gedanke des gemeinen Besten in der deutschen Staats- und Rechtsentwicklung* (Darmstadt, 1968, first published 1934), 64, notes the reliance by central government on this claim to discredit the estates' position based on the possession of "privilege."

[80] This characterization is suggested by Karl Bosl, *op. cit.*, 209.

[81] For an inside glimpse of how Bavarian administration worked in the time of Maximilian I, see Josef Sturm, *Joh. Christoph von Preysing. Ein Kulturbild aus dem Anfang des 30 jährigen Krieg* (Munich, 1923), 137-41. Preysing was *Rentmeister* of the province of Landshut for some years.

erties and *verbriefte* (documented) personal and collective immunities were a weak line of defense.

Elsewhere events followed the same trend. In Tyrol a strongly entrenched estates organization, which included peasant deputies from sixty or so self-governing rural communes,[82] could not prevent, though it tried throughout the sixteenth century, the construction of a state administration responsive to the centralizing interests of the county's Habsburg rulers.[83] Beginning in the 1490s, the emperors Maximilian I and Ferdinand I, acting as sovereigns of Tyrol, were able to expand the competence of their *Regierungen*, their central administrations in Innsbruck and Meran, to the point where "Spanish political practices" (Ferdinand had grown up in Spain and favored Spanish advisers) were seriously interfering with the exercise of "ancient and recent liberties and constitutions" by imposing "obligations, debts, and duties which have not been freely granted and entered into by us."[84] The normal way of enforcing such "obligations" was by "calling up" legal cases from local courts to the appellate division of the prince's central administration, where Roman procedures were in the charge of mostly "foreign" jurists.[85] While the estates discussed grievances and, from time to time, translated these into territorial legislation—some of it quite far-reaching in its democratic thrust[86]—the centralizing of governing functions in the ruler's hands continued on course. When Ferdinand II ascended in 1565 as the first of the Habsburg princes to give his undivided atten-

[82] For a map of these peasant *Gerichte*—rural administrative and judicial governments—see Fritz Steinegger and Richard Schober, eds., "Die durch den Landtag 1525 . . . erledigten 'Partikularbeschwerden' der Tiroler Bauern . . . ," *Tiroler Geschichtsquellen* No. 3 (1976).

[83] Peter Blickle, *Landschaften im alten Reich*, 159-254; Jürgen Bücking, *Frühabsolutismus und Kirchenreform in Tirol (1565-1665)* (Wiesbaden, 1972); Joseph Egger, *Geschichte Tirols* II (Innsbruck, 1876); Albert Jäger, *Geschichte der landständischen Verfassung Tirols* (Innsbruck, 1881-1885, reprint Aalen, 1970). Jäger covers estates and diets only to 1519 but is especially explicit on peasant representation. See also Josef Hirn, *Erzherzog Ferdinand II von Tirol. Geschichte seiner Regierung und seiner Länder* (Innsbruck, 1885-88) II, 1-72. Tyrol was unique in the empire in that peasant representatives sat even in the territorial ruler's *Geschworene Rat* whose members—nobles, burghers, and peasants—were chosen by the territorial diet.

[84] From estate grievances presented to diet of 1523 (the first diet of Ferdinand I as territorial ruler). LA Tir *Tiroler Landtagsakten* 1523, Fasz. I (no pagination).

[85] Jürgen Bücking, op. cit., 59-60. Id., *Kultur und Gesellschaft in Tirol um 1600. Des Hippolytus Guarinonius' 'Grewel der Verwüstung menschlichen Geschlechts' (1610) als kulturgeschichtliche Quelle* (Lübeck and Hamburg, 1968), 132-33.

[86] Especially the so-called Meran articles, which were accepted as part of the territorial constitution of 1525. See Josef Macek, *Der Tiroler Bauernkrieg und Michael Gaismair* (Berlin, 1965), 206-15. See also the *Landtagsabschiede*—recesses of Tyrolean diets— 1520 to 1590s in LA Tir Cod. 48.

tion to Tyrol, the gradual assumption of all important governing functions by princely bureaucrats was well under way. This trend was to be fully accomplished in the following century, during which the Tyrolean estates ceased to play an active role as coordinate partners in government.[87]

A similar sequence of developments brought strong central rule to Württemberg, and this in spite of the unusually favorable political situation originally enjoyed by the estates of that duchy.[88] Led by rich and well-connected urban patricians (the duchy's nobility took little part in politics, preferring to think of itself as "residents and free" [*inwoner und frei*] rather than "subjects" [*landsassen*]),[89] the Württemberg estates had, since the middle of the fifteenth century, struggled successfully to reach a position equal with, and on occasion superior to, the territorial ruler's. In 1498 they had stripped a duke of his title and assumed executive power during the minority of his successor. In 1514 they pressed upon this new ruler, Ulrich, the Treaty of Tübingen, intended, and from then on regarded, as a declaration of fundamental laws and rights and exacting, in exchange for financial help against debts and a threatening peasant revolt, important constitutional concessions, including the right of approval over all taxes and a vote on questions of war and peace. During the fifteen years of Ulrich's exile, while Württemberg was formally under the governance of the Habsburgs, the estates strengthened their hold on affairs. Annual diets, standing committees, supervisory authority over local bureaucrats, a ban on "foreigners" in important posts established the *Ehrbarkeit*— the class of urban honoratories dominating the estates organization— as a powerful presence in Württemberg politics.

But events after 1534, the date of Ulrich's return to his throne, laid bare the fragile foundation on which this power rested. The estates were not called on to take a part in the introduction of the Reforma-

---

[87] Peter Blickle, *Landschaften im alten Reich*, 232-33, argues for the loss of verve and interest on the part of the estates resulting from the erosion of their liberties during the seventeenth century. This judgment is borne out by the absenteeism afflicting Tyrolean diets in the late sixteenth century. See LA Tir *Tiroler Landtagsakten*, Fasz. 10, for years 1584-1604 for scores of letters from knights excusing and explaining their absence from diets.

[88] Walter Grube provides an overview of the early history of estates in Württemberg in "Stände in Württemberg" in Peter Blickle *et al., Von der Ständeversammlung zum demokratischen Parlament. Die Geschichte der Volksvertretungen in Baden-Württemberg* (Stuttgart, 1982), 31-50. Id., *Der Stuttgarter Landtag 1457-1957* (Stuttgart, 1957). F. L. Carsten, *Princes and Parliaments*, 1-52.

[89] HStA St A34, Bü lc, No. 16. On the position of the nobility in old Württemberg, see Karl Siegfried Bader, *Der deutsche Südwesten*, 99-100.

tion, the act that made Ulrich for a time a popular ruler in his realm. Far from continuing to meet annually, assemblies were rarely convened during the remainder of Ulrich's reign, to 1550, and as far as the duke was concerned, the Tübingen treaty was dead. Ulrich's successors, Christoph and Ludwig, were more cooperative, the former bent to compromise by the weight of his huge debts. As a result, the estates' position improved during the time of these two sovereigns (1550-1593). But toward the end of the century, the accession of a Calvinist ruler with absolutist ambitions, Friedrich I, reversed the situation once again, and this time drastically. A territory-wide administration had been in place since the 1530s.[90] Its control center, the *Oberrat*, functioned as the highest authority in both politics and law; "secret matters"—items touching the person of the prince—were handled by the *Hofrat*, the duke's own privy council, with its jurist members and its attached chancellery under a jurist chancellor. Lawyers had occupied places in the Württemberg government since the 1460s.[91] Their number increased rapidly following the "reformation" of the duchy's *Landrecht* in 1555 with its heavy infiltration of Roman practices. Protests against this influx were a regular feature of estate meetings in the 1550s and 1560s, but they availed nothing. In the 1550s, also, church and religious life was organized under a *Kirchenrat* with a "political" and a "spiritual" section under a single head, the "Director of the Church Council," a layman. The *Rentkammer* capped a sprawling financial administration, the control of which became one of the chief bones of contention when, in the 1590s, estates and duke, the latter aided by aggressive jurist advisers like Dr. Mathäus Enzlin, confronted each other on the question of a standing army.[92]

It is not easy for a modern observer to discover why the prince was able so easily to defeat his parliament on this and related issues. The estates controlled the towns and their circumferent rural district, from which they drew their economic and political strength. Their members sat on every important body of local government. This entrenchment notwithstanding, power in Württemberg shifted decisively from the assembly to the palace. The gruff and haughty manner displayed by Friedrich I toward his estates makes this transition ostentatiously clear. A timid reminder of the obligations owed by a Christian ruler to his loyal people was put down as "so much idle chatter," and the duke fol-

[90] Walter Bernhardt, *Die Zentralbehörden des Herzogtums Württemberg und ihre Beamten 1520-1629* (Stuttgart, 1972-1973), 1-64; Irmgard Kothe, *Der fürstliche Rat in Württemberg im 15. und 16. Jahrhundert* (Stuttgart, 1938).

[91] *Ibid.*, 17-18.

[92] F. L. Carsten, *op. cit.*, 43-47.

lowed this rebuke by serving notice that "whoever acts against our interests will be punished as it seems fit to us and according to our pleasure."[93] And when the estates' central committee once raised its voice against an arbitrary action by his government, Friedrich retorted that "it is not the committee's place to comment on matters that do not concern them. Let them refrain from such talk in the future," he added, menacingly, "or we will show them who is prince in the land." He concluded: "We mean this with all seriousness,"[94] and there could be little doubt of the conviction behind his words, or of his resolve, indeed his eagerness, to act on them.

Even where the political tone was more moderate and the ruler's pretensions less autocratic, as in Saxony, the estates found plenty to complain about as, from about the 1550s, the state raised its demands for scarce economic resources and tightened its hold on the essential organization of society. Ducal bureaucrats in all parts of Saxony interfered at will to alter traditional patterns of public and private life. They set aside judgments of local courts and arbitrarily transferred cases which, "according to ancient custom and tradition, and by force of clear privileges, freedoms, and common laws," belonged to local instances and private jurisdictions.[95] Most disturbingly, they encouraged disloyalty among the subjects of noble landowners (*"ungehorsam und widderwillen irer herschafft"*)[96] in order—it was suspected—to attach people more firmly to the duke's own political apparatus: the *Amtmann* and his deputy, a revenue officer called *Schösser*, their assistant the *Geleitsmann*, supported by bailiffs, foresters, lake masters, scribes, and detachments of armed men on horse and foot (*Knechte zu Ross und zu Fuss*). These functionaries were considered by many a blight on the land, even where the *Amtmann* was himself a knight, as were most of the complainants.[97] Higher taxes throughout the century (dutifully voted by the assemblies)[98] provoked protests against the enormous cost of maintaining this sprawling officialdom as well as a princely establishment beginning to take on the luxurious style considered necessary by the middle of the sixteenth century.[99] Excises were levied on beer

[93] *Württembergische Landtagsakten* 2. Reihe, vol. 2 (ed. Eugen Adam, Stuttgart, 1911), 41. This was in 1599.

[94] *Ibid.* vol. 1 (1910), 518.

[95] StA Wei Reg. Q, No. 19, 9ʳ.

[96] *Ibid.*

[97] Woldemar Goerlitz, *Staat und Stände unter den Herzögen Albrecht und Georg 1485-1539 (Sächsische Landtagsakten* I, Leipzig, 1928), 100-12.

[98] F. L. Carsten, *op. cit.*, 202-28.

[99] In 1565, the elector August documented a request for money with the following recent expenses: the wedding of his daughter, 200,000 fl.; the Danish war, 150,000 fl. to

and wine (the *Tranksteuer*) to help reduce ducal debts. A tax on fortunes (*Landsteuer*) paid by townspeople and villagers, and the *Türkensteuer* defrayed the regular costs of government and the price of current and past wars. Special taxes were raised frequently to cover emergencies,[100] always over the protest of estates, who nonetheless did their duty by approving and helping to collect them.

Loudest among the complaints were charges of violence done to patrimonial justice by new statutes and the central courts upholding them. The chief culprit was the superior appellate court in Leipzig, which had several professional lawyers sitting among its nine judges and was backed by the learned opinions of the Leipzig law faculty and the academic jurists on the duke's council, the court of final appeal in the duchy.[101] The arbitrary transfer of "trivial" or "ordinary" cases from their places of original instance to this high tribunal was a constant source of friction between the dukes' government and the nobles, prelates, and cities meeting in assembly. The estates regularly voiced their fear that the government was bent on undermining their traditional status as privileged corporations.[102] In fact—a fact clear in retrospect and at least discernible at the time—this privileged position was becoming increasingly anachronistic as government mandates sought to bring an ever larger portion of the country's common life under the prince's power to prescribe and proscribe. In 1555, Elector August's *Landesordnung* tried to gather so many details of public behavior in its legislative net that little of the duchy's life remained free of regulation. The new code laid down rules for institutions from courts and consistories to guilds and schools, and it controlled conduct, from setting prices and taking interest down to the choice of clothing, the drinking of toasts, gambling, dancing, and blaspheming. Needless to say, enforcement

date; war services owed to the emperor, 60,000 fl.; attendance at two meetings of the imperial electors, 100,000 fl. See Johannes Falke, "Die Regierungszeit des Kurfürsten August 1565-1582," *Mitteilungen des königlich-sächsischen Alterthumsvereins* 21 (1871), 86-87.

[100] Ernst Müller, "Die Ernestinischen Landtage in der Zeit von 1485 bis 1572 unter besonderer Berücksichtigung des Steuerwesens," *Forschungen zur Thüringischen Landesgeschichte* . . . (Weimar, 1958), 188-228.

[101] Christian Gottfried Kretschmann, *Geschichte des churfürstlich-sächsischen Oberhofgerichts zu Leipzig* (Leipzig, 1804). On central institutions in Saxony see Karlheinz Blaschke, *Sachsen im Zeitalter der Reformation* (*Schriften des Vereins für Reformationsgeschichte* 185, 1970), 19-33.

[102] Woldemar Goerlitz, *op. cit.*, 161-93. Goerlitz also notes (171-72) that Saxon knights liked to appeal their cases to the dukes themselves, placing their reliance on the prince's arbitration justice. For examples of cases so judged by Duke Georg of Albertine Saxony, see *ibid.*, 170-71.

was always much less energetic, and certainly less effective, than the intentions behind such legislation. Even in the long run the overall objective of social control was not achieved. Endless successions of new mandates repeating identical strictures are eloquent evidence of failure in this enterprise. Nothing resembling absolutism can be identified in Saxony until the late seventeenth century. Still, the inhibiting effect of such legislation, backed by a solidly emplaced corps of officials, should not be underestimated. From the middle of the sixteenth century on, the prince's assumption of the role of universal law maker and law enforcer was, to the protesting groups, persuasive evidence of how far the redistribution of prerogatives had gone in their society.

The Protestant Reformation of the sixteenth century further raised the pitch of political confrontations. Whether they embraced it as promise or resisted it as a threat, governments everywhere in the empire seized the evangelical movement as a convenient occasion for bringing the church under control and thus achieving dominion over all activities tied to ecclesiastical jurisdictions and the practice of religion.[103] The Lutheran Reformation thus offered unprecedented possibilities of expansion to the early modern state. Conversely, without the hospitable environment of the princely territory, the Reformation could scarcely have withstood its external and internal enemies or survived the organizational turmoil of its early years. Reforming a territory was always a political act. Normally it was accomplished by the publication of a new church constitution (*Kirchenordnung*) issued under the name of the ruling prince or, in the case of free cities, under the authority of the governing magistrates.[104] Estates rarely participated in this action, or in the intricate theological and legal deliberations preceding it. A century of mostly futile, at best fragmentary, efforts to subject the church to some kind of reform had created a vast reservoir of public support for swift strokes by resolute governments, irrespective of a ruler's or magistrate's stance for or against Protestantism. Disciplining the clergy, particularly restricting monks and friars, was coming to be accepted as a political responsibility, as was the resolution of disputes among fractious theologians. Everywhere the church was in urgent need of material help, on a scale that only the government could organize.[105]

[103] Karlheinz Blaschke, "Wechselwirkungen zwischen der Reformation und dem Aufbau des Territorialstaates," *Der Staat. Zeitschrift für Staatslehre, öffentliches Recht und Verfassungsgeschichte* 9 (1970), 347-64.

[104] See the many Protestant *Kirchenordnungen* gathered in Sehling.

[105] For Saxony, this need has been shown in detail by Susan C. Karant-Nunn, *Luther's Pastors. The Reformation in the Ernestine Countryside* (Philadelphia, 1979).

In these circumstances the church visitations carried on from the late 1520s, first in Protestant, later also in Catholic, states naturally led to the building of territorially organized church administrations under the aegis of the prince. This was the pattern as much in Catholic as in Protestant lands. The need to keep Protestantism outside one's borders, to check it where it had succeeded in crossing them, and to alter the conditions that had enabled it to gain a foothold demanded as much vigilance from an orthodox ruler as deviant sects and evangelical revolutionaries did from a Lutheran prince. Acting on these urgent requirements, Ferdinand II of Tyrol assumed the right to make decisions "in all matters touching religion" (in allen Religionssachen) in his realm,[106] and Wilhelm V of Bavaria declared that "concerning the punishment of meat-eating, Sunday work, and similar transgressions in religion, we hold these to be a part and dependency of the territorial ruler's jurisdiction, and for this reason it is the office of our government to observe, note, and punish them."[107] Most of the members of the Spiritual Council (Geistliche Rat) established by Albrecht V as the supreme ecclesiastical authority in Bavaria were "political," that is to say laymen. Many of them were jurists. From its instauration in 1570, this body's prior approval was required before a priest could be installed in a clerical living in Bavaria. The immediate occasion for this measure was the need for action against the country's nobles who appointed evangelicals to churches under their patronage. But a subsidiary, and certainly the ultimate, aim was to impose means of direct control over the territory's ecclesiastical organization.

Central administrative bodies like the Geistliche Rat were natural aggrandizers of their own responsibilities. The Saxon consistory at Leipzig is a case in point. Its members argued vigorously in 1554 for an increase in their number and an enlargement of the powers placed in their hands. Add another theologian or another jurist to the two of each kind already serving, they said ("but we want a sensible, experienced, honorable man, not a venomous, quick-tempered hothead") and give us "potestas coercendi, as the papal church had it," and we will then be able to cope with "the enormous toil and labor of the consistories' daily work."[108] A steady stream of religious mandates poured from such consistories in all regions, Protestant and Catholic. Whether these regula-

---

[106] Quoted in Jürgen Bücking, Kultur und Gesellschaft in Tirol, 69. This order rested on earlier ones to the same effect by the Emperor Ferdinand, issued in 1564.

[107] BHStA Mu Altbayerische Landschaft 1158, 87v. This formula is used repeatedly in the reigns of Albrecht V, Wilhelm V, and Maximilian I to turn down complaints and protests. E.g., Altbayerische Landschaft 1190, 119r.

[108] StA Dr, "Des Consistorii zu Leipzig Bedenken . . . 1554," Loc. 9356, 19r and v.

tions promoted the Reformation or favored the Counter-Reformation, the permanent result was always an augmentation of political power not only over the church—*de jure Kirchenhoheit* in Protestant, *de facto* dominance in Catholic sections—but also over society at large.

Foremost among the results of this expansion of power was the integration of the feudal nobility in the bureaucratic state. This task, too, was powerfully aided by the ruler's actions for or against the Reformation. An instance is the defeat of the lay cup movement among Bavarian nobles, which weakened the feudal classes there decisively vis-à-vis their prince, Albrecht V.[109] Another example occurred in the Austrian duchies, where Ferdinand I waged his struggle against the nobility as a battle to reverse the evangelicalism that had taken hold among them and their dependents. In territories moving toward Protestantism, the confiscations of church properties supported, at least in the short run, the rulers' struggle to gain financial independence from their estates.[110] As bishoprics and monastic domains were secularized in Protestant territories, the state's bureaucratic structure was enriched by the addition of new or enlarged administrative districts. Elite schools for the training of a faithful cadre shut nobles out of automatic access to government careers. The "police" measures inseparable from the establishment of the Reformation or the attempt to suppress it (parish visitations and other means of information gathering, mandates and directives, censorship and "book visitations") further increased the opportunities for state intervention. The levelling of religious belief and practice was among the principal aims of these measures. But beyond trying to standardize doctrine and observance, they also sought to promote conformity to norms laid down for secular life and considered vi-

[109] Alois Knöpfler, *Die Kelchbewegung in Bayern unter Herzog Albrecht V* (Munich, 1891), shows how Albrecht V, originally acommodating to the nobles' aspirations for the lay cup, came in 1564 to see the movement as an attempt at a political *fronde* rather than as a genuine religious manifestation. See especially 149-58. See also Brigitte Kaff, *Volksreligion und Landeskirche. Die evangelische Bewegung im bayerischen Teil der Diözese Passau* (*Miscellanea Bavarica Monacensia* 69, Munich, 1977), who sees evangelical doctrine as "Integrationsfaktor der Adelsopposition" (350) and the struggle against it as an exercise in power politics. See also Stefan Weinfurter, "Herzog, Adel und Reformation," *Zeitschrift für historische Forschung* 10:1 (1983), 1-39.

[110] F. L. Carsten, *op. cit.*, 431, 437, disagrees with the common judgment that this was so in Protestant regions. Their huge debts, so Carsten, forced princes to sell off confiscated lands at once, minimizing their gains. The final judgment on this question is still out. When Ulrich introduced the Reformation to Württemberg in 1535, he gained an additional 100,000 fl. annually from confiscations, only 24,000 of which went to the maintenance of the clergy. See Walter Bernhardt, *Die Zentralbehörden des Herzogtums Württemberg*, 50.

tal to the general welfare and the common good.[111] This drive toward uniformity was not a new undertaking originating in the middle of the sixteenth century. The princely state's endeavor to exert some leverage on its subjects' political and spiritual lives was nearly a century old. It had gathered a momentum that carried the Reformation with it. Indeed, by the middle of the sixteenth century the princely state had reached such an advanced stage in the pursuit of sovereignty that no practical alternative existed to the establishment of the Reformation as a territorial church.[112]

So formidable a threat to the survival of ancient autonomies evoked strong responses, and the confrontations of territorial assemblies with their prince and his agents furnished the most propitious occasions for voicing opposition. In the manner of the practical politics of the age, this resistance was focussed on particular, concrete, and immediate goals, most of them defensive in objective. Only occasionally did opposition rise to assertion of principle or statement of basic purpose. But the inference from thousands of sharply detailed grievances and doggedly reiterated complaints was ready to be drawn. The perceived menace issued from the territorial state and was a function of its very nature as an aggregation of power. As wielders of this power, the prince and his surrogates, jurists foremost among them, were hostile forces. The resistance to Roman law was therefore part and aspect of a broad and sustained defensive reaction against what was seen by the affected parties as the decisive—and to them the most threatening—political trend of the age: the forward march of the dominant state.

EVENTS and personalities articulated this trend differently in every region, but under its motley of expressions the direction is unmistakable. The Saxon dukes, for example, showed themselves for the most part accommodating toward their estates, responding courteously to complaints and giving assurances of their respect for everyone's rights and immunities. This entente, established early in the sixteenth century in both the Albertine and the Ernestine parts of the duchy,[113] kept out

[111] This point is made for Tyrol by Jürgen Bücking, *Kultur und Gesellschaft in Tirol*, 69, but it is equally valid elsewhere.

[112] This argument is made for Saxony, and by implication for other Protestant territories, by Karlheinz Blaschke, "Wechselwirkungen . . ." in *loc. cit.*, 356-63.

[113] For the Ernestine part: C.A.H. Burkhardt, ed., *Ernestinische Landtagsakten I: Die Landtage von 1487-1532 (Thüringische Geschichtsquellen* N.F. 5, Jena, 1902). For the Albertine part: Woldemar Goerlitz, *op. cit.* Duke Georg of Albertine Saxony was particularly successful in establishing and maintaining a harmonious relationship with his estates: *ibid.*, 108-09, 112, 133, 481-82.

much of the rancor intruding elsewhere into the relations between prince and assemblies. But it also lulled the latter into a state of passivity from which they could not rouse themselves when, later in the century, more autocratically tempered rulers made harsher demands.[114] By then—in the reigns of Moritz and August, when the Wettin lands were united once again—estate protests concerned themselves mainly with local economic hardships, especially taxation, and with perfunctory-sounding objections to bureaucratic invasions of jurisdictional privileges.

In Bavaria, by contrast, angry disputes over the policies of Duke Wilhelm IV in the early fifteen hundreds set the tone for succeeding reigns, during which wary estates never relaxed their guard against sovereign intrusions. The voluminous grievance literature produced by this political contest leaves no doubt that sixteenth-century Bavaria experienced a serious erosion of particular rights to the advantage of the central power. This shift took such forms as the introduction of summary judicial procedures, imposition of unwanted uniformity in religion, bureaucratic willfulness, and a general indifference on the part of government to the country's accustomed liberties. As elsewhere, there was inconsistency in the estates' position on what the state should and should not do. This point has been made in an earlier chapter. While condemning assaults on local and personal liberties, estates also pleaded for swifter government action against a host of social ills enumerated in grievance after grievance. The constitutional problem inherent in these pleas for more aggressive state intervention went unrecognized because, in the absence of anything approaching a developed theory of estate rights, all political opposition was formulated in *ad hoc* terms. On the other hand, a clear line was drawn by implication at least between the retention of vital rights and the loss of them to a superior power. All estates, in all parts of Bavaria, acted as the accusing parties in their attempt to hold this line.

The stormy reign of Wilhelm IV (1508-1550) offers a good illustration of how weighty these rights were held to be by both sides in the struggle.[115] Backed by his maternal uncle, the emperor Maximilian I,

---

[114] On this later period in Saxon history, see the articles by Johannes Falke, "Zur Geschichte der sächsischen Landstände. Die Regierungszeit des Herzog Moritz 1541-1546," *Mitteilungen des königlich-sächsischen Alterthumsvereins* 21 (1871), 58-115; "Die Regierungszeit des Kurfürsten Moritz 1547-1554," *ibid.*, 22 (1872), 77-132; "Die Regierungszeit des Kurfürsten August 1553-1561," *ibid.*, 23 (1873), 59-113; "Die Regierungszeit des Kurfürsten August 1565-1582," *ibid.*, 24 (1874), 86-134.

[115] F. L. Carsten, *op. cit.*, 350-74; Max von Freyberg, *Geschichte der bayerischen Landstände und ihrer Verhandlungen* II (Sulzbach, 1829), 3ff.; M. Doeberl, *Entwick-*

this headstrong ruler emerged from the estates' tutelage during his minority eager to rid himself of restrictions placed on his sovereignty by the Bavarian assemblies[116] whose members had, since the early fourteenth century, enjoyed broad immunities in their respective enclaves as well as a strong voice in the administration of the state.[117] Chief among the young duke's counselors in his effort to turn a new leaf was Dr. Leonhard von Eck, the Siena jurist who had been his tutor and, since 1512, served him as the closest of his advisers. Wasting little sympathy on ancient traditions, Eck urged Wilhelm to govern without the estates, advice that matched the prince's own autocratic inclinations. But debts, the hobble of all governments, as well as the rising costs of Wilhelm's ambitious policies in the empire, forced him early in 1514 to call the estates to Munich.[118] Trouble was bound to ensue. Although the granting of monies from taxation had, as elsewhere, become habitual in Bavaria,[119] it was still assumed as a matter of principle that the territorial ruler should cover court and government expenses out of the revenues of his own domains.[120] When they wished to chasten a ruler, estates fell back on this expectation. To obtain the financial relief he desperately needed, Wilhelm had therefore to agree to the estates' terms.

Taken together, these conditions placed severe restrictions on the duke. A small group of "daily councillors" named by the estates were to govern with him until he reached the age of twenty-four. Assembly leaders began to appoint ducal officials and dismiss those they dis-

---

lungsgeschichte Bayerns (3rd ed. Munich, 1916) I, 375-79; Sigmund Riezler, *Geschichte Baierns* IV (Gotha, 1899), 7ff.

[116] On the composition of Bavarian estates in the sixteenth century: Max Spindler, *Handbuch . . .* II, 502-15, 565-85. Those entitled to a seat in the Bavarian diets were listed in the official *Landtafel*: nobles possessing duty-free (*abgabenfrei*) estates, prelates who were heads of bishoprics or abbeys, and cities and towns directly under the duke's jurisdiction. In 1522, for example, the *Landtafel* listed the following *Landstände*: 808 nobles, 80 prelates, 32 cities, and 74 market towns. Peasants were not represented as their property was not free, even though they were personally free. Actual participants in diets were far fewer than the above numbers suggest. In 1519, in Munich, the following turned up: 43 nobles and knights, 20 prelates, and the deputies of 14 cities and 6 market towns.

[117] The Bavarian estates' grants of liberties are printed in Gustav von Lerchenfeld, *Die altbaierischen landständischen Freibriefe mit den Landfreiheitserklärungen* (Munich, 1853).

[118] The documents in BHStA Mu *Fürstensachen* 427 and 428 convey a vivid impression of the dukes' financial problems. They were at all times preoccupied with negotiations for long- and short-term loans, even for small sums from Jewish lenders to meet creditors' demands.

[119] See Karl Bosl, *Die Geschichte der Repräsentation*, 61-63.

[120] Hans Schmeltzle, *Der Staatshaushalt des Herzogtums Bayern im 18. Jahrhundert* (Stuttgart, 1900), 1, shows that jurists argued this view as late as the eighteenth century.

trusted, including Eck himself. They also organized a standing committee to guard estate interests between diets. And they compelled the duke to make solemn confirmation of all territorial rights and liberties bestowed in the past. A special committee of thirty-two nobles, sixteen prelates, twelve city deputies, and four representatives of market villages used the auspicious moment to vent the estates' indignation at the lavish and wasteful style of the prince's court, and at the prominence there of "a powerful clique of favorites," foreign-born men for the most part, who teamed up against the interests of the country and shielded the young duke from "stout men of native stock" to whom he should be turning for advice. "These parasites," the estates charged, "will permit no assault on our liberties to be punished." They do not want the estates to meet "because we interfere with the unbridled pursuit of their own interests." It is no wonder that "as soon as our assembly adjourns, the country's liberties are regarded as a dead letter. . . . How can good government exist under such conditions?"[121] The importance attached by the assembly to these sentiments is evident in the record kept of them: a large folio of over six hundred leaves preserving all speeches and documents in nearly verbatim paraphrase and true copies.[122] Nor did the estates relax the pressure once they had gained the upper hand. The duke's attempt to evade the 1514 agreement led, later that same year, to a new confrontation in the course of which the spokesman for the estates delivered a stinging lecture on what privileges, rights, liberties, and autonomies meant to those who were fighting to preserve them.

This spokesman was Dietrich von Plieningen, a Swabian noble and man of letters, a doctor of laws who had studied in Italy and then entered the service of Albrecht IV of Bavaria but now represented the estates in their cause against Albrecht's son Wilhelm.[123] The censorious words and combative actions of the Munich meeting earlier in the year had brought a rebuke from the emperor Maximilian in the form of a mandate enjoining the estates from "venturing to take unto themselves authority and responsibility [in the duchy], constituting themselves a government, and forming unions and associations in exercise of their

[121] From the protocols of the diet sessions recorded in BHStA Mu *Altbayerische Landschaft* Lit. 357, 61ᵛ-63ᵛ. Also Franz von Krenner, *Der Landtag im Herzogtum Baiern vom Jahre 1514* (Munich, 1804), 92-96.

[122] BHStA Mu *Altbayerische Landschaft* Lit. 357. The record is printed in part in Franz von Krenner, *op. cit.* A brief summary is in Max Spindler, *Handbuch* II, 300.

[123] On the interesting career of Dietrich von Plieningen see the brief biography by Franziska Adelmann, *Dr. Dietrich von Plieningen zu Schaubeck* (*Ludwigsburger Geschichtsblätter* No. 28. Ludwigsburg, 1976).

so-called liberties. All this," the emperor had written, "has brought harm and humiliation to the territorial prince, undermined the empire, and attacked the majesty of the emperor himself."[124]

Responding to this denunciation, and speaking for the estates in the name of its twelve-member executive committee, Plieningen read a lesson in the meaning of freedoms.[125] They were purchased, he reminds emperor and duke, for large sums of money over a long period of time. Declared, confirmed, and renewed many times in the course of centuries, they not only set down what each countryman has the right to possess, do, and enjoy in the land, but also give warning "distinctly and in clear, circumstantial words," that "if a prince of Bavaria should ever launch an attack on [the estates'] freedoms and lay oppression upon his subjects, these same subjects shall be empowered to form a union against him, and they shall not be thought to have acted against their duty in so doing." Numerous reaffirmations of these declared freedoms prove, Plieningen notes, that "they have long been in use by the estates, and are so used to this day, and that on the evidence of their charters and seals the estates have had the power to act on them, and still have that power." The estates claim no more than what is contained "in their old freedoms and in the established interpretation of these freedoms." They want nothing new. They ask "only that their ancient and dearly bought liberties remain unimpaired." If continually frustrated in this legitimate and just desire, they will have no recourse but "to refuse all obedience, aid, and counsel to the princes," leaving them to suffer "self-caused need, penury, and destruction." There would be "nothing unnatural" in such an act of last resort. It is self-defense, "which is an action nature permits to everyone. For when a man is unrightfully deprived of what is his own," Plieningen concludes, "the natural law tells him that he may protect himself. Such a man has not appointed himself a judge. He has only become a defender of his person and of his property."

Plieningen's words tell us something about the value of rights and freedoms to those who cherished them. Far from being abstractions in a contest of principles, they were goods and possessions bought (mostly with tax grants), managed, and treasured as investments in things of real and lasting value yielding palpable rewards. Estate deliberations constantly refer to "the ancient purchased freedoms [*die alten erkauf-*

---

[124] Max von Freyberg, *op. cit.* II, 124-25.

[125] Plieningen's speech is in BHStA Mu *Altbayerische Landschaft* Lit. 357, 118ᵛ-129ʳ, following the text of Maximilian's mandate (112ᵛ-118ʳ). The Bavarian dukes were not personally present at assembly meetings. In accordance with general practice, all that was said and done (*Handlungen*) took the form of written exchanges.

ten freiheiten]" and to rights "bought by us or by our ancestors for large sums of money."[126] Authenticated copies of original contracts exchanging cash for freedoms were prized as irrefutable evidence of liberties properly acquired and legitimately enjoyed. Plieningen sent a fat volume of them to the emperor to support his plea, and estates had collections made whenever they sensed a peril.[127] After the troubles of 1514, for example, it was suggested to the Bavarian diet that such a volume would be invaluable if proof and exact citation were needed in the future. A committee chosen to this end therefore invited all estate members to send copies of any and all documents in their possession, and from these a selection was made, and subsequently printed.[128] "No prince on earth," wrote the committee of twelve to Duke Wilhelm at that time, "has the right to use his power arbitrarily and in violation of law and fairness."[129] "Even a little worm curls up and defends itself," said Plieningen to the duke, "when he is about to be stepped on by a large animal."[130]

Their point made and accepted by the duke, whose penury left him little choice, the estates granted the much needed tax (with a warning about creeping poverty among "*die armen leut*" on whom—it goes without saying—fell most of the actual burden),[131] receiving in exchange a "New Confirmation of the Country's Freedoms."[132] But this document, and the agitation that led up to it, marked the zenith of estate ascendancy in Bavaria. Having patched up a quarrel with his disgruntled brother Ludwig, Wilhelm decided on joint rule with him, thus depriving the estates of the important leverage they had enjoyed earlier when the two princes were bidding for allies against each other. He also began to recall his banished advisers, including Leonhard von Eck, who became Wilhelm's chancellor in 1519. Eck's skill in opening up new sources of income for the state decreased the dukes' dependence on the estates' taxing powers.[133] The best the estates could do two years after

[126] E.g., Franz von Krenner, *op. cit.*, 107.

[127] The Munich archive holds many such collections, some hastily written, others calligraphic productions. E.g., BHStA Mu G.R. 992.

[128] They are printed again in Gustav von Lerchenfeld, *op. cit.* On the circumstances of the collection, see *ibid.*, ccccxx-ccccxxviii.

[129] BHStA Mu *Altbayerische Landschaft*, Lit. 357, 228ʳ.

[130] *Ibid.*, 228ᵛ.

[131] *Ibid.* Lit. 358 ½ 162ᵛ.

[132] It is bound in *ibid.* Lit. 357. It is printed in Franz von Krenner, *op. cit.*, 489-573 side by side with the "New Declaration" of 1516.

[133] Eck's preoccupation with the problem of independent revenues is evident in his correspondence with Wilhelm and Ludwig. See the letters printed in Wilhelm Vogt, *op. cit.*, e.g., 383.

the high point of their influence was to insert a plaintive clause in the "New Declaration of Liberties" of 1516 to the effect that "grave and notable denials, interventions, and obstructions have been directed against these our documented freedoms, which have been little honored in the duchy."[134] Among liberties ignored or contravened, they said, was the ducal promise "to appoint able men of the country to our council, men who are nobles and laymen, not learned doctors."[135] Had this undertaking been adhered to, it would, of course, have put a stop to the bureaucratic state, and the princes were not prepared to abide by it. They also, in due course, succeeded in transforming the estates themselves by coopting their executive committee into a standing organ for negotiations between country and government.[136] Mid- and late-six-teenth-century diets continued routinely to register complaints, but no new Dietrich von Plieningen arose to threaten the dukes with a limitation of their power, not to mention a rebellion against it. Maximilian I called only two diets during his long reign (1598-1651), both of them when large debts forced him to overcome his strong distaste for power sharing. By Maximilian's time, in any case, the estates had been reduced to a largely symbolic role.

Plieningen's advocacy of the estates' cause serves as a reminder that anti-legal sentiments were not indiscriminate among the critics of Roman law. As a jurist and an experienced negotiator, Plieningen was not only resourceful in parley and debate, but also shrewd and inventive about finding in classical and medieval sources an intellectually respectable base of support for his clients' position. Estates gladly availed themselves of such expertise. Roman law (and canon law as well) offered a number of useful arguments against centralized rule. This was scarcely the main thrust of the Justinian corpus. Yet, since the fourteenth century its authority had often been appropriated by proponents of limited and distributed power to suggest constitutional alternatives to the unitary claims of ambitious rulers.[137] The right of self-defense was argued from a passage in the *Digest* (43.16.27). Political consent was traced to a famous sentence in *Codex* 5.59.5 which declared (in a quite different context) "what concerns them all should be approved by all."[138] *Digest* 50.17.20 legitimized interpretations "in favor of liberty"

---

[134] BHStA Mu *Altbayerische Landschaft* Lit. 358 ½, 149ᵛ.

[135] Franz von Krenner, *op. cit.*, 533.

[136] Karl Bosl, *op. cit.*, 134-39.

[137] Quentin Skinner, *The Foundations of Modern Political Thought* (Cambridge, 1978) II, 124-33.

[138] "Quod omnes similiter tangit, ab omnibus comprobetur." The context was guardianship and curatorship.

278 — The Heart of Resistance

in all cases "where a grant of freedom is in doubt."[139] There was even
an allusion to the proposition that sovereigns, too, are subject to the
law: the so-called *digna vox* of *Codex* 1.14.4 asserted that "it is a statement worthy of the majesty of the ruler for the prince to profess himself
bound by the law. For our authority depends upon the authority of the
law." These passages from the *corpus* made effective starting positions
for champions of the politics of particularism.[140] Much as they deplored the machinations of jurists in the employ of their princes, therefore, estates were prepared to accept their services in their own cause.

Examples of this readiness to meet the adversary on his own ground
may be taken from all German territories. The Bavarian estates, facing
their duke and his formidable chancellor, found another able spokesman in Dr. Peter Baumgartner, who negotiated on behalf of the executive committee in 1519.[141] The estates of Württemberg were aided in
their confrontation with Duke Christoph by a staff of "councillors and
orators" some of whom had earlier been in the duke's employ.[142] This
was a common situation. Learned advocates speaking for estates were
often on simultaneous retainer to the government they opposed. It was
skill and experience that counted more than loyalty to cause. Dr. Wolfgang Baumgartner represented the Tyrolean estates in the 1540s.[143]
The estates of Hessen employed lawyers to press their case "with legal
words suitable to these matters."[144] Mecklenburg estates employed
corporate syndics from 1531, a number of them distinguished jurists
with university appointments.[145] Nobles in Saxony instructed lawyers
to argue their beer-brewing claims "not from the old tradition but from
the common, imperial, written laws instead." Every association of
knights had a syndic or two in its pay to provide members with legal

[139] "Quotiens dubia interpretatio libertatis est, secundum libertatem respondendum
erit."
[140] For the use of some of these passages in the middle ages, see Brian Tierney, *Religion,
Law, and the Growth of Constitutional Thought*. On the elements in Roman law that
could be used to limit state power, see Helmut Coing, "Das Recht als Element der europäischen Kultur," *HZ* 238 (1984), 10. See also E. H. Kantorowicz, "Kingship under the
Impact of Scientific Jurisprudence" in *id., Selected Studies* (Locust Valley, N.Y., 1954),
158-59. Jan Rogozinski, *Power, Caste, and Law. Social Conflict in Fourteenth-Century
Montpellier* (Cambridge, Mass., 1982), shows how Roman law was used to limit royal
authority and shore up communal and seigneurial authority. See especially 89-95.
[141] BHStA Mu *Altbayerische Landschaft*, Lit. 362, 26ʳ.
[142] F. L. Carsten, *op. cit.*, 31-32.
[143] LA Tir *Tiroler Landtagsakten*, Fasz. 375, 134ʳ.
[144] *Hessische Landtagsakten*, ed. Hans Glagau (Marburg, 1901) I, 64.
[145] Hermann Krause, *System der landständischen Verfassung Mecklenburgs in der
zweiten Hälfte des 16. Jahrhunderts* (Rostock, 1927), 49-57.

opinions and to act as *Fürsprecher* in political negotiations.[146] In 1565, nobles and cities in Saxony joined in deploring the paucity of law lectures in the duchy's universities. This, their spokesmen charged, reduced the number of law graduates, which made it difficult to find qualified spokesmen. They asked that "three readers of law be appointed with no duties other than to give regular lectures."[147] Every town of any size had its syndic to supply legal counsel and speak for the city in the deliberations of territorial assemblies. Such a man—as the town fathers of Wismar wrote to their colleagues in Rostock while preparing for a diet in 1552—"is indispensable" nowadays, for "when city people were first oppressed and burdened with [taxation] demands they had then no one to defend their ancient usages, freedoms, and time-honored customs."[148] In political advocacy as much as in private litigation there was no substitute for the experienced lawyer, his book knowledge, his verbal skills, and his professional ties to his counterparts in the adversary camp.

On the other hand, little intellectual substance was required to make the estates' case, and nothing in the way of a political philosophy was ever formulated to link the struggle against centralism with a coherent set of legal or constitutional postulates. The basic line of defense against intrusions from above was, simply, to appeal to the principle of fairness, to the force of long usage in history, and to the remembrance of an erstwhile order of things far superior on ethical grounds to the current drift. Instances of such plain political thinking lie scattered in the sources of estates negotiations. Deep in a controversy over regency and guardianship during the minority of Landgrave Philip, the estates of Hessen tried to have it acknowledged in 1509 that (speaking in the cumbersome phraseology of political dilettantes) "as jurisdiction has been transferred in time from subjects, who held such power in the past, to governments, but no person can now be found to exercise this power for the government, we conclude that the jurisdiction over, and the administration of, this principality rests with the general estates, and nowhere else."[149] Against this view of the source and origin of power in a state, the regents, a few years later, affirmed the ultimate responsibility of the territorial ruler. With greatly superior force of rhetoric they warned the estates that

---

[146] StA Wei, Reg. Q, No. 82, 38ʳ-70ʳ; Volker Press, "Die Reichsritterschaft im Reich der frühen Neuzeit," *Nassauische Annalen* 87 (1976), 109.

[147] StA Dr, Loc. 9350, No. 10, 9ᵛ.

[148] Karl von Hegel, *Geschichte der mecklenburgischen Landstände bis zum Jahre 1555*, 201-02.

[149] *Hessische Landtagsakten* I, 66.

No subject may make a law against the interest of his prince, and should he do so, such a subject will have acted illegally and wrongly because he thereby diminishes the prince's authority and power. . . . Every prince has it in his own charge to protect himself and his subjects from harm and danger. The better to accomplish this task, territorial rulers are accustomed from time to time to seek aid and counsel from certain of their subjects, which the latter are obliged to give. But subjects do not have the power to make laws for the prince . . . , to issue orders how he shall instruct his officials and their assistants . . . , to call assemblies and enter into associations. . . . For to defend and guard subjects is the proper office of the territorial sovereign, and to this end he is served by nobles, burghers, and peasants who pay him rents and dues, and obey him with their bodies and their worldly goods. This princely office, for the performance of which he is supported by rents and revenues, cannot be usurped by the estates, to whom it does not belong. If the latter think they are oppressed or wronged by their prince or by some other person, they should seek re-dress according to the rules set down in the common written laws, which tell us everything that is right in these matters.[150]

This, of course, was the doctine that prevailed, in Hessen and elsewhere. From Landgrave Philip's coming of age in 1518 the Hessian estates played but a small role in the affairs of the principality. In other territories, too, the pleas of estates spokesmen made little headway against the rulers' contention that they, and they alone, were the true and legitimate protectors of the common good. Assemblies could do no more than restate their right to be consulted "on all matters touching the country's prosperity or ruination,"[151] or reassert that it was wrong and unwise to depart from tradition[152] and from "what the old laws clearly express and make known,"[153] or ask princes to recollect their "bounden duty to keep the said freedoms."[154] Such pleas found hearing

---

[150] *Ibid.*, 225-28. This is from a memorandum by the Hessian regents to the elector of Saxony on the approaching diet of Kassel in 1514. On the estates in Hessen, see Ludwig Zimmermann, "Zur Entstehungsgeschichte der hessischen Landstände," *Zeitschrift des Vereins für hessische Geschichte und Landeskunde* 63 (1952), 66-82; F. L. Carsten, *op. cit.*, 150-82.

[151] Johannes Falke, "Die landständischen Verhandlungen unter dem Herzog Heinrich von Sachsen 1539-1541," *Archiv für die sächsische Geschichte* 10 (1872), 44-45.

[152] F. W. Müller, *Die elsässischen Landstände* . . . (Strassburg, 1907), 58-59.

[153] LA Tir *Tiroler Landtagsakten*, Fasz. I, Landtag Innsbruck, 1499, 1ʳ.

[154] From the Tübingen contract, Württemberg, 1514, printed in Werner Näf, ed., *Herrschaftsverträge des Spätmittelalters* (*Quellen zur neueren Geschichte* Heft 17, Bern, 1951), 76.

only when a crisis, usually financial, left rulers without any other choice. More often they produced nothing but a perfunctory response followed by a replaying of the scene at another diet.

This same pageant was also acted out on the smaller stages of rural communities where village associations were resisting intrusions from a number of quarters in the later fifteenth and the first quarter of the sixteenth centuries.[155] Self-governing in the vital affairs of daily life and work, and strongly disposed to remain so, villagers made effective use of grievance procedures in order to raise their complaints for public discussion. When frustrated in their expectations of relief, they resorted to direct action, occasionally to violence. The strong bond that linked village neighbors in these struggles—a bond made concrete in unchanging common customs and rituals, as we have seen[156]—was formed of specific freedoms vested in each village association and enumerated in its basic law. These freedoms consisted of property rights, including inheritance, sale, and removal; petty courts in which to try local offenses; communal assessment of taxes; fishing, hunting, netting, and foraging privileges; limits to duties owed to the ground lord, with precise amounts, measures, and duration stipulated; and the right to appoint and instruct communal servants such as the bailiff, the herd, the *Dorfschreiber*. The ritual proclamation of these freedoms was the most important ceremonial event at annual village meetings, to which each male neighbor was obliged to go, and at which the ground lord was normally represented by an appointed official. Villagers considered themselves free to the extent that they possessed and were able to make use of these acknowledged liberties. "For these are our ancient rights,"

[155] Karl Siegfried Bader, "Entstehung und Bedeutung der oberdeutschen Dorfgemeinde," *Zeitschrift für württembergische Landesgeschichte* N.F. 1 (1937), 287 stresses the difficulty of generalizing from the varied evidence illustrating the history of the late medieval village. On the village, see also *id.*, *Studien zur Rechtsgeschichte des mittelalterlichen Dorfes* (Graz, etc., 1962-1967); Walter Grube, "Dorfgemeinde und Amtsversammlung in Altwürttemberg," *Zeitschrift für württembergische Landesgeschichte* 13 (1954), 194-219; Rudolf Wilhelm, *Rechtspflege und Dorfverfassung* (*Verhandlungen des historischen Vereins für Niederbayern* 80, Landshut, 1954); Walter Scherzer, "Die Dorfverfassung der Gemeinden im Bereich des ehemaligen Hochstifts Würzburg," *Jahrbuch für fränkische Landesforschung* 36 (1976), 37-64; Peter Blickle, "Die staatliche Funktion der Gemeinde. Die politische Funktion des Bauern" in *id.*, *Deutsche ländliche Rechtsquellen* . . . (Stuttgart, 1977), 205-33; *id.,´ Deutsche Untertanen. Ein Widerspruch* (Munich, 1981).

[156] On the nature of this bond, see Karl Siegfried Bader, *Studien zur Rechtsgeschichte* II, 40. Good illustrations of how this community bond translated into community action are given in Albert Jäger, *Geschichte der landständischen Verfassung Tirols* (Innsbruck, 1881-1885; reprint Aalen, 1970) I, 38ff.

as a rural district in Tyrol put it, "and this is our freedom, namely that we can do as we please with what belongs to us."[157]

It has often been noted that political consciousness and political activity intensified greatly in rural communities from the late fifteenth century on.[158] The explanation is that villagers began around that time to feel pressured by two hostile processes going on simultaneously. One was the territorial state's attempt to stretch its authority over this most basic of the state's units of government, trying to accomplish that goal by means of increased taxation and by seeking to exert direct control over village officials and village legislation.[159] The other source of pressure was the economic squeeze issuing from landlords who, hard up themselves, were anxious to maximize the payments, contributions, and labor owed them according to old traditions. Added to imperial taxes also raised on the backs of rural folk, these were heavy burdens to bear. In attempting to make them less crushing, villagers, like the spokesmen for territorial estates, avoided theoretical formulations of their complaints and desires, asking in plain language for the removal of objectionable conditions and threatening innovations. Let an end be made of serfdom. Let personal freedom be enlarged and independence be secured vis-à-vis the administrative and judicial prerogatives of the groundlord and his henchmen. Taxes should be reduced and the legal status of the old privileged orders curtailed, especially that of the clergy. The heavy hand of the territorial power on the local scene was widely resented; peasant demands make this clear. They wanted to see this presence diminished.[160]

Objections to the "new written law" and its omnipresent doctors were made in this context. The reasons were the same as those given in meetings of territorial diets. Jurists destroy local courts by overturning and removing cases. They set their sights on a uniform legal system in which particular customs will wither away. They favor central direction, looking with impatience upon the preservation of local usages. They draw their ideas from academic disciplines alien to the living traditions of society. Rural spokesmen, too, made use of arguments from

[157] *Ibid.* I, 591.

[158] Peter Blickle, *Die Revolution von 1525* (Munich, 1975), 127-33.

[159] Winfried Schulze, *Bäuerlicher Widerstand und feudale Herrschaft in der frühen Neuzeit* (Stuttgart, 1980), 63-69.

[160] Peasant demands are summarized by Horst Buszello, "Die Staatsvorstellung des gemeinen Mannes im Bauernkrieg," *HZ* Beiheft 4 (N.F.): "Revolte und Revolution in Europa" (1975), 290-95 and by Peter Blickle, "Auf dem Weg zu einem Modell der bäuerlichen Rebellion" in *id. et al.*, *Aufruhr und Empörung? Studien zum bäuerlichen Widerstand im alten Reich* (Munich, 1980), 296-308.

Roman law when it suited them.[161] But they had learned by the 1520s that this law favored the rich over the poor and supported the stronger against the weaker. Above all they knew that it was a force promoting conformity, and that this bent turned it into a danger to the survival of all those singular features of ordinary existence on which their daily lives as they knew them depended. This is why they opposed it.

Like protestations issuing from territorial estates, rural opposition to encroaching state power gained few victories, and these few were transitory. Once the 1525 revolution had been beaten down, "legitimate" authority was everywhere reinforced, armed opposition made a crime, and political resistance in any form defamed by calling it a sin against God.[162] As we saw in an earlier chapter, "Christian freedom" came to be defined as a condition exclusively spiritual in its rightful expression. Evangelical virtues of submission and patience were extolled in catechisms and sermons, and given official sanction in formal pronouncements of doctrine. Resistance to authority, all grumbling even, was proclaimed in these pronouncements to be an ungodly act of disobedience. Protestant and Catholic governments were as one in regarding such proclamations as the most fitting conclusion to decades of religious and political turmoil.

ON EVERY plane of the social order, then, the thrust of opposition was channeled into protests and accusations directed against concentrated rule and preeminent authority. The loudest clamor came from the ranks of the nobility, whose members had most to lose in the transfer of jurisdictions and for this reason used every meeting of territorial assemblies to voice their concern.[163] The imperial knights were especially

[161] The question of Roman law and the German peasantry—did it help or hinder the peasants? Did they oppose or favor it?—is examined by Gustav Aubin, "Der Einfluss der Rezeption des römischen Rechtes auf den deutschen Bauernstand," *Jahrbücher für Nationalökonomie und Statistik* III. Folge, 44 (1912), 721-42; and Alfred Stern, "Das römische Recht und der Bauernkrieg von 1525," *Zeitschrift für schweizerische Geschichte* 14 (1934), 20-29. See also Karl-Heinz Burmeister, "Genossenschaftliche Rechtsfindung und herrschaftliche Rechtssetzung. Auf dem Weg zum Territorialstaat," *HZ* Beiheft 4 (N.F., 1975), 171-85; and Jürgen Bücking, "Der Bauernkrieg in den habsburgischen Ländern als sozialer Systemkonflikt, 1524-1526" in Hans-Ulrich Wehler, ed., *Der deutsche Bauernkrieg 1524-1526 (Geschichte und Gesellschaft.* Sonderheft 1, 1975), 189.

[162] Winfried Schulze, *op. cit.*, 73-76.

[163] See the interesting analysis of the Bavarian nobility given by Heinz Lieberich, *Landherren und Landleute. Zur politischen Führungsschicht Baierns im Spätmittelalter* (Munich, 1964). Lieberich shows that the legally and socially distinct groups into which the Bavarian nobility fell were brought together in the *Landschaft* by the need for a common

vociferous in defending the mainstay of their status as "free noblemen" and in asserting their right to exercise this autonomy.[164] Since the early fifteenth century they had organized against the double threat of impoverishment at the hands of townsmen and absorption in territorial and urban states. They could foresee being "usured to death" (*ausgewuchert*) by their urban suppliers and "sitting amidst the townspeople and the peasants as lords and nobles are now situated among the Swiss"[165]—in other words, disappear as an estate. Unlike free cities, imperial knights lacked the resources to guarantee their survival as residents *in*, not subjects *of*, the princely realm.[166] No move by territorial rulers to make them *landsässig*—legally integrated in the territory as men "settled" in the land—could therefore be let go unchallenged. By and large they prevailed, ever vigilant against attempts to further curtail their particular rights, but coming to accommodations with princes who no longer saw them as a threat to their sovereignty. In this way they managed to hold on to their increasingly anachronistic social and political position until well into the eighteenth century.[167]

High-handed interference with petty justice brought on the most sustained protests. A litany of complaints testified to the state's success in trying to control, if not take over, particular jurisdictions.[168] "Your Electoral and Princely Grace's officials meddle in our [patrimonial] courts," runs a typical objection made by Saxon prelates and knights at

---

front against the expansion of state power. On the German nobility in general, see Helmut Rössler, ed., *Deutscher Adel 1430-1555* (Darmstadt, 1965).

[164] Gerhard Pfeiffer, "Studien zur Geschichte der fränkischen Reichsritterschaft," *Jahrbuch für fränkische Landesforschung* 22 (1962), 173-280; Volker Press in *loc. cit.*, 101-22.

[165] From complaint by knights at the Imperial Diet of Speyer, 1542, quoted in Karlheinz Blaschke, "Frühkapitalismus und Verfassungsgeschichte," *Wissenschaftliche Zeitschrift der Karl-Marx-Universität Leipzig* 14 (1965), 438.

[166] As the Württemberg knights declared in the 1520s: ". . . dass wir auch von fürsten und herrn des fürstenthumbs Wirttemberg nye für land sässen sonder ynwoner des fürstenthumbs und für fry edelleut ye und allwege geacht und gehallten werden." HStA St A34, Bü 1c, No. 16.

[167] Volker Press in *loc. cit.*, 115-22; Karl Siegfried Bader, *Der deutsche Südwesten*, 165-66, 171. On the imperial knights in the sixteenth century, see also Johanna Maria van Winter, *Rittertum. Ideal und Wirklichkeit* (Munich, 1969) and Christian von Arnswaldt, *Die Lüneburger Ritterschaft als Landstand im Spätmittelalter* (Göttingen, 1969).

[168] For examples of the actual operation of *niedere Gerichtsbarkeit*—the most important and valuable right bestowed by grants of immunity—see, for Tyrol: Albert Jäger, *Geschichte der landständischen Verfassung Tirols* I, 480-509; for Bavaria: Rudolf Wilhelm, *Rechtspflege und Dorfverfassung*, 1-8; for Saxony: Martin Luther, *Die Entwicklung der landständischen Verfassung in den wettinischen Landen* (Leipzig, 1895), 36-37; also Hans Tütken, *Geschichte des Dorfes und Patrimonialgerichtes Geismar . . . (Studien zur Geschichte der Stadt Göttingen* 7, 1967), 246-75.

the Diet of Jena in 1518. "When a man is wounded or killed on a road or by-way running through our jurisdictions," they go on to explain, these officials "strive to have the case moved to one of Your Grace's courts where they themselves sit in judgment."[169] Malefactors are treated more leniently before these ducal bars, it is—probably incorrectly—charged, which results in the loss of judicial business to holders of lower justice. "When we undertake to punish our people for larceny or other felonies, they run off to the duke's court or to the *Amtleute*, from whom they obtain an injunction ordering us to cease our efforts to bring them to trial." "Many cases are taken from those who possess hereditary justice [*Erbgericht*] and given to the state [*oberkait*]," the Saxon nobles summarized in 1523, in uncharacteristic understatement.[170] At the beginning of the seventeenth century they were still saying this: ". . . trivial matters removed from us . . . all appeals accepted . . . cases involving a much lower sum than the required sixty florins taken on . . . the rightful authority of local government [*untern obrigkeit*] tampered with, . . . justice itself violated"[171] . . . "insignificant peasant matters" brought before the high courts . . . "all cases without distinction accepted by Your Electoral Grace's appellate court, although they have not yet been heard in the lower instance . . . ; citations, inhibitions, injunctions" raining down from the upper benches,[172] and so on. Personal expressions of grievance by Saxon nobles convey a sense of how it felt to be interfered with in this manner. One Gottfried von Nitzschwitz described as follows his running conflict with the *Schösser*, the official responsible to the elector for his district. He intervenes at will in my hereditary court, the noble wrote in 1602, and goads my subjects into insubordination and defiance:

> And if I then have them brought before my own court and fine them for flagrant disobedience, the *Schösser* writes to me, saying that I must not touch them, indeed must return their fines and leave them unmolested, or he will come in person to rescind all my decisions. . . . He then instigates a lawsuit against me, instructs his advocates to charge me with wrongdoing, and becomes a complainant against me in the trial over which he himself presides, thus acting simultaneously as interested party and as judge.

[169] StA Wei Reg. Q, No. 17, 127ʳ.

[170] From grievances by nobility of Vogtland presented at Diet of Altenburg, 1523, *ibid.*, No. 18, 132ʳ, 133ʳ, 137ʳ.

[171] From a long memorandum on judicial affairs submitted by nobles of all Saxon districts in 1601. StA Dr, Loc. 9359, 171ʳ-174ʳ.

[172] StA Dr, Loc. 9359 (1601), 110ʳ; Loc. 9362 (1609), unpaginated.

Such trespassing on a lord's authority, Nitzschwitz protests, has not been seen or heard heretofore in the land.[173]

Similar complaints were heard in other parts of the country. Bavarian nobles suspected that it was the aim of their duke "to alter the *natura feudi* and transform our ancient investitures."[174] It was the prince's ambition, they charged, to ruin them.[175] Local and private legal matters are made into "state cases." A noble's vassal who has been seen eating meat on a fast day is interrogated, tried, and punished by the *Rentmeister* himself.[176] The government's response to this particular complaint was returned, *mutatis mutandis*, to every other kind of grievance. "Meat eating or laboring on forbidden days pertain to the cause of religion [*der religion anhengig*]," Duke Maximilian declared, "and religion is under the jurisdiction of the territorial prince whose high government has special supervision over it."[177] Pleas to "let justice run its accustomed course"[178] produced no results. Monasteries and cathedral chapters, too, complained of such jurisdictional infringements.[179] These were especially galling in a Catholic state. The charge was made (in the reign of Duke Wilhelm V in 1595) that nobles unable to prove ancient Bavarian stock were stripped of the traditional right to sit as judges in their seigneurial estates.[180] Others—knights, mostly—faced brusque denial or cavalier disregard of their competence over lesser crimes committed within the borders of their lands. "Such has not been the custom and it is not fair," the concerned Bavarian landlords lamented, vainly of course.[181]

The very same charges were addressed to the Bishop of Bamberg by knights and towns constituting the estates in that ecclesiastical terri-

[173] "Gravamina und Gebrechen Anno 1602," StA Dr, Loc. 9359, 40ʳ-41ʳ.

[174] From grievances presented by Bavarian nobility in 1579. BHStA Mu *Altbayerische Landschaft* 1158, 28ʳ, 64ʳ, and many other places.

[175] One stratagem, of which Bavarian nobles were especially afraid, was to break up a noble's holdings following the death of his male heir by refusing to transfer his benefice to his widow or daughter. See the protest of knights in the early years of the reign of Maximilian I in BHStA Mu *Altbayerische Landschaft* 1185, 97ʳ-105ʳ; 109ʳ-117ᵛ.

[176] BHStA Mu *Altbayerische Landschaft* 1158, 33ʳ and ᵛ, 34ʳ, etc. The German term for "state cases" is *Vitztumhändel*, originally cases of "high" justice, involving capital crimes or large sums of money, reserved to the ducal official formerly called *Vitztum* (*Vice dominus*), i.e., the ruler's deputy. By the sixteenth century, the *Vitztum*'s duties had been taken over by the *Rentmeister*.

[177] *Ibid.*, 87ᵛ.

[178] *Ibid.*, 36ʳ.

[179] E.g., "Gravamina der stift und clöster" for Diet of 1588, BHStA Mu *Altbayerische Landschaft* 1172, unpaginated.

[180] *Ibid.* 1185, 99ʳ.

[181] *Ibid.* 1207 (from year 1612), unpaginated.

tory.[182] "Learned doctors deprive us of our hereditary rights," they protested. "They deal with us according to their whims against the nobility's old laws, good customs, and ancient traditions."[183] Minor cases—"battery, abuse, slander, debt, and so on"[184]—were removed willy nilly from town and rural courts to the bishop's bench, where "only the officials' [amptleute] and judges' testimony is given credit and our people's word counts for nothing."[185] "And no matter how solid is our evidence of the unfairness [unpilligkeit] done to us, they simply answer that what they do is the correct procedure at the territorial court. But this procedure they change overnight so that they may do with us as they please."[186] In Tyrol, from the second half of the century, the practice of second- and third-instance courts of issuing "revisions" of judgments first given by local tribunals led to repeated assertions that "no man knows any longer what is right and what is wrong in our land."[187] "No one to go before foreign courts" (niemand vor fremde gericht) was a rallying cry in Tyrol, where "foreign" might be a place only an hour's ride away. "Every legal action should be heard before its rightful authority in the first instance"[188] was another version of this challenge to the prevailing drift. In fact, justice was becoming an administrative prerogative, as most complaints make clear. The Tyrolean Bergrichter—administrators of mining districts—"have taken over all judicial business, regardless of its importance or of the amounts of money involved. They decide them either by arbitration or by judicial action, as they see fit."[189] All groups participating in the Tyrolean diet protested against Revision und abforderung der acta, the prerogative of higher courts to send for the file of a case for review of its verdict, a move that threatened to deprive patrimonial, town, and village courts of their function. Such revisions, the estates noted, are made by "foreign councillors . . . unacquainted with the customs of the country."[190] The survival of venerated customs and long-standing traditions is best protected, they argued, by competent local courts. Throughout the 1590s and early 1600s, however, the Tyrolean estates found fresh

[182] On the estates in the Bishopric of Bamberg, see Siegfried Bachmann, *Die Landstände des Hochstifts Bamberg*. . . .

[183] From grievances presented at *Rittertag* in 1503, StA Bamb B28, No. 1, 2ʳ.

[184] *Ibid.*, 19ʳ. See also *ibid.* No. 13, 5ᵛ.

[185] *Ibid.* No. 1, 5ʳ and ᵛ.

[186] *Ibid.*, 18ᵛ.

[187] From grievances presented to Diet of Innsbruck, 1573, LA Tir *Tiroler Landtagsakten* Cod. 45, 191ᵛ.

[188] *Ibid.*, 179ʳ.

[189] *Ibid.*, Fasz. 375 (1547), unpaginated.

[190] *Ibid.*, Cod. 45, 193ʳ; 194ʳ.

reasons to complain of "continuing intervention and new and unaccustomed disorder created by the . . . government."[191]

The judicial aspects of the change documented in these examples[192] have been discussed in another chapter. But their consequences go far beyond the erosion of particular justice. It was not only that local courts were trivialized in the centralization of the territorial justice system. Much more fundamental is the shift occurring in peoples' attitude toward authority, its origin, and their own involvement in its exercise. Nearby, familiar jurisdictions were ceasing to be sources of certainty and competence, and this change in the location of real power affected not only law, but also government and religion. Definitive proclamations were now made from the center. As the residents of the district of Stertzing in Tyrol complained in 1573: "we can no longer have hope of obtaining certainty of judgment [in our local courts], but must wait to receive this in the third instance, from the legal doctors and jurists who sit on the high courts." Which, they contended, "is ruinous to the poor and is irksome even to the rich," for not everyone, the villagers wrote, plaintively, "is willing to waste his time and substance on waiting for long-delayed verdicts."[193] Rulers and their legal advisers could supply excellent arguments for a policy of systematic undercutting of lesser jurisdictions. Patrimonial and other local courts were often lax in enforcing laws. They prevented the uniform application of rules and standards across the territory.[194] Above all they could not be effectively controlled. Writing to Duke Georg of Landshut, a Bavarian *Rentmeister* confessed the impotence of his sub-officials when it came to enforcing the duchy's statutes against blaspheming, gambling, and similar moral offenses. "Your Grace's *Ambtleut* say that when they try to interdict or punish such an offense in the district court, their people simply run to a noble's domain, where they can gamble at will."[195] Accurate weights and measures—a major concern at the time and one on which rulers were quick to take up the role of protectors of the public interest—were defeated by the refusal of seigneurial lords to admit government inspectors to their lands for the *Mühlbeschauen*, the annual

[191] *Ibid.*, Fasz. 10 (1601), unpaginated. On the "revisions" by appellate courts in Tyrol see also Jürgen Bücking, *Kultur und Gesellschaft in Tirol . . .* , 132-33.

[192] For more evidence of the same kind, see Herbert Helbig on Jülich-Berg: "Fürsten und Landstände im Westen des Reiches . . ." in Heinz Rausch, ed., *Die geschichtlichen Grundlagen der modernen Volksvertretung* II (Darmstadt, 1974), 169-77.

[193] LA Tir Cod. 45, 212^r.

[194] For evidence from Bavaria for this, see Volkmar Wittmütz, *Die Gravamina der bayerischen Stände . . .* , 16-24. Wittmütz, however, doubts that the attempt to undermine lower justice in Bavaria was systematic (21).

[195] BHStA Mu *Fürstensachen* 211, 1^r.

examination of mills.[196] In these and many similar ways did private jurisdictions—legal and political—obstruct the path of the unitary state. This was the crux of the case against particular privileges. And this is why governments were bent on reducing and weakening immunities wherever they could. If sheer numbers of complaints signify, this goal was not far from being reached by the middle or late years of the sixteenth century.

It is this frame that lends perspective to the accusations, aimed at every sixteenth-century government, of summary justice, bureaucratic meddling, centripetal decision making, and autocratic rule. True to the legalistic and litigious habits of the age,[197] most of this protesting concerned courts and judicial procedure. But the real object of attack, and the source of the severest anxiety, was the state's great enterprise: the centralization of political power. All groups gathered in the diets saw this as a real and immediate peril to the survival of their political and social world.

Though rarely rising above the trivial in the incidents of aggression deplored, protests and complaints never fail to point to the origin of this threat. And in their very profuseness and ubiquity they suggest something of its amplitude. Each fresh intervention is described as an *unerhörte neuerung*, an "unheard-of innovation": the new requirement that cities and towns in Bavaria must draw up registers of wards and guardians, for example. Names had to be supplied, the fortune of each ward, the occupation to which each is trained, and so on. Not that they have anything to hide, the towns protest. But the law itself is "a new and heretofore unheard-of demand."[198] Town magistrates in Bavaria were ordered to submit accounts of revenues and expenditures to the duke's financial officers. The books, the townsmen charge in 1588, are "not merely requested but requisitioned or confiscated. We are not trying to hide careless or dishonest reckoning," they say, protesting against what only a few years ago was an occasional interference by an over-eager *Rentmeister* but has now become "a general and permanent procedure [*ein general und durchgehendts werck*]" and as such "an in-

---

[196] E.g., an instance in Bavaria: BHStA Mu, *Kurbayern Äusseres Archiv* 694, 114ᵛ-115ʳ, also for inspection of butchers, shopkeepers, and publicans. Also *ibid., Altbayerische Landschaft* 1185, 100ᵛ.

[197] A good sense of the period's legalism is conveyed by Herbert Obenaus, *Recht und Verfassung der Gesellschaften mit St. Jörgenschild in Schwaben* (Göttingen, 1961) who concludes from his examination of this large association of knights that "Das ganze Vorgehen der Gesellschaft ist auf Recht gestellt" (79), and "Sicherung der Rechtsstellung und Durchsetzung der Rechtsforderungen der Mitglieder: das ist die 'Politik' der Gesellschaft mit St. Jörgenschild" (90).

[198] BHStA Mu *Altbayerische Landschaft* 1172 (1588), unpaginated.

sufferable innovation" which, if allowed to go unchecked, will lead to "the destruction of our entire land."[199] More symbolic, but no less disturbing in its implication for urban self-government in Bavaria, was an "innovation" concerning the swearing-in of town councillors. Old councillors used to administer the oath to their newly chosen colleagues. But now—in 1595—the ducal *Pfleger* has usurped this right and, for good measure, has also disallowed annual elections of town councillors who are now permitted to remain in office until dead or removed for cause. All of this, the townsmen say in their complaint, goes against "our ancient well-ordered constitutions."[200]

The response to the burghers' protest could not have calmed the anxiety aroused in them by the new measures. But it does throw a sharp beam of light on the opposing principles at work. The new manner of choosing town councillors and taking their oath of office, Duke Wilhelm wrote, has been established "for express, rational, and well-considered reasons [*aus sonderbaren vernunfftigen und wolbedachten ursachen*] and is in the urban estate's own best interests."[201] In all probability, this reply was not a mere piece of hypocrisy. The duke no doubt believed the new measure to be true and just; his advisers certainly did. But the affected townsmen must have seen it in a different light. To them it was a serious, potentially a fatal, blow to the survival of their habitual political institutions, and therefore to their autonomy. As part of the same process, Tyrolean burghers with longstanding possession of sealing rights found themselves denied the use of that power by officials who "proclaim in front of the church that citizens who have always sealed their own documents may no longer on pain of heavy fines issue a letter except as validated by the *Pfleger* or his recorder."[202] Cities and towns in Württemberg complained in the 1580s of state interference in their age-old right to control immigration. If refused permission to settle, or if the waiting period is too long to suit them, newcomers simply go before a ducal administrative court where they obtain an injunction ordering the magistrates to admit them. This, the towns protest, does great harm especially to local tradesmen and artisans.[203]

[199] *Ibid.*

[200] *Ibid.* 1185 (1595), 130ʳ and ᵛ.

[201] *Ibid.*, 134ʳ.

[202] From grievances of rural districts in Tyrol, 1525, Fritz Steinegger and Richard Schober, eds. in *loc. cit.*, 38.

[203] From grievances of towns and market villages in Württemberg, 1583. HStA St A34, Bü 13b. These developments originated in the aftermath of the victory of Charles V at Mühlberg. See Eberhard Naujoks, "Stadt und Stadtregiment der Reichsstädte" in Peter

Elsewhere, *Pfleger* and *Amtmänner*, acting "against our ancient customs and usage" but clearly carrying out government policy,[204] abrogated people's rights freely to sell their products[205] or their land,[206] gather fire wood and building lumber,[207] trap rabbits and deer "in my gracious lord the elector's woods, which our forefathers have done, but now it is denied to us,"[208] raise dogs to chase off wild game,[209] go about their own affairs without fear of being pressed into service to do labor or provide transport.[210] In countless other ways people were treated "like mere subjects [*untertanen*] until no ordinary man may now be secure in the possession of his town's or village's customs, usages, and rights."[211] When appeals against such high-handed interference were made to higher echelons, officials turned deaf. "No one gets a reply or a disposition from them, and things are allowed to remain in their wrongful state. In this way are nobles and indeed the whole country deprived of their freedoms, of their ancient traditions, and of their good old customs."[212] Covert or open demands for greasing palms were common (*und gehen die Schmiralia . . . vast in schwung*),[213] and excessive fines and court costs extracted by bureaucrats sitting as judges brought the whole justice system into disrepute.[214] Official contempt for customary rights was proverbial. "*Amtleute* are heard to say in a boastful manner that they do not care a straw about our territorial constitution and our freedoms," complained the Bavarian estates in 1595,[215] and no observer could fail to recognize that bureaucratic disregard of venerated traditions and the innumerable instances of arrogant and capricious (*mutwillig*) behavior by headstrong officials reflected governmental intentions. This must be the chief reason why

Blickle *et al.*, *Von der Standeversammlung zum demokratischen Parlament. Die Geschichte der Volksvertretungen in Baden Württemberg* (Stuttgart, 1982), 103-19.

[204] As made clear by official replies to grievances in the margins of the documents cited.

[205] E.g., wine in the district of Persen in Tyrol. LA Tir, *Tiroler Landtagsakten*, Fasz. II, unpaginated. This and the following examples are typical.

[206] Grievance of Bavarian prelates and monasteries, 1595, BHStA Mu *Altbayerische Landschaft* 1185, 85ᵛ.

[207] E.g., Ernestine Saxony: C.A.H. Burckhardt, ed., *Ernestinische Landtagsakten* I, No. 36.

[208] *Ibid.* Also StA Dr, Loc. 9356 (1554), 28ᵛ-29ᵛ.

[209] Saxony, 1565: StA Dr, Loc. 9350, No. 10, 10ᵛ.

[210] E.g., Württemberg: HStA St A34, Bü 1b, No. 2; Saxony: StA Dr Loc. 9355, 172ʳ and ᵛ; Bavaria: BHStA Mu *Altbayerische Landschaft* 1172, unpaginated.

[211] HStA St A34, Bü 1b, No. 2.

[212] *Hessische Landtagsakten* I, 187.

[213] Bavaria, 1572: BHStA Mu *Altbayerische Landschaft* 1158, 8ᵛ.

[214] StA Wei Reg. Q, No. 18, 142ʳ.

[215] BHStA Mu *Altbayerische Landschaft* 1185, unpaginated.

estates were so delinquent in following up on the standard government response to all grievances: to submit the names of offending officials and give the details of infractions charged to them. Supplying such information was not merely a hazardous undertaking. It would have been a useless exercise, for the root cause of the systematic debilitation of estate rights was the aggrandizing state itself led by its ambitious prince abetted by his teams of innovating counsellors. This powerful combination proved impervious to the estates' charges of victimization by arbitrary bureaucracy, summary justice,[216] religious regimentation,[217] and general ill use.

It must not be thought that anxiety about vanishing rights and crumbling immunities shut out all other concerns. To judge by the numbers of particular grievances, immediate economic worries counted most heavily: clearly these were uppermost in the minds of individual knights, townspeople, and villagers. Incongruously—as has been pointed out several times in these pages—all pleas and suggestions for redress asked more, not less, of central governments. Hardly a single offending or vexing condition was amenable to anything less than territory-wide solutions.[218] From towns came objections to the devaluation of currency and the influx of "base alien coins";[219] to preemptive buying (*Vorkauf*) of grain, hops, dairy products, and cattle—causing artificial scarcity and high prices—and to unfair competition by rural tradespeople living beyond city walls (weavers, millers, and butchers selling their handiwork cheap, and village landlords drawing low-priced beer); to "Italian and foreign peddlers" crying their wares from town to town, depriving established shopkeepers of their custom; to unapprenticed and masterless artisans bidding low against honest craftsmen; to greedy lumber merchants flouting the old rule that logs

[216] E.g., Württemberg, 1599: "geschwind und ungewonliche process . . . gleich mit der execution procedirt." *Württembergische Landtagsakten* 2. Reihe I, ed. Eugen Adam (Stuttgart, 1910), 2, 31; Bavaria, 1580s: BHStA Mu *Altbayerische Landschaft* 1190, 63ʳ, 64ᵛ; Saxony, 1609: StA Dr, Loc. 9362, 31ʳ-33ᵛ.

[217] Saxony, 1565: StA Dr, Loc. 9350, No. 10, 10ʳ; Bavaria, 1605: BHStA Mu *Altbayerische Landschaft* 1190, 100ʳ-119ʳ.

[218] The following summary is based on a number of comprehensive grievance documents. For Württemberg: *Verzaichnis und kurzer Extract aller gravaminum und Beschwerden so von den Stätten unnd Ämbternn im Fürstentum, auf den Landtag Anno 1583 inn Schrifften zur Kanzlei überschickt worden seyen* in HStA St A34, Bü 18d; also *ibid*. Bü 13b (for 1552-1553) and A36, Bü 18, consisting of fifty documents sumitted by towns and districts; Saxony: the documents and summaries published by Johannes Falke as given in note 114; for Tyrol: LA Tir *Tiroler Landtagsakten*, Fasz. I-II, 8-10, 375; Cod. 45; 2902, 2929; for Bavaria: the documents in BHStA Mu *Altbayerische Landschaft* Lit. as listed in the notes to the present chapter; for Bamberg: StA Bamb B48, No. 23.

[219] E.g., *Ernestinische Landtagsakten* I, No. 324.

floating down river must be held for three days when passing a town so that burghers could buy the wood they needed; to "Fugger and his company" with their monopolies on silver and copper (this notably from Tyrol); to the general moral decline in society as evidenced by blaspheming, gambling, and—especially—heavy drinking. Villagers complained of the proliferation everywhere of boars and wild pigs. They appended graphic descriptions of the ravenous and omnivorous devouring done by these beasts, and protested against the hobbling of peasants' dogs with wooden trammels to prevent their chasing after the invading game. "Things are so bad now," the elders of a market village in Württemberg wrote in 1583, "that our hired hands, tired out from a whole day's sweaty labor in the field, can take no rest at night, being forced to guard fields and orchards from these marauders."[220] Villagers also pleaded for help against habitual offenders such as landless rural workers who grazed their cows on private meadows, and they denounced seigneurial or princely *Forstmeister* who interfered with their rights to snare birds, net or angle fish, gather acorns and firewood, and so on. Nobles, for their part, took exception to poachers, to "servants without masters," and to roaming bands of soldiers and other vagrants who made the land unsafe. They handed in long accounts of their endless quarrels with nearby towns over brewing rights and called on governments to enforce or set aside, as the case might be, the *Bierbann* and *Biermeile*—the space within which "foreign" beer could not be sold.[221] Everyone complained of bad roads and rickety bridges, of high taxes and the mounting cost of everything, above all of the terrible consequences of war. From the "plain people and submissive subjects of the communes of Upper and Lower Seefeld" in Tyrol came this appeal for a reduction of taxes made to Ferdinand I in 1556. It is one of many such pleas. We are begging for relief, the villagers write

> because, wretched people that we are, we have been miserably ruined by Spaniards, Italians, and Schmalkaldics in the recently concluded wars, during which roving bands and foragers endangered our lives, seized what little we own in hay, straw, food, bedding, and domestic furnishings, slaughtered or drove away our cattle, set the torch to our houses, stole without a penny's compensation whatever took their

[220] HStA St A34, Bü 18b, unpaginated.

[221] For an interesting account and explanation of the economically vital issue of beer brewing in Saxony see Eberhard May, *Die Entwicklung der sächsischen Bierbrauerei* (Borna-Leipzig, 1905). For a collection of legal opinions on the laws and legal rights involved, see StA Dr, Loc. 9665, 1^r-22^v.

fancy, and drove us, our wives, and our children out of our homes and into the forests to look for safety.[222]

Countless such supplications were written in the empire in the age of Italian campaigns and religious wars. They describe what for a large number of people was the stark reality of life.

Taken together, these shared perceptions of the actual conditions of existence in town and countryside must have reinforced—if, indeed, they did not generate—the widespread sense of loss, instability, and imperilment pervading public attitudes in the later sixteenth century. This mood is vividly conveyed by the grievance documents, in which an uneasy apprehension that a world is being lost integrates a multiplicity of special concerns into a common expression of anxiety and dismay. Rights and freedoms defined and sanctioned this vanishing world. Every sign that the structure of rights and freedoms was being dismembered brought protests, plaintive or angry as circumstances allowed. Roman law and Roman lawyers were seen as the most destructive agents of this dismantling operation, and it is easy to understand why this was so. Their place at the head of the advancing state had made them inviting targets at which to aim expressions of frustration, outrage, and fear. More than a disagreeable nuisance in civic life, written law and its learned practitioners had come to stand as the symbol of all that seemed offensive and perturbing in the approaching new world, which was a world in which lawyers were the first citizens.

Even where the legal order itself was not in question—in Saxony, for example,[223] and in Tyrol—blame and excoriation came down upon academic jurists and the *doctorische Recht* of which they were the keepers. A Tyrolean pasquil of the 1550s puts these sentiments in a nutshell.

> The learned laws are everywhere,
> Destroying our country fair;
> Our rights and freedoms they impugn,
> No man's inheritance is immune.
> We must take arms against this foe,
> Or wretched to our graves we'll go.[224]

---

[222] LA Tir *Tiroler Landtagsakten*, Fasz. 8, unpaginated.

[223] Despite the argument made by Tullius von Sartori-Montecroce, *Über die Reception der fremden Rechte in Tirol . . .* (Innsbruck, 1895), Roman law was not a major concern of the Tyrolean estates, whose records give few indications of objection to Roman law on legal grounds.

[224] From a pasquil printed in Tyrol around the middle of the sixteenth century. Printed in *ibid.*, 9.

Beginning in the 1520s, when Ferdinand I began to promote imperial law in his Austrian duchies, the plea to "proceed not by the written laws, but by the ancient customs of this County"[225] was not silenced in Tyrol. It was still made, in identical words, in the early seventeenth century: "In matters touching the County, let us not proceed, judge, and conduct our affairs by using the common [imperial] law, but let us stay with our native Tyrolean law, and, where this is silent, go back to the old customs and usages." If this is done, the estates spokesmen concluded, "no innovations will be brought into our land."[226] In every part of the empire, voices deplored the lawyer's divisive effect on society. "Too many doctors on the high court" was a common outcry.[227] The solution: to name "honorable and sensible men" to the appellate courts, men "who are of the country and who are not doctors."[228] Such a "natives only" policy was in large part intended to halt the legification of state bureaucracies[229] (it was, of course, also meant to create jobs for nobles and old-family burghers; hence: "newcomers [*neuhergekommene*] must not be preferred").[230] Estates members felt much safer with "native-born countrymen in offices and posts"[231] men who "have inheritance and property in the district or the country,"[232] than under an administration run by "the learned and foreign born [*Gelerten und frembden*]."[233] From the latter kind little sympathy could be expected, and even less concern for prized freedoms and traditions. Hence the lasting antagonism to written law and to the legal profession, the circumstances of which have been the subject of this book.

Not everywhere did the prince's rule and the lawyer's prod replace the old order of rights and privilege. In Württemberg estates recaptured their strength in the seventeenth century and dominated politics in that

[225] From Innsbruck diet, 1525. LA Tir Cod. 48, 212r; also *ibid.*, Fasz. II (1525), unpaginated.

[226] *Ibid.*, Cod. 2902, 73.

[227] E.g., Bavaria, 1501, quoted in Eduard Rosenthal, *Geschichte des Gerichtswesens* . . . I, 144.

[228] From deliberations of Württemberg estates preparing for diet of 1514, *Württembergische Landtagsakten* 1. Reihe, ed. W. Ohr and E. Kober (Stuttgart, 1913) I, 141.

[229] E.g., BHStA Mu *Altbayerische Landschaft* 355, 51r and v; *ibid.* 1158, 2v; 1185, unpaginated; StA Dr, Loc. 9362, 51r-52v; *ibid.* 9356, 13v, 125r; HStA St *Tomi actorum* 5, 64r; *ibid.* A34, Bü 18b, *passim*; LA Tir *Tiroler Landtagsakten*, Fasz. II, unpaginated; Georg von Below, *Landtagsakten von Jülich-Berg 1400-1600* (Düsseldorf, 1895-1907) I, 133-35, II, 5, 9, 43, 277, 343, 461-62, 662-63, 678.

[230] BHStA Mu *Altbayerische Landschaft* 1180, unpaginated (1593).

[231] LA Tir *Tiroler Landtagsakten* Fasz. I, unpaginated.

[232] *Ibid.* Fasz. II, unpaginated.

[233] *Ibid.* Cod. 45, 193r (1573).

duchy throughout the next.[234] But Württemberg was an atypical case in Germany.[235] In nearly every one of the empire's territories, princely autocracy and juristic discretion gained steadily in substance as estates dwindled into shadows of their former selves. Late in the sixteenth century a plaintive tone of acquiescence speaks from the documents in which assemblies were waging this conflict, as if they were now asserting their grievances under duress of a force too strong or too cunning to be resisted. We hear such a note in the dejected comment of spokesmen for Bavarian towns as they met in diet in 1588. It is given here as one for many. Having, with the concurrence of the duchy's nobles and clergy, once again recounted the old complaints of unredressed assaults on their liberties, "of which we have good, written copies in our possession," the townsmen pause to wonder how much longer they will have the vigor and spirit to uphold these freedoms. "For," they say,

> if these our rights continue to be reduced, in violation of the explicit letter of our territorial charter of freedoms, it is not difficult to imagine how few of us will feel the desire, or see any reason, for taking so much trouble, facing so many dangers, bearing such great costs, and doing all the other things necessary for acquiring privileges and freedoms in the future.[236]

The ruler to whom it was addressed could not have mistaken this discouraged remark for a threat. In the 1580s the Bavarian estates had no means left for making threats. Nor could it have displeased the bureaucrats who sat in the prince's councils. They must have read it as an agreeable sign that their endeavors were about to be crowned with success. The plaintive strain of resignation sounding in the deputies' words told them that their antagonist was running out of strength, and that their effort to build the efficient state was now well on the way to being won.

---

[234] See Erwin Hölzle, *Das alte Recht und die Revolution* (Munich and Berlin, 1931) for a vivid, though tendentious, portrait of Württemberg in the eighteenth century. A more authoritative source is James Allen Vann, *The Making of a State. Württemberg 1593-1793* (Ithaca, N.Y., 1984), especially Chapters 3-5.

[235] F. L. Carsten, *op. cit.*, 147-48.

[236] ". . . ist unschwer abzunehmen, das man hinfüran vil mühe zuhaben, gefahr zu übersteen, uncosten aufzuwenden, und anderes zu tun, damit man dergleich privilegia und freiheiten erlangt, weder lust noch ursach haben würde." From "Gravamina der städt und märkt" (1588), BHStA Mu *Altbayerische Landschaft* 1172, unpaginated.

INDEX

Library of Congress Cataloging-in-Publication Data

Strauss, Gerald, 1922-
Law, resistance, and the state.

Includes index.
1. Roman law—Reception—Germany. 2. Lawyers (Roman law)
3. Law—Germany—History and criticism. 4. Religion and law.
5. Law and politics. I. Title.

KK941.S77 1986   349.43   85-43315
                  344.3
ISBN 0-691-05469-X (alk. paper)